An Imperfect Union

Studies in Legal History

Published by The University of North Carolina Press
in association with the American Society for Legal History

Editor: Morris S. Arnold

Editorial Advisory Board

An Imperfect Union

Slavery, Federalism, and Comity

Paul Finkelman

The University of North Carolina Press *Chapel Hill*

© 1981 Paul Finkelman

All rights reserved

Manufactured in the United States of America

Cloth edition, ISBN 0-8078-1438-5

Paper edition, ISBN 0-8078-4066-1

Library of Congress Catalog Card Number 79-27526

First printing, January 1981

Second printing, July 1982

Third printing, May 1985

Library of Congress Cataloging in Publication Data

Finkelman, Paul, 1949–
  An imperfect union.

  (Studies in legal history)
  Bibliography: p.
  Includes index.
  1. Slavery in the United States—Legal status of
slaves in free states.   I. Title.   II. Series.
KF4545.S5F56   346'.73'013   79-27526
ISBN 0-8078-1438-5
ISBN 0-8078-4066-1 pbk.

For Simon and Ella,

who always gave their son books to read

Contents

Acknowledgments

This book began in a unique seminar on slavery and law at the University of Chicago Law School, taught jointly by one historian— Stanley N. Katz—and two lawyers—Owen Fiss and the late Harry Kalven. Each year the specific topic changed and new course material was examined by students and teachers. It was truly an exciting intellectual experience as all members of the seminar learned and discovered together. I was fortunate to participate in the seminar three times, twice as a student and the third time as a coteacher with Stan Katz. During the second year of the seminar we examined the law of abolition and manumission. Law, particularly constitutional law, is not easily divorced from politics. Thus we also used various political materials, including sections from the Lincoln-Douglas debates.

At one meeting Owen Fiss voiced his disbelief in the fears Lincoln expressed in his "House Divided Speech" and throughout the debates with Douglas. He could not understand why Republicans or abolitionists could talk about a "slave power conspiracy" to nationalize the peculiar institution. As a rather brash graduate student, I decided to explain to Owen, on his own terms, how slavery could have been forced on the North. I wrote a hypothetical Supreme Court decision in which the right of slave transit and long-term sojourn with a slave could have been upheld. In it I projected how the Supreme Court could have applied past doctrine to a series of cases involving masters who brought their slaves into the North. I then discovered that such a case, *Lemmon* v. *The People* (1860), actually existed in New York and might have been brought to the high court had not the Civil War begun. This led to the discovery of other cases involving slave transit in both the North and the South. Five years later I can offer this book as a final answer to Owen's question.

Along the way I have been aided and befriended by numerous people. Stan Katz has had a profound impact on the direction and development of this book and my other scholarly pursuits. While I was in graduate school he allowed me to join the slavery and law seminar as a coteacher. He has remained a constant source of help, wisdom, and friendship since I began working with him. Stan's optimism, confidence, and good humor have kept me going through gloomy Chicago winters. His good counsel and advice have been enormously helpful. His friendship has been a delight.

John Hope Franklin was my first teacher at the University of Chicago and has remained a good counselor and friend. As a teacher he gave his time and energy to me throughout graduate school and afterward. As a scholar and a friend he has shared much with me, has taught me many things, and has been an inspiration.

A number of scholars have read all or part of this book for me. William Wiecek took a great deal of time from his own work to give me a detailed critique of the entire manuscript. I have not always followed his advice, but my book is better because of his unselfish help.

Louis Gerteis also read the entire manuscript, carefully telling me where I was wrong. Long conversations with him helped me to sharpen my ideas, particularly about the nexus between law and politics in the antebellum period. Kenneth Kusmer, who read portions of the manuscript and argued with me about them, has also remained a close and supportive friend since our graduate school days.

Harold Hyman read an earlier version of this book and took an active interest in seeing that it was published. He also agreeably read revisions and saved me from a few blunders. Don E. Fehrenbacher sent me the galleys from his book on Dred Scott so I could incorporate some of his findings here. Walter Ehrlich discussed his work on Dred Scott with me and gave me new insights into the case. Gerhard Casper, Keir Nash, Lawrence Friedman, Robert Abzug, Thomas D. Morris, Sam McSeveney, Michael Johnson, Ralph Ketcham, Otey Scruggs, and Michael Weinberg all read parts of the manuscript and offered useful suggestions. My fellow graduate students at Chicago, Martha Fineman, Ricardo Meana, and Stephen Ekovich, also read and dissected portions of it. Matt Schaaf, my research assistant at the University of Texas, was extremely helpful in the final preparation of this manuscript. S. E. Foster, Sam Broverman, June Ailin, and Guadalupe Arabzadegan helped proofread the galleys and prepare the index.

Lewis Bateman at The University of North Carolina Press has shown enormous patience and faith in me and my work. He has been prodding me for four years, as I suppose any good press editor should. I thank him for doing it. Sandra Eisdorfer, also an editor at The University of North Carolina Press, has overseen the editing of this book with great skill and dedication. Buzz Arnold has been a superb editor for Studies in Legal History. His critical comments and questions have saved me from many errors of fact and interpretation. He has spent more hours going over portions of this manuscript with me than either of us cares to count. Jan McInroy was a meticulous copy editor who found and corrected many errors.

As is the custom, I absolve all those named in this acknowledgment from the mistakes in fact, judgment, and interpretation that others may find in this book. Any faults that remain are probably due to my not heeding their advice.

Parts of this book were published in *Louisiana Studies* [now *Southern Studies*] and *Reviews in American History*. I am particularly grateful to John Milton Price, the editor of *Southern Studies*, who published an earlier version of the last chapter. Portions of this book were read as papers at meetings of the Missouri Valley History Conference, the Great Lakes Regional History Conference, the Missouri History Association, the American Historical Association—Pacific Coast Branch, and the Organization of American Historians. The editors of these journals and the commentators, participants, and audiences at those meetings allowed me important forums in which to express tentative ideas.

The research for this book would not have been possible without the aid of the staffs and librarians of the following institutions: the University of Texas at Austin, Washington University, University of Chicago, University of California at Irvine, Houghton Library of Harvard University, the Historical Society of Pennsylvania, the New-York Historical Society, Columbia University, Oberlin College, the National Archives, and the Library of Congress. Larry Boyer at the American-British Law Division of the Library of Congress provided aid above and beyond the call of duty and job requirements. His knowledge of legal sources and his ability to find uncataloged materials and track down isolated facts and cases made my research much easier. I would also like to thank Marlene McGuirl, chief of the American-British Law Division, Bruce Martin of the Reader Services Division, and Dan Burney of the Rare Book Room at the Library of Congress; Judith Wright and Richard Bowler at the University of Chicago Law Library; Janet Steed, Yvonne Wilson, and Pamela Lazare at the University of California at Irvine; Richard Holland at the University of Texas Perry-Casteñada Library; and Roy Mersky, Mickie Voges, Virginia Wise, Jim Hambleton, and James Murray at the University of Texas Law Library.

My friends Abe and Carol Wagner lent me their house, office, and typewriters while I lived in California. In Washington, D.C., Abe's company, Analytical Assessments, gave me office space and the use of their facilities. Janet L. Gray helped in ways too numerous to detail. Larry Kleiman, Robin R. Reynolds, Carol and Ron Leprohon, Eileen Boris, Arthur Cohen, Elinor and Arthur Handman, Louis Cohen, Jack and Katie Zammito, Roy and Pam Finkelman, Barbara and Allan Block, Julia Fitzgerald, Steve and Laney Sacks, Triss and Bob Stein, and Marian and Larry Kobrin have all provided friendship, love, moral support, and places to stay as I traveled around the country doing research.

The following grants and fellowships, institutions and foundations supported the research necessary to produce this book: University of Chicago, Urban Studies–Ford Foundation Fellowship; Andrew W. Mellon teaching fellowship at Washington University; National Endowment for the Humanities summer stipend; the University of Texas Research Institute; American Philosophical Society; Project '87; the American Bar Foundation Fellowship; and the J. Franklin Jameson Fellowship, given jointly by the American Historical Association and the Library of Congress.

An Imperfect Union

Is it consistent with this purpose of perfect union, and perfect and unrestricted intercourse, that property which the citizen of one State brings into another State, for the purpose of passing through it to a State where he intends to take up his residence, shall be confiscated in the State through which he is passing, or shall be declared no property, and liberated from his control?

> Justice Clerke, dissenting in *Lemmon* v. *The People* [*of New York*], 1860

. . . we are of opinion, that an owner of a slave in another State where slavery is warranted by law, voluntarily bringing such slave into this State, has no authority to detain him against his will, or to carry him out of the State against his consent for the purpose of being held in slavery.

> Chief Justice Shaw, in *Commonwealth* [*of Massachusetts*] v. *Aves*, 1836

Introduction

Slavery and the Conflict of Laws

Between the American Revolution and the Civil War the United States became a nation that was, in the words of Abraham Lincoln, "half slave and half free." One consequence of this division was the gradual development of a law of slavery in the South and a law of freedom in the North. While similar in most other respects, the legal systems of the slave and free states diverged quite sharply on questions involving the status of Negroes. Most obviously, the South allowed slavery and presumed that all blacks were slaves; the North did not allow slavery and presumed that all people were free.

At a glance these differences in law and ideology seem to have had little direct effect on the sectional conflict of the antebellum period. While New Yorkers, for example, might have thought Virginians should not own slaves, the New York courts had no power to interfere with Virginian slaves. Thus the laws of the two states would not come in contact or conflict with each other.

The separation of laws operated only so long as slaves remained in slave states. If slaves entered free states—as runaways, transients, or sojourners—important legal problems often arose. Free-state judges had to decide the status of slaves brought before them. In reaching a decision a judge would have to determine which law to enforce: the law of the free state, which did not recognize slavery, or that of the slave state, which did recognize the "peculiar institution." In deciding such a case a judge relied on that area of law known as "conflict of laws" or "choice of law." The two terms are suggestive of the problem and the process of solving it. The laws of one state were "in conflict" with those of another, and the judge literally had to make a choice of which law to apply.

In making his choice, a judge in the antebellum United States was guided by three general sources of legal authority. First were the commands of the United States Constitution and any relevant federal laws. The status of fugitive slaves was not subject to state legislation or common law because this area of the law was preempted by the Constitution's Fugitive Slave Clause and ultimately by two federal statutes implementing it. Second were the dictates of a state's constitution, common law, and statutes, which would be subject to judicial interpretation and enforcement. They also might be balanced against the third source of legal authority: the general theories of comity and international law. Comity is the courtesy or consideration that one jurisdiction gives by enforcing the laws of another, granted out of respect and deference rather than obligation. For example, a free state might recognize the slave status of a slave within its jurisdiction because the free state viewed harmony within the Union and respect for other states as a higher value than its own ideology of freedom. Such comity, for whatever field of law, was indispensable in a union of states, for if states refused to recognize and enforce each other's laws, interstate relations would collapse and the Union would founder. Ultimately, of course, a breakdown in interstate comity, combined with numerous other factors, led to precisely this result.

As long as slaves stayed in the South, cases involving the conflict of laws would not arise. But in an expanding nation, tourists, travelers, and migrants often entered free states with their slaves. Such movement across state lines led to important court battles and to a denial of comity by courts on both sides of the Mason-Dixon line. Indeed, before cannons were fired at Fort Sumter, judges and legislatures in both sections were taking "shots" at each other through court opinions and statutes.

Two late antebellum cases provide an example of the kinds of legal problems created by a Union that included both free and slave states.

The Case of Jonathan Lemmon

In 1852 Jonathan Lemmon and his wife wanted to move from their home in Virginia to Texas. They sailed to New York City, where they planned to secure direct steamship passage to Texas. Since they were moving from one slave state to another, they brought their eight slaves with them. But while in New York waiting for passage to Texas they were served with a writ of habeas corpus to bring before Judge Elijah Paine of the superior court "the bodies of eight colored persons . . . confined and restrained of their liberty . . . under the pretence that they were slaves." A week later Paine "discharged the colored Virginians" under an 1841 statute that prohibited all slavery within the state. Appeals to New York's two highest courts were unsuccessful, and before the case could be brought to the United States Supreme Court, the Civil War began.[1]

1. *Lemmon* v. *The People*, 20 N.Y. 562, 564–65 (1860).

The Lemmons and their supporters felt that the New York courts had committed a great injustice and, more important, that the New York statute and courts threatened the very Union itself. The Lemmons had not wanted to establish slavery in the Empire State. They had not even allowed their slaves out of the hotel room. They had only exercised their rights as citizens of the United States to travel, with their legal "property," through another state. To deny them the right of mere transit through another state was, in the words of a dissenting justice on New York's highest court, "a gross violation of those principles of justice and comity which should at all times pervade our interstate legislation, as well as wholly inconsistent with the general spirit of our national compact."[2]

The Case of Nancy Wells

In November 1846 Edward Wells, a Mississippi planter, took his slave Nancy to Ohio, where he executed a deed of manumission for her. This charitable act resulted from the circumstances of Nancy's birth: while her mother was also a slave owned by Wells, her father was Wells himself. In 1848 Edward Wells died, bequeathing three thousand dollars and some other property to his mulatto daughter. The executor of Wells's estate refused to give Nancy Wells her legacy because he claimed she was still a slave under the laws of Mississippi.[3]

In an 1859 opinion Justice William Harris of the Mississippi High Court of Errors and Appeals ruled that the Ohio manumission was invalid in Mississippi. He declared that the policy of Mississippi was to discourage the growth of a free black population anywhere in the United States. Thus Harris refused to enforce Nancy's manumission —that is, he refused to give comity and full faith and credit to the laws, constitution, and judicial decrees of Ohio, which declared Nancy to be free. Harris supported this position by aggressively attacking Ohio's pro-freedom policy. He concluded that the "obligations of comity" were "mutual and reciprocal, as well as voluntary," and "no State in this confederacy may violate that comity towards others, and thereby impose obligations on such others not previously existing." Justice Harris believed that Ohio, by allowing Nancy's manumission "and conferring rights of citizenship *there*, contrary to the known policy of Mississippi," had violated interstate comity, and Mississippi was not required to recognize Nancy's freedom. Ohio

2. Ibid. 644.
3. *Mitchell* v. *Wells*, 37 Miss. 235, 235–37 (1859).

could "neither confer freedom on a Mississippi slave, nor the right to acquire, hold, sue for, nor enjoy property in Mississippi."[4]

State Sovereignty and the Federal Union

The questions raised by these and many other antebellum cases went to the heart of a major constitutional problem: what was the meaning of comity between sovereign states of the federal Union? The sovereignty of the individual states was limited by their obligations to the Union. The Constitution recognized these obligations in article IV, which provided that "Full Faith and Credit shall be given each State to the public Acts, Records, and judicial Proceedings of every other State" and that "The Citizens of each State shall be entitled to all Privileges and Immunities of Citizens in the several States." The Constitution also provided that fugitives from justice should be "delivered up" on "Demand of the executive Authority of the State from which" they fled. Finally, fugitive slaves escaping from one state to another were not "discharged from such Service or Labour" by the laws of the state into which they escaped, but were to be "delivered up on Claim" of their owners.[5] These meager provisions were all that the Founding Fathers left to guide the states as to how they should interact with one another on the issue.

The least ambiguous clause, requiring fugitives from justice to be returned, has been the least controversial. In only a few instances have state governors refused to return convicted or accused criminals to the scene of their alleged crimes. Yet even this process was complicated by slavery and race. As early as 1791 the governor of Virginia refused to allow the extradition of Virginians accused of murdering Indians in Pennsylvania and of kidnapping a free black and bringing him back to Virginia. These two refusals to return accused criminals led to the passage of the Act of 1793, which enforced the Fugitive Slave Clause and the Fugitive from Justice Clause of the Constitution.[6] In 1839 Governor William H. Seward of New York refused to deliver three free blacks to Virginia authorities so that the blacks could be tried for helping a slave escape. Seward argued the men had broken no laws that were recognized by New York State or by "civilized countries" and thus the Fugitive from

4. Ibid. 264.
5. U.S., *Constitution*, art. IV.
6. William R. Leslie, "A Study in the Origins of Interstate Rendition: The Big Beaver Creek Murders," 57 *American Historical Review* (Oct. 1951) 63.

Justice Clause did not apply in their case.[7] Twenty years later, in a similar case, Governor William Dennison of Ohio refused to surrender a free black accused of helping a slave escape from Kentucky. The Ohio attorney general told Dennison that the black had committed no "crime, under the laws of this State [Ohio], or by the common law" and thus the extradition request should be rejected. The state of Kentucky then sued in the United States Supreme Court, asking for a writ of mandamus ordering Dennison to deliver the alleged criminal. In a decision reminiscent of Chief Justice John Marshall's opinion in *Marbury* v. *Madison* (1803), Chief Justice Roger B. Taney chastised Governor Dennison for refusing to act on the Kentucky request, but Taney declared that the United States Supreme Court lacked the power to issue the writ of mandamus or compel Dennison to return the alleged criminal.[8] Conflict between Kentucky and Ohio on this issue was not new. In 1846 a Kentucky court refused to allow the extradition of two of their citizens to Ohio, after it was alleged that they had kidnapped a free black in Ohio and enslaved him in Kentucky.[9]

Although these examples are isolated incidents, the refusals of northern and southern governors to surrender fugitives from justice indicate slavery's potential for disrupting comity and interstate relations. Perhaps the best known example is the enforcement of the Fugitive Slave Clause, which led to substantial conflict, particularly in the three decades before the Civil War.[10] Cases in the courts and conflicts in the streets resulted from attempts to enforce the clause.

7. Frederick W. Seward, *William H. Seward: An Autobiography from 1801 to 1834 with a Memoir of His Life and Selections from His Letters, from 1831 to 1846* (New York: D. Appleton and Company, 1877), 428–29, 437–38, 463–65, 528–31. Seward also refused to allow the extradition to Georgia of a man accused of larceny for "the stealing of a negro woman-slave"; ibid., 546–47, 554–56. See also *Richmond Enquirer*, 12 Jan. 1840.

8. *Kentucky* v. *Dennison*, 24 Howard (U.S.) 66, 68, 109–10 (1861). *Marbury* v. *Madison*, 1 Cranch (U.S.) 137 (1803).

9. *The State of Ohio vs. Forbes and Armitage, Arrested Upon the Requisition of the Government of Ohio, On Charge of Kidnapping Jerry Phinney, and Tried Before the Franklin Circuit Court of Kentucky, April 10, 1846* (N.p., 1846). The difficulties created by race relations have also undermined this clause in more recent times. In 1950 Governor G. Mennen Williams of Michigan refused to sign extradition papers for Haywood Patterson, one of the Scottsboro Boys who had escaped from an Alabama prison; Dan T. Carter, *Scottsboro: A Tragedy of the American South* (Baton Rouge: Louisiana State University Press, 1969) 413.

10. Although most attacks on the Fugitive Slave Laws came after 1830, northern states passed "personal liberty laws" to protect free blacks from kidnapping in the eighteenth century and throughout the early nineteenth. See Thomas D. Morris, *Free Men All: The Personal Liberty Laws of the North, 1780–1861* (Baltimore: Johns Hopkins University Press, 1974).

While the drama of the return or rescue of a fugitive slave provided vast amounts of propaganda for northern abolitionists and southern fire-eaters, the constitutional obligation (although not the process of rendition itself) was fairly clear from the wording of the Fugitive Slave Clause. Whether they liked it or not, northerners were part of a political compact that provided for the rendition of fugitive slaves.[11] Thus, as Staughton Lynd has noted, "abolitionists sought to undermine the Constitution's authority"[12] because in the Fugitive Slave Clause and other places, the Constitution supported slavery. It was northern distaste for returning fugitive slaves, rather than the wording of the clause itself, that led to a breakdown of interstate relations over this issue. A more elaborate clause might have made the rendition process smoother, but such elaboration was not necessary for antebellum Americans to understand what the clause was supposed to accomplish.

The Full Faith and Credit and Privileges and Immunities clauses were more ambiguous. States could and did deny privileges and immunities to citizens of other states. Full faith and credit were not always given to out-of-state judicial decrees. Such denials of comity, by both the North and the South, were partially responsible for the dissolution of the Union. The memory of such problems also motivated the adoption of certain sections of the Fourteenth Amendment.

For a master traveling with slaves such as Jonathan Lemmon or an emancipated slave such as Nancy Wells seeking to recover property in another state, the meaning of "Full Faith and Credit" and "Privileges and Immunities" was of critical importance. One way of understanding the comity provisions of the Constitution in the antebellum period is to examine how they were applied to problems of slavery and freedom. Slavery, after all, was the acid test for the comity provisions. No other institution ever placed such stress on the Union. Slavery and freedom, as incompatible ideals, could not be expected to coexist in both equality and harmony within the same political framework. As long as slaves remained in their home states little interstate friction would occur. But why have the Union

11. See Morris, *Free Men All*, and Stanley W. Campbell, *The Slave Catchers: Enforcement of the Fugitive Slave Law, 1850–1860* (Chapel Hill: University of North Carolina Press, 1970). It is clear that free states had a constitutional obligation to return fugitive slaves, even if it was unclear how that obligation should be carried out. Harold Horowitz, for example, has noted, "However state legislatures and courts might otherwise wish to resolve this choice-of-law question [fugitive slaves], the Constitution in this instance declared which state's policy would be subordinated"; Harold W. Horowitz, "Choice-of-Law Decisions Involving Slavery: 'Interest Analysis' in the Early Nineteenth Century," 17 *UCLA Law Review* 588 (1970).

12. Staughton Lynd, *Class Conflict, Slavery, and the United States Constitution* (Indianapolis: The Bobbs-Merrill Company, 1967) 154.

if movement was so circumscribed? If transit and sojourn with property, including slaves, were not allowed, then a basic reason for union and nationhood no longer existed.

The Right to Travel and the Antebellum Crisis

Slaveholders who came into the free states could usually be divided into four categories: transient, visitor, sojourner, or resident. These terms were generally tied to temporal definitions, but such definitions had to be flexible. A transient was someone traveling from one state to another (usually from a slave state to a slave state), passing through a free state. Being "in transit" implied continuous movement. A visitor was someone entering a free state with a definite intention to return to his or her home state at some time in the near future. A sojourner intended to leave a free state at some unspecified time in the future. A resident, of course, planned to remain in the free state.

The nuances and distinctions between these statuses have been examined with great care. It is clear from the cases studied that strict definitions were impossible for antebellum courts and legislatures. Ultimately the issue became one of comity: would a free state recognize the status of a slave from another state? This has been designated here as the "transit question" because that, after all, was the lowest common denominator. In a discussion of the right of transit with a slave, however, one must understand how masters were treated if they chose to visit, sojourn, or reside in the free states.

Today the right to travel is accepted as a basic freedom of all Americans. Through the comity provisions of article IV, the Commerce Clause of article I, and the Fourteenth Amendment, the Supreme Court has developed the "constitutional right to travel from one State to another," which "occupies a position fundamental to the concept of our Federal Union. It is a right that has been firmly established and repeatedly recognized."[13] One recent aspect of this development has been to strengthen the rights of persons after they migrate to a new state.[14] As Jacobus tenBroek has noted, "If you may be denied substantial rights after arrival, if you may be barred

---

13. *United States* v. *Guest*, 383 U.S. 745, 757 (1966). See also *Crandall* v. *Nevada*, 6 Wallace (U.S.) 35 (1868); *Edwards* v. *California*, 314 U.S. 160 (1941).

14. For example, *Shapiro* v. *Thompson*, 394 U.S. 618 (1969), invalidating residency requirements for welfare recipients; *Dunn* v. *Blumstein*, 405 U.S. 330 (1972), limiting residency requirements for voting; and *Memorial Hospital* v. *Maricopa*, 415 U.S. 250 (1974), applying *Shapiro* to health care.

from common callings and resources of the community available to others, if opportunities of life and livelihood may be withheld from you on a discriminatory basis, then the right to go there is emptied of substance and meaning."[15] Yet many antebellum Americans had precisely this problem. Most of the decisions protecting the rights of travelers have come since the Civil War. For antebellum travelers protections were less certain.

Without the Fourteenth Amendment and before the modern development of the Commerce Clause,[16] a master in transit could rely only on the Privileges and Immunities Clause for constitutional protection of his slave property. The classic antebellum interpretation of this clause was enunciated by Justice Bushrod Washington in his circuit court opinion in *Corfield* v. *Coryell* (1823).[17] Washington held that the Privileges and Immunities Clause protected, among other things,

> the right to acquire and possess property of every kind,
> and to pursue and obtain happiness and safety; subject
> nevertheless to such restraints as the government may justly
> prescribe for the general good of the whole. The right of the
> citizens of one state to pass through or reside in any other state,
> for the purposes of trade, agriculture, professional pursuits, or
> otherwise; to claim the benefit of the writ of habeas corpus; to
> institute and maintain actions of any kind in the courts of the
> state, to take, hold, and dispose of property, either real
> or personal.[18]

The United States Supreme Court was never asked to apply this clause, or Washington's interpretation of it, to transit with slaves. Had this happened in the late antebellum period, Taney's court possibly would have sustained the right of transit with slaves. Any decision on the subject would have precipitated a major constitutional and political crisis, for by 1860 many state courts had taken an inflexible position on slave transit. Harold Hyman has argued that "[u]ntil 1860 political palliatives salved the major sectional irritants. Parties continued to operate; democracy and federalism worked well enough." It was commonly believed, Hyman maintains, that the Constitution had "institutionalized commendable practices

15. Jacobus tenBroek, *The Constitution and the Right of Free Movement* (New York: National Travelers Aid Association, 1955) 12.

16. For early use of the Commerce Clause, see *Mayor of New York* v. *Miln*, 11 Peters (U.S.) 102 (1837); *Passenger Cases*, 7 Howard (U.S.) 283 (1849); and *Cooley* v. *Board of Wardens of the Port of Philadelphia*, 12 Howard (U.S.) 299 (1851).

17. *Corfield* v. *Coryell*, 6 F. Cas. 450 (1823).

18. Ibid. 456.

of political democracy, [and] perpetuated the happy arrangements of federalism. . . . ."[19] However, in the area of slave transit, federalism and comity were hardly "happy arrangements." On the contrary, well before the secession crisis of 1860–61, the comity provisions of the Constitution were usually ignored when state courts decided cases involving slavery and the rights of free blacks.

This breakdown of comity did not begin immediately after the Union was created. Rather, interstate cooperation eroded gradually. In the early years of the nation, the free states tried to accommodate their slaveholding neighbors who traveled or sojourned in the North. The slave states meanwhile recognized and accepted the acts and judicial decisions of free states that emancipated visiting slaves. Later, as sectionalism grew, the cooperation disappeared. Robert Cover has recently argued that the problem of slaves passing through free states "was settled in most of the North" by 1840,[20] but this was hardly the case, since much of the important litigation and legislation on slave transit was not established until after that date. The trend certainly began before 1840, but it developed over a much longer period than most historians have heretofore recognized. By 1860, however, most northern states refused to allow even the most minor transit with slaves. At the same time, most southern states refused to recognize or uphold freedom based on free-state residence or sojourn, or even direct emancipation in a free state. In only a few states, such as Kentucky and Illinois, was comity granted when the war came. But the firing on Fort Sumter was only a military manifestation of a judicial and legislative war that had been going on for some time between the states.

The American Civil War has been described as a "Constitutional Crisis"[21] and a "Crisis in Law and Order."[22] Antebellum Americans discussed "political issues cast in constitutional terms."[23] As Arthur Bestor has forcefully argued, "the very form that the conflict finally took was determined by the pre-existing form of the constitutional system."[24] Indeed, secession was a logical alternative to the Union because it was a *federal* system. One critical but long-overlooked aspect of the federal Union was the system of interstate comity that

19. Harold M. Hyman, *A More Perfect Union: The Impact of the Civil War and Reconstruction on the Constitution* (New York: A. A. Knopf, 1973) 3, 4.

20. Robert Cover, *Justice Accused: Antislavery and the Judicial Process*, (New Haven: Yale University Press, 1975) 161.

21. Arthur Bestor, "The American Civil War as a Constitutional Crisis," 19 *American Historical Review* 325–52 (1964).

22. Phillip S. Paludan, "The American Civil War Considered as a Crisis in Law and Order," 77 *American Historical Review* 1013–34 (1972).

23. Hyman, *A More Perfect Union* 5.

24. Bestor, "Civil War as Constitutional Crisis" 326–27.

began to break down as early as the 1820s and was well on the road to self-destruction by the 1840s. The antebellum constitutional crisis centered on such obvious and tangible issues as slavery in the territories, slavery in the District of Columbia, the interstate slave trade, and of course the rendition of fugitive slaves. Indeed, the tremendous emphasis on fugitive slaves has led one legal historian to the erroneous conclusion that the "great cases of the twenty years preceding the Civil War were almost all fugitive cases."[25] Yet, along with the fugitive cases and perhaps underlying them was the problem of comity and interstate transit raised in such great cases as *Groves* v. *Slaughter* (1841);[26] *Strader* v. *Graham* (1850);[27] *Dred Scott* v. *Sandford* (1857);[28] and *Lemmon* v. *The People* (1860). After all, if the existing states could not agree to accept each others' laws and decisions, if they could not agree to give "Full Faith and Credit" to the institutions of other states, how could they be expected to return escaped "property" or to agree on the constitutions of new states?

As *Lemmon* v. *The People* and *Mitchell* v. *Wells* show, by 1860 the issue of interstate comity threatened to intrude on the national political scene. The extension of slavery into the North through a Supreme Court decision in a case such as *Lemmon* had become one more element of what Free Soil and Republican politicians called "the Slave Power Conspiracy." By 1860 even moderate and conservative Republicans were beginning to accept parts of this conspiracy theory. Thus Francis Lieber, a conservative Republican and a former professor at the University of South Carolina, thought that "[e]ach institution of government was being strangled by an outreaching slave power."[29] The state courts were not exempt from this process. Indeed, some Republicans and other northerners feared that the crisis in the territories over the role of slavery in the federal system would soon be displaced by a crisis over slavery and freedom in the established states. When Lincoln campaigned for Republican candidates in 1859, he warned that a Democratic victory might set the stage for a "new Dred Scott decision that is to carry slavery into the free States."[30] As the fears of Lieber and Lincoln indicate and the decisions of the courts show, the constitutional crisis that led to war was in part a crisis over federalism—partly because of the nature of

25. Cover, *Justice Accused* 161.

26. *Groves* v. *Slaughter*, 15 Peters (U.S.) 449 (1841).

27. *Strader* v. *Graham*, 10 Howard (U.S.) 82 (1850).

28. *Dred Scott* v. *Sandford*, 19 Howard (U.S.) 393 (1857).

29. Phillip S. Paludan, *A Covenant with Death: The Constitution, Law, and Equality in the Civil War Era* (Urbana: University of Illinois Press, 1975) 79–80.

30. Roy P. Basler, ed., 3 *The Collected Works of Abraham Lincoln* (9 vols. New Brunswick, N.J.: Rutgers University Press, 1953–55) 423.

slavery and partly because of the nature of the Union, the Constitution, and the legal system. As Harold Hyman succinctly put it, "the quarrels of a century ago not only shaped the Constitution, the Constitution shaped the quarrels."[31]

Conflict of Laws and Slavery

Although political and constitutional questions were at the heart of cases involving slave transit, the cases themselves were usually presented as part of what Supreme Court Justice Benjamin N. Cardozo called "one of the most baffling subjects of legal science, the so-called *conflict of law*."[32] A legal case presents a conflict of laws when the issue involves the laws of two or more jurisdictions. In the suit of Nancy Wells, for example, the judges had to decide whether to enforce the laws of Ohio, which would have made her a free person, or the laws of Mississippi, under which she might still be a slave.

At the founding of this country, conflict of laws was one of the most undeveloped fields in Anglo-American jurisprudence. Indeed, not until the publication of Joseph Story's *Commentaries on the Conflict of Laws* in 1834 was there a generally accepted treatise on the subject in the United States. According to David Cavers, Story "used doctrine eclectically and emphasized case law in the manner of the common law jurist" that he was. For theoretical analysis Story relied primarily on the work of seventeenth-century Dutch scholars, particularly that of Ulric Huber.[33] Story borrowed from Huber three main principles of international law from which cases involving conflicting jurisdictions could be determined: (1) Laws have no force beyond the territorial jurisdiction of a state. (2) All persons found within any jurisdiction "whether their residence is temporary or permanent" are subject to the laws of that place. (3) Nations and states "from comity admit" that the laws of other nations and states ought to "have the same force every where" as long as "they do not prejudice the power or rights of other governments, or of their citizens." These principles were derived, not from any civil or natural law, but from "the convenience and tacit

31. Hyman, *A More Perfect Union* xvii.

32. Benjamin Nathan Cardozo, *The Paradoxes of Legal Science* (New York: Columbia University Press, 1928) 27.

33. David F. Cavers, *The Choice-of-Law Process* (Ann Arbor: The University of Michigan Press, 1965) 3–5. One of the few law review articles on slavery and conflict of laws finds that "[m]ost slavery cases, then, were litigated at a time when the American conflicts tradition was in its birth"; "American Slavery and the Conflict of Laws," 71 *Columbia Law Review* 76 (1971).

consent of different people."[34] Indeed, without such rules for international conduct, no trade, travel, or even diplomatic relations would be possible.

Added to these maxims were two conflicting rules concerning personal status and comity in general. Huber thought that every person was "recognized everywhere to have the capacity which he has in his native country, and enjoys everywhere the rights which persons of that capacity there enjoy or are subject to." But no application of comity was possible "when any sovereign power might be seriously inconvenienced in its actions by observing this rule."[35] Although Huber recognized slavery as a legitimate status under international law, his maxims raised major problems when a slave was taken from his native land and brought into a new jurisdiction where slavery "seriously inconvenienced" the sovereign power. Similar problems were of course raised when a free black entered a state where slavery was the usual status for Negroes.

Joseph Story felt that the "true foundation" of international law was based on "[m]utual interest and utility, from a sense of the inconveniences, which would result from a contrary doctrine, and from a sort of moral necessity to do justice in order that justice may be done to us in return." But Story maintained that "no nation is under any obligation to give effect to the laws of another nation, which are prejudicial to itself or its citizens," including anything "which is injurious to their public rights, or offends their morals, or contravenes their policy, or violates a public law."[36]

Moving from general principles to the specific problem, Story asserted that "foreign slaves would no longer be deemed such after their removal" to free states. This maxim was subject, in Story's eyes, only to the restraint found in the Fugitive Slave Clause of the United States Constitution.[37]

Some American courts, judges, and state legislatures were unwilling to accept Story's theories completely. In some states the Constitution was read more broadly to protect slaves in transit. In terms of choice of law, or conflict of laws, judges had basically four options from which to choose. First, they could grant comity to all visitors, based on a desire to maintain interstate harmony and friendship, even at the expense of local laws and institutions. Under this option

34. Joseph Story, *Commentaries on the Conflict of Laws* (1st ed. Boston: Hilliard, Gray and Company, 1834) 30.

35. Ulric Huber, 1 *The Jurisprudence of My Time (Heedensdaegse Rechtsgeleertheyt)*, translated by Percival Gane (2 vols. Durban, South Africa: Butterworth, 1939) 16, 22.

36. Story, *Commentaries* 34, 95.

37. Ibid. 93, 95, 97.

masters visiting the North, like the Lemmons, would be allowed
to retain their slaves; conversely, slave states would uphold the
freedom and rights slaves attained while living in the North. Second, judges could balance free-state interests against slave-state
interests. Thus, a free state might allow a slave to travel across the
state, but not to stop and work there. Or a state might declare a
slave free if that slave had been hired out in a free state, but not free
a slave who accompanied the master on a long pleasure trip in the
North. Jurists attempting to decide cases on this basis would soon
find themselves involved in making careful distinctions among transit, residence, sojourn, and domicile. Some states relied on specific
time spent in the state. For example, before 1847 Pennsylvania
freed visiting slaves after a six-month sojourn, but freed the slaves
of immigrants coming into the state the moment they decided to
make Pennsylvania their state of residence. Ultimately, most states
rejected such careful delineations among residence, sojourn, and
transit, or specific time limits, in favor of more inflexible rules. The
Lemmons were not allowed even the most minor transit with their
slaves, and Nancy Wells was not allowed to claim her legacy in
Mississippi, even though she herself did not want to live in or even
enter that state. The third option, which most states ultimately
adopted, was the enforcement of the *lex fori* (law of the forum) and
rejection of the *lex loci* (law of the state of residence) of the slaves
involved. Thus, New York enforced its own law against the Lemmons (*lex fori*) and absolutely rejected their *lex loci* (in this case the
law of Virginia). Similarly, Mississippi enforced its *lex fori* at the
expense of the *lex loci* of Ohio. Finally, states could ignore all issues
of local policy or conflict of laws theory, by deferring to the United
States Constitution. Here state jurists would try to decide cases
solely on the basis of what they perceived the Constitution to require
in article IV. A strict construction of article IV might have led to
the conclusion that only fugitive-slave property was protected by
the Constitution. A broader view might have led to a more flexible
interpretation. Resorting to federalism probably could have resulted
in any of the three previously mentioned results, at least before the
Dred Scott decision in 1857. After that case it might have been
logically argued that slave property was protected in the free states,
but that free blacks could claim no protections under the United
States Constitution.[38]

38. Don E. Fehrenbacher, *The Dred Scott Case: Its Significance in American Law
and Politics* (New York: Oxford University Press, 1978) 58–61 overstates the importance of the distinctions between transit, sojourn, residence, and domicile. See chapter 7 of this volume for a more detailed discussion of this issue. There is little secondary literature on slavery and the conflict of laws. The previously cited law review

All four of these conflict of laws options were used in the antebellum period. It seems likely, however, that these theories of law did not in themselves always determine state policy. Rather, they were used when necessary or convenient to justify or supplement the policies of judges and legislatures, especially during the period between 1836 and 1861 when questions of slave transit were complicated by the increased politicization of slavery.

The *Somerset* Precedent

The most important judicial precedent on slavery at the Founding was the British case of *Somerset* v. *Stewart* (1772).[39] In that case William Murray, Lord Mansfield, Chief Justice of the Court of King's Bench, ruled that a slave brought to England could not be compelled to leave the realm and could apply for a writ of habeas corpus if forcible removal was attempted. This case was well known throughout the new American nation, and a major theme of this book is the application of *Somerset* to American law. In 1827 *Somerset* was limited by William Scott, Lord Stowell, presiding justice of the High Court of Admiralty, in the case known as *The Slave, Grace* (1827).[40] Grace had lived in England, where she might have claimed her freedom under *Somerset*. Instead, she returned to the West Indies where she later sued for her freedom. Lord Stowell ruled that Grace had been entitled to her freedom only while she was in England; when she returned to a slave jurisdiction her status as a slave re-

---

articles are useful, but flawed. "American Slavery" in particular is replete with factual errors, and the analysis of too few cases leads to inaccurate interpretations and oversimplifications. Cover, *Justice Accused*, and Morris, *Free Men All* are quite useful, although neither directly confronts the transit question. Indeed, Cover seems to think it was not an issue at all. William M. Wiecek, "*Somerset*: Lord Mansfield and the Legitimacy of Slavery in the Anglo-American World," 42 *University of Chicago Law Review* 86–147 (1974); William M. Wiecek, *The Sources of Antislavery Constitutionalism in America, 1760–1848* (Ithaca and London: Cornell University Press, 1977); and David Brion Davis, *The Problem of Slavery in the Age of Revolution, 1770–1823* (Ithaca and London: Cornell University Press, 1975) 469–522, all deal with the period before 1780 in a sound and useful manner. And all three, particularly Wiecek, *Sources of Antislavery Constitutionalism*, refer to later developments, but do not cover them in great detail.

39. *Somerset* v. *Stewart*, Loft (G.B.) 1 (1772); 20 Howell St. Tr. (G.B.) 1 (1772). For a discussion of the background to *Somerset* and the arguments of counsel, see A. Leon Higginbotham, Jr., *In the Matter of Color: Race and the American Legal Process: The Colonial Period* (New York: Oxford University Press, 1978) 313–68.

40. *The Slave, Grace*, 2 Haggard Admiralty (G.B.) 94 (1827).

attached itself to her. A second theme of this book traces the development in American law of the problem presented in *The Slave, Grace*.

The policies set down by state courts are a primary focus of this book. The majority of the cases examined come from state appellate courts. Evidence from the reported state cases, as with any other historical evidence and sources, presents its own special problems. Antebellum court reporting varied a great deal from state to state. Pennsylvania, for example, offers a rich source of printed cases, including some from county courts. Rhode Island, on the other hand, did not have even official supreme court reports until 1845. Most states did record the decisions of their highest court, but not all decisions were reported. Even in so meticulous a state as Massachusetts some important cases brought before the Massachusetts Supreme Judicial Court were not officially reported. Wherever possible in this book, state reports have been supplemented by accounts in newspapers, pamphlets, magazines, law journals, and casebooks. Given the controversial nature of slavery, it is likely that most of the important cases were reported somewhere.

Another problem is the selectivity of legal sources. Most of the cases used in this study were argued before appellate courts. Yet in the antebellum period (or today) most cases were never appealed to higher courts. It is therefore impossible to know the actual number of cases like those of Jonathan Lemmon or Nancy Wells. It is equally impossible to know how many slaves actually spent time in the free states, while in transit or on visits with their owners.[41] Undoubtedly many more slaves were entitled to their freedom because of transit or residence in a free state than actually attained it. The evidence here shows only that some slaves did become free in this manner and how state courts and legislatures dealt with the problem.

In focusing on the reported decisions of the antebellum courts, one is able to see how the legal system and the society it served responded to slavery and how that system was exploited by politicians and activists on both sides of the Mason-Dixon line. These cases show that the antislavery movement was particularly adept at using the legal system to attack slavery, especially in the area of slave transit. The personal liberty laws, enacted in most free states to give due process rights to blacks claimed as fugitive slaves, were only moderately successful. Their intent, after all, was procedural. At best they could only stall the eventual rendition of fugitive

41. John Hope Franklin, *A Southern Odyssey: Travelers in the Antebellum North* (Baton Rouge: Louisiana State University Press, 1976) is the only study of southerners visiting the North. Franklin has a useful chapter on slaves who came with their masters, some of whom voluntarily returned to the South.

slaves.[42] In transit cases, on the other hand, the attack was substantive and if successful led to permanent liberty for the slave. Moreover, the laws and decisions freeing slaves in transit were direct attacks on the institution of slavery in one of the few areas where it could be reached by northerners. These cases also reveal that racism and negrophobia in the North were more complicated phenomena than many historians have realized. While many in the free states discouraged the growth of a black population in the North, the judiciaries and the legislatures often went out of their way to free slaves in transit. This practice, of course, led to a growth of the free black population in those states. However blacks were despised in the North, courts and legislatures were willing to free slaves even if it meant an increase in the free black population.[43]

Very few federal cases dealt with slavery and comity. In antebellum America a person's legal status was usually determined by state law. Nevertheless, a few major United States Supreme Court cases, as well as lower federal court cases, did deal with slavery and transit.

State Courts and the Antebellum Crisis

Charles Fairman has written, "Unless one has patiently examined the involved chronology—to distinguish between what was cause and what was consequence—and has looked squarely at the hard alternatives inherent in the facts, he cannot know the context within which the Court acted. Without full knowledge a reasonable judgment may not be made."[44] Much of the involved chronology of the antebellum legal battle over slavery is found in the records of the state courts, as well as those of the lower federal courts and the United States Supreme Court. Indeed, Fairman's statement must be extended to include the state courts, for much of the debate in the 1850s in the Supreme Court, and in the political arena, over such issues as *Dred Scott*, slave expansion, secession, and the "slave power" makes sense only in the context of state court decisions dealing with slavery and the conflict of laws.

42. See Campbell, *Slave Catchers*, and Morris, *Free Men All*.
43. The best study of northern attitudes toward blacks is Leon F. Litwack, *North of Slavery: The Negro in the Free States, 1790–1860* (Chicago: University of Chicago Press, 1961). However, Litwack does not analyze the issues or cases studied here. Thus, his conclusions must be modified in the light of these cases freeing blacks and allowing them to live in the free states.
44. Charles Fairman, *Reconstruction and Reunion, 1864–1888, Part One* (New York: Macmillan Company, 1971), 90.

The declared policy of the state courts and legislatures, as well as major federal court cases, helped create the constitutional crisis that led to the Civil War. These policies and the decision making of antebellum jurists reflected the assumptions, attitudes, and fears of antebellum Americans. The decisions of the state judges and the statutes of their legislatures demonstrate how a nation of states was well on its way to dissolving its judicial and legal bonds when secession completed that process. The cases show that interstate comity and harmony were severely tested by slavery and that ultimately slavery undermined and destroyed interstate relations. Most of all, these cases illustrate how individuals and legal institutions attempted to cope with a problem that was, in legal terms, insurmountable.

Chapter 1

The Privileges and Immunities of the Masters: Slavery and Comity at the Founding

In 1787 the Founding Fathers failed to provide adequately for the interstate movement of slaves. Slavery was a critical issue at the Constitutional Convention, and slave transit, through the *Somerset* case, had already emerged as a legal issue. But, for the reasons discussed below, southern delegates did not push the issue of slave transit in 1787.

By 1861 southern leaders regretted the lack of foresight by their political forebears. Thus, in the Confederate Constitution they went out of their way to rectify what had been done—or not done—in 1787. The Confederate Constitution shows what might have been accomplished in 1787 to insure greater comity for slave property in the United States. An examination of what the Confederate Constitutional Convention accomplished can lead to a better understanding of the problem of slavery and comity under the United States Constitution.

Comity in Two Constitutions

The Confederate Constitution of 1861 was a true child of the United States Constitution. The two are identical in format and nearly so in content. Almost all the substantive changes in the newer document reflected the southerners' profound distrust and distaste for centralized government. As Charles Lee has concluded, "The Confederate Constitutions are principally significant . . . [because] they represent the ultimate constitutional expression of the state rights philosophy and state sovereignty concept in nineteenth century America."[1]

Yet, in one important area the Confederate Constitution severely

---

1. Charles Robert Lee, Jr., *The Confederate Constitutions* (Chapel Hill: University of North Carolina Press, 1963) 150.

limited state power in an explicit attempt to create a more unified Confederacy. Article IV of the federal Constitution had been inserted to insure that interstate relations would not be hampered by conflicting laws of the different states. Under section 1 of these comity provisions, the "public Acts, Records, and judicial Proceedings" of one state were to be given "Full Faith and Credit" in all other states;[2] section 2, which Alexander Hamilton "esteemed the basis of the Union,"[3] guaranteed that citizens of any one state were "entitled to all the Privileges and Immunities of Citizens in the several States"; it further provided that fugitives from justice and runaway slaves be returned to the states from which they escaped.[4] These provisions insured that citizens of one state would have political, economic, civil, and procedural legal rights when traveling through, visiting, migrating to, or doing business in other states. Without such provisions, legal relations between the states would have rested on the unenforceable and unpredictable legal theories of the international law of comity or *jus gentium* (law of nations).

In article IV of the Confederate Constitution these provisions were not weakened to give more power to local judges and state legislatures. Rather, they were strengthened to insure greater protection for the "cornerstone" of the Confederacy, slavery. The Confederacy retained the original wording of the Full Faith and Credit Clause. The wording of the Privileges and Immunities Clause was also left intact, but the following was added: "[A]nd [the citizens of each State] shall have the right of transit and sojourn in any State of this Confederacy, with their slaves and other property; and the right of property in said slaves shall not be thereby impaired." A similar change was made in the Fugitive Slave Clause, by inserting the words *Lawfully carried*, so that runaway slaves could be recaptured in a state, whether they had escaped into another state or been lawfully brought into the state and then escaped.[5]

These changes were designed to insure that, no matter what any state might do about slavery within its own borders at some future time, the movement of masters with their slave property would not be hindered. The changes, which were apparently passed without debate,[6] were probably more symbolic than necessary. It would have

2. U.S., *Constitution*, art. IV, sec. 1.

3. Clinton Rossiter, ed., *The Federalist Papers* (New York: New American Library, 1961), *Federalist No. 80*, 478.

4. U.S., *Constitution*, art. IV, sec. 2.

5. Confederate States, *Constitution*, art. IV, sec. 2; Lee, *Confederate Constitutions* 110.

6. 1 *Journal of the Congress of the Confederate States of America, 1861–1865* (7 vols. Washington: Government Printing Office, 1904–05) 881–83.

been unlikely that the Confederate founders could have imagined the day when any of the seceding states would abolish slavery. As symbols they represented rights the slaveowners thought they had under the federal Constitution but which had never been explicitly written into the compact of 1787. Like the provision guaranteeing slavery in the Confederate territories,"[7] these additions to the Constitution seem to form a declaration of just causes for the seceding states: they had been denied full access to the territories, or felt such denial imminent, and had been denied comity by the northern states. Secession was justified.

Slavery at the Constitutional Convention

On the third day of the 1787 Constitutional Convention, Edmund Randolph of Virginia spoke at length of the "defects of confederation." While as yet "no commercial discord had arisen among any states," the "federal government could not check quarrels between the states," and disruptions of the peace seemed inevitable. A new government was necessary, which "ought to secure . . . against dissentions between members of the Union, or seditions in particular states." The new government would be national in scope and could better provide "common defence, security of liberty, and general welfare."[8]

For the next three months the delegates worked on a document that would bind the thirteen newly independent states into one nation.[9] While creating a strong national government, the founders had to protect and placate many important local interests. State sovereignty, individual rights, legal and political institutions, sectional needs, and economic interests all competed for a voice and a share in the new national government. Among the most critical of

7. Confederate States, *Constitution*, art. IV, sec. 3.

8. Max Farrand, ed., 1 *The Records of the Federal Convention of 1787* (4 vols. New Haven: Yale University Press, 1937) 18–19, 30.

9. At the convention, James Wilson of Pennsylvania thought a strong Union would be in the tradition of the Revolution. He read the Declaration of Independence to the convention, "observing thereon that the *United Colonies* were declared to be free & independent States; and inferring that they were independent, not *Individually*, but *Unitedly* . . . "; Farrand, 1 *Records* 334. If this attitude toward interdependence of the states was more or less universally held at the convention, it may explain why the comity provisions of article IV were so general and why there was little debate over them. Wilson's contention would imply general agreement that the states should grant special and flexible comity to citizens of the other states. In this sense article IV is a reaffirmation of basic principles as well as a statement of interstate obligations.

these issues, and the one that demanded and received a great deal of protection, was slavery. While not yet the great moral and political issue it would become half a century later, slavery nonetheless affected many of the convention's most crucial decisions. Representation, taxation, commercial regulation, domestic tranquility, state sovereignty, and interstate relations were all complicated by slavery. James Madison accurately "contended" while debating the structure and representation in the new national legislature

> that the States were divided into different interests not
> by their difference of size, but by other circumstances, the
> most material of which resulted partly from climate, but
> principally from the effects of their having or not having slaves.
> These two causes concurred in forming the great division of in-
> terests in the U[nited] States. It did not lie between the large &
> small States: it lay between the Northern & Southern. [A]nd
> if any defensive power [in the Congress] were necessary,
> it ought to be mutually given to these two interests, (as a
> security ag[ain]st the encroachments of each other).[10]

Although many delegates were hostile to slavery, no one proposed outright abolition under the new government. As Winthrop Jordan has noted, "manifestly the Convention could not consider even the eventual termination of domestic slavery; propositions on this head would have sent half the delegates packing."[11] While the delegates who disliked slavery hoped to curb the institution whenever possible, a small but vociferous proslavery group fought tenaciously to protect and strengthen slavery. Whenever this group apprehended a danger to slavery, its members raised a protest, made a deal, or threatened to start packing. Through bluster, compromise, and political blackmail over the question of union itself, they secured power and protection for slavery.

Led by delegates from Georgia and South Carolina, the proslavery group gained a series of important concessions in the areas of taxation, representation, the slave trade, and fugitive slaves.

10. Farrand, 1 *Records* 486. The quote in parentheses was in Madison's original notes, but was later deleted by him. See also Winthrop D. Jordan, *White over Black* (Baltimore: Penguin Books, 1968) 321–23, and Staughton Lynd, *Class Conflict, Slavery and the United States Constitution* (Indianapolis: The Bobbs-Merrill Company, 1967) 185–213, for discussions of slavery and sectionalism at the Founding.

11. Jordan, *White over Black* 323. In the heat of debate over the Three-Fifths Clause, Gouverneur Morris of Pennsylvania said he "would sooner submit himself to a tax for paying for all the Negroes . . . than saddle posterity with such a Constitution"; Farrand, 2 *Records* 223. These remarks appear to be rhetorical, for they were never repeated or considered, and are the only ones at the convention calling for an end to slavery.

More critical, perhaps, were the negative protections that restricted the central government to only those powers enumerated in the Constitution.

On paper the explicit compromises over slavery seem relatively equitable. Slavery was given representation on a three-fifths basis, but owners would be taxed at the same rate if and when direct taxes were levied; the importation of slaves, which both northerners and most southerners found morally objectionable, could be abolished by Congress, but only after twenty years. In the intervening grace period, Georgia and South Carolina could import the slaves they claimed to need so desperately. An additional trade-off, involving the Commerce Clause, may have been part of this compromise. General Charles Cotesworth Pinckney of South Carolina felt that "it was the true interest of the S[outhern] States to have no regulation of commerce," but a number of factors, including the "Eastern States . . . liberal conduct toward the views of South Carolina" with regard to the slave trade, made him think "it proper that no fetters should be imposed on the power of making commercial regulations."[12] Finally, masters were granted the right to recover their runaway bondsmen.

The apparent equity of these compromises soon faded as the new nation implemented its constitution. Direct taxes based on the three-fifths compromise were never levied. As Gouverneur Morris of Pennsylvania argued at the convention, "It is idle to suppose that Gen[era]l Gov[ernmen]t can stretch its hand directly into the pockets of the people scattered over so vast a Country." Morris and Rufus King of Massachusetts both felt the exports produced by slave labor ought to be taxed, but this idea was categorically rejected by the South.[13] While the slave states were never taxed for their slaves, they did gain an increment in their congressional delegations based on the slave population. While the three-fifths clause might "lean" "to freedom, not to slavery" as Frederick Douglass would later claim,[14] no provision for representation based on slaves would

12. Farrand, 2 *Records* 450. Luther Martin of Maryland, who opposed this compromise, noted, "[T]he Eastern states, not withstanding their aversion to slavery, were very willing to indulge the Southern States at least with a temporary liberty to prosecute the slave trade, provided the Southern States would, in turn, gratify *them*, by laying no restriction on navigation acts"; Luther Martin to constituents, in Jonathan Elliot, ed., 5 *The Debates in the Several State Conventions on the Adoption of the Federal Constitution as Recommended by the General Convention at Philadelphia, in 1787* (5 vols. Philadelphia: J. B. Lippincott, 1896) 497.

13. Farrand, 2 *Records* 22–23.

14. Philip S. Foner, ed., 2 *The Life and Writings of Frederick Douglass* (4 vols. New York: International Publishers, 1950–55) 372.

have leaned even further toward freedom. In the long run, free states gained nothing from the clause, while the slave states gained greater congressional representation and thus a disproportionate influence in the federal government.

The slave trade would be prohibited twenty years later, but, as Madison predicted, the period produced "all the mischief that can be apprehended from the liberty to import slaves."[15] When the clause was written into the Constitution, many thought it would lead to the eventual end of slavery. The Reverend Isaac Backus told the Massachusetts ratifying convention: "[A] door is now open hereafter to [abolish the slave trade] . . . and each state is at liberty now to abolish slavery as soon as they please. . . . And, as an honorable gentleman said some days ago, 'Though we cannot say that slavery is struck with apoplexy, yet we may hope it will die with a consumption.'" More to the point was James Wilson's summation before the Pennsylvania ratifying convention: "I consider this as laying the foundation for banishing slavery out of this country; and though the period is more distant than I could wish, yet it will produce the same kind, gradual change, which was pursued in Pennsylvania." Wilson felt that "[i]f there was no other lovely feature in the Constitution but this one, it would diffuse a beauty over its whole countenance. Yet the lapse of a few years, and Congress will have power to exterminate slavery within our borders."[16] Members of the Pennsylvania Society for Promoting the Abolition of Slavery, the Relief of Free Negroes Unlawfully Held in Bondage, and for Improving the Condition of the African Race—the Pennsylvania Abolition Society, as it was usually known—were less sanguine than their neighbor Wilson. Nevertheless, they wrote their counterparts in London, "We rejoice in the prospect of the good effects of this part of the proposed Constitution of our Country, inasmuch as it will afford when it shall be exercised the first instance of a Sovereign power by a public acknowledgement doing homage to the Christian principle of 'doing to others what we would wish them to do to us.'"[17]

Many northerners felt slavery could not survive without a constant influx of new slaves from abroad. Southern delegates knew otherwise. They had seen slavery survive quite well during the Revolution and immediately after the conflict, even though there had been no active overseas trade. Nevertheless, no southern dele-

15. Farrand, 2 *Records* 415.

16. Elliot, 2 *Debates in the Several States* 149, 452, 484.

17. Letter to the London Society for the Abolition of the Slave Trade, Minutes of 20 Oct. 1787, Pennsylvania Abolition Society Papers, microfilm reel 1, Historical Society of Pennsylvania (hereafter cited as HSP), Philadelphia.

gates contradicted the northern assumptions and expectations that the prohibition of the slave trade would lead to an end to slavery.[18] Not only did the slave trade clause fail to end slavery, but it was only marginally useful in ending the African slave trade. James Madison, who bitterly opposed the leniency of the clause, admitted to the Virginia ratifying convention, "The Union in general is not in a worse situation. Under the Articles of Confederation, it might be continued forever; but, by this clause, an end may be put to it after twenty years.... A tax may be laid in the mean time."[19] Yet, despite concerted efforts on the part of the British navy to end all slaving in the northern hemisphere, the slave trade continued after it was legally abolished in 1808. The national government, with few exceptions, showed little interest in suppressing the trade and enforcing the laws against it. Presidential requests for stronger sanctions against slavers and appropriations for stricter enforcement were rare, and when they were made, Congress ignored them. The United States consistently refused to join Great Britain in a bilateral effort to end the Atlantic slave trade. Not until the Lincoln administration did Congress provide "appropriations commensurate with the vastness of the task" of suppressing the slave trade. This act was possible only because proslavery congressional delegations were no longer in a position to stop appropriations and legislation. In any event, the Slave Importation Clause allowed twenty years of additional importations but in the long run did little to end slavery itself.[20]

The hastily drafted and accepted Fugitive Slave Clause proved the most vexatious, if not the most important, part of the Constitution directly bearing on slavery. On 28 August 1787 Pierce Butler and Charles Pinckney of South Carolina[21] moved to amend the section concerning fugitives from justice by inserting the words "to require fugitive slaves and servants to be delivered up like criminals." James Wilson objected that the states would have to pay for the upkeep and incarceration of the slaves, while Connecticut's Roger Sherman protested that there was "no more propriety in the public seizing and surrendering a slave or servant, than a horse." Butler then "withdrew his proposition in order that some particular

18. See W. E. B. DuBois, *The Suppression of the African Slave-Trade to the United States of America, 1638–1870* (Cambridge: Harvard University Press, 1896) 61–62. For a different interpretation, see speech of Frederick Douglass in Foner, 2 *Frederick Douglass* 472–73.

19. Elliot, 3 *Debates in the Several States* 453.

20. DuBois, *Suppression of African Slave-Trade* 91; W. E. F. Ward, *The Royal Navy and the Slavers: The Suppression of the Atlantic Slave Trade* (New York: Schocken Books, 1970), 138–61 and *passim*.

21. Two Pinckneys from South Carolina attended the convention: General Charles Cotesworth Pinckney and his younger, more strident cousin, Charles Pinckney.

provision might be made apart from" the article on fugitives from justice. The next day Butler introduced the Fugitive Slave Clause as a separate article to follow the article on fugitives from justice. It was agreed to without debate or formal vote.[22] The clause provided little indication of how it was to work, or what indeed it was to accomplish, other than allowing a master to regain somehow the services of slaves who had run away to other states. As interpreted by Congress and the courts, however, this clause stimulated a direct attack on northern moral sensibilities and fundamental notions of due process.[23]

In the long run the clause and its enabling legislation did little to protect or retrieve southern "property,"[24] but it did inflame sectional hostilities. Perhaps debate at the convention would have sharpened the focus of the clause and indicated how it was to be implemented. At the time, however, fugitive slaves were only a minor concern, and the clause was offered late in the convention. So vague was the clause that the antifederalist leader George Mason argued that "[n]o real security could arise" from it because it "only meant that runaway slaves should not be protected in other states." Neither Mason nor anyone else could foresee a federally regulated Fugitive Slave Law with marshals and special commissioners. Madison could answer Mason only by saying, "This is a better security than any that now exists," because "[a]t present, if any slave elopes in any of those states where slaves are free, he becomes emancipated by their laws; for the laws of the states are uncharitable to one another in this respect," but the Fugitive Slave Clause "was expressly inserted, to enable owners of slaves to reclaim them."[25] The delegates returning to North Carolina agreed with Madison, and told their governor that "[t]he Southern States have also a much better Security for the Return of Slaves who might endeavour to Escape than they had under the original Confederation." Charles Cotesworth Pinckney was the most optimistic, telling the South Carolina House of Repre-

---

22. Farrand, 2 *Records* 443, 453–54.

23. See Thomas D. Morris, *Free Men All: The Personal Liberty Laws of the North, 1780–1861* (Baltimore: Johns Hopkins University Press, 1974), for an excellent study of northern reaction to the fugitive slave laws. Also see William M. Wiecek, *The Sources of Antislavery Constitutionalism in America, 1760–1848* (Ithaca and London: Cornell University Press, 1977), especially chaps. 7 and 8.

24. The most recent work on the Fugitive Slave Law of 1850, Stanley W. Campbell, *The Slave Catchers: Enforcement of the Fugitive Slave Law, 1850–1860* (Chapel Hill: University of North Carolina Press, 1970), argues that the 1850 law was effective. However, Campbell finds only 298 fugitives returned in eleven years (at 207), while in 1850 alone the U.S. Census reported 1,011 slaves as runaways (at 6). This return rate is hardly illustrative of effective law enforcement.

25. Elliot, 3 *Debates in the Several States* 458, 453.

sentatives, "We have obtained a right to recover our slaves in whatever part of America they may take refuge, which is a right we had not before."[26]

The existing records of the northern state conventions do not indicate a single discussion of the clause. *The Federalist* fails even to mention the clause, much less explain it. As in the previously examined clauses, slaveowners won concessions with the Fugitive Slave Clause, while those opposed to slavery gained nothing.

The most important safeguard the proslavery delegates wanted was protection from abolition. In the heated debate over representation, Pennsylvania's Gouverneur Morris initiated what was perhaps the most forthright discussion of slavery at the convention: "Either this distinction [between North and South] is fictitious or real: if fictitious let it be dismissed & let us proceed with due confidence. If it be real, instead of attempting to blend incompatible things, let us at once take a friendly leave of each other. There can be no end of demands for security if every particular interest is to be entitled to it." Pierce Butler answered for the South with equal candor. Economic gain or even a guaranteed majority in Congress were not what the South wanted. "The security the South[er]n States want," Butler claimed, "is that their negroes may not be taken from them which some gentlemen within or without doors, have a very good mind to do."[27] Ten days later Charles Cotesworth Pinckney reiterated the point when he demanded "some security to the Southern States ag[ain]st an emancipation of slaves and taxes on exports. . . ."[28]

Although no specific clause insured against emancipation, the structure of the federal government as a whole did so. Because there was no specific clause allowing or authorizing emancipation, most supporters of the Constitution concluded that the national government would be powerless in this area. But a number of antifederalists were not so sure. In the Virginia ratifying convention Patrick Henry noted, "Among ten thousand *implied powers* which they may assume, they may, if we be engaged in war, liberate every one of your slaves if they please. . . . Have they not power to provide for the general defense and welfare? May they not think that these call for the abolition of slavery? May they not pronounce all slaves free, and will they not be warranted by that power? This is no

---

26. Farrand, 3 *Records* 84, 254–55.

27. 1 ibid. 604–5.

28. 2 ibid. 95. Earlier, Charles Cotesworth Pinckney expressed concern "that property in slaves should not be exposed to danger under a Gov[ernmen]t instituted for the protection of property"; ibid. 593–94.

ambiguous implication or logical deduction."[29] Other Virginians saw the Slave Importation Clause as allowing the federal government to end slavery, although their fear does not seem to be based, like the hopes of many northerners, on the unrealistic assumption that slavery would die out without the trade. The Virginians, after all, knew from their experience during the Revolution and Confederation period when the slave trade was illegal in that state, that slavery could survive without a constant influx of fresh Africans. Rather, some Virginians misconstrued the clause to imply that after twenty years the government could end slavery. The fears of these antifederalists were based more on their concern for the misuse of power by a strong central government than on the wording of the Constitution itself.

Most southern politicians apparently agreed with Madison that slavery was secure under the new Constitution because "there must be some degree of confidence put in their agents, or else we must reject a state of civil society altogether." Governor Edmund Randolph of Virginia had reservations about the necessary and proper clause because its "ambiguity may injure the states . . . by gradual accessions" of power to the national government. Nevertheless, he gave the Constitution a clean bill of health with regard to slavery. In answering attacks on the Slave Importation Clause, he demanded, "*Where* is the part that has a tendency to *the abolition of slavery?* . . . Does it affect the existing state of slavery?" He then used his position as a member of the Virginia delegation to drive home the point. In doing so he showed that those northerners at the convention, like James Wilson, who thought that the clause would lead to the end of slavery were either incredibly naive or were indulging in wishful thinking. Randolph told the Virginia state convention, "Were it right here to mention what passed in convention on the occasion [of the debate of the Slave Importation Clause], I might tell you *that the Southern States, even South Carolina herself, conceived this property to be secure by these words.* I believe, whatever we may think here, that there was not a member of the Virginia delegation who had *the smallest suspicion of the abolition of slavery.* Go to their meaning. Point out the clause where this formidable

29. Elliot, 3 *Debates in the Several States* 589–90. Henry was correct and prophetic, as Lincoln used the war powers to free slaves under the Emancipation Proclamation. However, the proclamation applied only to those areas of the nation that had seceded and had not yet been subdued. It is unclear if, in the event of foreign war, a president would have been able to end slavery through the implied powers. Even during the Civil War Lincoln did not believe he had the power to end slavery in the loyal slave states.

power of emancipation is inserted." The governor offered the Fugitive Slave Clause to prove "the absurdity of the supposition" that
the Constitution would allow abolition. If a Virginian could capture
a runaway in one state, could "it be seriously thought that, after
taking him and bringing him home, he could be made free?"[30]

General Charles Cotesworth Pinckney, who at the convention had
been adamant in his demands for protection of slavery, was evi-
dently quite satisfied with the implicit guarantees and protections
he obtained for the institution. During the debate over ratification
in South Carolina he told that state's house of representatives:

> We have a security that the general government can never
> emancipate them, for no such authority is granted; and it is
> admitted, on all hands that the general government has no
> powers but what are expressly granted by the Constitution, and
> that all rights not expressed were reserved by the several
> states. . . . In short, considering all circumstances, we have
> made the best terms for the security of this species of property it
> was in our power to make. We would have made better if we
> could; but on the whole, I do not think them bad.[31]

Slavery and Article IV

In one important area, however, the Constitution failed to provide
adequate security for slaveholders. While the Constitution, and thus
the national government, implicitly recognized slavery, nothing in
the Constitution obligated the states to recognize it. While the national government might be constrained from legislating against
slavery, the states were limited only by the Fugitive Slave Clause.
On all other aspects of slavery, the states were free to legislate as
they saw fit. The control and regulation of slavery would come under
the general police powers of the individual states, powers that were
left intact in the new Constitution. As Alexander Hamilton told the
New York ratifying convention, "Were the laws of the Union to new-
model the internal police of any state; were they to alter, or abrogate
at a blow, the whole of its civil and criminal institutions; were they
to penetrate the recesses of domestic life, and control, in all respects,
the private conduct of individuals,—there might be more force in
the objection" to the Constitution. But, happily such was not the
case.[32] On the direct question of slavery, General William Heath

---

30. 3 ibid. 458–59, 470, 598–99.
31. Farrand, 3 *Records* 254–55.
32. Elliot, 2 *Debates in the Several States* 267–68.

told the Massachusetts convention, "Each state is sovereign and independent to a certain degree, and the states have a right, and they will regulate their own internal affairs" as they saw fit.[33] Thus, "by the new Constitution, every particular state is left to its own option totally to prohibit the introduction of slaves into its own territories."[34]

While slaveowners might be protected from *federal* interference, the only guarantee from the states was that some method would be worked out to recover fugitive slaves. When traveling through, visiting, or sojourning in another state, a master's slave property would be protected only if the host state cared to protect it. Yet, without the freedom to travel with their bondsmen, slaveholders would lose important rights, which they expected to secure under the new Constitution. As counsel for a slaveowner would argue on the eve of the Civil War, if laws were allowed prohibiting masters from passing through free states with their slaves, then "the non-slaveholding States could pen up all slaveholders within their States as effectually as the slave is himself confined."[35]

Under British rule the American colonists were guaranteed freedom of movement by virtue of their imperial citizenship. Slavery and the slave trade were protected by the crown and were legal in all the colonies. Article IV of the Articles of Confederation provided that

> free inhabitants of each of these states, paupers, vaga-
> bonds, and fugitives from justice excluded . . . shall have
> free ingress and regress to and from any other State, and shall
> enjoy therein all the privileges of trade and commerce, subject
> to the same duties, impositions and restrictions, as the
> inhabitants thereof respectively; provided, that such restric-
> tions shall not extend so far as to prevent the removal of
> property, imported into any State, to any other State of
> which the owner is an inhabitant.[36]

While this clause gave the free citizens of one state the right to travel in other states, it is difficult to determine how the clause

33. 2 ibid. 115.
34. 2 ibid. 40.
35. *Lemmon* v. *The People*, 20 N.Y. 562, 580 (1860).
36. *The Articles of Confederation and Perpetual Union*, art. IV. When the articles were being debated, South Carolina attempted to insert the word *white* between *free* and *inhabitants*. According to Donald L. Robinson, *Slavery in the Structure of American Politics, 1765–1820* (New York: Harcourt Brace Jovanovich, 1971), 153–54, this amendment was rejected because the delegates were in a hurry to finish the Articles, and not for any major substantive reasons. If haste was indeed the reason for not including the word *white* and thus explicitly limiting comity to "free white inhabit-

applied to slaves. The phrase "property, imported into any State" might have protected all types of property. But if one state refused even to recognize a certain type of property, or banned it, then importation could be hampered. While the Articles of Confederation were in effect, every northern state banned the importing and/or exporting of slaves. More important, as will be examined below, Pennsylvania limited the right of sojourn with a slave.[37] Because of their short life under wartime and postwar conditions, the Articles were never tested. However, the Deep South states viewed the protections for their peculiar institution as inadequate and wanted them strengthened in the new Constitution.

The Constitution of 1787 did little to clarify the meaning of its comity provisions with regard to slavery. Article IV provided that "Full Faith and Credit shall be given each State to the public Acts, Records and Proceedings of every other State" and that Congress could pass laws to "prescribe the manner in which such Acts, Records and Proceedings shall be proved, and the Effect thereof." "Full Faith and Credit" might have meant free states were obligated to recognize the master-slave relationship created in a slave state. However, such "Full Faith and Credit" could be a two-edged sword. By the same logic, a slave state might be obligated to recognize the status of freedom gained by a slave while visiting a nonslave state, just as a state would be obligated to recognize a divorce granted by the laws of another state. No cases were ever brought to a federal court on this subject, and Congress never passed legislation bearing on it.

The debate on this clause at the convention was short and not very helpful. The original draft of the clause ended with the first sentence and did not refer to Congress. Hugh Williamson of North Carolina did not understand "precisely the meaning of the article" and offered the similar clause in the Articles of Confederation as a substitute. William Johnson of Connecticut and James Wilson "supposed the meaning to be that Judgments in one State should be the ground of actions in other States, & that acts of the Legislatures should be included, for the sake of Acts of insolvency &c—." Charles Pinckney moved to recommit the section and add a clause concerning bank-

---

ants," then South Carolina and other Deep South states may have felt no obligation, under the Articles or the Constitution, to grant comity to free blacks from other states. The understanding that "free inhabitants" in the Articles applied only to whites may very well have carried over into the more broadly worded provision for comity in the Constitution.

37. Arthur Zilversmit, *The First Emancipation: The Abolition of Slavery in the North* (Chicago: University of Chicago Press, 1967) 106–8, 120, 148–53, 156–69.

ruptcies, and foreign bills of exchange.[38] The clause was then sent to a committee consisting of Wilson, Johnson, Nathaniel Gorham of Massachusetts, and two southerners, Edmund Randolph of Virginia and John Rutledge of South Carolina. Five days later it was reported out of committee and the current wording accepted without debate or formal vote. The substance of Charles Pinckney's amendment was left out of this clause but was incorporated into article I,[39] which may indicate that the clause was to have a general meaning, as Johnson and Wilson argued.

If the Full Faith and Credit Clause was meant to give legal recognition to slavery in nonslave states, it is likely that the southerners at the convention would have said something to that effect. The debates in the state conventions provide even less help in interpreting the clause. Only in Virginia was it even mentioned. Here the antifederalist George Mason questioned the extent of congressional power to "declare the effects" of acts of other states. Madison's answer was honest, if not terribly informative: "[I]t appears to me that this is a clause which is absolutely necessary. I never heard of any objection to this clause before, and have not employed a thought on the subject."[40]

The next section of article IV is equally vague. "The Citizens of each State shall be entitled to all Privileges and Immunities of Citizens of the several States." This clause provoked little debate, either at the convention or in any of the ratifying conventions. Hamilton's only reference to it in *The Federalist* was that as "the basis of the Union" the clause ought to be enforced by a national judiciary.[41] It was apparently accepted by all concerned as a shortened, but equally meaningful version of the more elaborate Privileges and Immunities Clause in the Articles of Confederation.

Although the clause was clearly meant to protect the rights of

38. Farrand, 2 *Records* 447; U.S., *Constitution*, art. IV, sec. 1.

39. Farrand, 2 *Records* 448, 489.

40. Elliot, 3 *Debates in the Several States* 584–85. Madison's brief mention of the clause in *Federalist No. 42* is a little more illuminating, for he suggested that it would provide for more fair state trials where citizens of different states were involved.

41. See Rossiter, *Federalist Papers, Federalist No. 80*, 478. Debate between Morris and Wilson over the exact wording of article I, section 8, giving Congress the power to define certain crimes, suggests that no one at the convention had any precise ideas about the exact nature of comity or international law. James Wilson thought it was "ridiculous" and "would have a look of arrogance" for Congress to be given the power to define the law of nations. Morris thought certain "offences" could be defined, but agreed the law of nations was "often too vague and deficient to be a rule"; Farrand, 2 *Records* 614–15. This vagueness and uncertainty on the part of the delegates may in part explain the lack of specificity in article IV.

citizens from one state who might be traveling, visiting, or doing business in another state, the wording was ambiguous. For example, was Virginia obligated, under this clause, to recognize the citizenship of a black from Massachusetts, who had the franchise and other rights of citizenship in his home state? Or was Virginia in this case merely obligated to treat the black as Virginia would treat a native free black? Was Massachusetts, on the other hand, obligated to recognize the privileges and immunities of a slaveowner to control his "property" as he saw fit, or was the master-slave relationship to be governed by local law, even if that local law worked to end the relationship by freeing the slave? Could a free black citizen from Massachusetts, traveling in a slave state, demand the right to testify in court against a white, because he had that right in his home state? And, by the same token, could a slaveowner visiting the North demand that the relevant testimony of his own slave be excluded, should he find himself in a legal controversy?

Comity is the granting of rights by one nation or state to the citizens of another. Without such rights a union of states would be worthless. Yet, according to Supreme Court Justice Joseph Story, "comity is, and ever must be, uncertain. That it must necessarily depend on a variety of circumstances, which cannot be reduced to any certain rule."[42] Article IV was designed to create a certain rule, namely that the states of the new national Union would recognize the laws and judicial proceedings of other states and grant privileges and immunities to the citizens of other states. Even under ideal circumstances, the conflict of laws between the states would create problems. With the factors of race and caste added, the issues might prove insurmountable unless the fundamental law of the nation, the Constitution, declared clear and unambiguous rules from which to proceed. Unfortunately, article IV of the new Constitution was not so helpful. And even in the early years, the interstate movement of masters with their slave "property" raised legal problems in some states. As slavery grew into a major political, social, and moral issue, these problems complicated and undermined interstate relations.

The *Somerset* Precedent

When the Privileges and Immunities Clause was read at the convention, there was no real debate over it. However, Madison does report that Charles Cotesworth Pinckney was not satisfied. "He seemed

42. Joseph Story, *Commentaries on the Conflict of Laws*, (1st ed. Boston: Hilliard, Gray and Company, 1834) 29.

to wish some provision should be included in favor of property in slaves." Perhaps because of this objection, the South Carolina delegation opposed the clause and Georgia was divided, while the other nine state delegations in attendance favored it.[43] It is likely that Pinckney was concerned with slave movement and masters in transit when he raised the objection.[44] Throughout the convention the proslavery representatives had been adamant about protecting their property. It seems odd, therefore, not that Pinckney made the suggestion, but that it was not pursued. Three likely explanations may be offered. Pinckney may have felt the problem too remote or insignificant to worry about; he may have felt it would be impossible to win concessions on this point and chose discretion over valor; finally, he may have been convinced by his colleagues or upon reconsideration that precedent and the existing clause offered enough protection to slave property.

For a number of reasons it is unlikely that Pinckney or any of the other slaveowners at the convention saw the free movement of masters with their slaves as an insignificant or remote problem. Vitriolic debates over slavery had occurred throughout the convention. Only six days before Pinckney's objection, on 22 August, the final debate on the Slave Importation Clause had taken place. Connecticut's Roger Sherman began with an attempt at conciliation. Sherman "disapproved of the slave trade" but was willing to let it continue for a few more years in order to preserve harmony in the Union. Sherman's reasoning could hardly have reassured the proslavery group, since he "observed that the abolition of slavery seemed to be going on in the U.S. & that the good sense of the several States would probably by degrees compleat it." Oliver Ellsworth, also of Connecticut and also taking a conciliatory approach, thought "Slavery in time will not be a speck in our Country. Provision is already made in Connecticut for abolishing it. And the abolition has already

43. Farrand, 2 *Records* 443.
44. At the time of this debate each section of article IV was denominated as a unique article. Thus, the Fugitives from Justice Clause of the present Constitution was called article XV and the Fugitive Slave Clause became article XVI of the draft constitution. The current Privileges and Immunities Clause was then article XIV. Because Pinckney raised his objection when article XIV was debated (rather than at the time of the debate on the Fugitives from Justice article), it seems that he was not referring to fugitive slaves. This assumption is strengthened by the fact that the Privileges and Immunities Clause of the Articles of Confederation specifically protected property "imported into any State, to be removed to any other States of which the owner is an inhabitant." Slaves in transit would of course have been an important type of property protected by this clause. It seems fair to assume that Pinckney wanted that property protected in the Constitution.

taken place in Massachusetts."[45] With such evidence before them, the proslavery men could not have doubted that at some future time slavery might be banned in a considerable number of states.

On their side of the debate, delegates from the Deep South made it clear that slavery was here to stay. Charles Pinckney asserted, "If slavery be wrong, it is justified by the example of all the world. He cited the case of Greece[,] Rome & other antient [*sic*] States; the sanction given by France[,] England, Holland[,] & other modern States. In all ages one-half of mankind have been slaves." He warned that any "attempt to take away the right" to import slaves "will produce serious objections to the Constitution. . . . " His cousin, Charles Cotesworth Pinckney, would "consider a rejection of" the Slave Importation Clause "as an exclusion of S[outh] Carol[in]a from the Union." Because "S[outh] Carolina and Georgia cannot do without slaves" he did not think his home state "would stop her importations of slaves in any short time." Hugh Williamson of North Carolina "thought the S[outhern] States would not be members of the Union if the clause should be rejected." John Rutledge was most adamant of all: "If the Convention thinks that N[orth] C[arolina], S[outh] C[arolina] & Georgia will ever agree to the plan, unless their right to import slaves be untouched, the expectation is vain."[46]

If the Deep South delegates, many of whom were staunch supporters of a strong federal government, were willing to jeopardize the Constitution over the slave trade, they must have felt that slavery was absolutely necessary for the success of their states. Much of the North, on the other hand, had ended or appeared likely to end the institution. Conflict between the states should have appeared inevitable. As a historical precedent, travel and interstate movement should have seemed the likely impetus for such conflict. In the debate on the slave trade, John Dickinson, a Quaker from Delaware, "Considered it as inadmissible on every principle of honor & safety that the importation of slaves should be authorized" by the Constitution. To buttress his argument Dickinson noted, "If Eng[lan]d & France permit slavery, slaves are at the same time excluded from both those Kingdoms."[47] Dickinson was referring to the fact that, although slavery was legal in French and British colonies, its legal status was uncertain in France and Britain. In both nations slavery had been declared contrary to the law of the metropolis, and although in 1787 some slaves existed in each country, the status of property in man was precarious.

45. Farrand, 2 *Records* 369–71.
46. 2 ibid. 371–73.
47. 2 ibid. 372.

The earliest modern French case occurred in 1552, when a Spanish slave escaped to Metz. In refusing to return the slave, the French commander stated under "l'ancienne et bonne coutume de France" the slave had become instantly free when he touched French soil.[48] This understanding of French law was reaffirmed in 1571 when a shipowner brought some blacks to Bordeaux to be sold, but they "were ordered released by the parlement of that city on the ground that slavery did not exist in France." The position was strengthened a century later, when Minister of the Marine De Pontchartrain declared that thenceforth "Negroes brought into France would be free upon their arrival." An edict of 1716, by the Royal Council of State, allowed colonists to bring their slaves to the metropolis, but only under strict conditions. A slave could be brought only to learn a trade or be instructed in the Catholic faith. The master needed permission of the governor or commandant of the colony before leaving for France and had to register the slave within eight days after entering France and later at the Admiralty in Paris. Failure to comply with these rules could free the slave and subject the master to a one-thousand-livre fine.[49] While runaway slaves would be returned to their masters, the masters were not allowed to sell their slaves in France, nor could slaves in France be seized for debt. In 1738 a *déclaration* at Versailles limited the residence of slaves to three years, after which they would be confiscated. Masters in France at the time of the *déclaration* had one year in which to register their slaves. Under this new law, slaves taken to Paris had to be registered there and registration upon entering France had to be completed on the day of entry, rather than within eight days.[50]

Under French law slavery did not exist. The laws allowing slaves in France were designed to accommodate colonists visiting the metropolis. In passing these laws the French government acknowledged that slavery could exist only by positive law. Without strict

48. John Codman Hurd, 1 *The Law of Freedom and Bondage in the United States* (2 vols. Boston: Little, Brown, 1862) 338.

49. Shelby T. McCloy, *The Negro in France* (Lexington: The University of Kentucky Press, 1961) 12, 14, 25–26. McCloy notes that the laws were rarely enforced "because of the inconvenience it would have caused their owners, the West Indian planters, who brought them as their valets and maids." In France, as in so many other places, the law and the practice of slavery were often at odds.

50. *Code Noir, ou Recueil d'Edits, Declarations et Arrets Concernant les Esclaves Négres de l'Amérique* (Paris: Chez les Libraires Associez, 1743) 106–17. The slaves confiscated under the 1738 act were not, however, freed. Rather, they were to be sent back to the American colonies and sold or hired out for the benefit of the government. See also McCloy, *Negro in France* 26–27; William R. Riddell, "*Le Code Noir*," 10 *Journal of Negro History* 326 (July 1925).

adherence to the specific requirements of these laws, slaves taken to France would be free. The most important case under these laws was *Boucaut* v. *Verdelin* (1738). Boucaut and other slaves escaped to Paris *before* Verdelin could register them. Even Verdelin's counsel agreed that a slave became free the moment he touched French soil, except when protected by positive law. The French Admiralty court ruled that the provisions of the 1716 law had not been completely fulfilled; thus under "l'ancienne et bonne coutume de France" the slaves were free.[51]

Boucaut v. *Verdelin* was "the only [French case] similar to that of Somerset."[52] In both cases slaves taken to the metropolis escaped from their masters and were declared free by the courts. Both cases also affirmed the principle that only through positive law, strictly followed, could slavery exist in either England or France.

For the makers of the American Constitution *Somerset* v. *Stewart* (1772) was the most important, and the most misunderstood, slave case in Anglo-American law.[53] Just exactly what *Somerset* decided is still being debated, over two hundred years after Lord Mansfield's opinion. Until recently, most scholars felt it brought a de jure end to slavery in England, even though many recognized that de facto slavery existed there until the imperial emancipation of 1832. Many contemporary lawyers and politicians, in both Britain and America, also believed that *Somerset* ended slavery in the mother country. This idea persisted in the United States throughout the antebellum period and has been perpetuated by many scholars. Recent scholarship contends that such an interpretation is far too broad.[54] Even the strongest of revisionists, however, will concede that at the very least *Somerset* determined "a master could not remove a slave from the realm against the slave's will, and a slave could secure a writ of habeas corpus to prevent such removal."[55]

Even at its narrowest, the holding in *Somerset* could have posed a major threat to slaveowners if it were incorporated into the legal systems of nonslave states. While a slaveowner might take his slave *into* a free state, he might not be able to take the slave *out* of the state. Interstate transit for slaveowners would be severely limited.

51. Hurd, 1 *Law of Freedom and Bondage* 341–44.

52. 1 ibid. 341–42.

53. William M. Wiecek, "*Somerset*: Lord Mansfield and the Legitimacy of Slavery in the Anglo-American World," 42 *University of Chicago Law Review* 87 (1974). *Somerset* v. *Stewart*, 20 Howell St. Tr. (G.B.) 1 (1772).

54. Jerome Nadelhaft, "The Somersett Case and Slavery: Myth, Reality, and Repercussions," 51 *Journal of Negro History* 193–208 (1966); Wiecek, "*Somerset*" 87–88.

55. Wiecek, "*Somerset*" 87. See also a more updated discussion in Wiecek, *Sources of Antislavery Constitutionalism*. This book is also important because it shows how *Somerset* affected antislavery thought.

If the master tried to remove the slave and habeas corpus proceedings were initiated, then the substantive question of slavery in a free state would come before the court. In many northern states the master would have little chance of retaining his "property." In England the Virginian Charles Stewart was unable to send his runaway slave, James Somerset, back to America. Would a time come when a Virginian would be unable to send his slave back from Massachusetts or Pennsylvania?

Somerset may have gone further, however, than merely restricting the travel of masters with slaves. Under its most narrow holding, a slave could gain access to the courts only on a habeas corpus proceeding if there was an attempt by the master to remove the slave from England. However, Lord Mansfield's opinion also declared that "[t]he state of slavery is of such a nature that it is incapable of being introduced on any reasons, moral or political; but only by positive law, which preserves its force long after the reasons, occasion, and time itself, from whence it was created, is erased from memory. It is so odious, that nothing can be suffered to support it but positive law." If this dictum were extended to the American states, then, as in France, from the moment a slave set foot on free soil his chains would be broken forever.[56]

Although scholars disagree as to the accuracy of the Mansfield quotation on the odiousness of slavery, it is clear that this quotation was widely circulated and believed in Britain and America. Americans and Englishmen, including the knowledgeable abolitionist Granville Sharp, interpreted *Somerset* as ending slavery in England.[57] And this understanding went beyond the literate population. One Virginia slave attempted "to board a vessel for Great Britain . . . from the knowledge he has of the late Determination of Somerset's Case." Another Virginia master complained that his runaways were bound for England "where they imagine they will be free (a Notion now too prevalent among the Negroes, greatly to the Vexation and Prejudice of their Masters)."[58] Even if all Americans understood Mansfield's decision only to be a limited one, it would nevertheless have convinced slaveholders of the need to protect slave property in transit.

56. Hurd, 1 *Law of Freedom and Bondage* 191, 344.

57. Wiecek, "*Somerset*" 141–46; Nadelhaft, "The Somersett Case and Slavery" 193–94. As late as 1851 the Georgia Supreme Court erroneously agreed with attorneys that *Somerset* had ended all slavery in England, but argued that the decision did not apply to the United States; *Neal v. Farmer*, 9 Ga. 555, 557–61 (1851).

58. Gerald W. Mullin, *Flight and Rebellion: Slave Resistance in Eighteenth-Century Virginia* (New York: Oxford University Press, 1972) 131; Also see David Brion Davis, *The Problem of Slavery in the Age of Revolution* (Ithaca and London: Cornell University Press, 1975) 278, and Wiecek, "*Somerset*" 117–19.

James Somerset had been a fugitive in England when his master attempted to send him out of the realm. The founders knew of the case and understood its implications perhaps to be greater than they were. It is likely that the case was in part responsible for the Fugitive Slave Clauses in the Northwest Ordinance and the Constitution.[59] What is surprising, though, is that the impact of the case was no greater. From the available evidence at the time, it would seem the founders should have regarded *Somerset* as a threat to all transit with slaves.

The southerners at the convention may have thought that it would be impossible to win more concessions on slavery and that a protection of fugitive slaves was more important than a protection against the states interfering with transit. Yet, if the proslavery delegates thought transit was important—and Pinckney's statement plus the fame of *Somerset* indicate they must have considered the problem— then it would have been out of character for them not to put up a fight over the issue. The day after Pinckney made his plea for a protection of slaves as a privilege and immunity, Butler introduced the Fugitive Slave Clause, which met much resistance. Still, Butler persisted and the clause was accepted. Surely a seemingly innocuous clause, protecting one's property while in transit or sojourn could have been added, or at least suggested. It would not even have had to use the strained euphemism of "other persons" or "persons held to service," but could have simply been applied to all property. Charles Cotesworth Pinckney was already on record as saying that without "some security to the Southern States ag[ain]st an emancipation of slaves" the South would not join the Union. During the slave trade debate James Wilson and John Dickinson had been willing to deny the South's demands because Wilson thought "they would never refuse to Unite because the importation might be prohibited." However, most of the other delegates agreed with Roger Sherman, who "said it was better to let the S[outhern] States import slaves than to part with them, if they made that a sine qua non."[60]

It seems likely that a sine qua non over the right of unmolested transit would have met little resistance. The southerners did not make transit an issue, not because they thought they would lose or because it was an unimportant issue. Rather, as things stood, based on current free-state law and the guarantees of the Constitution under consideration, they probably thought such a clause was unnecessary.

59. Nadelhaft makes this argument in "The Somersett Case and Slavery" 202. That *Somerset* was widely reported in the United States is best demonstrated by Wiecek, *Sources of Antislavery Constitutionalism* 40–41.

60. Farrand, 2 *Records* 443, 453–54, 95, 372, 374.

The Emergence of Free States

By 1787 Massachusetts, New Hampshire, and Vermont (the four-teenth state) had ended slavery through express constitutional pro-visions or judicial interpretations. Connecticut, Rhode Island, and Pennsylvania had enacted gradual emancipation statutes. By the end of 1787 every state except Georgia had in one way or another at least temporarily prohibited the importation of slaves from Africa. More important, some states, including New York and Virginia, had restricted the importation of slaves from other states, and both New York and Virginia freed illegally imported slaves.[61] Yet, in none of these states was any indication apparent that bans on slavery or slave importation would lead to an implementation of the abolition-ist tendencies of *Somerset*. In fact, although no state attempted to apply the *Somerset* rule to emancipate slaves entering a free juris-diction, many specifically guarded against that possibility through positive legislation protecting masters in transit. Others simply ignored the question.

Slavery in Massachusetts never formally ended. During the Revo-lution many slaves asked for and obtained their freedom, or "simply absconded and depended upon the weight of public opinion to sustain them in their behavior." The Massachusetts Constitution of 1780 contained a "free and equal clause" that was applied to all men, including slaves. In a series of 1783 cases, commonly known as the Quock Walker Cases, this clause was used to free Walker and protect his new employers in a damage suit initiated by Walker's former master. Although some slaves were held in Massachusetts after the Quock Walker Cases, the 1790 census reported none in the state. By that date community pressure militated against anyone who admitted he owned a slave. Indeed, "[w]hen public opinion would no longer tolerate slavery, it disappeared" in Massachusetts.[62] Never-theless, the Quock Walker Cases seem to have had little effect on outsiders bringing their slaves into the state. Not until 1836, in *Commonwealth* v. *Aves*, would the Supreme Judicial Court interfere with the rights of transients traveling in Massachusetts with their slaves.[63]

How slavery ended in New Hampshire is "surrounded with . . . obscurity and ambiguity." In any event, by 1800 no slaves were in

61. *Laws of Virginia, 1778* 471–72; *Laws of New York, 1785–1788*, chap. 68, p. 121.
62. John D. Cushing, "The Cushing Court and the Abolition of Slavery in Massa-chusetts: More Notes on the 'Quock Walker Case,'" 5 *American Journal of Legal History* 137, 134, 144 (1961).
63. *Commonwealth* v. *Aves*, 18 Pick. (Mass.) 193 (1836); see also chap. 4 of this volume.

the state. Because of its remote location, New Hampshire has no recorded legal cases on slave transit.[64]

The Vermont Constitution of 1777 expressly prohibited slavery, and this position was reaffirmed in a 1786 statute that declared "the Idea of Slavery is expressly and totally exploded from our free Government." The statute noted that some owners were transporting their liberated slaves out of the state, so that they could be sold. Anyone attempting to enslave or transport "any subject of this State" could be fined.[65] The words "any subject" imply that a slave in transit, who would not be a "subject" of Vermont, could be taken from the state. Apparently, then, in 1786 at least, Vermont was willing to grant to foreign travelers who had slaves with them the right of unmolested transit. The only Vermont court case touching on the question of slave ownership affirms this interpretation. In *Selectmen* v. *Jacob* (1802)[66] the state supreme court held that a bill of sale for a slave purchased in 1783 in another state by a citizen of Vermont was not binding in Vermont: "Our State constitution is express, no inhabitant of the State can hold a slave; and though the bill of sale may be binding by the *lex loci* of another State or dominion, yet when the master becomes an inhabitant of this State, his bill of sale ceases to operate here."[67] The implication here is that if the owner were not a resident or inhabitant of the state, but only a sojourner, the *lex loci* of another state would be upheld, along with the bill of sale. The constitution, the statute, and the court all agreed that the prohibition against slavery applied only to Vermont residents, both black and white.

The haphazard manner of ending slavery in the three most northern New England states and the corresponding confusion in the meaning of their constitutional provisions reflect the relative unimportance of slavery in those three states. Since Connecticut had the largest number of slaves of any New England state and Rhode Island's smaller population was 6 percent black, it is not surprising that these two states gave more thought to the problems of slavery and emancipation. That citizens of both states were intimately involved in the African slave trade and commerce with the South may also explain their greater sensitivity to the ramifications of emancipation. Similarly, Pennsylvania had a substantial slave population and in 1780 was surrounded by slave states. The legislature seemed

64. Zilversmit, *First Emancipation* 116 and *passim*.
65. Ibid.; John A. Williams, ed., *The Law of Vermont*, 14 *State Papers of Vermont* (Montpelier, 1966) 100.
66. *Selectmen* v. *Jacob*, 2 Tyler (Vt.) 192 (1802).
67. Ibid. 192, 199.

well aware of the problems that could develop in a Union including both slave and free states.

In 1771 and 1774, Connecticut prohibited the importation of slaves. The wording of the 1774 law implied that the intent of its framers was not to interfere with interstate or, at the time, intercolonial, movement. The statute prohibited the importation of slaves "to be disposed of, left, or sold within this state." A gradual emancipation act of 1784 provided that all children born to slaves would become free at age twenty-five. Under these laws citizens of other states could come and go as they chose, bringing their slaves with them. Even a child born in Connecticut while the slave mother and master were in transit was not affected by the gradual emancipation statute. Not until 1792 did Connecticut ban the exportation of slaves, and even that statute applied only to residents of the state. As long as an out-of-state visitor did not attempt to leave a slave in Connecticut, no authorities would interfere with the movement of owners with their property. As in Massachusetts, the Connecticut Supreme Court would abruptly change this policy of unmolested transit in the 1830s.[68]

In 1774 the colonial legislature of Rhode Island banned the importation of slaves, and "rendered immediately free" any slaves brought in. The law had a number of exceptions; the first is worth quoting in full: "PROVIDED, nevertheless, That this law shall not extend to Servants of Persons travelling through this Colony, who are not inhabitants thereof, and who carry them out with them when they leave the same."[69] Coming two years after *Somerset*, this statute seems to be a direct attempt to insure that the British decision would not affect the colony of Rhode Island.

During the Revolution, however, Rhode Island did give direct statutory recognition to one aspect of *Somerset*. In its narrowest interpretation, *Somerset* held that a slave in Britain could not be forced to leave the realm. In 1779 Rhode Island passed an "Act prohibiting slaves being sold out of the State against their Consent." Although it did not affect slaves in transit, it did prohibit any Rhode Island resident from selling slaves out of the state. The seller could be fined and the slave freed. What makes this law particularly interesting is that it was not protecting the right of a slave who was to be free at some future date. Rather, the state felt that for slaves

---

68. Zilversmit, *First Emancipation* 4 and *passim*; *Statute Laws of the State of Connecticut, 1821* (Hartford: H. Huntington, 1824) 385–86; *Statute Laws of the State of Connecticut, Book I* (Hartford: Hudson and Goodwin, 1808) 624–25; *Jackson v. Bulloch*, 12 Day (Conn.) 38 (1837).

69. *Rhode Island Laws and Statutes, 1774*, 49–50.

to be carried off "against their Consent, to perpetuate their Slavery in foreign Parts remote from their Friends and Acquaintance, is against the Rights of human Nature, and tends greatly to aggravate the Condition of Slavery. . . . " In 1784 Rhode Island passed a gradual emancipation statute, which prohibited the importation of new slaves but apparently did not affect the right of transit found in the 1774 statute.[70]

Pennsylvania's gradual emancipation law of 1780 was the most detailed of the pre-Constitution state acts. It provided for registration of all slaves then in the state and the eventual emancipation of all children of those slaves. All slaves brought into the state would be freed. However, this law had two critical exceptions. "Delegates in Congress from other American states, [and] Ministers and Consuls" were allowed to bring their "domestic slaves" into the state and keep them there as long as they held those offices. "Persons passing through or sojourning" in Pennsylvania and "not becoming resident therein" were also permitted to bring slaves with them. However, these sojourners could keep their slaves in the state for only six months, after which they would be freed.[71]

By 1787 the harshest limitation on slave transit was the six-month provision of Pennsylvania's law. Even the most ardent proslavery advocates might have agreed that six months' transit was a reasonable time, and anyone asking for more might indeed be stretching the bounds of comity and the bonds of union. With precedents such as these, it is no wonder the southerners at the Philadelphia Constitutional Convention did not press for a clause protecting transit. They already had a Privileges and Immunities Clause that seemed to guarantee such rights. And if there were any doubt of the meaning of the clause, the free states seemed willing to bend over backward to accommodate the needs of the slaveowners. Since comity had been given freely by the nonslave states, why disrupt the convention to gain redundant protection in the Constitution?

Besides those states that were doing away with slavery, five others had legislated on the subject of slave importation and movement. In New York, New Jersey, Delaware, Maryland, and Virginia an imminent emancipation of slaves appeared unlikely. Madison told the Virginia ratifying convention that New York and New Jersey "would, probably, oppose any attempts to annihilate this species of property" by the national government because they "had made no attempt, or taken any step, to take them from the people."[72] The

70. Ibid., *1779*, 5–7; and *1784*, 6–8.

71. 1 *Laws of the Commonwealth of Pennsylvania* (4 vols. Philadelphia: N.p., 1810) 492–96.

72. Elliot, 3 *Debates in the Several States* 459.

laws passed by these slave states could serve only to reinforce the feeling that comity on slave transit would be an intrinsic part of the Union.

All five states wanted to end the African slave trade and to slow or reverse the growth of the state's slave population. All five therefore passed laws prohibiting the importation of slaves. These states were quite willing to punish those among their own citizens who illegally imported slaves. They were also careful to protect the rights of travelers, visitors, and even those forced to take up temporary residence as refugees from war zones. Persons in all these categories were allowed to bring slaves with them.[73]

By 1787 slavery was being abolished or had already been ended in six states north of the Mason-Dixon line. Only in Pennsylvania, however, was even the slightest restriction placed on interstate transit with slaves. As the new nation grew, problems of interstate movement and slavery developed. Yet it seems clear that the founders from all sections of the nation were intent on beginning their nation in a spirit of comity and accommodation, if not complete harmony and understanding. For the moment, the bargain over slavery and free movement, which seemed implicit at the 1787 convention, worked quite well, at least for white Americans.

73. Zilversmit, *First Emancipation* 155; *Laws of the State of New Jersey, 1703–1800* (New Brunswick: N.p., 1800), 311–13; *Laws of New Jersey, 1786*, 239; *Laws of New York, 1785*, 120; and *1788*, 475–79; *Laws of Virginia, 1778*, 471–72, *1780*, 307–8, *1787*, 182–83; 2 *Laws of the State of Delaware* (2 vols. New-Castle, Del.: 1797) 884–88, 941; *Laws of Maryland, 1783*, chap. 23; *1794*, chap. 66; and *1796*, chap. 67.

Chapter 2

The Limits of Federalism: Comity and Slave Transit in Pennsylvania, 1780–1847

Until the abolitionist agitation of the 1830s made slavery a national issue, the question of slave transit remained a minor aspect of that complex area of law known as conflicts, or choice of law. Although slave states and free states had competing interests and ideologies, they nevertheless tried to accommodate each other in a spirit of comity and national unity. Pennsylvania, for example, gave statutory and judicial protection to the slave property of out-of-state visitors who stayed less than six months. New York, after 1817, gave similar protection, with a nine-months transit.[1] Other northern states passed no legislation on the subject and often made no attempt to interfere with slaves in transit. Pennsylvania, with the first gradual emancipation statute and the strictest legislation on transit, generated a large number of cases. An in-depth examination of these cases illustrates the problems of public policy and law that resulted from slaves coming into the North and reveals that in the nation's first half century a state with a strong antislavery ideology was willing to grant comity to slaveholders from other states. Courts gradually tightened their interpretations of Pennsylvania's statutes, however, to make it more difficult to retain slaves in the state. This process was completed in 1847, when the legislature repealed the six-months law and thus refused comity to any traveling slaveowner. The result of this repeal and the judicial and legislative trends in other states will be examined in subsequent chapters.

Pennsylvania Regulates Slavery: 1780 and 1788

Perhaps no state in the Union felt the tensions of slavery and freedom so keenly as Pennsylvania did. The state was a leader in the

1. 1 *Laws of the Commonwealth of Pennsylvania* (4 vols. Philadelphia: Bioren, 1810) 492–93; 2 *The Revised Statutes of New York* (3 vols. Albany: Crowell, Van Benthuysen and Burt, 1836) 661–64.

"First Emancipation," even though total abolition did not come until 1847. The state's population was never more than 5 percent slaves, but slaves were concentrated more heavily in certain southern and western areas and in Philadelphia.[2] In 1780 Pennsylvania was surrounded by slave states and was often visited by slaveowners. As the nation's capital, Philadelphia drew visitors and residents from all over the nation, many of whom brought their personal "servants" with them. At the same time, the state's population included many Friends and revolutionary patriots who adamantly opposed slavery. Although the Quakers had abdicated political control of the state, they were still quite influential. In addition, Philadelphia had the nation's first active antislavery society, the Pennsylvania Abolition Society—or, as it was officially known, the Pennsylvania Society for Promoting the Abolition of Slavery, the Relief of Free Negroes Unlawfully Held in Bondage, and for Improving the Condition of the African Race.

In 1779 a Presbyterian legislator, George Bryan, "planned and executed" the passage of a gradual emancipation statute. Bryan's cause was aided by the Quaker abolitionist Anthony Benezet, who lobbied hard for the measure.[3] The law, passed in 1780, reflected a determination to end slavery but not to inhibit Pennsylvania's growth or economy. Under the act, all children of slaves born in the state were free, but they remained apprentices until age twenty-eight. Slaves currently in the state had to be registered before 1 November 1780, or they would become instantly free. Congressmen and "Ministers and Consuls" were allowed to retain their domestic slaves indefinitely while in the state. Other persons, visiting or traveling with slaves, were allowed to hold their slaves for six months. Any slave kept in Pennsylvania longer than six months was instantly free. As Chief Justice William Tilghman of the Pennsylvania Supreme Court would point out many years later, *"Pennsylvania had a right to give freedom to every person within her territory, however impolitic the extreme exercise of that right might have been, considering the situation of some of her sister states."* The six-months clause must therefore be seen as a specific granting of comity to the slaveholders of other states who might want to visit Pennsyl-

2. Arthur Zilversmit, *The First Emancipation: The Abolition of Slavery in the North* (Chicago: University of Chicago Press, 1967) 85–98, 124–37, 201–8.

3. For a legislative history and background of the 1780 act, see Edward R. Taylor, *Slavery in Pennsylvania* (Baltimore: Lord Baltimore Press, 1911) 78–79; Edward Bettle, "Notices of Negro Slavery as Connected with Pennsylvania," in 1 *Memoirs of the Historical Society of Pennsylvania* 405–11 (1864); Zilversmit, *First Emancipation*, 124–39; William M. Wiecek, *The Sources of Antislavery Constitutionalism in America, 1760–1848* (Ithaca and London: Cornell University Press, 1977) 85–90; and George Bryan Papers, box 4, HSP.

vania. Another clause of the 1780 statute indicated that the "situation of those [sister] states was neither unthought of nor neglected."[4] This clause allowed for the recapture of fugitive slaves and specifically exempted fugitive slaves from gaining freedom through the six-months clause. Finally, slaveowners moving into the state could retain their slaves for six months, during which time they could indenture the slaves for seven years, or until age twenty-eight if the slave was a minor. Indentures contracted in other states were also valid, so long as they did not exceed these age and time limits.[5]

The 1780 law was amended almost immediately so that "[c]itizens of other states compelled by the enemy to take refuge in Pennsylvania with their slaves" would be exempt from the act during the war. In 1782 the settlement of a boundary dispute between Pennsylvania and Virginia led to an extension of the registration period for slaveowners living in certain counties.[6]

Not until 1788 did any major change occur in the state's statutory regulation of slavery. In that year the Pennsylvania Abolition Society successfully lobbied for an additional act[7] "FOR preventing many evils and abuses arising from ill disposed persons availing themselves of certain defects" in the 1780 act. This new statute prohibited the removal of pregnant slaves, so that their children would be born as "slaves for life" rather than as servants until age twenty-eight. It also prohibited the removal from the state of any slave or servant for a term of years without that person's consent. Most important for an understanding of comity, the 1788 law clarified the status of slaves owned by people moving to the state "with an intention to settle and reside." Such slaves would be freed immediately, rather than after six months. Visitors could still bring slaves for six months and migrants could bring indentured slaves with them.[8] A number of cases under this act involved determining when a visitor became a migrant. Pennsylvania was the first of many states, both slave and free, to use "intention to reside" as a test of whether a slave had become free.

Although the legislature took great care in passing these stat-

4. *Commonwealth v. Holloway*, 2 S. & R. (Pa.) 304, 306 (1816).

5. 1 *Laws of the Commonwealth of Pennsylvania* 492–96. The fugitive slave provision of the 1780 law is particularly important, in that it was the first such statute in the nation and preceded the Fugitive Slave Clause of the U.S. Constitution by seven years.

6. Ibid. 496.

7. Minutes of 7 and 21 Jan. 1788, and 7 Apr. 1788, Pennsylvania Abolition Society Papers, microfilm reel 1, HSP; also see Edward Needles, *An Historical Memoir of the Pennsylvania Society for Promoting the Abolition of Slavery* (Philadelphia: Merrihew and Thompson, 1848) 34.

8. 2 *Laws of the Commonwealth of Pennsylvania* 443–46.

utes, they nonetheless stimulated a great deal of litigation, much of which was necessary to clarify the ambiguities presented by any pioneering legislation. But the complexity of the issues involved prompted many of the cases—questions of property rights versus human rights, the complications of conflict of laws, federalism, and the newness of both the state and the nation.

The Six-Months Law

Since most existing court records are appellate court records, there are few recorded cases dealing with just the six-months clause. Once the facts of a six-months visit to Pennsylvania were proved, an owner had scant legal ground on which to base his case. Miers Fisher, an attorney for the Abolition Society, obtained the freedom of one slave by proving to a judge that there had been a six-months transit. No trial was held and no attorney for the owner was recorded. The judge was George Bryan, who went to the state supreme court in 1780, after his gradual emancipation act was passed.[9] Another example is the case of William Steel and Peter. During the Revolution Steel, "an American officer," brought a slave, Peter, into Pennsylvania, and after six months Peter was freed. Many years later Peter sued for back wages, and the facts of his freedom were recorded in an appeal in that case. Peter's case may indicate that although a master might not contest the freedom of his slave, he might nevertheless be able to retain control of the freedman and benefit from his labor.[10]

Besides the difficulty of winning a case where a six-months stay was proved, the cost of litigation had also to be considered. An owner who sought to defend his property rights did so at his own expense. On the other hand, slaves with strong freedom claims were usually supported in their legal actions by the Abolition Society. As early as 1785 the society began to argue cases and investigate violations of the 1780 act. With the help of volunteer lawyers and a few wealthy

9. Bryan Papers, box 2, file 20, also see Thomas Altmore to Society, 5 Sept. 1787, Pennsylvania Abolition Society Papers, microfilm reel 2, vol. 1, no. 71. Case of Moses Johnson who escaped from his British master during the Revolution but was sold into slavery in New Jersey to a Pennsylvanian, who brought Johnson back to Pennsylvania. Johnson "obtained his freedom by the operation of the Act for the gradual Abolition of Slavery."

10. *Negro Peter* v. *Steel*, 3 Yeates (Pa.) 250 (1801). Sometimes it took many years for the law to be enforced. In *Jones* v. *Executors of Jonathan Rees* 4 Yeates (Pa.) 109 (1804), a slave brought into the state in 1781 did not win his freedom until 1799. Bryan Papers, box 2, file 20, HSP, contain records of a former master who forced his ex-slave to serve at sea. The former master was arrested for this crime.

patrons, the society began to harass masters holding slaves in Pennsylvania. This legal activism established a pattern that would be followed by other antislavery societies until the Civil War. In hundreds of cases the society aided blacks.[11]

In 1787 the society reported that a number of cases "pending in the Courts" had been successfully terminated and the Negroes "hath received their Liberty by Friendly Interview with their Claiments." Apparently the threat of litigation, by such leading attorneys as William Lewis, Jonathan Sergeant, William Rawle, and William Patterson of New Jersey, intimidated some owners into freeing their slaves without a court fight.[12]

Where out-of-court settlement was impossible, suits were initiated. Any violations, real or alleged, of the 1780 and 1788 acts were investigated. Out-of-state masters were carefully watched and brought to court if they stayed more than six months. Even before a six-months period had passed, if it appeared a case could be made that an owner had become a resident of the state, the society acted under the 1788 law.[13]

The first reported case dealing with slavery, *Pirate, alias Belt* v. *Dalby* (1786)[14] reflected the society's aggressive litigation strategy. Although Dalby had not kept his slave in the state for six months, the society still sued on Pirate's behalf. The case foreshadowed many of the legal arguments and interstate problems that would develop over slavery and comity within the Union.

The Abolition Society hoped to win a broad interpretation of the 1780 statute and have both *Somerset* and the Massachusetts judicial abolition adopted by Pennsylvania. Attorney William Lewis joined Pennsylvania Attorney General William Bradford in arguing that there was no positive law creating slavery in Pennsylvania and thus every construction ought to be in favor of liberty. Dalby's lawyer made a strong plea for interstate comity, arguing that Pirate was born a slave in Maryland and by the rule of *lex loci* he remained a slave in Pennsylvania.[15]

The court ignored the natural law arguments on behalf of Pirate and the international law arguments on behalf of Dalby. Instead, the court applied the 1780 statute to determine that Pirate was not free because he had not been in Pennsylvania more than six months.

11. Needles, *Memoir* 44–45.

12. Ibid. 29; minutes of 28 Nov. 1785, 5 Mar. 1786, and 11 Oct. 1790, Pennsylvania Abolition Society Papers, microfilm reel 1.

13. Minutes of 27 Feb. 1786, 28 Aug. 1786, 2 July 1787, 5 July 1790, and 30 May 1791, Pennsylvania Abolition Society Papers, microfilm reel 1.

14. *Pirate, alias Belt* v. *Dalby*, 1 Dallas (U.S. & Pa.) 167 (1786).

15. MSS dated 21 Apr. 1787, Bryan Papers, box 2, file 6.

One of the jurors in this case was Tench Coxe, a member of the Abolition Society, and the bench included George Bryan. But their well-known sentiments against slavery did not prevent a strictly legalistic interpretation of the statute.[16]

Aside from its legal aspects, *Pirate* v. *Dalby* was a prelude to the strain on interstate relations that antislavery organizations and comity cases would ultimately create throughout the nation. Dalby, a Virginian, first came to Philadelphia in 1784. During that visit a member of the Abolition Society initiated habeas corpus proceedings to free Pirate. Declarations were taken in September 1784, but the trial was delayed until April 1786. Because of this, Dalby was forced to return to Philadelphia over a year after his business there had been completed. Before returning for this "vexatious lawsuit," Dalby contacted his influential fellow Virginian, George Washington, who wrote the Philadelphia financier and patriot, Robert Morris, warning that if "the practice of this Society [Abolition Society] . . . is not discountenanced, none of those whose *misfortune* it is to have slaves as attendants, will visit the City if they can possibly avoid it; because by so doing they hazard their property; or they must be at the expense (and this will not always succeed) of providing servants of another description." Washington assured Morris, "[T]here is not a man living who wishes more sincerely than I do, to see a plan adopted for the abolition of it," but he felt it could be accomplished only through legislative action. He feared that agitation on the subject would do more harm than good and predicted it would threaten interstate harmony in the young nation if continued. He warned:

> But when slaves who are happy and contented with
> their present masters, are tampered with and seduced to
> leave them; when masters are taken unawares by these
> practices; when conduct of this sort begets discontent on one
> side and resentment on the other, and when it happens to fall on
> a man, whose purse will not measure with that of the Society,
> and he loses his property for want of means to defend it; it
> is oppression in latter cases and not humanity in any;
> because it introduces more evils than it can cure.[17]

Dalby's purse apparently measured up to that of the society, and he successfully defended his claim to Pirate. But it would be only a matter of time before all of Washington's fears, and more, began to materialize.

16. Ibid., at *Pirate* v. *Dalby*.

17. George Washington to Robert Morris, 12 Apr. 1786, in J. C. Fitzpatrick, ed., 28 *The Writings of George Washington* (39 vols. Washington: Government Printing Office, 1931–44) 407–8.

After *Pirate* v. *Dalby* the Pennsylvania Supreme Court heard numerous cases on technical issues concerning the acts of 1780 and 1788. Gradually the court narrowed the definition of permissible slavery in Pennsylvania. By the 1830s only bona fide travelers and exempt public officials could still bring their slaves into the state. While never moving as fast as the Abolition Society would have wished, the court ultimately leaned toward freedom in most cases.

One particularly thorny issue was the definition of "six months" and when "residence" under the 1788 act began, for under the 1780 act a slave could not gain freedom until six months had passed. But after 1788 the slaves of new residents became instantly free.

In 1789, in an unreported case, Justice George Bryan construed the meaning of residence quite liberally, *in favor* of the slaveholder. Frederick Lintz, a German Lutheran, arrived from Jamaica in May 1789 with his slave Mary. Lintz rented a house for three months and opened a grocery in that house. He talked about staying for good, but he was unsure and would not rent for a longer period. Before the three months were up he attempted to send Mary back to Jamaica, but illness prevented that. She then turned to the Abolition Society for aid, and Miers Fisher obtained a writ of habeas corpus. Fisher argued that Lintz "has given every evidence of becoming a resident. He has taken a house, opened a shop; bought goods as well as sold them." He argued that Lintz had been to Philadelphia a year earlier and "[b]efore the Negro debate he talked about returning after winter." The attempt to send Mary back to Jamaica indicated Lintz's desire to evade the 1788 act. Judge Bryan, however, rejected this theory. Instead, he declared "such is the Liberality of our laws, that foreigners, who arrive in Pennsylvania may not only carry on commerce, as elsewhere, by wholesale, but by retail, and may . . . choose their industry or artisan [*sic*], in any such manner as they are fit, for their support & maintenance while they sojourn in this State without being deemed residents or permanent inhabitants."[18] Thus Mary was remanded to Lintz.

Commonwealth v. *Chambre* (1794)[19] helped to define what constituted "six months" and reinforced the loose construction of "residence" in *Negro Mary* v. *Lintz*. Mrs. Chambre was a refugee from Santo Domingo who brought two slaves to the United States. After a residence of five months and three weeks she left Philadelphia for Burlington, New Jersey. The slaves ran back to Philadelphia and claimed their freedom because they had lived there for six *lunar* months. The court unanimously held that "the legislature

18. *Negro Mary* v. *Lintz*, unreported case dated 21 Apr. 1789, Bryan Papers, box 3, file 13.
19. *Commonwealth* v. *Chambre*, 4 Dallas (U.S. & Pa.) 143 (1794).

intended calendar months" and returned the slaves to Chambre. The most revealing aspect of this case was the prosecution's charge that Chambre left Pennsylvania "to avoid the operation of the [gradual emancipation] act." Her departure, only one week before the slaves would have been free under the act, supports this conclusion. The case indicates that some nonresident slaveowners were aware of the 1780 law and respected its force.[20] A year earlier, in fact, Haitian émigrés had petitioned the legislature to amend the gradual emancipation acts to allow them to bring slaves into the state. This attempt at diluting Pennsylvania's commitment to freedom was defeated, in part because of strenuous lobbying by the Abolition Society.[21]

Fifteen years later, in *Commonwealth* v. *Smyth* (1809),[22] a Pennsylvania court again had to determine what constituted "six months." In 1808 John Dowers moved from Trenton, New Jersey, to Philadelphia, where he rented a house for six months and brought his family to live. He told a witness he "intended to return within six months" and take the slave with him. Dowers did in fact take the slave back to Trenton "several times," but each time both master and slave returned to Philadelphia where Dowers's family remained. When the six-months lease expired, Dowers moved into a house owned by his father, in Philadelphia. In 1809 the slave deserted Dowers and was arrested. The Philadelphia Court of Common Pleas heard these facts and released the slave.[23]

The court decided Dowers was a permanent resident and thus the slave was free under the Act of 1788. Dowers came to Philadelphia "either to reside or to sojourn. He could not come to do both." The evidence indicated he had become a resident. Dowers's stated intention to remove the slave "was never carried out" and thus could not be taken into consideration. "If Mr. Dowers had taken the boy, (as he says he designed) back to Trenton, within six months, and kept him there, the present question would never have existed." This last conclusion by the court is logically inconsistent with the decision, because even if Dowers had taken the slave back, the slave would be free because he became instantly free when Dowers, as a new resident of the state, brought him into the state. But the court's most important statement was not on what might have been, but on what was. The court held that "taking him to Trenton several times, can have no operation to disprove the master's residence" and, more important, it could not interfere with the six-months clause. The

20. Ibid. 143–44.
21. Minutes of 7 Jan. 1793, Pennsylvania Abolition Society Papers, microfilm reel 1.
22. *Commonwealth* v. *Smyth*, 1 Browne (Pa.) 113 (1809).
23. Ibid.

court implied that even without residence, the slave would be free, because the six-months clause operated despite the occasional trips to New Jersey.[24]

But this case did not finally settle what constituted six months. *Butler et al.* v. *Delaplaine* (1821)[25] involved a seamstress who had occasionally taken a ten-year-old slave, Charity Butler, into Pennsylvania during the years 1788 and 1789. Over thirty years later Charity and her children ran away to Pennsylvania where they were captured by Sheriff Delaplaine, at whom a writ *de homine replegiando* (personal replevin) was directed.[26]

No one disputed that Charity had been in Pennsylvania at various times over a two-year period. But the jury determined she was never there for more than six consecutive months. Charity's counsel asked the judge to direct the jury to free Charity, because "a residence of six months in the whole, although compounded of periods shorter than six months each," with short intervals between these periods, would free a slave. The judge, however, thought that a residence under the 1780 law must be for six continuous months. He held that "different acts of residence, at different periods, cannot be tacked together, so as to make a whole: for each act of residence is a whole in itself."[27] The jury found against Charity.

On appeal, Charity argued that the 1780 law would be "easily liable to evasion." Her lawyer thought that under the trial judge's ruling a "slave might be brought in and kept here during life, if the owner took care to remove him occasionally for a day or two, so as to break the continuity of the sojournment." The Pennsylvania Supreme Court conceded that there might be "cases of a fraudulent shuffling backwards and forwards in *Pennsylvania*, and then into *Maryland*, and then back to *Pennsylvania*," but there was no evidence of such in this case. So the sojourn here had to be "a single,

24. Ibid.

25. *Butler et al.* v. *Delaplaine*, 7 S. & R. (Pa.) 378 (1821).

26. The writ *de homine replegiando* was a favorite of runaway slaves and abolitionists because it allowed for "numerous delays and exceptions" and, more important, a trial by jury. In areas hostile to slavery it was one way of obtaining freedom. Two years before Charity's case, Chief Justice Tilghman limited the use of this writ when he determined that fugitives were to "be delivered up, on a summary proceeding, without the delay of a trial in a court of common law"; *Wright* v. *Deacon*, 5 S. & R. (Pa.) 62, 63–64 (1819). Although one scholar has recently asserted that after *Wright* v. *Deacon* this writ could not be used in "any case involving a claim to a runaway," Charity Butler was nevertheless granted the writ; Thomas D. Morris, *Free Men All: The Personal Liberty Laws of the North, 1780–1861* (Baltimore: Johns Hopkins University Press, 1974) 11, 42. In Charity's case the writ was not used to delay the proceedings, as was done in *Wright*. Rather, she used it to test a legitimate, although unsuccessful, claim to freedom.

27. *Butler* v. *Delaplaine* 379–80.

unbroken one," for several clear reasons. "It was well known" to the legislature "that southern gentlemen . . . were in the habit of visiting this State, attended with their domestic slaves," and this was done "year after year." The springs at York and Bedford were "watering places frequented principally, and in great numbers, by families from Maryland and Virginia, attended by their domestic slaves. The same families with the same servants return in each season." A construction of the law making the six months cumulative "would amount to a prohibition—a denial of the rights of hospitality." It "would be an exclusion of the citizens of our sister States from these fountains of health, unwarranted by any principle of humanity or policy, or the spirit and letter of the law."[28]

Butler v. *Delaplaine* confirmed that the six-months clause generally meant a continuous, day-to-day, residence for six calendar months. Pennsylvania, through its statutes and courts, was willing to grant comity to bona fide sojourners and travelers who stayed less than six months. Indeed, it would even be possible for masters from other states to hire out their slaves in Pennsylvania for periods of less than six months. However, the court would not tolerate abuses or evasions of the law. In *Butler* v. *Delaplaine* the court asserted that "cases of a fraudulent shuffling backwards and forwards in *Pennsylvania,* and then into *Maryland,* and then back to *Pennsylvania* . . . might be fraud of the law" and thus lead to the freeing of the slave. But short of such evasions, slaveowners were free to bring their human property in and out of the state without penalty; Pennsylvania placed a higher value on comity than on human liberty.[29]

Slaves and Migrants

While the court may have been usually willing to grant comity to masters living in Maryland or Virginia, the court was less solici-

---

28. Ibid. 383–85.

29. Ibid. 383. An ironic nonlegal aspect of *Butler* v. *Delaplaine* made the victory less than complete for slaveowners. Charity Butler's owner hired an ambitious young lawyer, Thaddeus Stevens, to defend his claim to the slaves, and this experience with slavery helped turn Stevens into an abolitionist. It would strain historical and psychological interpretation to say this case was solely responsible for Stevens's uncompromising stand on slavery or that he spent the rest of his life atoning for his complicity in Charity's reenslavement. Nevertheless, as Stevens's biographer has noted, "The victory seems to have been ashes in his mouth. . . . This slave, whose hopes of freedom he had smashed, apparently taught the twenty-nine-year-old lawyer something he had not learned in books—that the law can be an instrument of terror as well as justice"; Fawn M. Brodie, *Thaddeus Stevens: Scourge of the South* (New York: W. W. Norton and Company, 1959) 33.

tous toward the property interests of slaveholders moving into Pennsylvania. This harsher attitude toward the actual importation of slaves is reflected in a series of cases involving masters who attempted to bring their slaves into the state as indentured servants.

The slaveowner wishing to move to Pennsylvania had two options: he could leave slaves behind, either through sale or hiring out; or he could bring slaves in as indentured servants. That many owners chose the latter indicates that one of the important side effects of the 1780 and 1788 laws was to allow for the gradual emancipation of slaves from other states. Masters who may not have wanted to or could not afford to free their slaves immediately could indenture them and take them to Pennsylvania. Thus some masters could prepare their slaves for freedom in a new locality, where free blacks had more opportunity and faced less restrictive legislation.

Indentures of slaves could last only until the slave reached age twenty-eight, unless the slave was already over twenty-one, in which case the indenture was for seven years. "Such an indenture between freemen" would not have been supported because it would not benefit the free minor, who gained full rights at age twenty-one. But the court upheld such indentures for slaves because the slave received "the most valuable of all considerations, *freedom*," and under most circumstances that freedom "ought to be supported."[30] However, the court was quick to void indentures that denied blacks a legitimate claim to freedom.

An example is the case of Robert, a twenty-four-year-old black, who in 1794 was released from his indenture. Although Robert had been brought into the state in 1779, his master neglected to register him under the Act of 1780 and instead signed an indenture with Robert in 1784. The court ruled that the failure to register Robert freed him immediately, and thus the indenture had to end when the already free man reached the age of his majority, his color notwithstanding.[31]

If it was an owner's negligence that freed Robert, it was ignorance of the law that freed the slave of Madame Boudineau, another refugee from Santo Domingo. Unlike her compatriot, Madame Chambre, Boudineau was apparently unfamiliar with the laws of her new residence. Perhaps her lack of knowledge can be attributed to a lack of interest, for she ultimately moved to France. However, as a slave-

---

30. *Commonwealth* v. *Hambright*, 4 S. & R. (Pa.) 218 (1818). See also *Pennsylvania* v. *Montgomery*, Addison (Pa.) 262 (1795). Some owners tried to avoid giving up indentured ex-slaves by removing them from the state. In 1783 Judge Bryan obtained the return of seven indentured blacks who had been forcibly taken to New York City; MSS dated 3 July 1783, Bryan Papers, box 2, file 17.

31. *Respublica* v. *Gaoler of Philadelphia County*, 1 Yeates (Pa.) 368 (1794).

owner she faced a dilemma in moving anywhere. She could not take her slave to France, because under French law he would have been free. Nor could she take him to any northern state and sell him. She could have legally sold her slave in the Deep South, but that would have been inconvenient. She could have kept her slave had *she* been interested in moving to a slave state, like New Jersey or Virginia. But she could not send her slave to either state and sell him there. The only option left was to indenture the slave for a period of time, thus gaining some economic recompense for bringing him with her. Having just left a slave jurisdiction and being in transit herself, Madame Boudineau, understandably perhaps, did not learn the details of Pennsylvania's statutes in time to make the indenture valid. At age twenty-five the slave sued for his immediate freedom. The court granted this freedom because there was "no evidence of any terms being agreed upon within six months after the negro was brought" into Pennsylvania.[32]

Madame Boudineau's problem was hardly unique. For slaveowners in transit many northern laws must have been unexpected and, indeed, incomprehensible. That Pennsylvania would take one's property merely because that property had been left in the state for more than six months was undoubtedly an unforeseen possibility.[33] As many of the Pennsylvania cases show, some slaveowners came to the state with no intention of evading the law or establishing slavery there. They merely wished to exercise their rights as citizens of other states or nations to visit a friendly neighbor without having their "property" arbitrarily taken from them. Nonetheless, they soon encountered just that inconvenience if they failed to follow Pennsylvania's laws scrupulously.

Indentures were also used by migrants settling in the state who wanted to bring their slaves with them and continue to enjoy their services for some period of time. While indentures were common for both blacks and whites, the court and the legislature were more willing to grant comity to indentures that would eventually free a slave than for indentures of white orphans and other children who might prefer to reach their majority in their home states. At the same time, the court also voided provisions in the indentures of slaves, in order to protect those slaves, while allowing similar provisions when whites were indentured. The end result of the court's

32. *Respublica* v. *Smith*, 4 Yeates (Pa.) 204 (1805).

33. This question also arose in slave states, where slaves sometimes sued for freedom based on Pennsylvania (and other free-state) residence. See, for example, the following Kentucky cases, discussed in chapter 7: *Violet and William* v. *Stephens*, Lit. Sel. Ca. (Ky.) 147 (1812); *Amy (a woman of color)* v. *Smith*, 1 Lit. (Ky.) 326 (1822); *Maria* v. *Kirby* 12 B. Mon. (Ky.) 542 (1851).

decisions was to protect the rights of whites, who would gain autonomy at age twenty-one, and to insure that blacks coming into Pennsylvania as indentured servants would gain their freedom.[34]

In *Commonwealth* v. *Edwards* (1813)[35] the court voided an indenture for a white orphan made in Virginia because there was "no express stipulation that the apprentice" could be removed from Virginia. Chief Justice Tilghman held that the indenture was enforceable only in Virginia, for "the consequences of a boundless license of removal would be monstrous." The judge added, however, "this opinion has no bearing on the case of negroes . . . [whose] condition depends in part on the singular nature of their case, and in part on the acts of assembly of our own."[36] The court implied that it would enforce an indenture made in another state if it worked to free a slave because Pennsylvania's public policy was to encourage freedom. But Pennsylvania was less concerned about a white, who would be completely free when he reached the age of majority. The Pennsylvania court also felt in the *Edwards* case that the state of Virginia did not wish its apprenticed orphans to be indentured in any other state. In refusing to recognize the indenture, Pennsylvania was actually granting comity to Virginia's law.

One might conclude from the dicta in *Edwards* that an indenture of a slave, which explicitly allowed for removal to another state, would be acceptable in Pennsylvania. However, *Commonwealth* v. *Hambright* (1818)[37] showed this not to be the case. A New Jersey master indentured his slave to serve until age twenty-eight "in *Pennsylvania*, or in any other state in which he should reside." But when the master returned to New Jersey the slave refused to accompany him. The master then had the slave jailed until he would agree to leave Pennsylvania. A petition for habeas corpus was filed, to which the master cited *Edwards* and claimed that the "express stipulation" made removal of the indentured slave legal.[38]

Chief Justice Tilghman refused to interpret his earlier decision in *Edwards* in this light. He ruled that under Pennsylvania's 1788

34. In *Commonwealth* v. *Longo*, 1 Browne (Pa.) 269n (1809), Tilghman acknowledged, "[W]e have no Act of Assembly, authorizing such binding" but felt "where the right of the master is clear, or where the law is doubtful, I am not prepared to say, that the indenture is void." It was "customary for negroes in Philadelphia, claimed as [runaway] slaves . . . to bind themselves for different periods . . . by way of compromise with their masters." Tilghman was willing to support indentures to age twenty-eight, in absence of any legislative authority, because he felt it would lead to more slaves being freed.

35. *Commonwealth* v. *Edwards*, 6 Binney (Pa.) 202 (1813).

36. Ibid. 204.

37. *Commonwealth* v. *Hambright*, 4 S. & R. (Pa.) 218 (1818).

38. Ibid.

statute, once an indentured slave was brought into the state he could not be forced to leave. Like the *Somerset* case in England, *Hambright* gave slaves the use of habeas corpus to prevent their removal to another jurisdiction. Unfortunately, unlike *Somerset*, the Pennsylvania decision was quite limited and applied only to those slaves indentured. Tilghman's reasoning was nevertheless extremely important. The chief justice argued that the statute of 1788 was passed to prevent indentured slaves from "being removed from the state of Pennsylvania to other states, where the laws did not afford them equal protection." Thus, in what may have been the first use of "equal protection" to serve the cause of racial justice, Tilghman ordered the slave released from prison and warned the master to "take care to make no attempt to carry him out of the state, against his consent."[39] At the end of the indenture period, the "protection" of Pennsylvania's statutes would free the black.

In a subsequent case a Maryland indenture was voided because, although it conformed to Pennsylvania law, it did not conform to Maryland law. The original indenture had been for ten years, but the master "remitted" the last three years in accordance with Pennsylvania's statute limiting indentures of adults to seven years. The slave was forty when the indenture began. When he reached age forty-five, the Pennsylvania court terminated the indenture and freed him, because under Maryland law no slave over age forty-five could be manumitted.[40] Thus, even though a forty-seven-year-old slave could be freed in Pennsylvania, the court enforced the earlier emancipation age based on the Maryland law under which the original indenture was written. This rather extreme example of comity contrasts with Pennsylvania's refusal to accept the legal New Jersey indenture that violated Pennsylvania's law. In terms of legal reasoning, Pennsylvania's decisions seemed inconsistent. In the New Jersey case the Pennsylvania court enforced the *lex fori* (law of the forum state) at the expense of the *lex loci* (law of the state in which the contract was made). In the Maryland case, the Pennsylvania court ruled in precisely the opposite way. While these rulings are based on contradictory conflict of laws theories, they include important common elements. In both cases the indentures had to satisfy

39. Ibid. 220–21.
40. *Russell* v. *Commonwealth*, 1 Pen. & W. (Pa.) 82, 83 (1829). In *Commonwealth ex rel. Taylor* v. *Hanson*, 3 Pen. & W. (Pa.) 237 (1831), the court upheld an indenture bringing two blacks into Pennsylvania because they had been indentured beforehand and then their indentures purchased by a citizen of Pennsylvania. This was not considered importation of slaves, because the blacks were indentured at the time they entered the state. The decision was also consistent with the court's policy of encouraging freedom, since it allowed for slaves to be freed in Pennsylvania.

two requirements: first, they had to be legal under the *lex fori*—that is, under Pennsylvania law; second, they had to be construed in favor of the slave. These cases underscore Pennsylvania's commitment to freedom, rather than a commitment to any strict rules of interpretation.

This commitment to freedom became more evident in two 1832 cases, *Commonwealth ex rel. Hall* v. *Cook* and *Commonwealth ex rel. Hall* v. *Robinson.*[41] Here the court decided that indentures could be enforced in Pennsylvania only if they were made *outside* the state and conformed to the laws of the state. A person bound to an indenture had to be "in a condition to receive an advantage from the contract." Such a condition could exist only for a slave outside the state, for upon entering Pennsylvania the slave of a prospective resident became instantly free, under the Act of 1788. It would thus be necessary for a person moving into Pennsylvania to know in advance what the laws of the state were and to execute an indenture before bringing a slave into the state. The owner had to be absolutely certain he wanted to move into the state, since there was no longer a six-months grace period for prospective residents. If the master came into the state with an indentured slave, the slave would have to remain in Pennsylvania, even if the master decided to return to his home state. However, if the slave came in without an indenture and the master decided to remain, the slave could not then be indentured, because he would be free under the 1788 law. However great the dilemmas for a master, the court had few doubts as to the correctness of the ruling. "In adopting this rule," Justice Milton C. Rogers wrote, "we impose no hardship on persons who may wish to introduce that class within the state. It is as easy to execute the indenture out, as in the state. It is presumed, that before they take a step of this kind they will inform themselves of the statutes of the state, and conform to the regulations which may be required."[42] In the fluid, mobile, and not always literate American society of the 1830s, such a presumption was likely to cause at least some masters to lose their property.

The dilemma of slaveowners moving into Pennsylvania was further complicated by a boundary dispute between Virginia and Pennsylvania. Because of this dispute many slaveowners in Westmoreland and Washington counties refused to register their slaves under the 1780 act. Many persons resident there felt that they were Virginians, since this was an era when state citizenship was more important than national allegiance. Others may have wished to

41. *Commonwealth ex rel. Hall* v. *Cook* and *Commonwealth ex rel. Hall* v. *Robinson*, 1 Watts (Pa.) 155 and 158 (1832).
42. Ibid. 159–60.

avoid the two-dollar-per-slave registration fee. On 31 August 1779, an agreement was reached between commissioners from the two states on the location of the border. Not until 23 September 1780 was that agreement accepted by a legislative resolution, and confirmation by statutory enactment did not come until 1 April 1784. In the meantime, an act of 13 April 1782 extended the time limit for registering slaves until 1 January 1783 for all those living in the disputed area on 23 September 1780.[43]

A number of Pennsylvania cases focused on the special problems of Westmoreland and Washington counties.[44] Two of them, *Respublica* v. *Blackmore* (1797) and *John, a negro man* v. *Dawson* (1799),[45] involved masters who had migrated into the disputed area after 23 September 1780, but before Pennsylvania had formally ratified the interstate agreement.

Samuel Blackmore, a Maryland slaveowner, purchased land in Pennsylvania in March 1780 and made arrangements to have his land sowed before he arrived in the fall. Blackmore planned to move in September but could not liquidate his Maryland property until December, when he finally came to his new home, bringing his two slaves with him. In 1782, when the registration extension was passed, Blackmore correctly registered them. Over a decade later, after Blackmore's death, the slaves were the objects of a habeas corpus proceeding against his wife, Aberilla.

Mrs. Blackmore argued that her husband should "be deemed an 'inhabitant' of *Westmoreland* county" as of the 23 September residence date, because by that time he had purchased land there and made preparations for moving. This argument was unacceptable to the court, which viewed residence as requiring a permanent physical presence that could not begin until after Blackmore had actually moved to the state.[46]

The court failed to acknowledge that Blackmore, and others similarly situated, were in an absolutely untenable position. When Blackmore bought his land "he could not know whether Pennsylvania would ratify the agreement made by the commissioners of the two states." Thus, he did not really know to which state he was moving. When the 1782 registration extension was passed "he availed himself of the proffered redress," doing "all in his power to

43. 1 *Laws of the Commonwealth of Pennsylvania* 496.

44. See, for example, *Campbell* v. *Wallace*, 3 Yeates (Pa.) 572 (1803); *Marchand* v. *Negro Peggy*, 2 S. & R. (Pa.) 18 (1815); *Lucy (a negro woman)* v. *Pumfrey*, Addison (Pa.) 380 (1799); *Giles (a negro man)* v. *Meeks*, Addison (Pa.) 384 (1799).

45. *Respublica* v. *Blackmore*, 2 Yeates (Pa.) 234 (1797); *John, a negro man* v. *Dawson*, 2 Yeates (Pa.) 449 (1799).

46. *Respublica* v. *Blackmore* 234, 236, 240.

comply with the laws of the country, and secure his property in" the slaves.[47] Unfortunately, the legislature and the court placed him in a position such that he had no legal way to secure his property. The fact that the 1782 extension could be claimed only by those owners who were residents on 23 September 1780 made it impossible for Blackmore to secure his slaves legally. But as a resident of Pennsylvania for more than six months, Blackmore could not then remove his slaves from the state. And of course, when he moved to Pennsylvania he could not have known that he had to reach the state by 23 September or lose his slaves.

In a similar case two years later, the court freed the slave John who had been imported after the 1782 registration extension was passed, but before it had expired. The master in this case claimed he had attempted to register John under the 1782 act but this argument was rejected by the court, which cited "a much stronger case on *habeas corpus* . . . against Aberilla Blackmore."[48]

Protecting Transients

The true test of comity in Pennsylvania was not the state's attitude toward masters settling in the state, but its treatment of bona fide transients and, to a lesser extent, its willingness to aid in the recaption and rendition of runaway slaves. Some fugitive cases thus bear indirectly on problems of comity and transit.

As indicated earlier, no appellate court cases are recorded in which slaves were freed after a six-months residence. Manuscript records indicate that such cases were heard in lower courts and most likely masters who lost these cases did not bother to appeal. A number of cases were reported, however, in which the state courts affirmed the right of a nonresident master to retain a slave in Pennsylvania for less than six months. Apparently blacks with even a tenuous claim to freedom could easily find legal help—usually from the Abolition Society—to argue their case.[49]

47. Ibid. 236.

48. *John* v. *Dawson* 499.

49. See *Pirate, alias Belt* v. *Dalby*, 1 Dallas (U.S. & Pa.) 167 (1786); *Commonwealth* v. *Chambre*, 4 Dallas (U.S. & Pa.) 143 (1794); *Respublica* v. *Richards*, 1 Yeates (Pa.) 480 (1795); *Jacob* v. *Executor of Jacob*, 2 Rawle (Pa.) 204 (1828); and *Cobean* v. *Thompson*, 1 Pen. & W. (Pa.) 93 (1829), all prosecuted by the Abolition Society. See generally the papers of the Abolition Society, which record their constant search for blacks who might need legal help. Edward R. Turner, *The Negro in Pennsylvania*, (Washington, D.C.: American Historical Association, 1911) 81–82, notes, "The Friends and abolitionists were particularly active in hunting up pretexts and instituting lawsuits for the purpose of setting at liberty the negroes of people who believed

In *Respublica* v. *Richards* (1795)[50] the supreme court not only affirmed a slave's status, but elaborated on the rights of a slaveowner who brought his property into the state for less than six months. The court also interpreted the 1788 addition to the gradual emancipation laws as a specific denial of the right to a writ of habeas corpus for all slaves brought into the state. The prosecution was initiated by the Abolition Society, which argued that no black, slave or free, could be forced out of the state. This stance of course was reminiscent of the most narrow interpretation of *Somerset*. However, such a broad reading of the 1788 statute was rejected by the court. The facts of the case reveal the problems of allowing any slave transit in a free state.

In 1795 Toby, a slave of General John Sevier, refused to leave Pennsylvania with the general's son, Major Sevier. Instead, Toby ran away. Major Sevier sought the aid of his brother-in-law, Samuel Richards, and the two men beat and subdued Toby, then sent him to New Jersey against his will. The major and Toby then continued on their way to Virginia. Richards returned to Philadelphia, where the Abolition Society procured an indictment against him for kidnapping.

The prosecution claimed that the 1788 statute's seventh section prohibiting the removal "by force or violence" of "any negro or mulatto" applied equally to slaves and fugitive slaves, as well as free blacks. The Abolition Society lawyers argued that this antikidnapping clause was meant to force all masters to go to court *before* they left the state with an alleged slave. Therefore kidnapping of free blacks would be prevented by giving *all* blacks in Pennsylvania, including fugitive slaves, the right to a hearing before their forcible removal. This interpretation might cause hardship to some masters, but the prosecution thought that the difficulties incurred would be "insignificant, when contrasted with the injurious consequences which must flow from their taking the reins into their hands solely."[51] Indeed, such an interpretation would have helped prevent kidnapping and would have eliminated the public subduing and beating of fugitive slaves in which Richards had been involved.

The court felt this interpretation of the law would be an unnecessary and unwarranted burden on the master. This interpretation

---

they were obeying the laws, but who neglected to comply with some technical point." Wiecek, *Sources of Antislavery Constitutionalism* 86–87, claims the Abolition Society in Pennsylvania and similar organizations in other states "were intensely litigious, so much so that they sometimes skirted the edges of barratry and maintenance."

50. *Respublica* v. *Richards*, 1 Yeates (Pa.) 480 (1795).

51. Ibid. 481–82.

would also negate the comity aspect of the six-months clause, since it would tend "to prevent the slaves of sojourners from being carried by force to other places or being prevailed on to remove thither."[52] Since Sevier's bondsman had been in the state less than six months, he was not free and the antikidnapping clause could not be used to prosecute Richards. Chief Justice Thomas McKean concluded that, once a Negro was proved to be a slave, not only did his master have "a right to seize and carry him away, but that, in case he absconded or resisted, it was the duty of every magistrate to employ all the legitimate means of coercion in his power, for securing and restoring the negro to the services of his owner."[53] On the other hand, had the slave stayed more than six months, the same magistrate would have been equally obligated to protect the black and punish anyone trying to force him out of the state.[54]

Pennsylvania's geographic location led to a greater problem of runaways than most northern states faced. In the 1780 statute the legislature specifically exempted runaways from the liberating aspects of the law. This was done without any coercion from the United States Constitution, which was of course not yet written, or from any clauses in the Articles of Confederation. The clause was inserted to help secure interstate harmony and comity in the new nation. The Constitution of 1787 and the federal Act of 1793 further regulated the rendition of fugitive slaves. Yet, like most legislation concerning slavery, these regulations failed to provide for all the complicated legal and human questions arising from the peculiar institution. Thus, while Pennsylvania might feel obligated, and even willing, to return fugitives,[55] the supreme court sometimes found that it was impossible to do so.

When a fugitive was captured within the state, the owner was given the option of emancipating the slave there and indenturing the now-free black. Under these circumstances the court did not require that the indenture be made before the slave entered the state, since "it would be a useless ceremony" to have the master and

52. Ibid. 482–83.

53. *Respublica* v. *Richards*, 2 Dallas (U.S. & Pa.) 224 (1795). This case was reported by both Dallas and Yeates, and while they do not differ in substance, each report contains some unique details.

54. This would later be affirmed in a federal court by Justice Bushrod Washington, in *Ex parte Simmons*, 22 F. Cas. 151 (1823).

55. In *Wright* v. *Deacon*, 5 S. & R. (Pa.) 62 (1819), Chief Justice Tilghman declared, "Whatever may be our private opinions on the subject of slavery, it is well known our southern brethren would not have consented to become parties to a constitution under which the *United States* have enjoyed so much prosperity, unless their property in slaves had been secured." Thus he would not interfere with the rendition of fugitive slaves under the constitutional clause and the Act of 1793.

slave leave the state, make out the indenture, and then return.[56] Under such an arrangement the runaway Susan was indentured and remained with her free husband in Pennsylvania, while her owner gained some economic recompense for the financial loss incurred by the humanitarian act of freeing her.[57] Even if a master refused to take advantage of this option, the court ruled that the child of a runaway, born in Pennsylvania, was free and could not be forced out of the state. This ruling, however, might apply only to those runaways who became pregnant after entering Pennsylvania, so that the child was literally conceived in freedom. The status of children of runaways or slaves in transit conceived in a slave state but born in Pennsylvania would "perhaps, be found to turn on different principles," although in the 1840s the court determined that they too were free.[58]

In concluding that the child of a runaway was free, the court was severely limiting the comity Pennsylvania would grant to the slave-owners of other states. The fugitive slave in Pennsylvania was still a slave, and thus it would not have been illogical to declare that her children were slaves as well, under the standard American rule that the status of a child of a black followed the status of the mother. The Pennsylvania court, however, leaned toward freedom and noted that the fugitive slave regulations applied only to slaves escaping into another state; since the child had not done so, the child was free. The court might have ruled that the child owed service until age twenty-eight, under the gradual emancipation statute, and allowed the owner to indenture the child. But even this concession to the master was denied, perhaps as an attempt to force the master to leave the mother in Pennsylvania, to care for her child. However, the Pennsylvania judges underestimated the capacity for inhumanity exemplified by at least one master, who left an infant in Pennsylvania and returned to Maryland with his "property," the child's mother.[59]

56. *Commonwealth ex rel. Hall* v. *Robinson*, 1 Watts (Pa.) 158, 160 (1832).

57. *Commonwealth ex rel. Susan Stephens* v. *Clements*, 6 Binney (Pa.) 206 (1814). One master felt he was coerced into agreeing to an indenture for his runaway slave. Nevertheless, the court upheld the indenture; *Stiles* v. *Richardson*, 4 Yeates (Pa.) 82 (1804).

58. *Commonwealth* v. *Holloway*, 2 S. & R. (Pa.) 305 (1816), suggested that children of slaves conceived in slavery but born in Pennsylvania might "turn on different circumstances." But, in *Commonwealth* v. *Auld*, 4 Clark (Pa.) 507 (1850) a slave catcher was convicted of kidnapping the son of a fugitive who was pregnant when she escaped. Thus, the son was conceived in slavery but born in freedom. The court held him to be free, and the kidnapping conviction was sustained.

59. *Commonwealth* v. *Holloway* 305–6. The Pennsylvania courts also refused to allow fugitives to be returned if they were under indictment for any civil or criminal

Congressional Immunity

A critical concession to national comity was the clause in the 1780 law that exempted "the domestic slaves attending upon Delegates in Congress from the other American states, foreign Ministers and Consuls" from the liberating aspects of the statute. Philadelphia was at the time the seat of the Congress under the Articles of Confederation. Later it would become the capital of the United States under the Constitution. With these honors went such obligations as protecting the property of domestic and foreign dignitaries.

For some citizens, however, the clause was too limiting. In 1791 a bill was introduced into the Pennsylvania legislature to allow "officers" of the United States government (not only congressmen and senators) to maintain their slaves in the state. Two committees of the Abolition Society petitioned the House of Representatives against this bill, and the society authorized its lobbyists to fight it. In January 1792 the lobbyists happily reported that the bill had been defeated.[60] Later that year a correspondent calling himself "Federalist" complained in the *American Museum* "that a foreigner, the subject of a friendly kingdom, shall during six months only be permitted to reside at the seat of general government under full protection of his person and property; and at the expiration of that period (N.B. without any trespass of his own) be compelled, by a particular state law, either to quit it, or to lose a property too often essentially necessary to him." "Federalist" thought the law was not "agreeable to the constitution of the United States and the law of nations."[61]

Despite the criticism, the law allowing diplomats and legislators to bring their slaves in Pennsylvania was not changed. Even after the seat of government was moved from Philadelphia to the Potomac, at least one congressman was allowed to visit Pennsylvania for more than six months without losing his slave. In this case[62] the court was willing to extend comity to a visiting congressman, in part because the law had not been changed even though the capital had and in part because any other action might have been viewed as a gratuitous attack on the South.

The first case to be argued under this clause was one of the most

---

offense. See *Commonwealth ex rel. Johnson, A Negro* v. *Holloway*, 3 S. & R. (Pa.) 3, 5–7 (1817); also see Turner, *Negro in Pennsylvania* 231 n. 15.

60. Minutes of 28 Feb. and 2 Jan. 1792, Pennsylvania Abolition Society Papers, microfilm reel 1.

61. 12 *American Museum* 292–93 (1792).

62. *Commonwealth ex rel. Lewis* v. *Holloway*, 6 Binney (Pa.) 213 (1814).

ironic in American legal history. The plaintiff was Pierce Butler, who twenty years earlier had been in Philadelphia as part of South Carolina's delegation to the Constitutional Convention. There he fought tenaciously to protect the rights of slaveowners; in fact, he introduced the Fugitive Slave Clause at the convention. Butler returned to Philadelphia in 1789 as a United States senator, a post that he resigned in 1796 but to which he was reelected in 1802. During his absence from the Senate he served as a member of the South Carolina legislature. However, from 1796 until his death in 1822 he maintained a house in Philadelphia where he usually resided. In August 1804 one of Butler's slaves, named Ben, came to the Abolition Society for help. Ben claimed that he had lived as a slave in Pennsylvania for eleven years and that Butler was preparing to take him to Georgia. Isaac T. Hopper, an officer of the Abolition Society, obtained a writ of habeas corpus from Judge Inskeep, of the Philadelphia Court of Common Pleas, and served the writ on Butler.[63]

While the Abolition Society provided a lawyer for Ben, Butler argued his own case. He claimed he was a citizen of South Carolina and thus exempt from the law. He also argued that Ben had never been kept in Pennsylvania for six consecutive months, except while Butler was a senator and exempt from the six-months provision. However, facts, including Butler's own admissions, showed that Ben had been kept in the state for eight consecutive months in 1804; this was enough to free him. The case was an important one, in part because of the principles involved, in part because of the issue. It was twice adjourned and strenuously argued. Ultimately, however, Ben was discharged from Butler's custody and became a free man.[64]

After losing this case in the state court, Butler sued Isaac Hopper in federal court to recover damages or custody of Ben.[65] In the earlier case Hopper had not been a litigant (he simply served Butler with the writ of habeas corpus) and thus the federal court could not simply reaffirm the holding of the state court (res judicata). The case was argued in the federal United States Circuit Court, where Justice Bushrod Washington was presiding at the time. Ultimately Justice Washington upheld the right of Pennsylvania to govern slave property in that state.[66]

Butler based his case on the fact that he was "a member of congress" and "a sojourner." Washington quickly disposed of the first

63. *Butler* v. *Hopper*, 4 F. Cas. 904 (1806); Lydia Marie Child, *Isaac T. Hopper: A True Life*, (2d ed. New York: Dodd, Mead, and Company, 1881) 98–103.
64. *Butler* v. *Hopper* 904–5; Child, *Isaac T. Hopper* 103.
65. See chap. 8 for a discussion of this case in federal district court.
66. *Butler* v. *Hopper* 904–5; Child, *Isaac T. Hopper* 103.

contention, noting that for some of the years he had kept Ben in Philadelphia Butler had not been in Congress.

Washington thought that Butler was a sojourner because while in Philadelphia he "left behind an estate which he cultivates, sometimes visits, (no matter how often, or how long in each year,) and whilst there, keeps house, and is even elected into the legislature of the state." Washington found these to be "circumstances . . . of prodigious weight . . . to repel the idea of a change of domicile." But the jury in the federal court found other evidence that convinced them Butler had in fact ceased to be a resident of South Carolina and had become a resident of Pennsylvania. Justice Washington would not overrule the Pennsylvania finding that Ben was free because his owner had become a resident of the state.[67] At this point Pierce Butler may have deeply regretted that he had not insisted on additional protection for slave property in the federal Constitution.

In 1814 the Pennsylvania court held that moving the capital to Washington or whether the Congress was in session had no effect on the special privilege granted to members of Congress. Langdon Cheves, a congressman from South Carolina, was allowed to retain his slave, even though he kept the slave in Pennsylvania for more than six months between two congressional sessions. Chief Justice Tilghman pointed out that it was almost impossible for some congressmen to return home after each session and to do so would be extremely inconvenient. Furthermore, Pennsylvania would never have passed legislation "the probable consequence of which would have been the banishment of congress from the state." Cheves could keep his slave in Pennsylvania as long as he remained a member of the national legislature.[68]

Compromise and Comity

Tilghman buttressed his opinion in the Cheves case by asserting, "We all know that our southern brethren are very jealous of their rights on the subject of slavery, and their union with the other states could never have been cemented, without yielding to their demands on this point."[69] While this reading of the accomplishments of the Constitutional Convention was questionable, it was an accurate statement of southern feeling, in 1787 and afterward. Such an attitude is quite useful in explaining the rulings of the Pennsylvania courts and the acts of the legislature in the nation's first fifty years. Pennsylvania felt obligated to protect the property of its

67. *Butler* v. *Hopper* 904–5; Child, *Isaac T. Hopper* 103.
68. *Commonwealth ex rel. Lewis* v. *Holloway*, 6 Binney (Pa.) 213, 218–19 (1814).
69. Ibid.

neighbors, both in returning fugitive slaves and in allowing for unmolested transit. This protection was attempted, even though the public policy of the state was opposed to slavery and favored freedom. Slaveowners permanently moving into the state were treated more harshly than those who were legitimate sojourners, transients, or visitors. In general, Pennsylvania tried to follow the *Somerset* rule of freeing slaves who touched the free territory of Pennsylvania and of allowing slaves access to the courts to protect their rights. However, as part of a Union that included slave states, Pennsylvania suspended the immediate application of *Somserset* for nonresidents. After six months *Somerset* went into effect, and thus Pennsylvania balanced the needs of freedom with those of the Union. Because Pennsylvania's own emancipation was gradual, some slaves were living in the state long after most were free and some blacks were under long-term indentures but would ultimately gain complete freedom.

By the mid-1830s the questions of law concerning Pennsylvania's 1780 and 1788 statutes were settled. After that date no appellate cases under those statutes were recorded. The courts now faced the problem of runaways.[70] Perhaps by this time few slaveowners were moving into the state, and those who visited were careful to conform strictly to the laws. Slaveowners continued to visit the state and to recapture runaways there. Both situations offended the sensibilities of many Pennsylvanians. The new abolitionist movement took root there in 1831 and the Pennsylvania State Anti-Slavery Society was formed in 1837. The older Abolition Society continued to function, but its role was diminished.[71] In 1842 the United States Supreme Court voided an 1826 Pennsylvania act intended to protect free Negroes who might be captured or kidnapped and claimed as fugitive slaves. All of these facts led to a new act, in 1847, which abolished the six-months clause for regular sojourners and the unlimited right of sojourn for congressmen and foreign ambassadors. The 1847 act formally ended an era of comity in Pennsylvania.[72]

70. Turner, *Negro in Pennsylvania* 279, notes that as early as 1789 slaves were running into Pennsylvania, where they thought they would become free. An advertisement in that year for a runaway noted, "The slaves in this state [Virginia] generally supposing that they may obtain their freedom by going to Pennsylvania makes it highly probable that he is in some part of that state."

71. Dwight L. Dumond, *Antislavery: The Crusade for Freedom in America* (Ann Arbor: University of Michigan Press, 1961) 189, and Needles, *Memoir, passim.*

72. *Prigg* v. *Pennsylvania*, 16 Peters (U.S.) 539 (1842); *Pennsylvania Session Laws, 1847,* 206–8. For a discussion of some fugitive slave cases in Pennsylvania and other states, as well as *Prigg*, see Paul Finkelman, "*Prigg* v. *Pennsylvania* and Northern State Courts: Anti-slavery Use of a Pro-Slavery Decision," 25 *Civil War History* (Mar. 1979) 5–35.

Chapter 3

Cooperation and Comity:
The Northern Rejection of *Somerset*

Unlike Pennsylvania, the rest of the North showed little interest in slave transit before the 1830s. Scattered statutes in a few states gave virtually unlimited rights of transit for masters with slaves. Some northern jurists were uncomfortable with the presence of slaves in their states, but before the 1830s no slaves were freed solely on the basis of transit or sojourn. Even long-term residence had little effect on the status of slaves in some states. The weakness of antislavery sentiment in some areas accounted for much of the lack of interest in the question of slave transit. Pervasive negrophobia, particularly along the Ohio River, made it unlikely that slaves in transit would be freed, for such acts would allow more free Negroes in those states like Indiana and Illinois where discrimination was most blatant.

But even in states where racism was less powerful, courts had either no opportunities or no inclination to free slaves in transit. The slow progress of gradual emancipation in New York and New Jersey made the transit question somewhat less important. The abolition societies in those states, as well as in Rhode Island and Connecticut, concentrated most of their efforts on protecting the rights of recently freed blacks or gaining manumissions for slaves. Nevertheless, some legal groundwork was laid for the eventual assault on the right of transit with slaves. The question had been raised in much of the North by 1830, when slavery no longer existed in that area and the presence of any slave provoked legal and political debates on the nature of the Union and the rights of free states to exclude slavery from their jurisdiction. As the slavery issue grew in importance in national politics, slave transit became a more important legal problem for the North. But in the period before 1830, northern jurists, like most of their neighbors, were able to avoid any direct confrontations over slavery, slave transit, and federalism.[1]

1. Edgar J. McManus, *Black Bondage in the North* (Syracuse: Syracuse University Press, 1973) 160–79; Pennsylvania Abolition Society Papers, microfilm reel 3, vol. 5, *HSP*, contains some records of legal cases in a number of northern states. Most involve manumission suits between the years 1785 and 1796. See also William M.

New York

In 1785, as a result of Quaker petitions, New York passed a statute to facilitate manumission. The statute also prohibited the importation of slaves for sale, but did not affect persons who migrated to the state with slaves or permanent residents of the state who imported slaves for their personal use. Slaves illegally imported or slaves sold after importation would be freed and the importers fined.[2] A 1788 statute prohibited the exportation of slaves for sale in other states or the sale of a slave in New York for the purpose of exportation to another state. Anyone moving out of the state could take previously owned slaves but could not buy new slaves. Like the anti-importation law, this act freed illegally transported slaves and subjected the exporter to fines. The statute made intent to remove for future sale, or sale and purchase with intent to remove, offenses, as well as actual removal. Thus a former owner could be prosecuted after the buyer and the slave left the state. Similarly, a purchaser and seller could both be prosecuted before actual removal took place. But once removal took place it would be possible for the slave to gain freedom only if the courts of another state extended comity to New York by enforcing the New York statute and freeing the slave.[3]

Wiecek, *The Sources of Antislavery Constitutionalism in America, 1760–1848* (Ithaca and London: Cornell University Press, 1977) 84–105; and Arthur Zilversmit, *The First Emancipation: The Abolition of Slavery in the North* (Chicago and London: University of Chicago Press, 1967).

2. *New York Laws, 1785*, chap. LXVIII; Edgar J. McManus, *A History of Negro Slavery in New York* (Syracuse: Syracuse University Press, 1966) 186; Thomas E. Drake, *Quakers and Slavery in America* (New Haven: Yale University Press, 1950) 94.

3. *New York Laws, 1788*, chap. XXXIX. See also *State* v. *Quick*, 1 Pennington (N.J.) 413e (1807), discussed below. In *Henderson* v. *Negro Tom*, 4 Harr. & J. (Md.) 282 (1817), the Maryland Supreme Court freed Tom after he was removed from New York and imported into Maryland. Tom gained his freedom not because Maryland enforced New York law, but because his owner failed to register him properly under Maryland law. In *Carney, a coloured man*, v. *Hampton*, 3 T. B. Mon. (Ky.) 228 (1826), the Kentucky Supreme Court refused to enforce New York's prohibition against selling slaves and then removing them from the state. The Kentucky court would not "believe" that New York "intended wholly to prevent the exportation of slaves" and thus ruled that a man who purchased a slave without any intention to export him and then later left the state had not in fact violated New York's law. Kentucky's inability to "believe" that New York could truly mean to end *all* exportation of slaves indicates how difficult it was for states to grant comity to each other's laws. In this case New York's interests were so alien to those of Kentucky that the latter state simply found it impossible to understand New York's law. Most likely, Kentucky viewed New York's law simply as a measure to punish slaveowners. New York, however, had the interests of the individual slaves in mind as much as the interest of ending slavery. Kentucky often freed slaves who lived in free states. At the time of

In 1799 New York passed a gradual emancipation statute, under which the children of all slaves born in New York after 4 July 1799 would become indentured servants. Sons would serve their mother's master until age twenty-eight and daughters until age twenty-five. In this and other features the statute resembled the earlier gradual emancipation statutes of Pennsylvania, Connecticut, and Rhode Island. The 1788 provision prohibiting the exportation of the children of slaves remained in force.[4]

Between 1801 and 1817 New York passed a number of statutes regulating slave importation and migration. Some importation was allowed under these acts, but the slaves brought in would ultimately gain their freedom. In 1801 the legislature allowed unlimited transit with slaves, but in 1810 the time was limited to nine months and this rule remained in force until its repeal in 1841. Under the 1817 law slavery came to an end in New York on 4 July 1827. After that time only transients and visitors could retain their slaves. Immigrants to the state could keep slave minors as indentured servants until they reached their majority. An 1828 revision of the law allowed part-time residents to take their slaves in and out of the state without penalty.[5] This, along with the leniency of the nine-months law, meant that interstate transit with slaves would be unhindered.

Because of the liberality of these laws only a handful of cases dealing with the interstate movement of slaves in New York are recorded, centering chiefly on provisions regulating the exportation and importation of slaves into the state. While the New York Manumission Society "worked hard to prevent the illegal export of slaves

---

this case slavery had provoked few sectional antagonisms. Nevertheless, Kentucky could not grant comity to New York because the conflict of laws between the two states was so great. This example underscores the extreme difficulty of adjudicating cases involving slavery and freedom at this time. On the illegal exportation of blacks from New York, see McManus, *Negro Slavery in New York* 170.

4. Zilversmit, *First Emancipation* 181–84; McManus, *Negro Slavery in New York* 174–75; *New York Laws, 1799*, chap. LXII.

5. *New York Laws, 1801*, chap. CLXXXVIII, *New York Laws, 1810*, chap. CXV, *New York Laws, 1817*, chap. CXCCVII; *New York Laws, 1841*, chap. CCXLVII. Unlike Pennsylvania, New York did not impose a residency test on slaveowners. Masters therefore could keep slaves in New York for long periods of time, if they owned land in other states where they claimed to be resident. One antislavery group claimed that there were "many instances of persons having estates in the South, who reside here [New York City], and keep slaves in defiance of the laws." As long as these slaves were not kept in the state for more than nine consecutive months, the slaves would not be free even if the master appeared to be a resident of the state. The antislavery organization quoted above also complained that slaves were kept in the state for more than nine months and still not freed; *The First Annual Report of the New York Committee of Vigilance* (New York: Piercy and Reed, 1837) 14–15.

from the state," no reported cases focus directly on the problem. Perhaps any prosecutions initiated by the society were so strong that they precluded appeals. But it seems likely from the decline in New York's black population after 1800 that substantial illegal exportation of blacks from the state did in fact take place.[6] Exporters of slaves were unlikely to be caught once they left the state, and thus prosecutions would have been difficult. Importers, on the other hand, were more vulnerable. A slave brought into the state and then sold contrary to the law was living proof that the law had been violated.

The first importation case to reach the New York Supreme Court was *Sable* v. *Hitchcock* (1800).[7] Sable, a New Jersey slave, had been legally brought to New York when her master migrated there and was sold by an executor after the owner's death. Sable sued for freedom, claiming that she had been imported and then sold, contrary to the 1785 law. The court ruled that this did not violate "the spirit of the act" because "[i]t ought not to be deemed to apply to those who act involuntarily, for the benefit of others, and in performance of a trust imposed by law."[8] In this case the New York court placed a higher value on the rights of a testator and his heirs than on the rights of a slave to freedom.

While *Sable* v. *Hitchcock* kept the slave in bondage, it was narrowly applied as a liberating precedent in subsequent cases. *Caesar* v. *Peabody* (1814)[9] involved a slave brought to New York when his owner moved there from Virginia. After financial reverses Caesar was sold for debt at a sheriff's sale. This transaction was deemed legal on grounds similar to those in *Sable* v. *Hitchcock*—namely, that the act was involuntarily performed for the benefit of others, in this case creditors. However, when the new owner resold Caesar the court freed the slave. The second sale was unnecessary and therefore constituted a sale after importation, even though the seller was not

6. *New York Laws, 1810*, chap. CXV. On the decline of New York's black population due to illegal exportation, see McManus, *Negro Slavery in New York* 169–70, 176. See also A. Judd Northrup, "Slavery in New York," 4 *State Library Bulletin of History* 295–98 (May 1900). See also *Thompson and Bowen's Cases*, 2 New York City-Hall Recorder 120 (1816). In this case a man was convicted of attempting to export free blacks from the state. There was no appeal from this jury-trial conviction, which led to the fining of one of the defendants and the imprisonment of the other. In *Lucy Brown f.w.c.* v. *Smith*, 8 La. Ann. (La.) 59 (1853) a Louisiana court upheld the freedom of a slave based on a residence of more than nine months in New York. This case is the only one I have found in which a slave stayed in New York longer than nine months and was freed by court action.

7. *Sable* v. *Hitchcock*, 2 Johns. (N.Y.) 79 (1800).

8. Ibid. 79, 83.

9. *Caesar* v. *Peabody*, 11 Johns. (N.Y.) 68 (1814).

the importer.[10] The *Sable* rule was also applied in *Helm* v. *Miller* (1820).[11] Here a slave was legally imported when his owner migrated to New York. The owner died in 1806 and his widow married Helm. In 1813 Helm sold the slave to Miller and when Miller refused to honor the note, Helm brought suit. Helm claimed that he sold the slave as part of the estate of his wife's first husband. However, the court found this, in and of itself, was not a legitimate reason for selling the slave, since the sale of the slave was "unnecessary in the administration" of the estate. Therefore the slave had been imported and then sold, contrary to the law of 1785. The note was voided and the slave freed.[12]

Immediately after deciding *Sable* v. *Hitchcock* in favor of the master, the New York court freed a slave in *Fish* v. *Fisher* (1800).[13] The slave Fish escaped to New York, where his master caught him. Rather than return to New Jersey, his master sold him to Fisher, on the condition that Fish be freed after twenty years. In a similar situation, Pennsylvania had allowed such transactions, because "[i]t would be a useless ceremony" to have the master take the slave out of the state and then sell his rights to another within the state.[14] New York had not yet banned the importation of slaves for personal use, and thus Fisher could have gone to New Jersey and purchased Fish as a slave for life. Nevertheless, however useless a ceremony it would have been to return the slave to New Jersey, without such an act the New York court decided that the slave had been imported. For when the master found Fish in New York and did not remove him, the owner "thereby made the change of residence of the slave his own act, and the slave, by the consent of the master, became domiciliated" in New York, which was "the same, in effect, as *bringing* him, in the first instance"; thus there was importation. The court also thought that the indenture for twenty years, when the slave was already twenty years old, amounted to an absolute sale, for the expected lifetime of the slave. Finding importation and sale, the court freed Fish.[15]

In a similar case a few years later, a New York judge ruled that

---

10. Ibid.

11. *Helm* v. *Miller*, 17 Johns. (N.Y.) 296 (1820).

12. Ibid. 296, 299.

13. *Fish* v. *Fisher*, 2 Johns. (N.Y.) 89 (1800).

14. Ibid. 89; *Commonwealth ex rel. Hall* v. *Robinson*, 1 Watts (Pa.) 158, 160 (1832). One reason for the difference in the ruling of the two states may have been the length of the indenture in Fish's case. Pennsylvania would not have allowed such a long indenture. It is possible that if the indenture had been for a reasonably short time the New York court would have ruled the same way Pennsylvania did thirty-two years later.

15. *Fish* v. *Fisher* 90. Also, see *Link* v. *Beuner*, 3 Caine (N.Y.) 325 (1805), for a similar case.

an indenture made in New Jersey for twelve years was "a mere evasion" of an 1810 law prohibiting the importation of slaves. The indenture was "void" because "the slave became free immediately upon her being brought" into the state.[16] Indentures such as this one and that in Fish's case led to the 1810 law, passed because people had attempted "to evade the existing laws of this state concerning the importation and transfer of slaves. . . ."[17]

In an 1817 case similar to *Fish* v. *Fisher*, the supreme court upheld the rights of a master to a slave who had escaped into New York and been sold.[18] Both the seller and the buyer were residents of another state at the time of the transaction, even though the transaction itself took place in New York, where the fugitive slave was captured. The court ruled that "it cannot be said that the domicil of the slave was changed to this state, by the assent of his master, by the adoption of the act of the slave in coming here."[19] Thus, there had been no importation to New York followed by a sale.

These cases show that New York's main interest during this period was to prevent any increase in the state's slave population; thus illegally imported slaves were freed. The work of the New York Manumission Society illustrates this point. In one eighteen-month period in 1796 and 1797 the society successfully obtained freedom for slaves in thirty-six separate cases. In twenty-nine of these cases the slaves had been illegally imported.[20]

But stopping slave importation did not mean interfering in slave transit. The most important factor in New York's treatment of slave movement during this period was the nine-months law. By allowing masters to keep slaves in the state that long, New York insured that a harmonious relationship would exist between that important northern state and her southern trading partners. Slaveowners were not likely to cross New York when moving to the western slave states, as they might cross Pennsylvania, Ohio, or Illinois. Nor were a great number of slaveowners likely to move into the state. But slaveowners came to New York City to do business and to Saratoga, Niagara Falls, and other "watering spots" for vacation.[21] These visitors could bring their slaves with them and stay a long time

16. *DuBois* v. *Allen*, Anth. N.P. (N.Y.) (2d ed., 1852), 128, 129–30. This case is undated but appears to have taken place sometime between 1810 and 1820.

17. *New York Laws, 1810*, chap. CXV. On long indentures, see McManus, *Negro Slavery in New York* 169.

18. *Skinner* v. *Fleet*, 14 Johns. (N.Y.) 263 (1817).

19. Ibid. 269.

20. Pennsylvania Abolition Society Papers, microfilm reel 3, vol. 5, p. 66.

21. The best study of southern travelers in the North is John Hope Franklin, *A Southern Odyssey: Travelers in the Antebellum North* (Baton Rouge: Louisiana State University Press, 1976).

without legal harassment. Only with the growth of antislavery sentiment in the 1830s and the election of the antislavery Governor William H. Seward was the spirit of comity terminated. In 1841 the nine-months law was repealed, and an era of interstate comity ended.[22]

New Jersey

New Jersey was the last northern state to end slavery. Indeed, the 1860 census reported eighteen slaves still in the state, although their actual legal status was as apprentices for life.[23] With the exception of some rather weak legislation dealing with the African and interstate slave trades, New Jersey took no action to end slavery until passage of the gradual emancipation statute of 1804. Various supplemental laws dealing with slavery led in 1820 to a comprehensive law regulating manumission, emancipation, the slave trade, and the interstate movement of slaves. Among other provisions, the law stated that any slave had the right to refuse to leave the state with his master. Visitors, transients, and their slaves "having a temporary residence" in New Jersey were exempt from this statute.[24] Final abolition occurred in 1846, when the few remaining slaves became apprentices. The unlimited right of transit and sojourn for nonresident slaveowners and their human "property" was maintained until 1865.[25]

Because New Jersey protected the rights of slaveowners only one case dealing with the problem of comity and slavery was recorded. *State* v. *Quick* (1807)[26] involved a slave purchased in New York and then brought to New Jersey. The case was a classic problem in the choice of laws. New York prohibited the selling of a slave for export. New Jersey, on the other hand, had no objection to the introduction of new slaves, provided they were purchased outside the state and not resold within the state. There was no New Jersey law that could free the slave. In reaching his decision, Justice William Pennington noted that if the slave was free under New York law, "it must be that

22. *New York Laws, 1841*, chap. CCXLVII.

23. Zilversmit, *First Emancipation* 222; Henry Schofield Cooley, *A Study of Slavery in New Jersey* (Baltimore: Johns Hopkins University Press, 1896) 438–39. As apprentices, these aged blacks had numerous privileges, protections, and rights that slaves were denied. Their former owners (and still their masters) were responsible for maintaining them in their old age.

24. *New Jersey Laws, 1820* 679–85; Cooley, *Negro Slavery in New Jersey* 429–40.

25. Lucius Q. C. Elmer, ed., *Digest of the Laws of New Jersey* (3rd ed. Trenton: Charles Scott, 1861) 801–10.

26. *State* v. *Quick*, 1 Pennington (N.J.) 413e (1807).

he was free before he was brought into this State; for the State of New York cannot extend into this State and attach itself to any act done here, in order to give him freedom." Pennington could have determined that under New York law the slave was free before he came to New Jersey, because the *intent* to export a slave purchased in the state was an offense, as well as the actual exportation. Also, since the exportation began with preparations in New York, the crime against New York law was committed *before* the slave ever reached New Jersey. Justice Pennington, however, did not interpret New York's law that way. Instead he ruled that the slave would be free under New York law only if the original purchase of the slave was made with the intent of illegally exporting the slave from New York. Since the purchase took place two years prior to the removal, Pennington held that the purchase had not been an attempt to evade the New York law; thus the slave was not freed.[27] The decision indicates a certain bias in New Jersey's willingness to grant comity. Unlike other northern states that leaned toward liberty while at the same time granting rights to nonresidents, New Jersey gave rights to all slaveowners and refused to enforce a New York law for the benefit of a slave owned by a New Jersey resident.

Upper New England

Until the 1830s the New England states exhibited a general willingness to grant comity to out-of-state slaveowners. In upper New England this tolerance was in part a function of comity and in part a result of the area's geography. In New Hampshire, Vermont, and Maine there were few slaves and no recorded instances of cases involving slave transit. Unlike Pennsylvania, New York, or Massachusetts, there were few statutes or cases on the subject because virtually no slaves came into northern New England.

In New Hampshire slavery appears to have withered away, without either statutes or explicit judicial decrees. Neither cases nor laws dealing with slave transit are recorded there before the 1840s. When transit became a political issue in the 1840s and 1850s the New Hampshire legislature passed laws freeing any slaves that

27. Ibid. 413e, 415e. McManus, *Black Bondage in the North* 173–79, argues that most New Jersey judges leaned toward freedom. Perhaps they did in manumission cases involving wills, promised freedom, and registration under the law of 1804. However, New Jersey was the most negrophobic state in the East and the last to take steps to end slavery. The decision in *State* v. *Quick* and the protection offered slaves in transit until the Emancipation Proclamation indicate that New Jersey was one of the least pro-freedom states in the North.

might be brought into the state. What little evidence there is indicates a profound distaste for the peculiar institution in the Granite State.[28]

After abolishing slavery in 1777 and prohibiting the exportation of Negroes and mulattoes out of the state in 1786, Vermont's legislature ignored slavery until the passage of various personal liberty laws in the 1840s and 1850s.[29] The one case dealing with a slave indicates the attitude of the Vermont Supreme Court toward slavery and comity. In 1802 the Board of Selectmen of the Town of Windsor sued Stephen Jacob for the maintenance of an "infirm, sick, and blind" black woman, whom Jacob allegedly purchased as a slave in 1793 and later abandoned. All parties in the case agreed slavery could not legally exist in Vermont. But counsel for Windsor claimed that a de facto slavery existed before Jacob abandoned the woman and thus he was responsible for her care. The state supreme court had to decide if the bill of sale from the 1793 purchase was admissible as evidence against Jacob. Without the bill of sale the case against Jacob would dissolve.[30]

Judge Royall Tyler ruled that the bill of sale was not valid in Vermont, because the state's constitution was "express" and "no inhabitant" could "hold a slave" in the state. Thus Jacob was not liable for the upkeep of the old woman. Tyler did admit that a bill of sale might be "binding by the *lex loci* of another State or dominion," but upon entering Vermont the contract became void and the slave became free. The only exceptions to this rule were for fugitive slaves.

28. Edward R. Taylor, *Slavery in Pennsylvania* (Baltimore: Lord Baltimore Press, 1911) 80 n. 46; Isaac W. Hammond, "Slavery in New Hampshire," 21 *Magazine of American History* 62–65 (1889). See *Burlington* v. *Fosby*, 6 Vt. 83 (1834), which involved "the slave of one Moore, a citizen of New Hampshire." Also, William Frederick Poole, *Anti-Slavery Opinions before the Year 1800* (Cincinnati: Robert Clarke and Company, 1873) 58. Poole claims the declaration in the New Hampshire Constitution of 1784 that "all men are created equally free and independent was constructed to mean that all persons *born* after 1784" were free. Thus Poole argues that New Hampshire had gradual emancipation. Poole cites no case or instance when such a construction was made. Most likely the "construction," if it can be called that, was made and enforced by public opinion. In *Semmes* v. *Sherburne*, 21 F. Cas. 1059 (1825), a slave gained her freedom after being taken to New Hampshire.

29. McManus, *Black Bondage in the North* 160; John A. Williams, ed., *The Law of Vermont*, 14 *State Papers of Vermont* (Montpelier, 1966) 100; *Compiled Statutes of the State of Vermont, 1851* (Burlington: 1851), chap. CI. In 1786, before statehood, Vermont passed "An act to prevent the sale and transportation of negroes and mulattoes out of this State." The law was repealed when Vermont entered the Union because it was thought to interfere with the Fugitive Slave Clause of the Constitution. Actually the law simply protected former slaves residing in Vermont and probably did not conflict with the Constitution. Its repeal suggests that the understanding of the Fugitive Slave Clause at this time was rather murky.

30. *Selectmen* v. *Jacob*, 2 Tyler (Vt.) 192 (1802).

Tyler asserted that the "good people of Vermont" would "submit with cheerfulness" to the enforcement of the Fugitive Slave Law, even though they might wish that the federal requirements were "more congenial to our modes of thinking." In the spirit of comity and nationalism that pervaded this period, Judge Tyler declared that Vermonters were "sensible . . . of numerous right blessings to us as individuals, and to the State as an integral of the Union."[31]

Tyler's decision might be read as strongly supportive of interstate comity toward slavery. He specifically limited his restrictions to "inhabitants of the State." Tyler might have allowed a sojourning master to retain his slave in Vermont. But the decision might also be seen as one of the earliest to imply that a state had a right to interfere with slave transit. Vermont, under Tyler's reading of the federal Constitution, was obligated only to respect the rights of a master under the Fugitive Slave Clause. Transit, which was not specifically covered in the Constitution, might not be a protected right.

Maine entered the Union as a free state in 1820. The state's first constitution declared that "all men are born equally free and independent." An act of 1821 prohibited the removal of "any person lawfully residing and inhabiting" in the state but contained no reference to fugitive slaves or slaves in transit. Slaves in both of these categories would not have been "lawfully residing and inhabiting" in the state.[32] Maine's geographical remoteness explains why few laws or cases concerning slavery are found among its records.

Lower New England

Unlike northern New England, Rhode Island, Connecticut, and Massachusetts had a great deal of contact with slaves and slaveholders. All three states were involved in the African slave trade. Gradual emancipation in two of them meant that a few slaves would be legally resident after most blacks in the states were free.

Rhode Island had the largest percentage of slaves in the New England states. Newport had been a leading port for the African

31. Ibid. 192–93, 197–98. See also *Glover* v. *Millings*, 2 Stew. & P. (Ala.) 28 (1832). Millings, a slave in Alabama, alleged he had lived in Vermont as a free man and had been a soldier there. Because of the inadmissibility of certain evidence the Alabama Supreme Court reversed the lower court decision freeing Millings. The facts presented in the case imply that Millings was born or raised in the North, and had been kidnapped and taken to the South.

32. *Maine, Constitution of 1819*, art. 1, sec. 1; *Maine, Revised Statutes, 1821*, chap. 22.

slave trade and later became a "watering hole" for southerners summering in the North. The Narragansett planters profitably exploited slavery on a scale equal to parts of the South.[33] In 1774 Rhode Island prohibited the importation of new slaves, but the law did not affect sojourners or visitors. A 1779 act prohibited the exportation of slaves who did not wish to leave the state, but again, the law applied only to Rhode Island residents. The gradual emancipation statute of 1784 also did not apply to slaves in transit, and until 1844 it appears that slave transit was generally allowed in Rhode Island.[34]

Since Rhode Island did not have a supreme court reporter until 1845, it is impossible to know if there were any cases that challenged the right of sojourning masters. It is likely, however, that such cases would have been reported elsewhere. The Rhode Island Manumission Society in this early period was concerned primarily with the proper enforcement of the gradual emancipation statute. Although the society apparently initiated a number of lawsuits on behalf of blacks, no record was kept of them.[35]

Until 1837 Connecticut allowed out-of-state masters unlimited transit with their slaves. The state's various statutes, revised in 1821, included the 1788 provisions allowing nonresident masters to take their slaves in and out of the state.[36] Only one reported Connecticut case deals with slave movement, and its result is unfortunately not known. In 1792 a Mr. Nichols was tried for illegally exporting two black children who were to be free at age twenty-five under that state's gradual emancipation statute. Because certain depositions were excluded at the trial, Nichols was acquitted.[37] A second hearing showed that Nichols had introduced forged evidence and a new trial was ordered, the outcome of which is unrecorded.[38]

The judicial abolition of slavery in the 1780s in Massachusetts had no immediate effect on the slaves of nonresidents. Only two cases concerning slavery and comity reached the Bay State's highest court before 1830. In 1810 William Greenwood sued Benjamin

33. Edward Channing, *The Narragansett Planters* (Baltimore: Johns Hopkins University Press, 1886); Irving H. Bartlett, *From Slave to Citizen: The Story of the Negro in Rhode Island* (Providence: The Urban League of Greater Providence, 1954) 5–24; Franklin, *A Southern Odyssey, passim*; Arline Ruth Kiven, *Then Why the Negroes?* (N.p.: Urban League of Rhode Island, 1973) 23 and *passim*.

34. *The Public Laws of the State of Rhode Island* (Providence, 1822) 441–44. For further discussion of these laws, see chap. 1 of this volume.

35. "Report of the Providence Society," 24 May 1798, Pennsylvania Abolition Society Papers, microfilm reel 3, vol. 5, p. 132.

36. *Jackson* v. *Bulloch*, 12 Day (Conn.) 38 (1837); *Laws of Connecticut, 1821*, tit. 22 and tit. 93.

37. *Hillyard* v. *Nichols*, 1 Root (Conn.) 493 (1793).

38. *Hylliard* v. *Nickols*, 2 Root (Conn.) 176 (1795).

Curtis for failing to fulfill a contractual obligation for the delivery of slaves in Africa, who were then to be transported to South Carolina. The contract for delivery had been made before the African slave trade was prohibited by federal law, but long after it had been prohibited by Massachusetts law. Nevertheless, the court enforced the contract over the strenuous objections of Justice Theodore Sedgwick. Chief Justice Theophilus Parsons reasoned that "[t]o maintain the action . . . is enjoined on us by the comity we owe another state." Only if the contract injured the state or citizens of Massachusetts or if it were for a consideration that Massachusetts found unacceptable, would it be void. Slaves were of course an illegitimate consideration in Massachusetts, but Chief Justice Parsons ruled that the contract could be enforced for the value of the slaves in money. Thus, Greenwood was able to recover the value of the goods he had shipped Curtis.[39]

What is perhaps most interesting about this case was the unchallenged statement of Greenwood's counsel that the common law would allow "an action for the price of a slave sold in a country where it is allowed" even though "slaves arriving in England are instantly free as they are here. . . ."[40] This interpretation was of course a misreading of *Somerset,* which was quite common in America. More important, it was not a correct statement of Massachusetts law. Slaves often arrived in Massachusetts with their masters during this period, and no one had ever challenged the master's right to remove them. Massachusetts courts held only that residents of the Bay State could not be held as slaves. But the counsel's argument was prophetic. A quarter of a century after this case the Massachusetts Supreme Judicial Court would in fact rule that slaves brought into the state were "instantly free."

Thirteen years after *Greenwood* v. *Curtis,* in *Commonwealth* v. *Griffith* (1823),[41] the court held that neither Massachusetts statute nor common law, nor the state's constitution could interfere with the recaption of a fugitive slave. Chief Justice Isaac Parker put aside his personal convictions because he felt obligated to enforce the federal Fugitive Slave Act, based on the assumption that the United States Constitution "was a compromise. It was a compact by which all are bound." Massachusetts had "entered into an agreement that slaves should be considered property." The case did not involve the validity or constitutionality of the federal Fugitive Slave Act. Rather, the issue was whether a slave could be captured and returned without a

39. *Greenwood* v. *Curtis,* 6 Mass. 358, 363, 378, 379–82 (1810).
40. Ibid. 362.
41. *Commonwealth* v. *Griffith,* 2 Pick. (Mass.) 11 (1823).

warrant sufficient under Massachusetts law. Parker felt that it could be accomplished legally without a state warrant because Congress prescribed the rules. Justice George Thacher disagreed. In dissent, he argued, "The laws here do not recognize a slave" and every person being a "freeman" was "entitled to all the privileges of a freeman," including the protection of unauthorized seizure. While southern states might allow seizure without a warrant, it did "not follow that the same may be done here."[42] Thus, in 1823 at least one Massachusetts justice was unwilling to give comity to the slaveowner, even when the slaveowner claimed it under federal law and the federal Constitution. And the rest of the court was willing to grant this comity *only* because of the specific clause in the United States Constitution. This position in itself was a major step away from the comity freely granted in *Greenwood* v. *Curtis*. In the next decade Massachusetts would follow this logic to its conclusion: that only fugitives could be considered slaves in Massachusetts and all others entering the state would be instantly free.

The Northwest Ordinance

In the northeastern states the problem of slaves in transit was considerably complicated by the fact that the population of all of these states at their foundings included at least a few slaves. Indeed, only in Vermont was slavery abolished outright, by express wording of the state's 1776 constitution. In all the other states judicial constructions of vaguely worded free-and-equal clauses found in state constitutions[43] or legislative acts for gradual emancipation were required to end slavery. All of these states except Vermont faced some confusion over the status of slaves within their jurisdictions.

42. Ibid. 11, 19–20.

43. Many early state constitutions contained "free and equal clause[s]" or some general declaration of the rights of men. In some instances, but not many, such clauses were interpreted to end slavery. The Declaration of Independence, for example, asserted that "all men are created equal" but no one at the time would have interpreted that to mean that slavery should not be tolerated in the nation. Article I of the Virginia Declaration of Rights (1776), which declared, "[A]ll men are by nature equally free and independent, and have certain inherent rights . . . namely the enjoyment of life and liberty . . ." was not intended to end slavery in Virginia. Chancellor George Wythe attempted to interpret the Virginia Declaration of Rights in this manner, but he was emphatically overruled by the Virginia Court of Appeals; *Hudgins* v. *Wrights*, 1 Hen. & M. (Va.) 134 (1806). For a discussion of this case, see Robert M. Cover, *Justice Accused: Antislavery and the Judicial Process* (New Haven: Yale University Press, 1975) 51–55, and ibid. 42–61 for discussion of free and equal clauses in early constitutions. See also John T. Noonan, *Persons and Masks of the Law* (New York: Farrar, Straus, and Giroux, 1976) 54–64. The New Hampshire Bill of Rights

In the states formed from the Northwest Territory it would appear that such confusions could not exist. In "the first and last anti-slavery achievement by the central government" under the Articles of Confederation,[44] the Northwest Ordinance of 1787 declared, "There shall be neither slavery nor involuntary servitude in the said territory, otherwise than in the punishment of crimes, . . . provided always, that any person escaping into the same, from whom labour or service is lawfully claimed in any one of the original states, such fugitives may be lawfully reclaimed, and conveyed to the person claiming his or her labour or service aforesaid."[45] Because of this clause the ordinance remains "a symbol of the Revolution's liberalism" even though Staughton Lynd has persuasively argued that the ordinance was part of a larger, and insidious, bargain on the whole question of slavery in the new nation.[46]

The clause led to the "common understanding" among the early settlers of the area as well as the general public of later generations, "that slavery was absolutely prohibited in the Territory Northwest of the Ohio."[47] In 1838, for example, United States Supreme Court Justice John McLean suggested that because of the Northwest Ordinance of 1787, Ohio could not allow slavery under its state constitution "without the consent of the original states." If this were not the case, then the ordinance's "import has been misconceived by the people of the state generally. They have looked upon this provision as a security against the introduction of slavery, even beyond the provisions of the constitution." Indeed, in McLean's view, it was just this provision that "has drawn masses of population to our state, who now repose under all the guarantees which are given on this subject by the constitution and the compact [Northwest Ordinance]."[48] This conception of the ordinance was also used as an im-

---

declared, "All men are born equally free and independent," but this was applied only to the children of slaves born after the Constitution was ratified. Massachusetts, on the other hand, interpreted a similar clause in its 1780 constitution to end all slavery in the state. As late as 1844, however, it was decided that the New Jersey Bill of Rights had not ended slavery in that state; *State* v. *Post*, 1 Spencer (N.J.) 368 (1845). See also the 1776 state constitution of Pennsylvania, which did not free slaves in that state, although it declared all men born free and equal.

44. Ulrich Bonnell Phillips, *American Negro Slavery* (New York: D. Appleton and Company, 1918) 128.

45. *Northwest Ordinance*, art. IV.

46. Staughton Lynd, *Class Conflict, Slavery, and the United States Constitution* (Indianapolis: The Bobbs-Merrill Company, 1967) 186; Jacob P. Dunn, *Indiana: A Redemption from Slavery* (Boston and New York: Houghton Mifflin and Company, 1900) 212–14.

47. Dunn, *Indiana* 219.

48. *Spooner* v. *McConnell*, 22 F. Cas. 939 (1837).

portant argument against those who attempted to legalize slavery in Indiana and Illinois.[49]

While it may indeed have prevented the introduction of slavery in the Northwest Territory and the states carved out of it, the ordinance did not remove the peculiar institution from north of the Ohio River. If article VI of the ordinance prohibited slavery, it and other articles of the ordinance implied that some forms of slavery could exist in the area. The Fugitive Slave Clause of article VI allowed the recaption of fugitive slaves from then-existing states. This clause was automatically extended to every state by the Fugitive Slave Clause of the federal Constitution written later that year.[50] Under the ordinance the franchise was restricted to "free male inhabitants," which implies a category of nonfree, or slave, male inhabitants. Similarly, only "free inhabitants" were to be counted when areas of the territory applied for statehood. Finally, the ordinance explicitly protected the property of the French inhabitants and other settlers who "professed themselves citizens of Virginia." The Jay Treaty of 1794 gave the same protection to the property of British subjects residing there. Thus, as one early historian concluded, "as to all the ancient inhabitants" of the Northwest Territory "slavery was lawfully permitted to exist until abrogated by the state constitutions."[51] Even after the states were formed, slavery and various forms of long-term servitude continued.[52]

These contradictions within the ordinance created a great deal of confusion over the status of slavery in the territory. In 1794, for example, Judge George Turner of the Northwest Territorial Court ruled that the slaves of Henry Vanderburgh, another territorial judge, were free by "the Constitution of the Territory." Vanderburgh and his agents immediately kidnapped and reenslaved the liberated

49. Robert McColley, *Slavery and Jeffersonian Virginia* (Urbana: University of Illinois Press, 1964) 180.

50. Lynd, *Class Conflict* 185–213. In a number of court cases, starting in 1837, Salmon P. Chase argued that the Fugitive Slave Clause of the U.S. Constitution did not apply to the Northwest Territory because of the Northwest Ordinance. He further argued that the Northwest Ordinance applied only to the states existing at the time it was passed. Chase felt that Ohio was not obligated to return fugitive slaves from new states, such as Kentucky and Missouri. His argument was rejected by every court that heard it.

51. Dunn, *Indiana* 219–20, 252. For litigation on this subject, see *Charlotte (of color)* v. *Chouteau*, 11 Mo. 193 (1847); *Charlotte* v. *Chouteau*, 21 Mo. 590 (1855); *Charlotte (of color)* v. *Chouteau*, 25 Mo. 465 (1857); *Charlotte* v. *Chouteau*, 23 Mo. 194 (1862).

52. N. Dwight Harris, *The History of Negro Servitude in Illinois* (Chicago: A. C. McClure and Company, 1904) 6–15, 99–123; Dunn, *Indiana* 314–16, 329–36, 348–49, 405–6, 429–34. See also Eugene H. Berwanger, *The Frontier against Slavery* (Urbana: University of Illinois Press, 1967) 7–59.

blacks. Indictments against the kidnappers failed. Turner eventually resigned his position under pressure from the proslavery leadership in the territory. Indiana Territorial Governor Arthur St. Clair
and others felt that the ordinance applied only to imported slaves
and not to those living in the territory before 1787.[53]

The same conclusion was also reached by the territorial court of
Michigan. In 1807 Justice Augustus B. Woodward held that a man
who owned slaves in Michigan before 31 May 1793 had a legal right
to them under the Jay Treaty. He also held that persons who owned
slaves in Michigan before 11 June 1796, could claim their services
until the blacks reached age twenty-five, at which time they would
become free under Canadian law. The judge felt obligated to reach
this decision because of the Supremacy Clause with respect to "all
treaties made" under the United States Constitution.[54] In a companion case, Justice Woodward struck a blow for freedom by holding
that the Fugitive Slave clauses of the Northwest Ordinance and the
United States Constitution did not apply to other countries. Thus a
slave escaping from Canada into Michigan would immediately become free. A lack of reciprocity on the part of Britain and her colony
made this decision an easy one to reach. While Woodward based his
decision primarily on the prohibitory clause of the Northwest Ordinance, he also cited *Somerset*, noting that it is "unquestionable that
the principle of the english [*sic*] law, as decided by Lord Mansfield, is
that a right of property cannot exist in the human Species. . . ." While
not dealing directly with slaves owned by American citizens, Woodward's dictum at least suggests that no slaveowner had the right of
transit with his human property across Michigan. Only the Jay
Treaty allowed the former British subjects any rights to their slaves,
because Woodward found that Michigan's "will is THERE SHALL BE
NEITHER SLAVERY, NOR INVOLUNTARY SERVITUDE IN THIS TERRITORY."
Woodward declared "*that a right of property in the human Species
cannot exist in this territory,*" except for slaves owned by the original
British settlers and fugitives covered by the Northwest Ordinance.
Any "*other man coming into this territory is by the law of the land a
freeman. . . .*"[55]

53. Dunn, *Indiana* 223–24. See also Francis S. Philbrick, "Law, Courts, and Litigation of Indiana Territory (1800–09)," 24 *Illinois Law Review* 15 (May 1929). Philbrick
finds at least two other instances in which courts freed slaves in the Indiana Territory.
The first was in 1798, when Judge John Cleves Symmes freed a slave brought into
what is now Illinois and a second in Indiana in 1806.

54. *Denison et al.* v. *Tucker*, 1 Blume 385, 390, 394, 395 [William Wirt Blume, 1
Transactions of the Supreme Court of the Territory of Michigan (Ann Arbor: University of Michigan Press, 1935)].

55. *Pattinson* v. *Whitaker*, 1 Blume 414, 416–18 (1807). The Michigan state constitution of 1835 provided that "[n]either slavery nor involuntary servitude shall ever

While the "ancient inhabitants" of the Northwest Territory perhaps were allowed to own slaves, persons moving into the area after 1787 appear to have been barred by the ordinance from maintaining such property. Nevertheless, slaves were brought into the territories. Many of the early settlers of Ohio, Indiana, and Illinois were southerners. Some undoubtedly came, as Justice McLean argued, precisely because they wished to reside where there would be no slavery.[56] For example, James Madison's protégé, Edward Coles, saw the ordinance's antislavery provisions in even larger terms. At considerable personal sacrifice, Coles took his many slaves to Illinois in 1819, purchased land for them, and freed them. Coles remained in Illinois and eventually became the state's second governor on a strong antislavery platform.[57] Many other southerners, however, wanted to bring slaves to the Northwest, not to free them, but to perpetuate the institution in their new home. For example, in 1796 four settlers in the "Illinois Country" of the Indiana Territory petitioned Congress for at least a partial repeal of the antislavery provision of the Northwest Ordinance. Three years later former military officers from Virginia petitioned for the right to bring slaves with them when they settled their military bounty land in the Indiana Territory. Although New York had passed special legislation for slaveholding veterans, the Congress was unwilling to be so generous.[58] In 1800, 270 residents of the Indiana Territory again petitioned Congress. They asked for the right to import slaves from other parts of the United States and hold all slaves for life, but free their sons at age thirty-one and daughters at age twenty-eight. The petitioners

---

be introduced into this state, except for the punishment of crimes of which the party shall have been duly convicted." A strong antikidnapping statute, designed to protect "any negro, mulatto, or other person of color" was included in the *Revised Statutes of the State of Michigan* (Detroit: J. S. Bragg, 1838) 623–24. With the exception of fugitive slaves from other states, no black could be "sent out of this state against his will." This law would seem to mean that owners had no right of transit across Michigan after 1838. No reported state cases deal with transit in Michigan. The remoteness of the state precluded any master's traveling through Michigan en route to another slave state. Since the state was an abolitionist stronghold, masters would have been quite foolish to bring slaves into Michigan.

56. William H. Brown, *An Historical Sketch of the Early Movement in Illinois for the Legalization of Slavery* (Chicago: Church, Goodman, and Donnelley, 1865) 12. See also *Spooner* v. *McConnell*, 22 F. Cas. 939 (1837). Also see Berwanger, *Frontier against Slavery, passim*.

57. Ralph L. Ketcham, "The Dictates of Conscience: Edward Coles and Slavery," 36 *Virginia Quarterly Review* 46–62 (Winter 1960).

58. Dunn, *Indiana* 284–90, 305; Willard C. MacNaul, *The Jefferson-Lemen Compact: The Relation of Thomas Jefferson and James Lemen in the Exclusion of Slavery from Illinois and the Northwest Territory with Related Documents* (Chicago: University of Chicago Press, 1915) 13–14.

could not "conceive any well-founded objections" would be made. In fact, they felt "[i]t cannot but meet with the support of those who are friends to a gradual abolition of Slavery" because "in the course of a very few years [the proposal] will in all human probability rescue from the vilest state of Bondage a number, and without doubt a considerable number, of Souls yet unborn." The United States Senate was so unimpressed with this appeal to humanity that it immediately, and permanently, tabled the petition. In 1802 a convention of settlers presided over by Territorial Governor William Henry Harrison wrote a more modest petition, which merely asked Congress to suspend the antislavery clause of the ordinance for ten years. However, the gradual emancipation scheme was not included, which implied that the petitioners hoped for perpetual slavery in the area. Needless to say, this and four other similar petitions were never acted on by Congress.[59]

Ohio

While Congress consistently refused to modify the antislavery provisions of the Northwest Ordinance, the territorial and state governments in Ohio, Indiana, and Illinois soon took matters into their own hands. Although slavery was never formally legalized in these places, it did exist and was sometimes supported by positive law and judicial enforcement.

In 1800 the Northwest Territory was divided into the Indiana Territory and the Ohio Territory. The latter became a state in 1803. In 1805 the Michigan Territory was partitioned from the Indiana Territory, which was divided again with the creation of the Illinois Territory in 1809. Because of this development the newer territories

59. Dunn, *Indiana* 297–99, 305–9; MacNaul, *Jefferson-Lemen Compact* 13–14. The 1803 petition was referred to a committee in the House in February 1803, which reported against it. However, at the next session it was again sent to a committee, this time consisting of three southerners who, not surprisingly, reported favorably on the request to allow slave importation into the territory. The report was referred to a committee of the whole, where it died; McColley, in *Slavery and Jeffersonian Virginia* 175–81, suggests that the success of cotton in the Southwest insured that slavery would not be introduced into the Northwest. "This marvelous plant, popularly supposed to be the agent of prolonging the life of slavery, probably had the opposite effect," by channeling slavery into one corner of the nation. McColley's theory presupposes that Congress would have allowed slavery to be introduced into the Northwest, which seems doubtful. More likely, such a development would merely have accelerated the conflict over slavery in the territories and the nation. The best discussion of slavery and the territories is Don E. Fehrenbacher, *The Dred Scott Case: Its Significance in American Law and Politics* (New York: Oxford University Press, 1978) 74–113 and *passim*.

inherited the laws of the older ones, although sometimes the laws were changed when the new territorial legislatures were created.[60]

Between 1788 and 1800 various laws were enacted regulating conduct toward slaves in the Northwest Territory without expressly providing for slavery or indentured servitude. This legislative activity indicates an awareness that slaves would be entering and leaving the territory, as well as living in it, even if slavery itself could not be introduced. Like New York and Pennsylvania, the Northwest Territory was willing to allow slave transit. In 1802 the Ohio territorial legislature began preparations for statehood by drafting a constitution that included an absolute ban on slavery. The constitution also prohibited indentures of Negroes "made and executed out of the State, or if made in the State, where the term of service exceed one year . . . except those given in the case of apprenticeship." In 1803 the new state legislature passed "An act to regulate black and mulatto persons," prohibiting the removal of blacks from the state, except upon application to a magistrate and subsequent arrest as an alleged slave by a sheriff. The law also provided that no black could "settle or reside" in the state "without a certificate of his or her actual freedom." An amendment added in 1806–07 required free blacks entering the state to give "bond not to become chargeable." After this time, various acts prohibited kidnapping and regulated the rendition of fugitive slaves, but at no time before the 1850s did Ohio legislate on the problem of slaves passing through the state.[61] During this early period Ohio's chief legislative concern was to limit black movement into the state. By demanding certificates of freedom and a bond from any black migrating to the state, Ohio was initiating a negrophobic policy that would be repeated in Indiana and Illinois.[62]

60. The Northwest Ordinance provided for the organization of a territorial legislature as soon as the territory had 5,000 free male inhabitants. Until that population was achieved, each territory was ruled by a territorial governor and appointed judges.

61. The best source for a summary of these laws is John Codman Hurd, 2 *The Law of Freedom and Bondage in the United States* (2 vols. Boston: Little, Brown, 1862) 115–20.

62. Enforcement of this law was lax. Indeed, one of the problems with understanding law and society is that many laws are not regularly enforced. Leon F. Litwack, *North of Slavery: The Negro in the Free States, 1790–1860* (Chicago: University of Chicago Press, 1961), and Berwanger, *Frontier against Slavery* perhaps present a skewed view of the negrophobia of the Midwest. While a number of midwestern states prohibited free blacks from coming within their borders, or required bonds for those that did, there is little evidence that these laws were actually enforced. The fact that courts in these states also freed slaves in transit—thereby adding to the free black population of the state—suggests that negrophobia may not have been as great as has been supposed. Certainly it could not overcome antislavery feeling in a number of northern states. An indication of the laxity of enforcement is

While Ohio was basically antiblack, the "feelings, manners and habits" of the people, as one judge put it, were "averse to slavery."[63] Thus in March 1808 slaves Milly and Naise were freed by an Ohio court after their Virginian master brought them to Ohio. Unfortunately, they were inveigled into returning to Virginia, where the courts refused to recognize their freedom.[64] Although the owner of Milly and Naise claimed to be in transit, the Ohio court rejected Virginia's law in favor of Ohio's prohibition on slavery. The court's rationale in this decision is unclear, but it appears to be an enforcement of Ohio's constitutional ban on slavery. This determination may have been reached because the slaves were used in some work capacity and may have been hired out.[65] In 1817 another Ohio court chose to recognize free-state law instead of a ruling by a slave-state court. A Kentuckian traced his runaway slaves to Ohio and seized them under a warrant issued by a Kentucky court. The case was then brought before an Ohio court, where it was shown that the blacks had been illegally purchased in Pennsylvania, contrary to that state's 1780 gradual emancipation statute. Here the Ohio court faced a classic choice of law question. Kentucky law said the blacks were slaves, while Pennsylvania law said they were free. In enforcing the Pennsylvania law, the Ohio court chose to support freedom at the expense of slavery.[66]

The Ohio Supreme Court heard only one case during this period that dealt directly with slave transit. In *Ohio* v. *Carneal* (1817)[67] a black man, Richard Lunsford, was held as a slave in Cincinnati by Thomas Carneal. Judge John McLean[68] thought slavery "repug-

---

found in David N. McBride and Jane N. McBride, eds., *Common Pleas Court Records of Highland County, Ohio (1805–1860)* (Ann Arbor: Edwards Letter Shop, 1959). Only one case, in 1811 (at 106), is found where blacks were actually sued (not prosecuted) for not giving bond after entering the state. However, a number of other cases suggest that slaves were brought to the county as apprentices and freed, without any bond posted for their future care.

63. "Charge to the Grand Jury," by Judge Crane, in Court of Common Pleas, Montgomery County, 1819, in Ervin H. Pollack, ed., *Ohio Unreported Judicial Decisions Prior to 1823* (Indianapolis: Allen Smith Company, n.d.) 222–24. Also see Berwanger, *Frontier against Slavery*, and Litwack, *North of Slavery* for discussion of antislavery feelings of settlers of Ohio. Court cases have been cited as evidence to show that Ohioans disliked slavery, since it is important for the reader here to understand that the opinions of jurists reflected—and often tried to reflect—the community they served.

64. *Lewis* v. *Fullerton*, 1 Rand. (Va.) 15 (1821).

65. Ibid.

66. *Jacob Kounts* v. _____, (1817), in Pollack, *Ohio Unreported Decisions* 255.

67. *Ohio* v. *Carneal*, (1817), ibid. 133.

68. At this time McLean was on the Ohio Supreme Court, where he served from 1816–22. He later served on the United States Supreme Court.

nant" but felt that under the federal Constitution Ohio was "bound to respect as property, to a certain extent, that which is made property by the law of a sister state." Carneal's claim to Lunsford was based on Kentucky law and had to be tested by the laws of that state. Fortunately for McLean's conscience and Lunsford's happiness, Carneal's title was deficient under Kentucky law and Lunsford gained his freedom.[69]

At the trial Lunsford proved that he had lived on and off in Ohio and had been hired out there. McLean realized it was "not strictly necessary" to comment on slavery and transit, but he thought it "not improper" to do so because of the importance and interest in the case. McLean plunged into this complicated problem with a long and sometimes contradictory discussion of slavery and comity. He referred to an unnamed Ohio Court of Common Pleas ruling "that whenever a person held in slavery by the laws of any state, shall enter the state of Ohio with the consent of his master, such a person is entitled to his liberty."[70] This extreme position antedated *Commonwealth* v. *Aves* (1836)[71] by two decades; if implemented, it would have made Ohio the most "pro-freedom" of any state. "Viewing the question abstractly," McLean found that the "immutable principles of natural justice" entitled all people to their freedom. But the federal Constitution modified both the law of nature and the Ohio Constitution. Thus, McLean felt constrained "to guard the liberty of a fellow creature on one hand," while not wholly disregarding rights "which have been sanctioned by the laws and policies of another state" on the other hand.[72]

McLean was positive that in most instances bringing a slave in and out of the state would free the slave. Indeed, if a man entered the state "with the intention of becoming a resident, and bring with him his slaves, one day, or one hour," it would be "sufficient to manumit them." The master who remained in Kentucky and hired his slave out in Ohio would also lose his slave. But McLean would not say that "every slave who sets foot within the state with his master's consent, has a *legal* right to claim his emancipation—or that a traveller may not pass through the state with his servant." He was uncertain what would happen "if the master consent that his slave should come into the state, to indulge or gratify the slave—or if he sent him merely on an errand" or if the slave followed his mas-

69. *Ohio* v. *Carneal* 133–39.

70. Ibid. 139–40.

71. *Commonwealth* v. *Aves*, 18 Pick. (Mass.) 193 (1836). This case is discussed in chap. 4 of this volume.

72. *Ohio* v. *Carneal* 139–40.

ter, who was traveling through the state.[73] These.questions could
be answered only when cases arose under them. For the moment
McLean would only assert the following principles:

> Employing the slave here by day and sending him across
> the river at night, is subterfuge which will not exonerate
> the master from the penalty of forfeiture, nor prevent the slave
> from demanding his liberty. . . . Such an evasion of the policy of
> the constitution can never be sanctioned. No citizen ought to
> introduce, either directly or indirectly, that which the consti-
> tution expressly prohibits. I am therefore prepared to say
> generally, wherever the master seeks a profit, by the labor if
> [*sic*] this slave in this state, he forfeits all right to the
> possession and services of such slave.[74]

This opinion put the state supreme court on record as opposing any
introduction of slavery or slave labor in the state, while hedging on
the legality of introducing a slave into the state for a short time.

McLean was supported by the two other judges on the court, who
wrote separate opinions. They agreed that Lunsford was free because Carneal's title was defective and because living and working
in Ohio had freed him. However, Justice Jessup N. Couch was more
certain of the rights a slaveowner might have in Ohio. He thought it
the "duty of the court to manumit the slave, if he is *unlawfully* held
to labor." But this right to freedom could exist only if the slave was
actually employed in Ohio. Couch did not "entertain the *doubts*" on
the subject of slave transit. He noted that Pennsylvania allowed
travelers six months in the state but thought it "extremely difficult
for the *legislature* or the *court* to fix any precise limit how long the
proprietor may retain his servant within the limits" of Ohio. Justice
Couch could not believe "that the moment the servant lands from
the Ohio river to travel through the state with the consent of the
owner, that our laws will proclaim his emancipation." Such a policy
"would destroy that *comity* which exists between the different states
as members of the Union. It would render Ohio, rising as it is in
wealth and respectability, an insulated state; and compel travellers
to pursue a circuitous journey around the limits of our jurisdiction
to avoid the danger of liberating their servants." Couch did not
believe that this was the intention of the state's constitution.[75]

Couch's position was adopted de facto, if not de jure, by Ohio in
this early period. Many transients passed through the state on their

73. Ibid. 140–41.
74. Ibid. 141–42.
75. Ibid. 148–49.

way west and undoubtedly they took their slaves with them. Only when antislavery forces became politically significant in the 1840s and 1850s would Ohio's attitude toward slaves in transit change.[76]

Indiana

While Congress ignored their petitions to allow slavery, the residents of the newly formed Indiana Territory turned to the territorial assembly to circumvent the Northwest Ordinance. In 1803, 1805, and 1807 legislation regulated slavery and free blacks in this "free" territory. These laws, based on Virginia and Kentucky statutes, reflected the southern origins of many of the settlers "who carried with them their love of slavery and their unreasoning prejudices against free Negroes."[77] The 1807 act (a culmination of earlier acts) was condemned in a petition to Congress as an act "for the Establishment of disguised slavery."[78] This act allowed a slaveowner to bring his bondsmen into the territory as indentured servants for a term of years agreed to by both parties. Since the slave was under the total domination of the master, however, virtually any form of indenture could have been forced upon the slave. Once in Indiana these indentured servants could be hired out or sold for their terms of service. If they refused to work they could be sold back to a slave state. Children of the indentured servants were also indentured, until age twenty-eight for females and thirty for males. Various registration procedures had to be followed, otherwise owners could forfeit their rights to the blacks' labor. However, the general thrust of these statutes was to protect a master's right to the labor of his slaves and their children.[79]

With these acts a de facto type of slavery was legally introduced into the territory. The number of slaves who could be brought into the territory was not limited, nor was the number of years for which it would be legal to import them. The laws do not indicate what would happen to third-generation servants born to mothers who had not yet reached age twenty-eight. It is quite likely they would have been viewed as servants until age twenty-eight or thirty as well. These laws provided for a workable system of involuntary servitude in an area that was theoretically free. In the Northeast, states

76. Berwanger, *Frontier against Slavery, passim*. See chap. 6 of this volume.

77. Henry Wilson, 1 *History of the Rise and Fall of the Slave Power in America* (2 vols. Boston: James R. Osgood and Company, 1872) 161–62.

78. Francis S. Philbrick, "Law, Courts, and Litigation of Indiana Territory," 12–13.

79. Hurd, 2 *Law of Freedom and Bondage* 123–36; Harris, *Negro Servitude in Illinois* 7.

were trying to abolish slavery gradually and painlessly; in Indiana the legislature was attempting to introduce slavery gradually and surreptitiously.

Most of the support for the 1807 law came from the part of the Indiana Territory that ultimately became Illinois. In 1810 the Indiana assembly, which by then represented what is now the state of Indiana, repealed the 1807 statutes. The assembly allowed existing indentures to stand but eliminated the export provisions, allowing only fugitive slaves to be taken out of the state against their will. Anyone else removing a black from the state could be disqualified from holding office and fined a thousand dollars. This clause does not, however, appear to have been aimed at stopping slave transit. Rather, it was designed to prevent the exportation of indentured blacks and the kidnapping of free blacks.[80]

Indiana's Constitution of 1816 outlawed slavery and also prohibited "any indenture of any negro or mulatto hereafter made and executed out of the bounds of this State." An 1816 antikidnapping law protected free blacks in Indiana but also punished anyone who harbored slaves or encouraged them to desert their masters. This clause would have applied to the harboring of slaves passing through the now-free state of Indiana, as well as those running away to it. Laws of 1819, 1823, and 1827 provided for the attachment of "slaves or indentured or registered colored servants," as well as their sale at execution. The 1827 act also allowed them to be assessed as taxable property.[81]

These statutes providing for the sale and taxation of slaves seem somewhat anomalous in a supposedly free state, especially in light of the state supreme court decision in *State* v. *Lasselle* (1820),[82] which prohibited all slavery in Indiana. In response to a writ of habeas corpus, Lasselle claimed Polly as a slave because she had been legally purchased in the territory while it was still under British control. In freeing Polly, Justice James Scott said it was unnecessary to "inquire what rights the first emigrants enjoyed." He simply held that when Indiana became a state "it was within the legitimate powers of the Convention, in forming our Constitution, to prohibit the existence of slavery. . . . " This the convention had done, and it was "an irresistible conclusion" that slavery could "have no existence in the State of Indiana."[83]

80. *Indiana, Revised Code of 1807*, 188.
81. Hurd, 2 *Law of Freedom and Bondage* 128–30.
82. *State* v. *Lasselle*, 1 Black. (Ind.) 60 (1820). This important case is omitted in Helen Tunnicliff Catterall, *Judicial Cases concerning American Slavery and the Negro* (5 vols. Washington: Carnegie Institution, 1926–37).
83. *State* v. *Lasselle* 60–63.

Whatever the constitution and courts said, the census found 190 slaves in the state in 1820 and 35 in 1830. "The idea which commonly obtained was that the Constitution could have no effect on preexisting slavery; that the property in slaves was a vested right, secured by the Ordinance, and could not be impaired."[84] This idea died hard, and the court's decision did not permeate the state for more than a decade. As so often happens with court-induced social change, a judicial decree did not guarantee instant and total compliance.

The question of slave transit across Indiana did not reach a court until December 1829, when Judge Morris of the Marion County Court freed the slaves of William Sewall. Sewall was a Virginian traveling through the state, en route to Illinois. Morris held that Sewall had "voluntarily relinquished his citizenship in Virginia, and brought his slaves with him, with the purpose and intention of settling in a free state." The slaves had asserted their freedom, which the owner contested. But, Morris asked, on what grounds could he claim the slaves? "He cannot as a citizen of Virginia, because he no longer sustains that character." The judge acknowledged the need for comity, implying that if the owner were still a citizen of Virginia and headed for a slave state, he could retain his slaves. But Morris saw a different rule of comity when the slaveowner was headed toward a free state: "The same rule that requires me to take notice that the laws of Virginia tolerate slavery, requires me to know that in Illinois it is prohibited. The comity due from us to Illinois, is not less than that which we owe Virginia." In addition, Judge Morris was bound by his own constitution, which prohibited slavery "in the strongest and most emphatic terms."[85]

In freeing the slaves Judge Morris indicated that slave property in transit between slave states was protected in Indiana, but in this case the situation was different. The judge concluded with a strong endorsement of federalism and comity:

> By the law of nature and of nations, (see Vattel 160) and the necessary and legal consequences resulting from the civil and political relations subsisting between citizens as well as states of this federated republic, I have no doubt but the citizen of a slave state, has a right to pass, upon business or pleasure through any of the states, attended by his slaves or servants; and while he retains the character and rights of a citizen of a slave state his right to reclaim his slave would be unquestioned. An escape on a journey through a free state,

84. Dunn, *Indiana* 434, 431.
85. *Sewell's Slaves*, 3 Am. Jur. 404, 404–7 (1830).

should be considered as an escape from the state where the master had a right of citizenship, and by the laws of which the service of the slave was due.

Morris was unsure what would happen if a slaveowner moved from one slave state to another, with citizenship in neither, but he believed that such a person ought to be allowed to reclaim any slave who escaped during the journey.[86] This of course would not have been a problem if Morris freed the slaves on the basis of Indiana law. But he did not free them under the law or constitution of his own state. Rather, the slaves gained their freedom because their master was not a citizen of any slave state and did not plan to become one. While leading to the freedom of the slaves, this decision was not a threat to interstate transit. On the contrary, Morris had supported the right of transit with slaves on the basis of the comity that Indiana owed the laws of the slave states.

Morris's decision was given legislative support a year later. In 1831 a new law declared "[t]hat the right of any persons to pass through this State, with his or her, or their negroes or mulattoes, servant or servants when emigrating or traveling to any other State or territory or country, making no unnecessary delay, is hereby declared and secured."[87] Any pro-freedom implications of Morris's decision were clearly overruled by this law.

This statute also required free blacks entering the state to post bond. Those not doing so could either be "hired out" for the benefit of the black or be removed from the state. This law was superseded by Indiana's 1851 constitution, which prohibited all blacks from entering or settling in the state. Both the law and the constitutional provision were later affirmed by various court cases. On the face of it, this constitutional provision and the legislation passed in 1852 to enforce it seem to have repealed the 1831 statute allowing transit with slaves, since they prohibited all blacks, slave and free, from entering Indiana.[88] However, interfering with slave transit—and the freeing of slaves brought into the state—was not the purpose of these legal innovations. Indiana certainly did not wish to interfere with slave transit if it meant that newly freed blacks would remain in the state. The new regulations were designed simply to keep all blacks—free, slave, or indentured—out of Indiana.

86. Ibid. 407.

87. *Indiana Revised Statutes of 1831*, chap. 66.

88. Ibid.; *Indiana Revised Statutes of 1852*, chap. 74, "An act to enforce the 13th article of the Constitution." See *State* v. *Cooper*, 5 Black. (Ind.) 258 (1839); *Baptiste* v. *State*, 5 Black. (Ind.) 283 (1840); *Hickland* v. *State*, 8 Black. (Ind.) 365 (1847); *Barkshire* v. *State*, 7 Ind. 389 (1856); *Hatwood* v. *State*, 18 Ind. 492 (1862).

Illinois

In 1812, two years after the Indiana territorial assembly repealed the 1807 indenture law, the Illinois territorial legislature moved in the opposite direction by affirming all laws of the Indiana Territory passed before the 1809 partition. Thus, importation and indenture continued in Illinois until statehood was achieved in 1818.[89] Consequently, a considerable number of blacks, indentured for long periods of time, lived in Illinois. In addition, many of these blacks had children who could also be indentured until age twenty-eight for females or thirty for males.

The 1818 Illinois Constitution ended slavery and prohibited long-term indentures but did not interfere with existing slavery or existing indentures. Former slaves could be indentured in Illinois for one-year periods. In addition, until 1825 slaves could be hired out for one-year terms as laborers at the Shawnee Town saltworks. Finally, while reaffirming existing indentures, the constitution said that the children of indentured blacks would have to serve only until ages eighteen and twenty-one, instead of twenty-eight or thirty for females and males, respectively.[90]

In 1819 Illinois passed the first of its numerous acts designed to keep Negroes out of the state. This law also prohibited masters from bringing slaves into the state to free them. From then until 1845 other acts regulated free blacks and the treatment of slaves. An 1827 statute prohibited the harboring of slaves owing service in Illinois or any other state or territory. The statute implied that slaves in transit could not run away and that those harboring such slaves might be prosecuted. An 1829 statute prohibited slaves who came to Illinois to be "hired for labor" from later suing for their freedom. While generally directed at fugitives, the statute would have also precluded freedom suits by sojourning or visiting slaves who came to the state with the master's consent.[91]

89. Hurd, 2 *Law of Freedom and Bondage* 132.

90. Illinois Constitution of 1818, art. VI, sec. 1, 2, 3. Don E. Fehrenbacher, *Dred Scott Case*, at 85, argues that these one-year indentures were "presumably renewable," and thus Congress "accepted this dubious compromise with servitude and admitted Illinois as a 'free' state." Fehrenbacher implies that the "presumably renewable" indentures led to a form of perpetual slavery. Indeed, Illinois did have perpetual slavery at the time of statehood, but the source of it was not blacks indentured in Illinois for one year. For in order for a black to be indentured in Illinois (except at the saltworks before 1825), the black had to be freed. After the one-year indenture was terminated, the presumption would be that the ex-slave was now free of all obligations and legal connections to the former master. The indentures perhaps were renewable, but the master could no longer coerce the now-free black into such an indenture.

91. These laws are described in Hurd, 2 *Law of Freedom and Bondage* 134–36.

Until 1845 Illinois afforded more comity to slaveowners in transit and more protection to slaveowners living there than any other northern state, with the possible exception of New Jersey. During this period numerous freedom suits failed, while those that succeeded resulted from the negligence of owners who improperly registered slaves and servants.[92] Only two transit cases appear to have reached the courts during this period.

In 1843 Judge John D. Caton ruled in a circuit court case that if "a master voluntarily bring his slave within the state, he becomes from that moment free, and if he escapes from his master while in this State, it is not an escape from slavery, but it is going where a free man has a right to go; and the harboring of such a person is no offense against our law; but the tie which binds a slave to his master can be severed only by the voluntary act of the latter."[93] Caton's lower court decision was not appealed. However, that same year the Illinois Supreme Court reached an opposite conclusion in *Willard* v. *The People* (1843).[94]

Sarah Liles was traveling from Kentucky to Louisiana, through Illinois, when her slave Julia escaped and was hidden by Julius Willard. Willard was indicted and convicted under the 1827 statute prohibiting anyone from harboring or secreting "a slave or servant owing service or labor to any other persons."[95]

In his appeal to the state supreme court Willard argued that the settled law of the land was "[i]f the master brings his slave into a State where slavery does not exist, such slave becomes free." Cases from Massachusetts, Pennsylvania, Mississippi, Missouri, Louisiana, England, and France were cited to support this position, for by this time much of the North had adopted the same view of slave transit. Citing Justice Joseph Story's treatise on the conflict of laws, Willard's counsel denied that comity could apply to slavery, which was "unnatural and artificial, and cannot exist beyond the jurisdiction creating it."[96] Further analysis showed that slavery was prohibited by the Northwest Ordinance and the state constitution. Thus, Willard had not harbored a fugitive slave but merely had helped a former slave who gained her freedom when her owner brought her to Illinois.

92. See a series of cases beginning with *Nance* v. *Howard*, Breese (Ill.) 182 (1828), and including *Phoebe* v. *Jay*, Breese (Ill.) 207 (1828); *Boon* v. *Juliet*, 1 Scam. (Ill.) 258 (1836); *Choisser* v. *Hargrave*, 1 Scam. (Ill.) 317 (1836); *Bailey* v. *Cromwell*, 3 Scam. (Ill.) 71 (1841); *Sarah, alias Sarah Borders* v. *Borders*, 1 Gil. (Ill.) 46 (1844); *Hays* v. *Borders*, 1 Gil. (Ill.) 46 (1844); *Jarrot* v. *Jarrot*, 2 Gil. (Ill.) 1 (1845).

93. Harris, *Negro Servitude in Illinois* 11–12.

94. *Willard* v. *The People*, 4 Scam. (Ill.) 461 (1843).

95. Ibid. 464, 463.

96. Ibid.

The Illinois attorney general agreed that "[t]he only question" was "whether or not the transit of a master with his slave, through this State emancipates a slave." Like Willard's counsel, the attorney general did not think the federal Fugitive Slave Law was at issue. The case was strictly a matter for the state of Illinois to decide, according to its own laws and constitution. He argued that Illinois "virtually secured" the right of transit by passing laws authorizing masters to restrain their slaves. Such laws did not exist in Massachusetts, Britain, or the other places cited on behalf of Willard. Among others, the attorney general cited Judge Morris's decision in Indiana upholding the right of slave transit.[97]

In upholding Willard's original conviction, Justice Walter B. Scates decided that Illinois "does most distinctly recognize the existence of the institution of slavery." The statute under which Willard was convicted was deemed constitutional, even though its main purpose was to facilitate the removal of fugitive slaves.[98]

Justice Scates went further, however, in explaining why this decision was necessary. If the state denied comity and free transit, "[i]t would be productive of great and irremediable evils of discord, of heart burnings, and alienation of kind and fraternal feelings, which should characterize the American brotherhood, and tend greatly to weaken, if not destroy the common bond of union amongst us, and our nationality of character, interest, and feeling." He noted that "[t]housands from Kentucky, Virginia, Maryland, Tennessee, and the Carolinas, and other southern States have sought and found free and safe passage with their slaves" across Illinois. "It would be startling, indeed, if we should deny our neighbors and kindred that common right of free and safe passage, which foreign nations would hardly dare." Similarly, since Illinois was obligated under international comity to grant a right of transit to non-Americans, without disturbing their property, "[m]uch less could we disregard their [United States Citizens'] Constitutional right, as citizens of one of the States, to all the rights, immunities, and privileges of the citizens of the several States."[99]

On these grounds Scates emphatically concluded that "the slave does not become free by the Constitution of Illinois by coming into the State for the mere purpose of passage through it." Thus Willard's conviction stood.[100]

97. Ibid. 465–68.
98. Ibid. 471.
99. Ibid. 471–72.
100. Ibid. 472.

Comity Rejected

The Willard decision was the last major northern-state case affirming the right of slave transit through a free state. By 1843 antislavery sentiment had begun to grow throughout the North. Many free states had court opinions or legislation that declared slaves in transit to be free. A number of southern states had freed slaves who lived, sojourned, or even merely visited in a free state. Yet Illinois still granted comity and dared not offend her southern neighbors. Five years after *Willard*, Senator Sidney Breese of Illinois would tell the United States Senate that "the courts of the slave States had been much more liberal in their adjudications upon the question of slavery than the free States. The courts of one of them (Illinois) had uniformly decided cases against the right of freedom." But, "in precisely similar cases the courts of Kentucky and Missouri . . . decided in favor of the rights of freedom."[101]

While the Illinois Supreme Court supported comity over freedom, the decision was attacked around the state. The *Chicago Express*, although it was a Democratic and antiabolitionist paper, nevertheless thought it "strange that the Supreme Court of the State of Illinois should be called upon to decide whether slavery exists in the State." In the paper's view, "If slavery exists" in Illinois, "it is high time to amend the Constitution." The *Alton Telegraph* thought that the decision was "in direct conflict with the decisions made upon the same question in Massachusetts and Pennsylvania, and what is regarded *now* as the settled law of the land."[102] Indeed, in 1843 Illinois was out of step with the rest of the North. While the *Willard* decision might have been consistent with northern legal opinions ten years earlier, by 1843 the legal consensus throughout the North had changed quite dramatically.

By 1832 slavery had become a major political issue in the nation. The Missouri crisis of 1820, the publication of *David Walker's Appeal* in 1828 and William Lloyd Garrison's *Liberator* in 1831, Nat Turner's rebellion, and the Nullification Crisis all focused national

101. Thomas Hart Benton, *Historical and Legal Examination of that part of the Decision of the Supreme Court of the United States in the Dred Scott Case* . . . (New York: D. Appleton and Company, 1857) 44–45. Breese overstated the case, especially given the time he made the statement. However, his judgment on this subject must be understood in light of his antiabolitionist beliefs. When Salmon P. Chase arrived in the Senate in March 1849, he received a communication from the antislavery Ohio congressman, Jacob Brinkerhoff, describing Chase's colleagues. Brinkerhoff warned Chase to beware of Breese, "who I know to be a cold-hearted, dough-faced scoundrel." Jacob Brinkerhoff to Salmon P. Chase, 26 Mar. 1849, Salmon P. Chase Papers, HSP.

102. Harris, *Negro Servitude in Illinois* 114–15.

attention on slavery.[103] Yet throughout all of this the state courts of the North maintained their desire for interstate comity and harmony. Only in Pennsylvania was any real attempt made to interfere with the movement of slaves. Even there, the six-months law remained in force to protect masters in transit. But in the decade of the 1830s this pattern began to change. Starting in Massachusetts and spreading to almost all of the North, masters were to be denied even limited transit with slave property. The legal harmony of the nation's first five decades was about to end.

103. Charles M. Wiltse, ed., *David Walker's Appeal in Four Articles; Together with a Preamble to the Coloured Citizens of the World* (New York: Hill and Wang, 1965); Stephen B. Oates, *The Fires of Jubilee: Nat Turner's Fierce Rebellion* (New York: Harper and Row, 1975); William W. Freehling, *Prelude to Civil War: The Nullification Controversy in South Carolina, 1816–1836* (New York: Harper and Row, 1965); John L. Thomas, *The Liberator: William Lloyd Garrison* (Boston: Little, Brown, 1963).

Chapter 4

The American Adoption of
Somerset: Massachusetts

Beginning in the 1830s Massachusetts initiated a change in policy toward slave transit that ultimately spread to most of the North. That Massachusetts pioneered in this rejection of comity for slaveholders is not surprising. Three factors influenced the change in legal and judicial policy. First, a well-organized abolition movement existed in Boston and other key areas of the state. A number of able lawyers, affiliated with the movement, were available and eager to argue cases as they arose. Second was the state's legal tradition of leaning toward freedom. Massachusetts was the first state to end slavery through court rulings, and its constitution and common law were, from the beginning, antislavery.

Finally, and perhaps most important of all, were the ability and prestige of the state's jurists. Chief Justice Lemuel Shaw of the Massachusetts Supreme Judicial Court was, without doubt, the most influential state jurist during his thirty-year tenure on the bench. His decisions on all subjects carried great weight. Thus, after he ruled emphatically in favor of freeing slaves in transit, it became much easier for other judges to reach similar results. Indeed, after 1836 northern judges who did not follow Shaw's precedent often felt obligated to explain their actions.[1]

Francisco's Case

The first hint of a change in northern judicial attitudes toward slave transit came in an unreported Massachusetts case in 1832. The New England Anti-Slavery Society initiated a habeas corpus action against a Mrs. Howard, who was visiting Boston with "Francisco, a

---

1. The best judicial biography of Shaw (perhaps the best for any American jurist) is Leonard W. Levy, *The Law of the Commonwealth and Chief Justice Shaw* (Cambridge: Harvard University Press, 1957); see also G. Edward White, *The American Judicial Tradition: Profiles of Leading American Judges* (New York: Oxford University Press, 1976), especially 55–63.

colored boy, twelve or fourteen years of age, (whom it was alleged that the defendant intended to carry to the Island of Cuba and there keep or sell as a slave). . . . "[2]

Mrs. Howard denied that Francisco was her slave and "stated in writing" that he was merely her servant, "that he was free, and that she did not claim him as her slave." Despite this protestation, witnesses testified that Francisco had been purchased as a slave and that, until the habeas corpus action began, Mrs. Howard had intended "to claim him as her slave in Havana, on her return there."[3]

Because Howard no longer claimed Francisco as a slave, but only as her free servant, the most important question before Chief Justice Shaw—that of the status of a slave voluntarily brought to Massachusetts—was in fact moot. Nevertheless, Samuel Sewall, the corresponding secretary of the New England Anti-Slavery Society, urged the court to appoint a guardian and remove the boy from Howard's custody. Sewall felt that Francisco had gained his freedom only by entering Massachusetts and that he would lose it if returned to Cuba. Charles P. Curtis, on behalf of Mrs. Howard, "contended that the court ought not to deprive her of the care of a boy, whom she had treated kindly, and who was attached to her, and desirous of going with her." He was certain that the boy's freedom, once established in Massachusetts, would be secure in Cuba.[4]

To resolve the dilemma, Shaw did, in the words of his biographer, "the most simple and sensible thing: he examined Francisco privately to determine his personal wishes." Francisco wished to remain with Mrs. Howard, which is what Shaw ordered. Although a minor, Shaw thought Francisco old enough to know his own mind. Also, because Mrs. Howard had "disclaimed to hold him as a slave" and "made a record of his freedom," Shaw felt that she could not "make him a slave again" in Cuba.[5]

While this case had no effect on the de facto relationship between Howard and Francisco, Shaw's dictum made clear that the relationship was not affected *only* because Howard did not claim Francisco as her slave. Had she done that, Shaw would "have ordered him to be discharged from her custody."[6]

---

2. *The Liberator*, 8 Dec. 1832; *In re Francisco*, 9 Am. Jur. 490 (1833).
3. *In re Francisco* 490.
4. Ibid. 491.
5. Ibid. 492; Levy, *Chief Justice Shaw* 62.
6. *In re Francisco* 491.

Commonwealth v. Aves

Four years later, *Commonwealth* v. *Aves* (1836)[7] tested Shaw's dictum. Med, a six-year-old slave girl, had been brought to Boston by Mrs. Samuel Slater of New Orleans. Mrs. Slater was visiting her father, Thomas Aves, and intended to remain in Boston for four or five months before returning with Med to New Orleans.

In August 1836, Levin H. Harris petitioned the Massachusetts court for a writ of habeas corpus. Although not a member of any abolition society, Harris acted on behalf of the Boston Female Anti-slavery Society, which pursued the case "with unfaltering zeal."[8] The petition stated that Med was "free by the law of Massachusetts," but that without judicial intervention she might be "unlawfully carried back to New-Orleans, and there made a slave." Harris noted that Med was a child with no known relatives, and thus he acted on her behalf.[9]

The petition was presented by Ellis Gray Loring and Samuel Sewall. They were later aided by the nonabolitionist Rufus Choate. Benjamin R. Curtis and his relative C. P. Curtis argued on behalf of Aves. Charles P. Curtis had opposed Sewall in Francisco's case, but this case was primarily a battle between the younger, Benjamin R. Curtis, and Ellis G. Loring. Two decades later, as a United States Supreme Court justice, Curtis would adopt Loring's arguments, and cite *Aves*, in his dissent in the *Dred Scott* case. Here, however, he fought hard to defend the interests of the slaveowner.[10] Arguments began at nine o'clock in the morning and continued until seven

7. *Commonwealth* v. *Aves*, 18 Pick. (Mass.) 193 (1836).

8. *Case of the Slave-Child Med: A Report of the Arguments of Counsel and of the Opinion of the Court in the Case of Commonwealth vs. Aves* (Boston: Isaac Knapp, 1836) 5; Henry Wilson, 1 *History of the Rise and Fall of the Slave Power in America* (2 vols. Boston: James R. Osgood and Company, 1872) 371. See also Boston Female Anti-Slavery Society, *Right and Wrong in Boston #2: Annual Report of the Boston Female Anti-Slavery Society Being a Concise History of the Case of the Slave Child Med* (Boston: Isaac Knapp, 1836); although no author is given, it is known that this pamphlet was written by Maria Weston Chapman.

9. *Case of the Slave-Child Med* 5.

10. *Dred Scott* v. *Sandford*, 19 Howard (U.S.) 393 (1857). The Boston Female Anti-slavery Society initially tried to retain United States Senator Daniel Webster to argue the case. "He was willing to serve provided" the case could be postponed "a few days." This was not feasible, and so "Rufus Choate, a man only second to him [Webster] in abilities, and whose heart is strongly favorable to anti-slavery, was employed." Lydia Maria Child to E. Carpenter, 4 September 1836, in John G. Whittier, ed. *Letters of Lydia Maria Child with a Biographical Introduction* (Boston: Houghton, Mifflin and Company, 1883) 20. Child's analysis of Choate's sentiments ultimately proved erroneous. By the 1850s he "was utterly hostile to the anti-slavery movement," ibid. 21n.

in the evening with only an hour and a half recess for dinner.[11] According to Chief Justice Shaw, the case was "fully and very ably argued" by both sides. Upon reading a printed copy of the case, United States Supreme Court Justice Joseph Story wrote Loring: "I have rarely seen so thorough and exact arguments as those made by Mr. B. R. Curtis and yourself. They exhibit learning, research and ability of which any man may be proud."[12]

All persons connected with the case realized its importance, for both Massachusetts and the nation. By 1836 all northern states freed slaves brought to live in their jurisdiction. Many southern courts also accepted this and freed slaves who had acquired domicile in the North and returned to the South. As we shall see in chapter 7, some southern states at this time even freed slaves who had lived in the North for only a short time. However, this policy, which was a function of southern comity to the North and recognition of the Northwest Ordinance, was on the wane. As Benjamin Curtis stated it, this was the first time that a court would decide whether "*a citizen of a slaveholding State, who comes to Massachusetts [or any other free state] for a temporary purpose of business or pleasure, and brings his slave as a personal attendant on his journey, may restrain the slave for the purpose of carrying him out of Massachusetts and returning to the domicil of his owner.*"[13]

Because this case set a major precedent and the attorneys for both sides were unusually talented, a close examination of the arguments is warranted. Both counsel discussed the ramifications of the case and any decision in it. In doing so they gave Chief Justice Shaw an opportunity to explore fully the legal theory and precedents, as well as the expected consequences, of his decision. While other courts reached different decisions after *Aves*, they were usually based on different circumstances of law, politics, and geography, rather than on new legal arguments. Indeed, not until the *Lemmon* case, in 1860, would a transit case be argued so fully and so well.

The Argument for Comity

On behalf of Aves, Benjamin Curtis argued that "by the law of . . . Louisiana," Med "is *now* a slave" and Massachusetts law would "allow the master to exercise" the "qualified and limited power over his slave" for "the purpose of carrying him out of the state."[14]

11. *Case of the Slave-Child Med* 4; *The Liberator*, 27 Aug. 1836.
12. *Commonwealth* v. *Aves*, 18 Pick. (Mass.) 193, 207 (1836); William W. Story, ed., 2 *Life and Letters of Joseph Story* (2 vols. Boston: Little Brown, 1851) 235.
13. *Case of the Slave-Child Med* 5.
14. Ibid.

This introduction led to a strategy based on three arguments: first, that allowing Med to remain a slave would not violate the laws or morals of Massachusetts; second, that freeing Med would violate the interstate comity established by the federal Constitution; and third, that the powerful *Somerset* precedent was not applicable to this case. If the court were to accept these arguments, then Med's slave status would be secured.

Before developing his arguments, Curtis tried to limit the case's scope by anticipating "an objection which is supported by high authority." This statement referred to Lord Mansfield's contention in *Somerset* that it was an "extreme difficulty" to adopt "the relation" of slavery "without adopting it in all its consequences." "All its consequences" would clearly have been "contrary to the municipal law" of Massachusetts, just as they were to the "municipal law of England."[15]

But Curtis saw *"no practical difficulty* in giving" a "qualified effect" to Louisiana law. He noted that the Fugitive Slave Clause of the federal Constitution gave a qualified effect to slavery in all the states without creating slavery in them. Logically, if Massachusetts could recognize the right of a slaveowner to claim a fugitive slave—without all the "consequences" of slavery corrupting the state—then it could do so in this case as well.[16]

On this point Curtis was quite successful. In presenting the counterargument, Ellis Gray Loring listed problems that might develop if slavery were allowed in the state—such as a slave's getting married, having children, committing a crime, or even killing a master in self-defense. But Chief Justice Shaw rejected these fears, noting in his opinion that "it is not contended that a master can exercise here any other rights of a slave owner," than those necessary to retain a slave "during his residence, and to remove him on his return."[17]

Curtis argued that allowing Aves to retain custody of Med would injure neither the laws nor the morals of Massachusetts. Restraining a slave would violate no statutes, because there were none on the subject. The only law remotely connected to the case was an antikidnapping statute prohibiting the restraint or confinement of a person "without legal authority." But Curtis argued that under Louisiana law Slater, or her agent Aves, did have such authority.[18]

However, while there might be no statutes prohibiting the confinement of Med, it might nevertheless be impossible to recognize the

15. Ibid.
16. Ibid.
17. Ibid. 26–27; *Commonwealth* v. *Aves* 18 Pick. (Mass.) 193, 205, 207 (1836).
18. *Case of the Slave-Child Med* 8–9.

Louisiana law making her a slave, because that law was in itself immoral. Curtis readily acknowledged that slavery was not "consistent with natural right." But the opinions of judges "as men, or as moralists" should have "no bearing on the question." The only question was "whether, when measured by the standard of *our* law, slavery is immoral?"[19]

Curtis told the judges they could "hardly declare in this case, that slavery is immoral" and a "pernicious and detestable" example for the citizens of Massachusetts, when, "before you rise from your seats, you may be called upon by the master of a fugitive slave, to grant a certificate, under the constitution, which will put the whole force of the commonwealth at his disposal, to remove his slave from our territory."[20] Slavery may have been inconsistent with the public policy of Massachusetts, but Curtis clearly demonstrated that it was not inconsistent with the United States Constitution. And Massachusetts was a party to that compact.

Curtis did not attempt to argue, as less skillful attorneys might have done, that the Fugitive Slave Clause applied to slaves in transit. But he used that part of the Constitution to underscore his argument that the morality of slavery was not a legitimate issue in an American court. Indeed, the overriding issue was interstate comity. He felt it "of the utmost importance" for the court to "keep in view the relations between" Massachusetts and Louisiana. Courts were closed to enemies, but open "to an alien friend, for personal actions." This case, however, demanded more than just the rules of international law. "What then," Curtis asked, "are the relations which we sustain" to Louisiana, "which ought to affect our public policy towards her citizens?" Curtis showed that at the Founding the South had left the question of slave transit "to the voluntary comity" of the free states and that this had worked quite well, until the present case arose. Indeed, "[v]ery soon after the adoption of the constitution" four free states passed laws allowing slave transit. Curtis asked what difference there was "between the policy of Pennsylvania, New York, Rhode Island, and New Jersey, and the policy of Massachusetts, on the subject of slavery."[21]

This argument set the stage for distinguishing *Somerset* from *Aves*. Curtis did not deny that *Somerset* "settled the law in England." But England was not America. Mansfield had asserted that slavery could be introduced "only by positive law." Curtis showed that throughout the Americas slavery had long existed without positive law. He then suggested that positive law might mean that law

19. Ibid. 11.
20. Ibid.
21. Ibid. 9–11.

"which at least *permits* the master to exercise acts of ownership over the slave." If so, then such law existed in the "principle which declares that the law of the domicil shall govern, as to the relations between foreigners, except in so far as it contradicts our own policy and laws."[22] Curtis had come full circle: Massachusetts had no law against Med being held as a slave and therefore ought to give comity to the Louisiana law that enslaved her.

A more important objection to *Somerset* could be raised, however. *Somerset* was the decision of an imperial court adjudicating the claims of a colonial subject, and thus "the question of national comity did not arise." England's public policy toward "her dependent colonies, was a very different thing from the public policy of Massachusetts" to "her sister States." Massachusetts had to give special consideration to the needs of her sister states: "It is also important to keep in view the relations which we sustain to Louisiana. She is not a foreign nation. We are bound up with her and the other slaveholding states, by the constitution, into a union upon the preservation of which no one doubts that our own peace and welfare depend."[23]

Curtis had reached his conclusion. Allowing Med to remain a slave would not violate the public policy of the Bay State. But denying Slater her claim *would* violate the public policy of maintaining harmonious relations with other states. Curtis rested his case by quoting Judge Morris's Indiana decision, that a master had "a right to pass, upon business or pleasure, through any of the States, attended by his slaves, or servants."[24]

The Argument for Freedom

Curtis's call for national harmony and comity would be repeated in other cases involving slave transit. Similarly, the detailed arguments made by Ellis Gray Loring would be repeated. Loring attacked Curtis's notion of comity from a number of directions. But the main thrust of his rebuttal was based on the immorality of slavery.

Loring began by noting that the petitioner was not a member of any antislavery society. This point was a shrewd attempt to remove the odium of abolition from the case. Abolitionists, in 1836, were generally regarded as social outcasts and troublemakers. The staid and formal Chief Justice Shaw, while opposed to slavery, was not

22. Ibid. 12.
23. Ibid. 12, 9.
24. Ibid. 13.

an abolitionist and disliked their radical tendencies. A few weeks before the *Aves* case, an alleged fugitive slave had been rescued from Shaw's courtroom while an officer was "maltreated in peril of his life." Although abolitionists condemned this violence, it is likely that Shaw blamed them for disrupting the sanctity of his courtroom. Even without this incident fresh in his mind, it is doubtful that Shaw would have been much affected by Loring's disclaimer. Of the three counsel for the petitioner, only Rufus Choate was not an active member of William Lloyd Garrison's New England Anti-Slavery Society.[25]

Loring then attempted to put Aves in a morally ambiguous position. He acknowledged the "inhumanity of separating mother and child," a point stressed by Curtis. This probable separation was "a painful feature of the case," but not the fault of the petitioner: "The responsibility of it belongs, however, wholly to that odious system, which is continually breaking up the domestic ties. It is slavery and not freedom that is separating mother and child." There was no "inhumanity in making" Med free so she could "be educated for usefulness and respectability." Loring even thought Med's mother would approve of her daughter's new status, however painful the separation. But the petitioner was willing to compromise: if Slater would "manumit her according to the law of Louisiana," the case would be dropped. "For the sake of placing her again in her mother's bosom," the "peril" of returning Med to "the midst of a slave city" would be risked.[26] The antislavery activists were willing to sacrifice a major legal victory with great precedential and propagandistic value for the welfare of the individual involved. However, the offer was rejected.

Loring began his legal argument by quoting an "eminent" judge from the Louisiana Supreme Court, that in "a matter of doubt" a court would "prefer the law of its own country, to that of the

---

25. Ibid. 14a; Levy, *Chief Justice Shaw* 72–78. Neither Loring nor Sewell signed the New England Anti-Slavery Constitution, since as lawyers they felt it would be inappropriate to do so. However, they joined the organization and became the leading antislavery attorneys in Boston; Wilson, 1 *Rise and Fall of Slave Power* 227. Four months after this case, Chief Justice Shaw's wife, Hope Savage Shaw, attended the annual fair of the Anti-Slavery Society. William Lloyd Garrison noted that Mrs. Shaw "is not better than any other woman; but then her attendance shows that our cause is by no means so odious as it once was"; Garrison to Mrs. Sarah T. Benson, 24 Dec. 1836, in Louis Ruchames and Walter M. Merrill, eds., 2 *The Letters of William Lloyd Garrison* (6 vols. Cambridge: Harvard University Press, 1971) 191–93. Garrison believed the *Aves* case helped change public opinion concerning his organization and cause, for through that case, abolitionists in Boston were able to appear as protectors of young children, rather than as troublemakers and radicals.

26. *Case of the Slave-Child Med* 8–9.

stranger."[27] Comity, Loring argued, was "founded on the consent of nations, and the need which is felt of reciprocal good office." But no such consent operated where slavery was concerned. Nor was there any "room for reciprocity." Taking the most narrow view, Loring noted that Massachusetts had no slaves; thus Louisiana could never be asked to give comity to their status. Nor did Louisiana, or most other southern states, give comity to the free black citizens of Massachusetts. But "in direct violation" of the Privileges and Immunities Clause of the Constitution, "colored citizens of the North, seamen or others, are forbidden by law from entering many of the Southern ports in this Union, on peril of being 'confined in jail'. . . ."[28]

These violations of comity were merely "specimens of the wholesale outrage and injustice" imposed on the citizens of Massachusetts

27. Ibid. 14. He was quoting Justice Alexander Porter's opinion in *Saul* v. *His Creditors*, 5 Mart. N.S. (La.) 569, 596 (1827).

28. *Case of the Slave-Child Med* 14–15. A full discussion of comity toward free blacks would require a chapter—or book—of its own. Briefly, South Carolina, Louisiana, Georgia, North Carolina, and Florida enacted various statutes to control free black sailors who landed at ports in those states. From 1822 on these Negro Seamen's acts caused considerable interstate, federal-state, and international problems. The British government complained that her free black citizens were seized and arrested. In 1844 the Massachusetts legislature sent Samuel Hoar to Charleston and Henry Hubbard to New Orleans to arrange a compromise on this issue. Both men were forced to leave the cities after government officials told them their lives were in danger and they could not be protected. See Wilson, 1 *Rise and Fall of Slave Power* 576–86 and William M. Wiecek, *The Sources of Antislavery Constitutionalism in America, 1760–1848* (Ithaca and London: Cornell University Press, 1977) 128–40. In *Elkison* v. *Deliesseline*, 8 F. Cas. 493 (1823), Supreme Court Justice William Johnson declared the South Carolina law unconstitutional, but this ruling was ignored by the state. During the oral arguments in *Aves*, Charles P. Curtis cited Johnson's decision to prove that South Carolina did give comity to Massachusetts. However, Justice Samuel Putnam interrupted to state that he knew of "one instance which has occurred, within three or four years, at Charleston," when a free black seaman was imprisoned; *Case of the Slave-Child Med* 33. In testifying before the Lunt Committee of the Massachusetts legislature, William Lloyd Garrison defended his organization and his growing anticonstitutionalism by showing that the South had denied comity to the citizens of the North. He asserted, "Why, sir, the south does with our colored citizens just as she pleased, in haughtiness of her heart, and the omnipotence of her oppression. They [free blacks] cannot tread upon her soil without being seized and thrust into a loathsome prison, and amerced with a heavy fine, which, if they cannot pay, often causes them to be sold into perpetual servitude to the highest bidder! . . . It is thus that the south adheres to our boasted Constitution. Where, then, are the rights of the citizens of this Commonwealth? Ay, sir, where are our STATE RIGHTS?"; *An Account of the Interviews Which Took Place . . . Between a Committee of the Massachusetts Anti-Slavery Society and a Committee of the Legislature* (Boston: Massachusetts Anti-Slavery Society, 1836) 8, 11. See also Jacob Harvey to Charles Sumner, 12 and 16 Jan. 1842 in Charles Sumner Papers, Houghton Library, vols. V:30 & V:31, for private discussion of this issue. See chap. 7 n. 86 of this volume for a fuller description of Louisiana's laws.

in the states "from whence" this "call for comity" came. Other out-
rages and denials of comity could be found throughout the South.
But, as Loring's argument implied, what could one expect from a
legal system that allowed something as outrageous and immoral as
slavery? In the South a man's race determined his status; in Massachusetts and before the law of God, things were different: "But white
or black skins are nothing here—this tribunal, like a greater, is no
respecter of persons."[29]

But, these remarks about the limits of comity were only preliminary. The more important objections were that "no people" were
bound to grant comity to a law that "offends their morals," "contravenes their policy," "violates a public law," or "offers a pernicious
example." Slavery, as Loring saw it, fit into all these categories.[30]

Loring accepted Curtis's contention that a moral standard could
be ascertained in a court only "by a legal standard." In cases where
legal precedents existed, Loring admitted that the abstract morality of slavery might not be relevant. But, this case was without precedent and not covered by the Constitution. Thus, Loring
"endeavor[ed] to show . . . the immorality of slavery."[31]

Loring traced the history of slavery as a problem in both natural
and positive law. He cited, among others, Grotius, Patrick Henry,
Thomas Jefferson, Justice Mansfield, and the Bible. He concluded
that slavery "is contrary to good morals;—a violation of the law of
nature, and of the revealed will of God. It therefore falls within the
first exception to the exercise of national comity."[32] Quite simply,
slavery was immoral.

Slavery also violated the public policy and laws of Massachusetts. The law of the state, he asserted, was, from 1772, that law
found in *Somerset.* Even if *Somerset* had been misinterpreted in
England and the colony, the free-and-equal clause in the new state's
constitution covered "the whole ground." This constitution "was followed by judicial decisions, applying its principles" to slavery in
Massachusetts.[33]

In addition to the constitution, statutes protecting civil rights and
liberties were also at odds with slavery. Massachusetts law would
"not permit a man to beat his neighbor, to kidnap and sell him into
exile, to forbid his marriage, to rob him of his children, to deprive
him of an education, [or] to plunder him of his earnings." Yet, these

29. *Case of the Slave-Child Med* 15.
30. Ibid. 16.
31. Ibid. 16–17.
32. Ibid. 17–20.
33. Ibid. 21. Curiously, Loring did not cite the Quock Walker Cases.

actions were all "component parts of slavery." And, "if the parts are forbidden," Loring asked, "is not that a prohibition of the whole?"[34]

Almost anticlimactically, Loring argued that slavery would set "a pernicious and detestable example" for the citizens of the state. There were of course no laws or cases to prove this. Instead, he quoted that most famous slaveowner, Thomas Jefferson, who wrote in *Notes on the State of Virginia* that slavery made tyrants of masters, who were "stamped by it with odious peculiarities."[35]

Loring devoted the second half of his oral presentation to showing why Curtis's constitutional arguments were erroneous. The Fugitive Slave Clause was "a barter of conscience, a violation of the express law of God," to which the North had unfortunately agreed. But no such compromise governed slave transit, and the court was free "to look to the will of God ('the perfect law of liberty') alone."[36]

Loring managed to avoid the law of God long enough to cite such precedents as *Butler* v. *Hopper, Ex parte Simmons*, and a number of other Pennsylvania cases, some southern cases, *Somerset*, and *In re Francisco*. He sarcastically noted of Judge Morris's opinion in *Sewall's Case* that "the decisions of the Indiana Courts" were "rarely referred to" in Massachusetts. Also, he found "evident mistakes of law" in Morris's opinion.[37]

Loring concluded with a long list of horrors that would occur if slavery was allowed in the state. His final plea reflects the frustrations of abolitionists and at the same time explains why cases such as *Aves* were so important to many northerners: "Let not the accursed system thrive amongst us. If we are to be restrained from attacking the giant trunk,—if we have even consented to let a single bough shoot over among us, to taint our air,—I trust by the blessing of Heaven we have yet strength and virtue enough to lop its luxuriance. God forbid that the deadly branches should bend over and strike root, to become in their turn, a parentstock, growing up in the soil of Massachusetts."[38]

34. Ibid.
35. Ibid.
36. Ibid. 23.
37. Ibid. 22–27.
38. Ibid. 27. Loring's reference was to the poisonous Upas tree of Java, Malaya, and India. I must thank Professor William Wiecek of the University of Missouri, Columbia, for this bit of information.

The *Aves* Precedent

On Saturday, 27 August, Chief Justice Shaw delivered a carefully argued, "diplomatic"[39] opinion for a unanimous court. Med was freed.[40]

Shaw felt the case presented an "interesting question," not because of any "doubt or difficulty attending it" but because of "its important consequences" for slaves and masters. What intrigued Shaw most was that this was a precedent-setting case. "Until this discussion," Shaw admitted, he "had supposed that there had been adjudged cases on this subject." He thought the "prevalent opinion among lawyers" was that "if a slave is brought voluntarily and unnecessarily within the limits" of Massachusetts, the slave became free, not so much because "breathing our air or treading on our soil, works any alteration in his *status*," but because there was no state law authorizing a master "to restrain the slave of his liberty . . . or forcibly to take him" from the state. But the perplexed Shaw found "no decided case on the subject reported." His decision would remedy this.[41]

Shaw reviewed the history of slavery in Massachusetts. He failed to mention the Quock Walker Cases, and observed that it was "not very easy to determine" how slavery was abolished in the state. But everyone agreed "if not abolished before, it was so by the declaration of rights," which declared "[a]ll men are born free and equal." "It would be difficult," Shaw thought, "to select words more precisely adopted to the abolition" of slavery. The "whole tenor" of Massachusetts policy had been "consistent with this construction."[42]

39. Levy, *Chief Justice Shaw* 64.

40. *The Liberator*, 15 Oct. 1836. Med was subsequently "bound out" to Isaac Knapp, the publisher of *The Liberator*, and became somewhat of a young celebrity among the Boston antislavery advocates. She was renamed Maria Sommersett by the Boston Female Anti-Slavery Society, which had financed her case. However, this name may not have stuck. In 1838 Ellis Gray Loring wrote to a manager at the Samaritan Asylum for Colored Orphans to inquire about Med's health. He offered to pay for a full-time nurse and was sending his own doctor as "a consulting physician." Loring, who had won her freedom in court, wrote, "I have full confidence in the Management of the Asylum, & doubt not every thing possible will be done for her health, & comfort. I feel a strong interest in her, & most earnestly pray that she & her mother may, one day, be reunited, *in freedom*." The actions of Loring and others indicate that the abolitionists, however paternalistic they were, were nevertheless concerned with the welfare of the blacks they felt they had "rescued" from bondage. Two years after she ceased being his client, Loring was still looking out for Med's best interests; Loring to Miss Sullivan, 8 Mar. 1838, Ellis Gray Loring Papers, letterbook, Houghton Library, Harvard University.

41. *Commonwealth* v. *Aves* 18 Pick. (Mass.) 193, 207–8 (1836).

42. Ibid. 208–10.

While Massachusetts policy was clearly against slavery, Shaw still had to take into account theories of comity and the United States Constitution. After reviewing the American and British cases cited by counsel for both sides, Shaw concluded that slavery was "contrary to natural rights, to the principles of justice, humanity and sound policy," but it was not contrary to the law of nations. It was in fact recognized by the United States Constitution and half the states. Massachusetts was bound to "take notice of those laws" of other states that created slavery, and could not declare them "unlawful and void."[43]

Shaw would not free Med by simply asserting the "higher" morality of Massachusetts. Instead, he gave an elaborate analysis of comity and slavery. The strongest argument for the master was that "the right of personal property follows the person, and ... by the comity of nations the same must be deemed his property everywhere." But Shaw found that this argument proved too much and strained the bounds of comity. For, under it, "if slavery exists anywhere, and if by the laws of any place a property can be acquired in slaves," then logically "the law of slavery must extend to every place where such slaves may be carried." This position was, of course, untenable. Therefore, Shaw concluded that comity could "apply only to those commodities which are everywhere, and by all nations treated and deemed subject of property."[44] Thus slavery was clearly excluded.

The master-slave relationship, therefore, could be determined only by local law. Shaw quoted the Louisiana Supreme Court to bolster this position: "The relation of the owner and slave is" in the slave states "a creature of municipal law." Thus, persons coming into Massachusetts became "subject to all its municipal laws," and "entitled [only] to the privileges which those laws confer." Slaves became free "not so much because any alteration is made in this *status*, or condition, as because there is no law which will warrant, but there are laws ... which prohibit, their forcible detention or forcible removable." These protections applied to all people, black and white, except fugitives.[45]

Shaw's decision was virtually a total application of *Somerset* to Massachusetts. A slave became free because the master could not lawfully restrain the slave. Shaw declined to consider what the slave's status would be should he return to the slave state with the master. Shaw also offered the South reassurance on three points.

43. Ibid. 215.
44. Ibid. 216.
45. Ibid. 217. Shaw was quoting *Lunsford* v. *Coquillon*, 2 Mart. N.S. (La.) 401 (1824). See chap. 7 of this volume for a discussion of this case.

First, he distinguished this case from that of a fugitive slave. Then he noted that an owner would be able to pass through a free state when returning home with a captured fugitive. Finally, Shaw felt it would be a different case if an owner moving from one slave state to another "necessarily passes through a free State, or where by accident or necessity he is compelled to touch or land therein, remaining no longer than necessary." Shaw declined to predict what would happen in such a case; instead, he noted that "our geographical position exempts us from the probable necessity of considering such a case."[46]

Aves Applied

Although the latitude of Massachusetts precluded migrants from one slave state passing through on their way to another slave state, slaveholders sometimes unintentionally brought their human property into the Bay State. In such cases Shaw's court showed little sympathy with the master. Twice in 1844 Shaw extended the doctrine pronounced in *Aves*.

In August 1844, the brig *Carib* arrived in Boston with a slave passenger, who had been placed on board in New Orleans and was to have disembarked in Cuba (a slave jurisdiction). But authorities there would not let the American slave land, and he remained on board when the ship continued on its journey to Boston. There "members of the abolition party" secured a writ of habeas corpus, and the case was brought before Shaw.[47]

Although the slave's master had not wanted him to come to Boston, Shaw ruled that he had been voluntarily brought there by his master's agent, and therefore the principles of *Aves* applied. The slave's parents lived in New Orleans, but he "preferred to remain" free in Boston. Justice Shaw obliged him.[48] Three principles of *Aves*

46. *Commonwealth* v. *Aves* 225. Abolitionists were jubilant over the outcome of the case. At an antislavery fair, they sold work bags "in commemoration of little Med's case, decided by Judge Shaw, in a manner so honorable to himself and his country. On one side was the representation of a Slave kneeling before the figure of Justice; underneath, these sentences were printed in golden letters: 'Slavery was abolished in Massachusetts by the adoption of the Bill of Rights as a part of the Constitution, A.D. 1780.' Slavery says of this law, 'Lo, 'tis cold and dead, and will not harm me.' Anti-Slavery replies, 'But with my breath I can revive it!' Then follows, 'The adjudication on the case of a slave brought into Massachusetts from another State, fifty-six years afterwards, Aug. 26, A.D. 1836'"; Ruchames and Merrill, 2 *Letters of Garrison* 193n.

47. *Commonwealth* v. *Potterfield*, 1 W.L.J. (Mass.) 528 (1844); *Commonwealth* v. *Potterfield*, 7 Monthly Law Reporter (Mass.) 256 (1844).

48. Ibid.

were applied in this case: first, since the black was not a fugitive slave, he could not be held in custody under the federal law; second, no Massachusetts law authorized his restraint or forcible removal from the state; and, third, by placing him on board the ship the owner made the captain his agent and acquiesced to the slave's going wherever the ship went. The agency theory seems strained here, since the owner had placed the slave on board intending that he be taken to Cuba. But this very fact could be construed to support Shaw's decision. If a slaveholding jurisdiction would not allow the slave to land—that is, would not grant comity to another slave jurisdiction—then Massachusetts might be under no moral obligation to grant comity either.

In October 1844 the Massachusetts court went one step further. Robert T. Lucas was a slave owned by Edward Fitzgerald, purser on the naval frigate *United States*. While at sea Fitzgerald had taken Lucas as his servant. Although a slave could not enlist, Lucas was "entered on the muster roll" as a landsman. Fitzgerald received Lucas's wages because he still owned Lucas. This arrangement had the approval of Secretary of the Navy A. P. Upshur. After two years at sea, the frigate returned to the United States, and its first port was Boston. Upon arrival two crew members obtained a writ of habeas corpus and Lucas was brought before Justice Shaw.[49]

Arguing for Fitzgerald, Benjamin F. Hallet claimed that Lucas was "lawfully entered in the service of the United States, [and] that his enlistment was a valid contract by the law of Virginia." He claimed that entering Massachusetts had been involuntary and the contract for Lucas's services was still in force. But, even if the contract was invalid, the case was exempt from the *Aves* doctrine because Fitzgerald did not voluntarily bring Lucas into the state.[50]

The omnipresent Samuel Sewall argued that the case did come within the *Aves* precedent, since "when his master placed him in the naval service of the United States, he thereby consented that he should go anywhere the ship might be lawfully ordered to, and took the chance of his being sent to a free port."[51]

In an "elaborate opinion" Chief Justice Shaw ruled that a contract with a slave was void because a slave could not make a contract. However, the contract for the slave's services, made between the master and the navy, was perfectly legal. But the navy "could acquire no greater right over the slave than the master himself had, and no greater right than any private person would acquire by such a contract." Expanding on the dicta of *Somerset* and *Aves*, Shaw

49. *Commonwealth* v. *Fitzgerald*, 7 Monthly Law Reporter (Mass.) 379, 380 (1844).
50. Ibid. 380–81.
51. Ibid. 380.

concluded that slavery was local, supported only by local (state) laws; therefore, as soon as the frigate left the waters of Virginia there was no longer any law that could make Lucas a slave. This reasoning applied to the United States government as well as to private citizens. Lucas was not a person "in the United States Service" as Hallet argued, because slaves could not be enlistees. Lucas was simply a slave under contract who had gained his freedom through the act of those who held his contract.[52]

Hallet had also argued that Lucas was in Massachusetts by accident or distress, rather than by the design of his master. But Shaw felt that Lucas's master had "consented that the slave should be carried anywhere that the ship might be sent" when he rented the slave's labor to the navy. Shaw left open the question of a vessel traveling from one slave state to another, which might "be cast away on the coast of a free state." This question was not before him. The logic of Shaw's opinion dictates that once any slave entered international waters with a master's consent, the slave became free. For the case at hand Shaw found that Lucas was neither a fugitive slave nor a sailor "lawfully enlisted." And when a slave was "casually" in Massachusetts "whether he is brought here voluntarily or not" there was "no law here to authorize his restraint." Lucas was discharged.[53]

The Slave's Right to Choose

Two facts were central to the outcome of these cases: blacks were actually claimed as slaves, and they either wished to remain in Massachusetts or were too young to make a reasonable choice. In 1839 a slaveowner moving to rural Massachusetts tried to retain her slave by denying both these assertions. Although the case never went beyond the Worcester County Court of Common Pleas, the Holden Anti-Slavery Society issued a pamphlet about the case containing a transcript of the testimony and notes from one of the attorneys.[54]

"Abstract Slavery," the pamphlet asserted, was something "everyone abhors; but slavery as it exists, so little is even yet known that most seem to regard it as mainly a nominal evil, and therefore, experience very little sympathy for those who are called slaves." The society published the pamphlet to help change this situation by

52. Ibid. 380–81.
53. Ibid. 382.
54. Holden Anti-Slavery Society, *Report of the Holden Slave Case* (Worcester, Mass.: Colton and Howland, 1839).

giving New Englanders a firsthand description of how slavery could operate, even in Massachusetts. The pamphlet shows why, in the view of so many northerners, absolutely no comity should be granted to slavery within their jurisdiction. The case underscores the connection between antislavery, the legal system, and the issue of slave transit and sojourn. In addition, the testimony of nonabolitionists indicates how the treatment of one person as a slave could create an uproar in a community. Although the alleged slave in Holden may not have been asked to work harder than other girls in the community, the method of her labor and the attitude of her mistress distressed the people of Holden.[55]

Anne, a thirteen-year-old black girl, had been brought to Holden from New Orleans, when her mistress, Mrs. Olivia Eames, moved back to her native Massachusetts. After Anne had been in Holden five months, four concerned citizens served Eames with a writ of personal replevin. The writ asserted that Anne was illegally deprived of her liberty and that Eames planned to take her back forcibly to the South and sell her. In accordance with a statute passed a few months after *Aves*, the writ of personal replevin would allow a jury to determine Anne's status.[56] Eames resisted the men who served the writ, and they took Anne by force. Eames then testified about the incident to a grand jury, which indicted the men for "devising and intending to deprive" Eames "of the voluntary service" of Anne.[57]

The question of Anne's freedom was not directly before the court, but was ancillary to the guilt or innocence of the men who had taken Anne from Eames. At the trial, the district attorney prosecuted the men on behalf of Eames. If the men were successfully prosecuted, the writ of personal replevin would have been quashed and no jury trial would have been held to determine Anne's status. Eames probably thought this was the best way of retaining Anne. Convicting four men for physically abusing her and forcibly removing her domestic servant seemed more feasible than trying to convince a jury in central Massachusetts that she could retain full custody of a girl whom she might some day attempt to sell as a slave. Indeed, a few years later, in a quite similar case, a Massachusetts antislavery man would be successfully sued for false imprisonment, after securing a writ to free a slave who did not want to be separated from her master.[58]

55. Ibid. 3.

56. Ibid., and "An Act to Restore the Trial by Jury on Questions of Personal Freedom," in *Massachusetts Acts of 1837*, chap. 221.

57. Holden Anti-Slavery Society, *Holden Slave Case* 32.

58. See *Linda* v. *Hudson* (1848), discussed below, pp. 121–22.

The prosecutor asserted that Anne was free "as soon as she came into this State" and "had the right to remain with or leave her mistress, as she saw fit." This, he noted in an oblique reference to *Aves*, had been decided by the "highest tribunal" of the state. The indictment itself declared that Anne was not restrained of any liberty but was voluntarily with Eames, a statement that of course begged the question of whether Anne was actually a slave or not. In her testimony Eames proved equally evasive. When Eames was asked if she planned to "carry Anne back as a slave," the prosecutor objected. When the objection was overruled, Eames simply said she *"never considered her property"* after coming to the North, and *"never* called her *property"* after coming "to this free country." After persistent questioning, however, she admitted, "It was my intention to go back—I don't know that I should have asked her [Anne's] consent to carry her back—can't tell what I should do—should carry her, if she was willing to go—I had no more interest in her than in any other . . . I never told her she was a slave or free." Numerous witnesses testified that Eames referred to Anne as her slave.[59]

Anne's status, in Massachusetts or New Orleans, was actually of only secondary importance to the prosecution. If the prosecution could prove that Anne wanted to remain with Mrs. Eames—whatever her status was—then the four men could be found guilty of conspiring to take her away from Eames against Anne's wishes. Eames of course testified that Anne did not want to leave her. Anne testified that she had never asked anyone to help her gain her freedom and she "never told" Eames she "wanted to go away and leave her." But on cross-examination Anne undercut this loyalty to her mistress. She admitted that Eames planned to take her back to New Orleans and sell her. When asked if she ever "express[ed] a wish to have your personal liberty" the prosecution objected but was overruled. Anne admitted telling two women she wished to be free, and she said her mistress had hit her in the head with a toasting iron for this act. She also confirmed she had carried "a great many pails of water in a day" and that her mistress told her to carry them on her head.[60] The spectacle of a young black girl carrying water pails on her head must have touched a nerve in the Massachusetts community, for a number of witnesses testified to this incident. Undoubtedly, such a sight appeared to them as a living symbol of the slavery they did not want in their state. Finally, Anne admitted that she knew her age only because Eames had recently told her

59. Holden Anti-Slavery Society, *Holden Slave Case* 5–6, 9–10, and *passim*.
60. Ibid., *passim*.

she was thirteen years old. Other witnesses noted that she had been neither to school nor to church meeting while in Holden. All of this testimony made Anne appear to be a slave in the free state of Massachusetts.

The defense planned to call fourteen witnesses to prove that Anne was kept as a slave, but it was necessary to use only two. These two women quoted Eames as calling Anne her slave, described the punishments she received for simple mistakes, told of Anne's being neglected and overworked, and confirmed that Anne said she wished her freedom. These statements were sufficient for the prosecutor, who concluded "the evidence abundantly justified the issuing of the process" and that the defendants ought to be acquitted. With no one to prosecute the men, the "jury immediately gave a verdict of acquittal." This action did not free Anne. It only freed the men who had served the writ of personal replevin on Eames. The question of Anne's status was decided later, in the case of *Anne* v. *Olivia Eames.* Eames initially hired an attorney to argue against the writ, but the case was "defaulted by consent" after Eames paid nominal damages to Anne for illegally holding her in servitude.[61]

In July 1841 Massachusetts Supreme Court Judge S. S. Wilde gave support to the Holden verdict in a similar case. A slaveowner named Ludlow came to New Bedford to visit his ailing father-in-law. His slave Lucy Fagins was brought to care for Ludlow's children, and a writ of habeas corpus brought the case before Justice Wilde. Ludlow did not argue that Lucy was a slave. Rather, he claimed she was free under Massachusetts law and voluntarily chose to remain with him. As Chief Justice Shaw had done in Francisco's case nine years earlier, Justice Wilde examined Lucy Fagins in his law library. There, away from the coercive presence of her master, Lucy said she wished to remain in Massachusetts as a free woman.[62]

Three months later, in *Commonwealth* v. *Taylor* (1841),[63] another slaveholder tried to convince the Massachusetts Supreme Judicial Court that she should be allowed to keep her slave in the state. Mary B. Taylor was visiting the state with her seven- or eight-year-old slave, Anson, when a writ of habeas corpus brought the case into court. Like Eames and Ludlow, Mrs. Taylor did not claim Anson as a slave. Indeed, Taylor asserted that she would take Anson back to Arkansas only with his consent. Chief Justice Shaw found this position rather self-serving. The "natural and strong feelings of

---

61. Ibid.
62. *The Philanthropist*, 28 July 1841.
63. *Commonwealth* v. *Taylor*, 3 Metcalf (Mass.) 72 (1841).

a child," Shaw noted, "which induce him to cling instinctively to those whom he has been accustomed to regard as his natural protectors, cannot be regarded as the exercise of a legal will, or of an intelligent choice." Shaw ruled Anson to be free and placed him in the hands of a guardian.[64]

According to the *Monthly Law Reporter*, Anson "seemed to be a bright, intelligent child, and remarkably cheerful and happy." While with his temporary guardian during the proceedings he sat as "apparently an unconcerned spectator." But, when Anson understood this new relationship was to be permanent "he broke out into most impassioned entreaties to be permitted to go back and see his father and mother and brothers and sisters, weeping bitterly and pleading with his guardian to let him go. The business of the court was suspended, while the child was led away, shrieking and begging to be suffered to go back to his father and mother."[65]

This decision was complicated by Shaw's previous ruling in *In re Francisco*. In that case Shaw allowed Francisco to remain with his former mistress and return to Cuba with her, because that is what he chose to do and because she did not claim him as a slave. These same conditions existed for Anson. However, Shaw felt Anson was "too young to exercise a free election, and therefore has no will on the subject" of whom he would remain with. Also, Anson was owned by Mr. Taylor, not his wife, and Shaw noted "she cannot bind him by her disclaimer" that the boy is not a slave. Finally Shaw thought it was Mrs. Taylor's "intention . . . to carry him back to Arkansas, to his former condition of slavery."[66] This opinion indicated that Shaw did not trust the state of Arkansas (or Mrs. Taylor) to enforce the free status that Anson had gained by being brought to Massachusetts.

Anson obviously was not pleased with the humanitarian result of this case. He would have preferred to be returned to his family. As "a child of such tender years," however, he had "no will, no power of judging or electing; and therefore his will and choice are to be wholly disregarded." Shaw might also have quoted Ellis Loring's argument from *Aves*: "It is slavery not freedom that is separating mother and child."[67]

64. Ibid. 72–75.

65. *Commonwealth* v. *Taylor*, 4 Monthly Law Reporter (Mass.) 275 (1841). As were other cases during this period, *Commonwealth* v. *Taylor* was reported in more than one source. Although these sources rarely contradict each other on major points, they often give different facts on nonessential aspects of the cases.

66. Ibid. 275; *Commonwealth* v. *Taylor*, 3 Metcalf 73 (1841).

67. *Commonwealth* v. *Taylor*, 3 Metcalf 73 (1841); *Case of the Slave-Child Med* 14a.

However much Anson objected to the result of his case, that objection resulted only from his status as a minor. Shaw noted that "a very different rule would apply" if the slave were considered "to have sufficient intelligence and capacity to judge of his own interests, and elect whether he would return with his master to a slave State, or be set at liberty here."[68] This situation applied in Francisco's case and was implied in the Holden case.

In Anson's case Mrs. Taylor's counsel cited an unnamed "case of a steward of a vessel." This slave-sailor had a wife and children in Maryland, and he "preferred returning there to be a slave, to abandoning them and remaining" in Massachusetts. His wishes were granted.[69] Similarly, in November 1857 the slave Betty also chose to remain with her owners. She was twenty-five and had a husband in Tennessee who was more important to her than freedom in Massachusetts. Chief Justice Shaw ordered that she be free to do as she chose and gave her a writ commanding "that all persons be interdicted and forbidden to interfere with her personal liberty in this respect."[70]

This writ may have been necessary to protect Betty from well-meaning but sometimes overzealous abolitionists. Two earlier cases illustrate this problem. In 1845, a Mr. Hodgson of Savannah, Georgia, was traveling with his slave, Linda, in western Massachusetts, when Linda allegedly told a black man she wished to be free. This statement was communicated to a Dr. Erastus D. Hudson. Hudson followed Hodgson and Linda from Springfield to Northampton, where at his request a writ of habeas corpus was issued and Linda was "arrested and brought before" a judge.[71]

When brought before the judge Linda claimed that she was there against her will and that she had not wanted the writ of habeas corpus issued on her behalf. The writ was quashed and Linda returned to her master. Linda then initiated a thousand-dollar damage suit against Hudson "for personal injuries and annoyance . . . in procuring her to be arrested under" the writ. The trial resulted in a hung jury. At a second trial Justice Wilde ruled that because the facts of the case did not show probable cause for Hudson's procuring the writ, the only question for the jury was one of damages. Wilde charged the jury that without probable cause Hudson "acted on his own hazard, and must take the consequences." The jury returned a

68. *Commonwealth* v. *Taylor*, 3 Metcalf 73 (1841).

69. *Commonwealth* v. *Taylor*, 4 Monthly Law Reporter 475–76.

70. *Betty's Case*, 20 Monthly Law Reporter (Mass.) 455, 458 (1857).

71. *Linda* v. *Hudson*, 9 Monthly Law Reporter (Mass.) 353, 354–55 (1848); *Linda* v. *Hudson*, 1 Cushing (Mass.) 385, 386–88 (1848).

verdict for Linda and found damages of $30.67 against Hudson. On appeal, however, Chief Justice Shaw ordered a new trial because the jury ought to have decided "upon the evidence, whether the complaint and petition made by the defendant" were made at Linda's "request and for her benefit." The third trial apparently led to a settlement; otherwise, it is likely that Hudson would have appealed again to the Massachusetts Supreme Judicial Court. Unlike other litigants, abolitionists had access to volunteer lawyers and financial backers for important cases. Indeed, in this case Hudson was well represented by A. C. Spooner and Wendell Phillips. Phillips "appeared under a special power of attorney," because as an anti-constitutionalist, Garrisonian abolitionist, Phillips had long before "renounced his oath as a counsellor and attorney of the court." After Shaw's decision ordering a third trial, *The Liberator* suggested that a law be passed to prevent such cases. "It would be a good kind of law," Garrison's paper declared, "which should decide that no human being has a *right* to be a slave." No one should "be condemned for endeavoring to prevent such an act *nolens volens* [consenting or not]."[72]

The most bizarre case involving alleged slaves in Massachusetts was *Commonwealth* v. *Robinson* (1837). In 1837 Mr. and Mrs. Henry Bright moved from Mobile, Alabama, to Mr. Bright's native Massachusetts. Mrs. Bright, also a New Englander, characterized herself as an "immediate abolitionist." They brought with them a five-year-old black girl whose slave mother had died in Alabama. Their intention was to reside permanently in Massachusetts where the child, Elizabeth, could be educated and grow up free.[73]

A few weeks after moving to Cambridge, Massachusetts, Elizabeth was abducted by the Robinsons, a black couple whose "characters stand high." The Robinsons feared that the Brights would return to the South and enslave the child. Immediately after the abduction the Brights explained their intentions and situation to Samuel E. Sewall and asked him to help recover the child. Bright then visited a black clergyman, the Reverend William Snowden, and at his suggestion drew a bond of five hundred dollars, which would be forfeited if Elizabeth were taken to a slave state. But still "the colored people would not give up the child." Bright then called on Ellis Gray Loring, "knowing that he was an influential abolitionist." Sewall had already talked to Loring, who "was satisfied that the child ought to be given up." Loring gave Bright a letter to that effect. The Brights then called on Mrs. Robinson, who acknowledged

72. Ibid., and *The Liberator*, 14 Apr. 1848.
73. *Commonwealth* v. *Robinson*, Thac. Cr. Cas. (Mass.) 488, 494 (1837).

that she had abducted the girl, but said the child was in the hands of two white women, whom she refused to name, but to whom she did agree to talk.[74]

The next day the Brights met with Eliza and Mary S. Parker. The Parker sisters "said they knew nothing of the little girl until the evening before, when Mrs. Robinson told them of her; that Mrs. Robinson had called on them that morning, and requested permission to bring the child to their house." The Parker ladies agreed the child ought to be returned, and one of them went to the Robinsons' with Mr. Bright. There Rev. Snowden said "that some of the colored people thought the bond was not sufficient," because the child could be sold for at least that amount. Later, at Loring's office, Mrs. Robinson declared "that, notwithstanding the white people wished them to give up the child, the colored people thought differently, and were determined not to give her up, unless there was some law to compel them."[75]

At this point Mr. Bright took out guardianship papers and sought a writ of habeas corpus, which Justice Shaw refused to issue. A civil suit was then initiated. A thousand dollars in damages were assessed against the Robinsons, and their property was attached. But they still refused to give up the girl, which was all that Bright wanted. Bright then complained to the grand jury, which indicted the Robinsons on three counts of kidnapping.[76]

After hearing evidence, in the trial for kidnapping, Judge Peter Oxenbridge Thacher charged the jury to consider both the facts of the case and the law of kidnapping. Good intentions were no defense: "To show that the defendants were free from an evil intent, and that they acted on high principles of humanity and benevolence, [does] . . . not avail for their acquittal, although it may speak much in mitigation of their punishment, especially if, by hastening to restore the child, they should acknowledge their fault." Thacher felt the Robinsons had "set their own will above the law."[77]

The Robinsons were found guilty of kidnapping and sentenced to four months in jail and fined two hundred dollars plus costs. They immediately appealed, but after finally releasing Elizabeth and paying the costs in the criminal case and Bright's costs in the civil case, the prosecutor, at Bright's request, entered a nolle prosequi and the case ended.[78]

74. Ibid. 489–94.
75. Ibid. 491–94.
76. Ibid.
77. Ibid. 499.
78. Ibid. 500.

An "Outrage upon Southern Rights"

The *Aves* case and its successors reflected the growing antislavery sentiment in Massachusetts. The courts responded to this sentiment as cases were brought before them. And, as long as the courts could support freedom without violating any specific federal laws or constitutional provisions, they served as a forum for liberty. Only when fugitive slaves, rather than slaves in transit, became the issue, did the Massachusetts Supreme Judicial Court refuse to free slaves. The Massachusetts courts, and particularly Chief Justice Shaw, were antislavery, but not abolitionist. Thus, in fugitive slave cases Shaw and his court saw their obligation to the federal Constitution as greater than any obligation to the Massachusetts constitution or to the higher law. This position would soon contrast markedly with that of courts and justices in Wisconsin, Pennsylvania, and other northern states.[79]

Nevertheless, the actions of Massachusetts courts were critical to the development of the impending crisis in interstate law and politics. *Aves* signaled the beginning of the end of interstate comity for slaves in transit. Since the Founding, slavery had been a divisive factor in American politics. The issue had been debated at the Constitutional Convention, in Congress, in state legislatures, and during elections. But until 1836 the northern courts had avoided this conflict. *Aves*, however, began a new trend. As one Boston Whig paper noted, "The great importance" of the decision "is easily perceived." It was "the first decision in any of the free States upon" the "precise point" that "a slave voluntarily brought here by his master becomes free." This conservative, antiabolitionist paper did not like the decision. It doubted that other northern courts would "consider themselves bound by this adjudication," but with civic and state pride concluded that "the high rank held by the Supreme Court of Massachusetts," gave "great weight to its decisions on this, as on other points."[80]

Any doubts about the importance of the precedent were dispelled in the next few years. The second edition of Joseph Story's *Commentaries on the Conflict of Laws*, published in 1841, carried the entire text of Shaw's decision in an extended footnote covering seven-

---

79. For Shaw's reaction to fugitive slave cases, see Levy, *Chief Justice Shaw* 72–108. In Wisconsin a major conflict arose between the supreme court of that state and the United States Supreme Court, over the enforcement of the Fugitive Slave Law of 1850. The case, *Ableman* v. *Booth*, 21 Howard 506 (1859) is briefly discussed in chap. 10. For Pennsylvania, see discussion of *Prigg* v. *Pennsylvania*, 16 Peters (U.S.) 539 (1842), in chap. 5.

80. *Boston Daily Advertiser*, 29 Aug. 1836.

teen pages. *Commonwealth* v. *Aves* was soon cited in almost every case dealing with slavery and comity. Some federal judges accepted the doctrine of *Aves*, and Shaw's reasoning was often paraphrased or quoted. Not surprisingly, as antislavery sentiment grew, many northern courts and state legislatures adopted the *Aves* doctrine.[81]

The South of course also reacted to the decision. In what was clearly a minority opinion, the *Louisville Advertiser* saw "nothing to irritate or alarm the South" because it was a perfectly constitutional and reasonable decision. If the courts were denied the power to make such decisions, the paper thought it would be easy for slavery to be forced on those states that did not want it. More representative, no doubt, was the *Augusta Sentinel*, which asked the "people of the South!" if they were "willing to sustain forever a confederation with states into which you dare. not travel with your property, lest that property becomes by law actually confiscated." *Aves* was the first of many cases that would be an "outrage upon Southern Rights."[82]

81. See, for example, *Polydore* v. *Prince*, 19 F. Cas. 950 (1837) and *Jones* v. *Van Zandt*, 13 F. Cas. 1040 (1843), accepting the principles of *Aves*. Besides law-related publications, the opinion was also printed in *Niles Weekly Register*, 24 Sept. 1836.

82. *The Liberator*, 8 Oct. 1836.

Chapter 5

The Northern Rejection of Comity: The East

Abolitionists and others opposed to slavery were quick to grasp the significance of the decision in *Commonwealth* v. *Aves*. In Massachusetts the state antislavery society cheerfully published the news of this "IMPORTANT DECISION" in its annual report. Singled out for special praise was "that watchful, heroic, unfaltering band, the Boston Female Anti-Slavery Society," which initiated the case. The Massachusetts society noted, "It is to woman, therefore, that humanity owes this great decision."[1]

At the National Women's Anti-Slavery Conference in 1837 two resolutions recognized the importance of transit. Angelina E. Grimké reminded her sisters that slavery would remain a national sin, if, among other things, the northern states "refuse to repeal those laws which recognize and secure the usurpation of the master over his slave." Lydia Marie Child urged the delegates to petition their state legislatures to repeal laws allowing slave transit.[2]

A year later abolitionists in New York questioned candidates for state office to discover who was "in favor of the repeal of the law which now authorizes the importation of slaves into this state, and their detention here as such for the time of nine months." Carefully drafted by Gerrit Smith and William Jay, this query was designed to elicit maximum antislavery results. It backfired, however, for both gubernatorial candidates, William Marcy (Democrat) and William H. Seward (Whig), replied that the nine-months law allowed only sojourn and not "importation." Seward won the election and ultimately supported repeal of the law.[3]

Besides questioning candidates and petitioning legislatures, antislavery activists took to the courts. Within a year after *Aves* other

1. Massachusetts Anti-Slavery Society, *Fifth Annual Report, 1837* (Boston: Isaac Knapp, 1837) 70.
2. *Proceedings of the Anti-Slavery Convention of American Women Held in the City of New York, 1837* (New York: William S. Dorr, 1837) 11, 8.
3. Thomas Hart Benton, 2 *Thirty Years View* (2 vols. New York: D. Appleton, 1857) 775–76; Richard H. Sewell, *Ballots for Freedom: Antislavery Politics in the United States, 1837–1860* (New York: Oxford University Press, 1976) 17.

courts faced similar cases. In terms of legal precedent, a minor revolution in jurisprudence was taking place. Between 1836 and 1860 every free state faced the *Aves* precedent through court cases, legislation, or constitutional provisions. With a few exceptions, the *Aves* precedent was ultimately accepted throughout the North. The most important states to reject *Aves*—Indiana, Illinois, and New Jersey—were negrophobic, Democratic strongholds and shared important borders with slave states. In addition, two had large southern-born populations and in all three the antislavery movements were relatively weak.[4]

By 1860 transit with slave property had no protection in most of the North. Fifty years of comity disappeared in less than half that time. From Maine to Minnesota, the North rejected interstate harmony in favor of antislavery. By the time of Lincoln's election, Free Soil meant not only that slavery would be excluded from the territories, but also that it would be kept out of the free states.

Connecticut

The first state to adopt *Aves* was Connecticut. In *Jackson* v. *Bulloch* (1837)[5] a black woman named Nancy Jackson applied for a writ of habeas corpus "alleging" that she was "illegally confined" by James Bulloch, "then residing in Hartford." Bulloch claimed he was a citizen of Georgia temporarily in Hartford to educate his children. He and his family intended to return to Georgia after this education was completed. While the children were in school Bulloch spent about half his time in Connecticut and half in Georgia.[6]

In a three-to-two decision, Chief Justice Thomas Williams ruled that Jackson could no longer be held as a slave. Applying the reasoning of Mansfield and Shaw, Williams stated, "[S]lavery is contrary to the principles of natural right and to the great law of love; that it is founded on injustice and fraud, and can be supported only by the provisions of positive law."[7]

The influence of *Aves* was evident throughout the case. Bulloch's counsel did not attempt to overcome the principles laid down by Shaw. He "expressly conceded that slavery was a system of such a character, that it can claim nothing by the law of comity . . . that it

4. *Aves* was also rejected by the California Supreme Court, in *Ex parte Archy*, 9 Cal. 147 (1858), and implicitly rejected by the Oregon Constitution, which prohibited all blacks from entering that state.

5. *Jackson* v. *Bulloch*, 12 Conn. 38 (1837).

6. Ibid. 39–40.

7. Ibid. 38–41.

was local and must be governed entirely by the laws of the state, in which it is attempted to be enforced." He further admitted that nothing in the federal Constitution was "applicable to this case" because that document only protected a master's right to a fugitive slave. Bulloch's counsel simply tried to prove that Connecticut law would allow a long-term transit or sojourn with a slave. Chief Justice Williams readily accepted this reading of the legal principles involved and did not "examine the authorities" cited by both counsel. Instead, he referred "to the able opinion of the supreme court of Massachusetts in the case of *The Commonwealth* v. *Aves.*"[8]

Even if the legal principles involved were the same for Connecticut and Massachusetts, the constitutions and statutes were not. Williams admitted, "[I]n this state we have not been entirely free from the evil of slavery; and a small remnant still remains to remind us of the fact." Williams also found nothing in Connecticut's constitution to free Jackson; the state's bill of rights was "certainly broad, but not as broad as that of the bill of rights in Massachusetts, to which it has been compared." Rather, it was "limited to those who are parties to the social compact," which excluded slaves. But, while Chief Justice Shaw could use only a broadly worded constitutional provision and foreign precedents to free Med, his Connecticut counterpart had positive law, in the form of two statutes, under which he could free Nancy Jackson. The anti-importation act of 1774 prohibited any slave from being "disposed of, left or sold within" the state. The act of 1784 declared any slave born after its passage free at age twenty-five.[9]

The application of these statutes to free Jackson required a judiciary more inclined to the rights of an individual black or to striking a blow at slavery, than to the interests of an owner or the necessity of preserving interstate harmony. Two justices, although sympathetic to Jackson's plight, found it impossible to read the statutes in

---

8. Ibid. 40–41. The importance of *Aves* in this case is underscored by correspondence between abolitionists Theodore Dwight Weld and Lewis Tappan. Weld was in Connecticut a week before oral arguments were heard. He asked Tappan to send him a copy of Ellis Gray Loring's argument in *Aves* so he could give it to Nancy Jackson's attorneys. Weld had already given them Shaw's opinion, but lacked Loring's argument. Weld also wrote to James G. Birney, suggesting that the latter meet him in Hartford because he (Weld) "should stay here to watch the progress of the cause and aid in whatever may be necessary"; Theodore Dwight Weld to Lewis Tappan, 8 June 1837, in Gilbert Hobbs Barnes and Dwight L. Dumond, eds., 1 *Letters of Theodore Dwight Weld, Angelina Grimké Weld and Sara Grimké, 1822–1844* (2 vols. New York: Appleton-Century-Crofts, 1934) 397–400; Theodore Dwight Weld to James G. Birney, 8 June 1837, in Dwight L. Dumond, ed., 1 *The Letters of James Gillespie Birney, 1831–1857* (2 vols. New York: D. Appleton-Century, 1938) 386–87.

9. *Jackson* v. *Bulloch*, 12 Conn. 38, 40–41, 44–45 (1837).

her favor. They viewed the statutes as applying only to permanent residents of Connecticut and not to sojourners who intended to leave the state. However, the dissenters found it "a source of gratification" that if their "views on this subject are erroneous," as the majority believed, "their effect will not be unjustly to deprive a fellow being of her liberty."[10]

Justice Williams responded to this opposition with a spirited defense of his interpretation of the laws. He understood Bulloch's position to be that visitors could bring slaves into Connecticut "in any number, and for any time their owners choose" if "they do not intend to remain here permanently, themselves; and they do not mean that the slave shall remain here for life." But such an interpretation would defeat the entire purpose of the legislation, which was aimed at gradually ending slavery in the state. Under this reading of the law, anyone might "go abroad and hire slaves, and bring them to labour in this state." Although the slave "could not be left here for life," he could "be hired for a term of years; and the contract of hiring for a term, would always prove that he was not to be permanently left." Soon slaves would "again become the cultivators of our soil." The chief justice's fears were not completely fanciful, for such practices had been going on in the Northwest Territory (and the states carved out of it) for some time.[11]

This could not of course have been the intent of the statute. Williams interpreted the word *left* to allow for transit through the state but not sojourn in it. Otherwise, any nonresident could "remove into this state with his slaves; and so long as he remains with them, they are not 'left'" in the state. Williams felt that "so long as he is a traveller, passing through the state, he cannot be said to have *left* her here." But Bulloch, with his family, were "residing here for years" and he allowed Nancy Jackson "to remain here, for almost two years." Thus Bulloch could not "claim the privilege of a traveller," although "he intended at some future time, to return with his family to his former residence."[12]

Under this interpretation of the statute, Jackson was free. Williams, however, did not stop here. He went on to analyze the 1784 statute, to show that on other grounds, namely, as a slave over the age of twenty-five, Jackson was also free. Tactically this strategy served two useful purposes. First, it illustrated the antislavery intent of the legislation. Williams noted that the 1774 act "aimed a blow at the increase of slaves; that of 1784, struck at the existence of slavery. The former was intended to weaken the system; the latter,

10. Ibid. 69.
11. Ibid. 47.
12. Ibid. 48–49, 50–51.

to destroy it." This reasoning bolstered Williams's antislavery interpretation of both laws. Williams then argued that "if one citizen could hold no person but those under 25 years of age as slaves, by a parity of reasons, no others among us could hold them for a longer period."[13] Although Williams was at the time only upholding Jackson's freedom, he may have been laying the groundwork for a future attack on slavery in Connecticut which would have freed any slave over twenty-five who was brought into the state. The interpretation of the 1774 statute freed only those slaves *left* in the state for some length of time; but Williams may have been looking to a time when all slaves, or at least all those over twenty-five, might be freed upon entering the state.

A year after this decision, the compiled laws of the state retained the 1774 and 1784 statutes without revision, indicating that the legislature saw no need to interfere with the *Bulloch* decision. A new statute, passed that year, increased the procedural rights of blacks claimed as fugitives. In 1848 the legislature abolished all slavery in the state but continued the section prohibiting any slave from being "disposed of, left, or sold" in the state. *Jackson* v. *Bulloch* was cited "for construction of this section." However, since the first section of the new law declared that "no person shall hereafter be held in slavery in this state," it is likely that *Bulloch* had in fact been superseded by this new, all-encompassing legislation. No cases were brought under this law. In 1857 all ambiguity was removed with a statute declaring that any slave "not having escaped from any other state" upon "coming into" Connecticut "or being therein, shall forthwith become and be free."[14]

In other New England states no cases concerning slave transit were reported. However, statutes to deal with the problem did exist. Rhode Island's 1774 act allowing slaves in transit to enter and leave the state remained in force until the adoption of the state's first constitution in 1843 and the revised statutes of 1844. The democratization following the Dorr War influenced the constitutional clause that declared, "Slavery shall not be permitted in this State." The revised statutes also provided for the maintenance, and assumed the emancipation of, any remaining slaves. The former guarantees of transit were not repeated in these revised statutes and thus were repealed.[15]

13. Ibid. 54.

14. Connecticut, *Revised Statutes, 1839*, tit. XLVII; Connecticut, *Revised Statutes, 1849*, tit. LI, *General Statutes of the State of Connecticut 1866*, tit. LVIII.

15. *Revised Statutes of the State of Rhode Island* (Providence: Sayles, Miller and Simons, 1857), chaps. 212 and 223. On the Dorr War, see Arthur May Murray, *The Dorr War: The Constitutional Struggle in Rhode Island* (New York: Chelsea House, 1970).

Vermont passed various personal liberty laws between 1840 and 1858 that made any form of slavery in the state difficult to maintain. The 1858 statute declared, "Every person, who may be held as a slave, who shall come or be brought or be involuntarily, in any way, in this State, shall be free." An 1857 New Hampshire statute freed any slave living in the state "with the consent of his or her master or mistress, or who shall come, or be brought into or be in this State involuntarily." That same year (1857) Maine passed a similar statute.[16] The statutes in these three states were probably more symbolic than necessary. Few southerners would have been foolish enough to bring their slaves to these abolitionist strongholds. Nevertheless, as symbols, this legislation undermined interstate harmony.

New York

In 1839 the New York State Assembly received some petitions for the repeal of the nine-months law. In 1840 a repeal bill died in committee. Most of the antislavery petitions in these two years concerned the passage of a personal liberty law giving a jury trial and other procedural rights to alleged fugitive slaves. The jury trial bill was passed in 1840, and the next year the state's growing antislavery movement concentrated most of its energies on the transit law. In 1841 the house received over fifty petitions calling for repeal of the nine-months law. On 29 March a bill was introduced and given unanimous consent for a second reading. Ten times the usual number of copies were printed. But the bill languished in a hostile committee as the legislative session drew to a close. On 22 May a similar bill was introduced in the state senate, read twice, and engrossed for a third reading. It passed the senate on 24 May and went to the house. The house passed it on 25 May and Governor William H. Seward signed it into law that same day. Two days later the assembly adjourned. Seward had supported the bill from the beginning, but the Democrats controlled the house and at the time of the bill's passage held a temporary majority in the senate. Democratic support for the repeal indicates the strength of statewide sentiment against slave transit.[17]

16. *General Statutes of the State of Vermont* (1863), tit. XXXII, chap. 109; *New Hampshire, Laws, 1857*, chap. 1955; *Maine, Laws, 1857*, chap. 53.

17. *New York House Journal, 1839*, 41, 69, 77, 148, 167, 170, 203, 336, 1150, 1219; *New York House Journal, 1840*, 157, 216, 247, 248, 250, 404, 405, 410, 466, 478, 583, 666, 855, 1193, 1270, 1274, 1444; *New York House Journal, 1841*, 44, 48, 57, 64, 77, 156, 176, 218, 292, 298, 303, 315, 332, 340, 358, 368, 381, 394, 409, 417, 446, 490, 547, 607, 616, 619, 638, 658, 709, 722, 734, 800, 939, 1013, 1051, 1115, 1362–64, 1381;

No major cases were decided after the repeal until *Lemmon* v. *The People* (1860).[18] However, in two obscure cases involving alleged fugitive slaves a state circuit court judge gave an indication of how New York's judiciary would treat slaves in transit. Both of these cases, and a number of cases in other states, can be understood only in light of the United States Supreme Court's decision in *Prigg* v. *Pennsylvania* (1842).[19] Although *Prigg* dealt with the Fugitive Slave Law of 1793, the case had important implications for transit.

Edward Prigg was convicted under Pennsylvania's 1826 personal liberty law for taking a black woman and her children out of the state without a warrant from a Pennsylvania magistrate. In declaring this Pennsylvania statute unconstitutional, Justice Joseph Story reached five major conclusions.

First, he found the 1793 federal Fugitive Slave Law to be constitutional.

Second, he declared that state laws interfering with the rendition of fugitive slaves were unconstitutional. Thus the Pennsylvania law of 1826 was unconstitutional and Prigg's conviction was overturned.

Third, Story determined that state officials could enforce the federal law of 1793 if they wished to, but they could not be required by the federal government to do this. Such a requirement would be an infringement on states' rights. Story also acknowledged that the states could refuse to allow their officers and officials to enforce the federal law. This dictum infuriated Chief Justice Taney, who realized that northern states might prohibit their public servants from participating in the rendition of fugitive slaves and close their jails, courtrooms, and other facilities to masters seeking their runaways. This is precisely what happened in a number of free states.[20]

Fourth, Story declared that masters had a "right of recaption," which would need no judicial enforcement or supervision. Thus, if a

New York Senate Journal, 1841, 480, 484, 487, 488–90, 507, 522–23; Frederick W. Seward, *William H. Seward: An Autobiography from 1801 to 1834 with a Memoir of His Life and Selections from His Letters, from 1831 to 1846* (New York: D. Appleton and Company, 1877) 464–65, 534, 541–42. Thomas D. Morris, *Free Men All: The Personal Liberty Laws of the North, 1780–1861* (Baltimore: Johns Hopkins University Press, 1974) 82–84.

18. *Lemmon* v. *The People*, 20 N.Y. 562 (1860). This case began in the New York Superior Court in 1852. It will be fully discussed in chap. 9.

19. *Prigg* v. *Pennsylvania*, 16 Peters (U.S.) 539, 613 (1842).

20. Ibid. 626–33. For an investigation of how northern courts turned *Prigg* into an antislavery tool, see Paul Finkelman, "*Prigg* v. *Pennsylvania* and Northern State Courts: Anti-Slavery Use of a Pro-Slavery Decision," 25 *Civil War History* (March 1979) 5–35. Story claimed he intended this decision to be a "triumph of freedom." In fact, it was attacked throughout the North as being blatantly proslavery. It became a pro-freedom decision only when applied by local judges in the North in certain cases.

master could capture a runaway "without any breach of the peace or any illegal violence," there was no need to take the slave before a judge or magistrate.[21]

Finally, Story declared that his decision did not prevent the states from passing police regulations to aid in the rendition of fugitive slaves or their removal from the state. Some northerners interpreted this to mean that free states were still allowed to protect free blacks from kidnapping.

While not directly concerned with transit, Story's opinion asserted that an owner returning home with captured fugitive slaves had "exemption from state regulation and control, through however many states he may pass" while "in transitu, to his own domicile." The Constitution would not support the proposition that "the moment he passes the state line he becomes amenable to the laws of another sovereignty, whose regulations may greatly embarrass or delay the exercise of his rights, and even be repugnant to those of the state where he first arrested the fugitive."[22] This position clearly meant that interstate transit with a fugitive slave would have federal protection. But Story made no mention of any other type of transit with a slave. Nor did this dictum indicate how much protection or under what circumstances a master might be protected. Did, for example, protection apply only to a quick and direct return, or could a master complete other business before being forced to return with a captured fugitive slave? Could a professional slave catcher, as the agent of a number of masters, incarcerate fugitives over a period of time and then return them all at once? How the dictum was to apply to other types of transit is also not known. Story may have felt that only transit with a fugitive slave was protected and not other forms of transit. This interpretation is consistent with some of his other legal theories, particularly those expressed in his *Commentaries on the Conflict of Laws*.[23] But other judges could easily have used Story's dictum to support and protect all transit with slaves.

Besides the major conclusions and the dictum on transit with fugitives, Story made a passing reference to one fact of the case

---

21. *Prigg* v. *Pennsylvania* 625.

22. Ibid. 624.

23. Joseph Story, *Commentaries on the Conflict of Laws* (2d ed. Boston: Charles C. Little and James Brown, 1841) 92–93. In this edition, published a year before *Prigg*, Story declared, "Independent of the provisions of the Constitution of the United States, for the protection of the rights of masters in regard to domestic fugitive slaves, there is no doubt that the same principle pervades the common law of the non slaveholding States of America [as in England with the *Somerset* case]; that is to say, foreign slaves would no longer be deemed such after their removal thither." He quoted Shaw's opinion in *Aves* in its entirety to support this position.

that could have affected slave transit. One of the blacks Edward Prigg took to Maryland had been conceived and born in Pennsylvania "more than a year after the said negro woman had fled and escaped from Maryland."[24] Thus, almost without notice the United States Supreme Court overruled one of the basic tenets of the law of freedom—that the child of a slave, born in a free state, could not be claimed as a slave by the mother's owner. Eventually the notion in Story's opinion that such a child could be claimed as a slave was rejected by Pennsylvania courts.

In 1846 a New York judge applied *Prigg* to a case involving a fugitive slave from Georgia. In his decision Justice John W. Edmonds avoided interpreting the repeal of the nine-months law. Nevertheless, he was extremely hostile to slave transit and made it clear that the New York judiciary would not look favorably on masters bringing their slaves into the Empire State.

In October 1846 a ship originating in Savannah, Georgia, entered New York harbor carrying a slave stowaway named George Kirk. Kirk had been discovered when the vessel was near the port of New York. The captain had immediately put Kirk "in chains, and confined him to the hold, with the intention of taking him back to Savannah." The captain acted under a Georgia statute authorizing ships' officers to capture stowaway fugitive slaves.[25]

In response to a writ of habeas corpus, the New York Court of Oyer and Terminer released Kirk. Justice Edmonds ruled that the Georgia law could "not operate beyond her territory" and that the captain was without authority to act. To allow the captain to hold the slave would "be in effect" to have the courts of New York "execute the laws of Georgia," and, in this case, to enforce a law that did not even take effect until the ship entered international waters and Georgia's "boundaries had been passed." Edmonds acknowledged the "obligation of one state to give full faith and credit to the public acts, and judicial proceedings of every other state." But Edmonds was "not aware" that full faith and credit had "ever been carried" to support laws that could be enforced only outside the

24. *Prigg* v. *Pennsylvania* 609.

25. *In re George Kirk*, 1 Parker Cr. R. (N.Y.) 67 (1846); *Matter of George Kirk*, 9 Monthly L. Rep. 355 (1846). The *Monthly Law Reporter* printed two reports of this case. It is more complete than the report in *Parker Cr. R.*, although that reporter (Parker) added a number of interesting details about the case. The most important is that this case was brought by "Lewis Napoleon" who was undoubtedly the same "Louis Napoleon" who brought the complaint six years later in *Lemmon*. This free black man apparently spent a great deal of time on the New York docks, watching, among other things, for any slaves who might be brought in or out of the city. He then swore out writs of habeas corpus and obtained excellent legal counsel through antislavery societies.

jurisdiction in which they were passed. If this were the case, then New York would be subject "to the jurisdiction of at least twenty-seven sovereignties."²⁶

Edmonds saw no place for the Fugitive Slave Law here because the captain could not claim the slave as his own and he was not the designated agent of the owner. While any citizen of Georgia might have the power to arrest a fugitive slave in that state, he clearly had no such power in New York. And New York could not be asked to enforce the Georgia statute giving them that power. This would have created the very extraterritorial effect of Georgia law to which Edmonds objected. While not explicitly saying so, the implication of Edmonds's decision was that New York would not recognize slavery outside the state where it was created, for that too would subject New York to the laws of many sovereignties.

While freeing Kirk, Edmonds did suggest a possible remedy for the ship captain. He noted a New York statute providing "that whenever a person of color, owing service in another state, shall secrete himself on board a vessel and be brought into this state in such vessel, the captain may seize him and take him before the mayor," and after a hearing the mayor could order the slave remanded to the captain. However, since the captain had not complied with the New York law, but had acted under the Georgia statute, which had no force in New York, Edmonds released Kirk. The captain immediately seized Kirk again and this time brought him before the mayor, who authorized his return to the captain. At the instigation of Judge William Jay, a leading abolitionist, the district attorney applied for a second writ of habeas corpus, directed to the "circuit judge."²⁷ The only circuit judge then in New York City was none other than Justice John W. Edmonds.

The question now before Edmonds was the constitutionality of the statute under which the mayor authorized Kirk's detention. Two objections were raised to this statute: first, that it had been repealed by the 1841 repeal of the nine-months law; second, that it was "repugnant" to the United States Constitution.²⁸

Edmonds ducked the first question by ruling that the law violated the Fugitive Slave Clause as interpreted by Justice Story in *Prigg*. Edmonds ignored the ambiguities in *Prigg* as to whether a law that aided rendition was unconstitutional. Instead, he boldly interpreted *Prigg* to mean "that the law of Congress may be truly said to cover the whole ground of the constitution" and "must supersede all state

26. *In re George Kirk*, 9 Monthly L. Rep. 355, 356–58.
27. Ibid. 359–64.
28. Ibid. 366.

legislation on the subject, and by necessary implication, prohibit it."[29] Edmonds adroitly freed a slave without having to interpret New York's recent repeal of the nine-months law. Any disruption of interstate comity had not been his fault, or New York's, because Edmonds had merely followed the guidelines set down by the United States Supreme Court. The implication was clear, however, that New York would favor the slave at the expense of the master.

A year later Edmonds heard the case of Joseph Belt, an alleged fugitive slave from Maryland. Belt had been captured on a New York City street and held incommunicado for two days while his captors waited for passage to Maryland. In the meantime, a writ of habeas corpus brought the case before Edmonds, where John Jay (son of Judge William Jay and grandson of United States Chief Justice John Jay) argued for Belt's liberty. Belt's alleged owner claimed that under *Prigg* Justice Edmonds had no jurisdiction in the case. Jay countered that *Prigg* allowed the state to interfere with the rendition of a fugitive slave if there was a "breach of the peace or illegal violence." Edmonds noted that Belt's captors had made neither a claim under the Fugitive Slave Law nor taken Belt before a federal judge to obtain a certificate of removal. Instead, Belt was kidnapped and held for two days. "If he [Belt's owner] can do this for two days," Edmonds warned, then "he can [do it] for two years or twenty. To justify this, would warrant every slaveholder in the nation to hold his slaves in this state as long as he pleases, notwithstanding slavery was unknown to our laws." This Edmonds would not allow. He would not decide if Belt was a fugitive slave because under *Prigg* that was beyond his jurisdiction. Instead, he freed Belt from the illegal restraint under which he was held.[30] While not relying on the repeal of the nine-months law, Edmonds nevertheless made it clear that transit with slaves would not be tolerated in New York.

Five years after the repeal of the nine-months law, in 1846, New Jersey, finally took steps to end slavery in the state. The remaining slaves were not freed, but instead became indentured servants for life. As such they were supported by their masters and had a certain degree of freedom. The Garden State tempered this "radical" move by also declaring that nonresidents could bring no more than "the usual number" of household slaves with them when they visited New Jersey. No court was ever asked to determine what "the usual number" of slaves was, and the statute remained on the books until after the Civil War.[31]

29. Ibid.

30. *In re Belt*, 1 Parker Cr. R. (N.Y.) 169, 181–82 (1848).

31. Lucius Q. C. Elmer, ed., *Digest of the Laws of New Jersey* (3d ed. Bridgeton:

Pennsylvania

Pennsylvania, the first state to limit slave transit in any significant way, did not attempt to stop it altogether until 1847. Between 1788 and 1847 various new statutes regulated the rendition of fugitive slaves and protected free blacks from kidnapping. The most important of these was declared unconstitutional in *Prigg* v. *Pennsylvania*.

Not until 1847 did the Pennsylvania legislature respond to the *Prigg* decision. Then, as if to make up for lost time, a new personal liberty law was passed with blinding speed. On 6 February 1847, the law was introduced in the House of Representatives, given three readings, and sent to the Senate that afternoon. By 3 March it had passed the Senate and was signed by the governor. The law was ostensibly designed to protect free blacks wrongly arrested as fugitives. But it was also an attempt to protect all blacks, free and fugitive, without violating the rules laid down in *Prigg*. The law withdrew all state support for the federal Fugitive Slave Act; no state judges could enforce the federal law and no state jails could be used to hold fugitive slaves. In the abolitionist strongholds of Pennsylvania, these provisions made it almost impossible for a slaveowner to recapture a fugitive without risking a breach of the peace. And, once a breach of the peace occurred, the right of judicially unsupervised recaption, as explained by Story, would no longer exist.[32] These provisions both suggest that antislavery had become a powerful political force in Pennsylvania by this time and also may indicate a sharp reaction to *Prigg* as an infringement of the right of Pennsylvania to protect its black citizens from arbitrary arrest.

As early as 1806 a Quaker abolitionist argued in a carefully reasoned pamphlet that the Constitution allowed the free states to prohibit slave transit.[33] Indeed, since 1780 numerous petitions had been presented, which "at times poured in like a flood," to repeal the six-months transit law. This campaign reached fruition in 1847, when the six-months clause was repealed in the new law. In addition, slaves were granted the right to testify in court "against any person whatsoever." Under this law any slave brought into the state

---

Elmer and Nixon; Trenton: C. Scott, 1861) 801–10; also see Arthur Zilversmit, *The First Emancipation: The Abolition of Slavery in the North* (Chicago: University of Chicago Press, 1967) 175–89, 215–22.

32. Morris, *Free Men All* 115–17; also see Stanley W. Campbell, *The Slave Catchers: Enforcement of the Fugitive Slave Law, 1850–1860* (Chapel Hill: University of North Carolina Press, 1970) 10–12, 99–101, 151–54.

33. John Parrish, *Remarks on the Slavery of Black People* (Philadelphia: for the author, by Kimber, Conrad and Company, 1806) 31.

could claim immediate freedom and have access to the courts to insure it. Such suits could be initiated by abolitionists and free blacks, who could advise traveling slaves of their rights. Any master attempting to restrain his slave might be faced with the black testifying against him in court. This right, which was not granted to blacks in any of the slave states, was of course a great breach of comity, as far as the slaveowner was concerned. Pennsylvania not only threatened the master-slave relationship with this statute, but also undermined the entire system of race control upon which slavery was based. Following the leads of Massachusetts, Connecticut, and New York, Pennsylvania had gone on record against all slavery in the state.[34]

The Pennsylvania courts quickly repudiated one implication of *Prigg* in *Commonwealth* v. *Auld* (1850),[35] which challenged the right of a master to enslave the children of a runaway. Alexander Burns was born in Pennsylvania only six months after his slave mother escaped from Maryland. Some eighteen years later he was lured into a wagon by a professional slave catcher named Martin C. Auld and against his will was driven to the Maryland home of his mother's owner. Auld was subsequently indicted for kidnapping. In his defense Auld argued three things: the state court had no jurisdiction in a case involving fugitive slaves; the 1847 statute was unconstitutional because it violated the *Prigg* doctrine; and Burns was a slave because his mother was a slave.[36]

Justice Frederick Watts, sitting at the Court of Quarter Sessions of Cumberland County, felt the 1847 statute was constitutional, since it did not deal with fugitive slaves, but with free blacks. He agreed that the state courts had no jurisdiction in any fugitive slave case, but he could not "perceive why the legislature of Pennsylvania may not pass a law to protect the free negroes and mulattoes within her own borders by punishing the crime of kidnapping."[37]

Watts then dealt with Burns's status. If Burns was a slave Auld could not be prosecuted for kidnapping. The rule that a black child followed the status of the mother was acknowledged but rejected. As early as 1816 the Pennsylvania courts freed the child of a fugitive conceived and born in Pennsylvania, but warned that if the child were conceived in a slave state the case would "perhaps, be found to turn on different principles."[38] Ignoring this dictum, Watts saw no

---

34. Edward R. Turner, *Slavery in Pennsylvania* (Baltimore: Lord Baltimore Press, 1911) 86. *Pennsylvania, Laws of 1847* 206–8.

35. *Commonwealth* v. *Auld*, 4 Pa. L.J. (Pa.) 515 (1850).

36. Ibid. 519–21.

37. Ibid. 521.

38. *Commonwealth* v. *Holloway*, 2 S. & R. (Pa.) 304, 305 (1816).

difference in principles. "However strongly we may be disposed to recognize the rights of slave owners in our sister states," he noted in an offhand acknowledgment of comity, "we cannot for a moment question the competency of our legislature to declare, that all children born within this state shall be free." Auld was thus found guilty of kidnapping and imprisoned.[39]

The first reported case to involve the 1847 repeal of the six-months clause came before the Philadelphia Court of Common Pleas in 1848. Lewis Pierce, a slave from New Orleans, was brought to Philadelphia by his master. There he successfully sued for his freedom. Judge King ruled that the constitutional question was "free from real difficulty," for the "State of Pennsylvania like any other independent sovereignty has the clear right to declare that a slave brought within her territory becomes *ipso facto* a freeman." Citing *Somerset* v. *Stewart*, he declared, "[T]his was and is a principle of the Common Law."[40]

While the lower courts in Pennsylvania freed slaves under the six-months repeal, the Pennsylvania Supreme Court never gave a definitive interpretation of the law. In two lengthy and rather bizarre cases, *Kauffman* v. *Oliver* (1849, 1850)[41] and *Passmore Williamson's Case* (1855),[42] the state court made numerous references, both direct and oblique, to the repeal but never completely explained how it should be interpreted. Both cases were also heard in federal courts where the repeal was mentioned. But coming as they do from federal judges, and coming as dicta, these interpretations are not much help in determining what Pennsylvania's policy was toward slaves in transit.

Kauffman v. *Oliver* appears to have been the perfect test case for an interpretation of the revised law. Yet for some unknown reason

39. *Commonwealth* v. *Auld* 521.

40. *In re Lewis Pierce*, 1 W. Legal Observer (Pa.) 14 (1849). This case, reported fully only in this obscure and short-lived law journal, was argued and decided in October 1848. The case is also cited in John Codman Hurd, 2 *The Law of Freedom and Bondage in the United States* (2 vols. Boston: Little, Brown, 1862) 73–74 n. 2. See also the case of *Maria* v. *Kirby*, 12 B. Mon. (Ky.) 542 (1851), in which the Kentucky court refused to accept the decision of a local Pennsylvania judge that a slave became free the moment she was brought to Pennsylvania. This case shows that local judges interpreted the 1847 repeal to mean that slaves brought into the state were immediately free. In 1860 a slave woman "was at once told that she was free" when her master brought her to Philadelphia. Nevertheless, she voluntarily returned to Virginia; Turner, *Slavery in Pennsylvania* 87.

41. *Kauffman* v. *Oliver*, 10 Pa. St. 514 (1849); *Oliver* v. *Kauffman et al.*, 18 F. Cas. 657 (1850); *Oliver* v. *Weakley*, 18 F. Cas. 678 (1853).

42. *United States ex rel. Wheeler* v. *Williamson*, 28 F. Cas. 682 (1855), and 28 F. Cas. 686 (1855); *Passmore Williamson's Case*, 26 Pa. St. 9 (1855); *Williamson* v. *Lewis*, 39 Pa. St. 9 (1861).

the question was never raised in the state court. In May 1847, two months after the new law was passed, Mrs. Cecilia Oliver brought twelve slaves from Arkansas to her native Maryland. En route they passed through Pennsylvania. In October the slaves ran back to Pennsylvania, where they were aided by Daniel Kauffman and others. Oliver alleged that Kauffman actually went into Maryland and urged the slaves to run away. After failing to recapture the slaves, Oliver sued Kauffman in the Cumberland County Court of Common Pleas; the action was one at common law to recover the value of the slaves. Kauffman did not deny any of the alleged acts. Instead, he argued that because the case involved fugitive slaves, Oliver's remedy lay with the federal rather than the state courts. The trial court gave judgment for Oliver, and the case was appealed to the Pennsylvania Supreme Court.[43]

Speaking for a unanimous court, Justice Richard Coulter reversed the decision against Kauffman on grounds of jurisdiction. He agreed with Kauffman that only the federal courts had jurisdiction in a case dealing with fugitive slaves and cited *Prigg* as the ruling precedent. He then discussed the common law aspect of the case, for, although Kauffman could be convicted of criminal charges only under the federal act, this might not necessarily preclude the common law action for damages. But this was possible only if Pennsylvania's common law recognized slavery and slave property. Coulter noted that *Somerset* "was decided before the Revolution" and "became the common law" of Pennsylvania, except as modified only by the Fugitive Slave Clause of the United States Constitution. Under this reasoning slavery did not exist in Pennsylvania, and no common law suit for the value of a slave could be maintained. Indeed, "even persuading the fugitive to fly, would be no offense in Pennsylvania, whatever it might be in Maryland."[44]

In reversing Kauffman's conviction the court made one of its strongest statements against the recognition of slavery in Pennsylvania. Yet it is curious that an even stronger statement was not made. Kauffman did not deny that he might have violated the federal Fugitive Slave Law. In fact, he used that argument to avoid the state court action. Kauffman, it seems, would have been on much stronger ground had he asserted that the blacks in question were not slaves at all. He could have argued that the blacks had been voluntarily brought to Pennsylvania by their owner after the six-months law had been repealed. Because of that, he might have argued they had become instantly free, and once free they would

43. *Oliver* v. *Kauffman* 657–58; *Kauffman* v. *Oliver* 517.
44. *Kauffman* v. *Oliver* 517.

always be free. Under this reasoning the blacks running back to Pennsylvania would not have been fugitive slaves, but free persons, going where they chose to go. But Kauffman did not argue along these lines, and the Pennsylvania Supreme Court did not have an opportunity to interpret the repeal of the six-months law.

Oliver then sued in federal court to obtain monetary damages that were allowed under the 1793 Fugitive Slave Law. Kauffman again failed to use the six-months repeal in his defense. Instead, he claimed that he was merely charitably aiding travelers whom he had no way of knowing were fugitive slaves. Although ten jurors thought Kauffman liable for damages, two did not, and the jury was dismissed. A second trial resulted in a monetary judgment against Kauffman.[45]

The meaning of the six-months repeal was also at issue in a series of cases involving Passmore Williamson. Most of Williamson's legal battles were fought in federal district court, before Judge John K. Kane, and as such they will be more fully discussed in chapter 8. However, the slave transit questions raised by his case were also argued in two different Pennsylvania courts.

Williamson was an official of the Pennsylvania Abolition Society. In July 1855 he was informed that three slaves had been brought into Philadelphia by their master, but that they were about to be removed from the state. The slaves belonged to John H. Wheeler, the United States minister to Nicaragua. Wheeler, en route to his diplomatic post, had stopped in Philadelphia for a few hours to attend to some personal business. Williamson and a number of blacks arrived at Wheeler's ship a few minutes before it was scheduled to sail. They boarded the ship and Williamson informed the slaves they were free under Pennsylvania law. Wheeler attempted to prevent his slaves from leaving, but was unsuccessful. As the slaves left with a group of free blacks, Williamson gave Wheeler his card and then he also left. Wheeler soon obtained a writ of habeas corpus from Federal District Judge Kane, commanding Williamson to bring the slaves into federal court. In his return of the writ, Williamson asserted he did not have the slaves in his custody and in fact that he had never had them in his custody. Judge Kane felt this was evasive, if not false, and cited Williamson for contempt. A bizarre series of hearings followed, along with an extended imprisonment for Williamson, which made him an antislavery martyr. The hearings before Judge Kane, which took place in federal district court, will be discussed in chapter 8.[46]

45. *Oliver* v. *Kauffman* 660; *Oliver* v. *Weakley* 678.
46. *United States ex rel. Wheeler* v. *Williamson*; *Passmore Williamson's Case*;

While in prison under Judge Kane's order, Williamson applied to the Pennsylvania Supreme Court for a writ of habeas corpus. Wheeler in turn complained to a grand jury about the abduction of his slaves, and five black men, who had helped Williamson rescue the three slaves, were indicted for riot, assault, and battery.

Before the Pennsylvania Supreme Court Williamson argued that he was illegally held by Judge Kane because the federal courts had never had any legitimate jurisdiction in the case. This argument was supported by the contention that the slaves became free the moment they entered the state and thus were not subject to the federal jurisdiction under the Fugitive Slave Clause or laws. Therefore Judge Kane had no authority to issue the writ and could not detain Williamson for his response to the writ. Williamson wanted the state court to free him from the clutches of a federal judge who disregarded the law and abused his power.

In deciding the case, Justice Jeremiah S. Black callously rejected the questions raised by Williamson. He refused to "go behind the proceedings in which" Williamson was incarcerated and to examine if "the sentence for contempt is void, because the court had no jurisdiction" over the entire issue. Instead, Black asserted the power of the federal courts to conduct their own affairs and a lack of power on the part of the state courts to interfere with federal court decisions. Justice Walter Lowrie concurred in the result but doubted that the federal courts legitimately had jurisdiction in the original case. This reasoning of course left Williamson in prison for resisting illegitimate or illegal authority, with no remedy open to him, except an appeal to the abuser of authority (Judge Kane) who had originally sent him to prison. In an unpublished dissent Justice John C. Knox asserted that when it appears from the record that a court did not have jurisdiction, it is permissible in a habeas corpus hearing to examine the facts behind an alleged illegal imprisonment. Doing so, Knox concluded that the slaves were free the moment they were brought into the state, thus Judge Kane had no authority over them.[47] Thus two justices were on record as interpreting the six-

---

John K. Kane, *Case of Passmore Williamson* (Philadelphia: Uriah Hunt and Son, 1856); *Narrative of the Facts in the Case of Passmore Williamson* (Philadelphia: Pennsylvania Anti-Slavery Society, 1855); Ralph Lowell Eckert, "The Ordeal of Passmore Williamson," 100 *Pennsylvania Magazine of History and Biography* 521–38 (1976).

47. *Passmore Williamson's Case*, 26 Pa. St. 9, 19, 24–27 (1855). Portions of Judge Knox's unpublished opinion are found in *Narrative of the Facts in the Case of Passmore Williamson* 18–21. The Western Anti-Slavery Society meeting in Ohio thought the state courts "had acquiesced in the monstrous claim of the slave power" and "thus the State Judiciary of Pennsylvania was thoroughly subdued, and the work that was desired by the slavepower really done," despite the fact that Williamson was released

months repeal to mean instant freedom for blacks brought into the state, while the other three members of the Pennsylvania Supreme Court had successfully avoided the issue.

The issue was not avoided, however, in the criminal trial of the five rescuers indicted for riot, assault, and battery. At their trial Wheeler testified that his slaves, Jane Johnson and her two sons, had not wanted their freedom and had been forced from his custody by the rioting blacks. However, in a dramatic gambit orchestrated by antislavery groups with the aid of the police department, Jane Johnson appeared as a surprise witness. She refuted all of Wheeler's testimony and then was hurried off from the courtroom under heavy police protection. Although she was willing to testify at this trial, she would not appear before Judge Kane because she assumed he would return her to servitude. Indeed, federal marshals were prepared to seize her and bring her to Kane when they heard she was testifying, but the city police protected her. Ultimately two of the defendants were convicted of assault on Wheeler (for threatening to cut his throat from ear to ear), fined ten dollars, and sentenced to one week in prison. They were acquitted on the other charges, while the remaining defendants were acquitted on all charges. These acquittals were no doubt influenced by the judge's charge to the jury "that when Col. Wheeler and his servants crossed the border of Pennsylvania, Jane Johnson and her sons became as free as he." Thus, despite the inconclusive interpretation of the six-months repeal by the state supreme court, a trial judge in Philadelphia concluded that the repeal freed all slaves coming into the state.[48]

In 1856 the Judiciary Committee of the Pennsylvania House of Representatives attempted to resolve the meaning of the six-months repeal. However, the committee split sharply on its interpretation of the law. A minority of the committee held that the repeal meant that all slaves, except fugitives, became free the moment they entered the state. The majority thought this interpretation was far too broad. They believed that the repeal

> hugs the wind closely, and sails between the rock of
> the Constitution on the one hand, and the whirlpool of its
> open repudiation on the other. It does not purport to take away

---

from prison and Jane Johnson retained her freedom; "Report of the Executive Committee," in Western Anti-Slavery Society Minutebook (LC), 14th annual meeting, 1856. At least one modern federal jurist suggests that the state court in this case, and similar ones, may indeed have had the power to release prisoners held on federal charges; see Richard S. Arnold, "The Power of State Courts to Enjoin Federal Officers," 73 *Yale Law Journal* 1385 (1964).

48. *Narrative of the Facts in the Case of Passmore Williamson* 11–17.

from their masters, the domestic slaves attending upon their persons, as they pass through this State. It does not prohibit the bringing of them within it. It only forbids the *bringing and retaining* of them here. It may affect the slaves of *sojourners*, but it cannot reach persons or slaves *in transitu*, because they are not both *brought and retained* within this Commonwealth.

Indeed, the majority of the committee believed that slave transit was protected by the United States Constitution and to interpret the repeal as interfering with transit would "disgrace our Commonwealth in the eyes of the civilized world. . . ."[49] This report, coming nearly a decade after the repeal, cannot be considered a definitive interpretation of the repeal. Rather, it must be seen as the opinion of Democratic politicians in Pennsylvania in an important election year.

Perhaps the best analysis of Pennsylvania's law came from an outsider. Missouri Senator Thomas Hart Benton acknowledged Pennsylvania's "right to repeal" the "sojourning law of 1780." But he felt the entire act of 1847 was "the exercise of a mere right, against the comity which is due to States united under a common head, against moral and social duty, against high national policy, against the spirit in which the constitution was made, against her own previous conduct for sixty years; and injurious and irritating to the people of the slave States. . . ." Benton thought the 1780 act "was just and wise, and in accordance with the spirit of comity which should prevail among States formed into a Union, having a common general government, and reciprocating the rights of citizenship. Benton was most disturbed at the repeal of the six-months clause of the 1780 act. Congress could counteract the ill effects of Pennsylvania's refusal to enforce the Fugitive Slave Law of 1793; in fact this was partially accomplished by the Fugitive Slave Law of 1850. But the repeal of the six-months clause was a "radical injury" for which there was "no remedy in federal legislation."[50]

Free Soil in the Northeast

By 1860 the states of the Northeast offered little hospitality to the master who brought his slaves north. Only in New Jersey could

---

49. *Report of the Committee on the Judiciary of the House of Representatives of Pennsylvania, in Relation to the Rights of Transit of Slave Property Through This State* (Harrisburg, 1856); Pennsylvania, General Assembly, House of Representatives, Committee on the Judiciary, *Minority Report in Relation to the Rights of Transit of Slave Property Through This State* ([Philadelphia?], 1856).

50. Benton, 2 *Thirty Years View* 774–75.

such slaves be kept without any legal problems. In Pennsylvania the statutory law was clear, even if there was no definitive court ruling on the subject. The repeal of the six-months law meant that any slave brought into the state was a free person. Lower courts in Pennsylvania had determined this on a number of occasions. It would only have been a matter of time before the Pennsylvania Supreme Court would have had an opportunity to rule on the question. The Civil War of course prevented such a ruling.

In the rest of the Northeast there was even less ambiguity. New York and all of New England were emphatically on record opposing any slavery within their jurisdictions. The precedents set by Chief Justice Lemuel Shaw in Francisco's case and *Commonwealth* v. *Aves* had become the law of the land, for this part of the nation.

Chapter 6

The Northern Rejection
of Comity: The West

In the nine free states west of Pennsylvania, slavery was prohibited by various acts of the national, territorial, and state legislatures. Six of these—Michigan, Wisconsin, Minnesota, Iowa, California, and Oregon—were quite distant from the usual traveling routes of most slaveowners. Consequently, their records contain few or no cases dealing with slave transit. Only California showed an inclination to allow transit with slaves.[1] Oregon was openly hostile to the presence of any blacks, slave or free.[2] The other four were antislavery and Republican bastions where neither slavery nor slave transit could expect any support. The scattered court records and statutes from these states indicate that slave transit would not have been tolerated, assuming that any master was foolish enough to risk his valuable property in them.[3]

Comity along the Ohio and Mississippi Rivers

The long river borders that separated the free states of Ohio, Indiana, and Illinois from the slave states of Virginia, Kentucky, and Missouri provided the setting for potential conflicts over slave transit and sojourn. The rivers themselves created artificial boundaries between slavery and freedom, which many masters ignored. It was

1. *In re Perkins*, 2 Cal. 424 (1852) and *Ex parte Archy*, 9 Cal. 147 (1858). For a detailed discussion of the western states not analyzed here, see Paul Finkelman, "A More Perfect Union? Slavery, Comity, and Federalism, 1787–1861" (Ph.D. dissertation, University of Chicago, 1976) 153–64.

2. See Finkelman, "A More Perfect Union?" Oregon's 1859 constitution prohibited the immigration of blacks into the state. The last vestiges of this clause were not repealed until 1971.

3. See Finkelman, "A More Perfect Union?" For Iowa, see also *Daggs v. Frazer*, 6 F. Cas. 1112 (1849) and *In the matter of Ralph, (A Colored Man) On Habeas Corpus*, 1 Morr. (Iowa) 1 (1839); and generally see V. Jacque Voegeli, *Free But Not Equal: The Midwest and the Negro during the Civil War* (Chicago: University of Chicago Press, 1967), especially 2, 38, 89, 166.

not uncommon for masters to take their slaves with them on short trips for business or pleasure into Ohio, Indiana, or Illinois. Some masters even allowed their slaves to enter these states without any supervision. Some sent their slaves across the river on errands, to earn money, to work land, or to help friends or neighbors. Sometimes these slaves refused to return to their masters and claimed their freedom on the basis of time spent in a free state. Other slaves simply used the opportunity offered by a visit to a free state to disappear, relying on their feet and their wits, rather than the courts, to free them.[4]

Besides the easy access to freedom provided by the close proximity of these three states to the slave states, the location of the rivers and the geography of the states had an important effect on east-west trade and travel. The Ohio River was one of the main routes to the West. Slaveowners moving from Virginia or Maryland to Kentucky, Missouri, Tennessee, or even the lower Mississippi area would probably have spent some time on the Ohio River. Most riverboats stopped on both sides of the river, which meant that a slaveowner might find himself and his slaves standing on free soil at some point during their journey across the nation. The overland route from east to west also went through these three states. Indeed, the better roads and later the better railroads in the North made it far easier to cross Ohio, Indiana, or Illinois than to cross Kentucky.

Thus, for Indiana, Illinois, and Ohio slave transit was a real and ever-present problem. Slave transit also created dilemmas in this part of the country that were not apparent in the Northeast. The economies of these states depended, in part at least, on travelers from and trade with the slave states. An immediate and absolute application of the *Aves* doctrine might have led to severe economic problems. It would have also led to a great number of blacks being freed in, and living in, these states. Many of the people in this area were southern-born and extremely negrophobic. As the many race riots in Cincinnati and the killing of the abolitionist journalist Elijah Lovejoy at Alton, Illinois, in 1837 indicate, large black populations (and the concomitant abolitionist activity) might not have been tolerated here.[5] On the other hand, refusing to free slaves

4. See, for example, *Strader et al.* v. *Graham*, 5 B. Mon. (Ky.) 173 (1844) discussed in chap. 7, where slaves used their easy access to Ohio and Indiana to escape Kentucky and make their way to Canada.

5. Leonard L. Richards, *"Gentlemen of Property and Standing": Anti-Abolition Mobs in Jacksonian America* (New York: Oxford University Press, 1970) 34–35, 40–43, 69, 92–101, 113, 122–50. There were major racially linked riots in Cincinnati in 1829, 1836, 1841, and 1843; William S. Lincoln, *Alton Trials* (New York: John F. Trow, 1838).

brought into these states might have allowed the covert introduction of slavery. It would have been very easy to hire out slaves for short periods of time on the free side of the Ohio or the Mississippi River. This practice would have undermined the value of free white labor in the eyes of many residents. It would also have destroyed the free-state institutions they were trying to establish. Such a lax policy would also have clashed with the growing antislavery sentiment, particularly in Ohio. Finally, these states felt political and intellectual pressures from some of their own citizens and the rest of the nation to follow the trend set by *Aves*. Judges who considered themselves within the mainstream of the profession found it difficult to resist the precedents of such an able jurist as Lemuel Shaw.

Each of the free states along the Ohio River dealt with the questions raised by slave transit and sojourn in a different way. While all three started from the same position, only Indiana resisted the political and judicial pressures for change. In Illinois the judiciary moved in one direction, while the legislature adopted an entirely different course. Naturally, in an age before judicial activism, the legislature wound up the winner, although the victory was ultimately incomplete. In Ohio the legislature and the bench were finally persuaded that no forms of slavery should be tolerated in that state.

Indiana

In 1831 the Indiana legislature explicitly declared that masters in transit could bring their slaves through the state without any interference from the courts. Twenty years later the Indiana Constitution of 1851 prohibited *all* blacks from entering the state. This was enforced by an 1852 statute that was upheld by the state supreme court in 1856 and 1862.[6]

Between 1831 and the end of the Civil War no cases concerning slaves in transit were brought before the Indiana Supreme Court, and there are no printed records of lower court cases on the subject. It is unlikely that the supreme court (or most of the lower courts) would have been sympathetic to the cause of any black who tried to assert freedom in Indiana.[7] The general policy of the state was to

6. *Barkshire* v. *State*, 7 Ind. 389 (1856); *Hatwood* v. *State*, 18 Ind. 492.

7. Voegeli, *Free But Not Equal* 170. Not all of Indiana was so solicitous to slaveholders. The reputation of the Midwest as negrophobic must be tempered with an understanding that a large minority of the population of that area—and often the majority in certain locales—was strongly abolitionist and at least moderately equalitarian. In 1849, for example, John Norris, a Kentucky master, captured his fugi-

discourage the growth of its black population. Freeing slaves in transit would have had the opposite effect. In the antebellum period many slaveowners undoubtedly crossed Indiana without difficulty.

Illinois and Ohio

Unlike Indiana, Illinois and Ohio were the scene of numerous transit cases. Both states had long borders with slave states and important river ports where ships carrying slaves often stopped. Abolitionist strongholds could be found in both states, although they were much more prevalent and powerful in Ohio. This is one of the main reasons for the contrast in the development of the law of slave transit between the two states. In Ohio antislavery sentiment grew to be quite strong, often militant, and was manifested in the political ascension of such leaders as Joshua Reed Giddings and Salmon Portland Chase. In Illinois, on the other hand, few antislavery politicians reached positions of power before the late 1850s.

The political power of the antislavery movement in Ohio and the talent of such abolitionist lawyers as Chase ultimately made Ohio a leader in the North's judicial war against slavery. Indeed, while Abraham Lincoln was defending the rights of slaveowners who visited Illinois, Chase and other Ohio attorneys were effectively attacking slavery in the courtrooms.[8] By 1860 slaveowners found

---

tive slaves in Cass County, Michigan, and attempted to return home with them. Outside South Bend, Indiana, the trip was interrupted by over 140 armed men led by Edwin B. Crocker, the county sheriff. After Crocker served Norris with a writ of habeas corpus, a local judge released the slaves. Norris obtained a warrant under an Indiana statute and the slaves were recaptured and jailed. But the local judge "instead of aiding the plaintiff in the recovery & safekeeping of his slaves according to law, . . . aided the mob in their rescue" and granted a second writ of habeas corpus. Norris declined to challenge this writ for fear of his life. The slaveowner later sued in federal court and won a $2,850 judgment; *Norris* v. *Newton*, 18 F. Cas. 322 (1850); *Norris* v. *Crocker*, 13 Howard (U.S.) 429 (1851). The above quotation is from Thomas Metcalfe to John J. Crittenden, 7 June 1850, John J. Crittenden Papers, v. 14, Library of Congress (LC), Washington. For another example of violent antislavery actions in Indiana see n. 39 in chap. 8.

8. Abraham Lincoln argued for the slaveowner and lost, in *In re Jane, A Woman of Color*, 5 Western L. J. (Ill.) 202 (1848). Despite Lincoln's legal talent, Jane and her ten children gained their freedom through residence in Illinois. In 1841, on the other hand, Lincoln had helped a slave gain her freedom in *Bailey* v. *Cromwell*, 3 Scam. 71 (1841). Lincoln's most recent, and sympathetic, biographer declares that this "illustrates the essentially pragmatic approach to the [fugitive slave] law he [Lincoln] and most other attorneys adopted"; Stephen B. Oates, *With Malice Toward None: The Life of Abraham Lincoln* (New York: Harper and Row, Publishers, Inc., 1977) 109–10. Lincoln's willingness to take the case of a slaveowner, when he was at the height of

statutory protection for their slaves, although not necessarily enthusiastic judicial support, in Illinois. In Ohio, on the other hand, they could expect no support in the legislature or the courts.

Illinois

Before Illinois could develop a policy for dealing with slaves in transit, the state had to emancipate the remaining slaves within its borders. Although slavery had been prohibited by the Northwest Ordinance and the Illinois Constitution, as late as 1845 there were slaves in the state, the descendants of slaves owned by the original French settlers of the area, who were exempted from the provisions of the Northwest Ordinance in a long series of decisions by the Illinois Supreme Court.[9] That court reversed itself on this issue in *Jarrot* v. *Jarrot* (1845).[10]

Julia Jarrot claimed "a right to hold" Joseph Jarrot "in perpetual bondage, as a descendant of an old French slave held in bondage" before 1787. After reviewing the history of slavery in Illinois, Justice Walter B. Scates freed Joseph, citing *Aves* and *Somerset* as the ruling precedents for his decision. He also cited a series of southern cases that held that slaves residing in, or born in, the Northwest Territory were entitled to their freedom. With an uncanny ability to ignore earlier Illinois cases, including many decisions he himself wrote, Scates concluded that in Illinois "[t]he presumption is in favor of liberty." Almost sixty years after the Northwest Ordinance was written, the Illinois Supreme Court finally concluded that the words "there shall be neither slavery nor involuntary servitude" meant that slaves could not be held there. The state constitution, with a similar clause, clearly freed any slave born in Illinois after

his prepresidential political career underscores the difference between Ohio and Illinois. Salmon P. Chase, Lincoln's counterpart in Ohio and a leading rival for the 1860 Republican presidential nomination, was at this very time building a political career that was strongly based on antislavery activity. Indeed, Chase was willing to sacrifice his election to the United States Senate in 1849 in order to insure the repeal of Ohio's black laws; Salmon P. Chase Diary, 1845–59, pp. 18–19 (manuscript) in Salmon P. Chase Papers, box 1, LC. See also, Louis S. Gerteis, "Salmon P. Chase, Radicalism, and the Politics of Emancipation, 1861–1864," 60 *Journal of American History* 42–62 (June 1973).

   9. For example, see *Nance* v. *Howard*, Breese (Ill.) 182 (1828); *Phoebe* v. *Jay*, Breese (Ill.) 207 (1828); *Boon* v. *Juliet*, 1 Scam. (Ill.) 258 (1836); *Choisser* v. *Hargrave*, 1 Scam. (Ill.) 317 (1836); *Williams* v. *Jarrot*, 1 Gil. (Ill.) 120 (1843). Many of these cases involved "indentured servants" whose term of service could be as long as eighty years.

   10. *Jarrot* v. *Jarrot*, 2 Gil. (Ill.) 1 (1845).

its adoption. Scates regretted "the impolicy or injustice of taking away one man's property by a fundamental law in order to restore another his liberty," but he left the question of morality "to be settled by the philanthropic, the good, the humane, and the just."[11]

A majority of the justices concurred in this opinion, although Chief Justice William Wilson was "not prepared to say, that if the plaintiff was a slave before the adoption of the Constitution, that he could now assert his liberty." Three judges dissented, presumably on the grounds that some type of slavery might still exist in the state. They wrote no opinion.[12]

Two years before *Jarrot* v. *Jarrot*, the state supreme court had heard the case of *Eells* v. *The People* (1843),[13] which suggested where the court stood on slave transit. Eells was indicted for harboring a slave from Missouri, contrary to Illinois law. Eells argued that this law was unconstitutional because only the United States Congress, according to *Prigg*, could legislate on the issue of fugitive slaves. The majority of the court, however, upheld the act because it did not interfere with the master's recovering a fugitive slave. Justice James Shield's majority opinion also suggested that the law was passed "to prevent the influx of that most unacceptable population." If blacks, slave or free, were unacceptable, then the Illinois court would not be anxious to free them in the state.[14] The Prairie State was not interested in actively opposing slavery if such a position meant that more blacks would live in the state.

Three judges, Samuel D. Lockwood, Thomas C. Browne, and Chief Justice Wilson dissented. Speaking for them, Lockwood noted that there was no proof the slave entered Illinois as a fugitive. "Did his master bring him here, and hire him out?" the judged asked. If so, "then he became free."[15] No Illinois precedents upheld that position. It is also difficult to determine whether Lockwood thought that just the act of bringing a slave into Illinois freed him or that the hiring out was the determining factor. The facts in *Eells* indicate that the slave was brought into the state by his master, but this was not discussed by counsel for Eells or the majority justices and Lockwood made only an oblique reference to it.[16] Earlier in the same session,

11. Ibid. 12.

12. Ibid. 32.

13. *Eells* v. *The People*, 4 Scam. (Ill.) 498 (1843).

14. Ibid. 511.

15. Ibid. 511, 513, 518.

16. Ibid. *Eells* was later appealed to the U.S. Supreme Court as *Moore* v. *The People of Illinois*, 14 Howard (U.S.) 13 (1852). The court determined that the Illinois statute under which Dr. Eells was prosecuted was not unconstitutional. In so doing the court cleared up any still existing misunderstandings about the power of the states to legislate on fugitive slaves: as long as the legislation appeared to benefit the

in *Willard* v. *The People* (1843),[17] the supreme court had determined that a slave voluntarily brought into the state did not automatically become free. There only Lockwood and Wilson had dissented, while Browne did not sit on the case. Although still a minority, the anti-slavery judges on the Illinois court were at least able to lay the groundwork for an eventual change in the state's policy toward slavery and slaves in transit.

In 1847, Chief Justice Wilson wrote a decision upholding his dissenting position in *Eells*. The case, *In re Jane, A Woman of Color*,[18] was heard by Wilson and Associate Justice Samuel Treat while both were riding circuit in Coles County. Jane and her four children had been brought to Illinois in 1845 by General Robert Mateson of Kentucky. Mateson owned land in both states but maintained his permanent residence and most of his slaves in Kentucky. Although he had brought slaves into Illinois before 1845, this was the first time he kept one there for more than a few months. Citing the common law, the United States Constitution, the Illinois Constitution, and Justice Bushrod Washington's decision in *Ex parte Simmons*, Chief Justice Wilson concluded that slaves voluntarily brought into Illinois were free. Neither Mateson's "declared intentions" nor his permanent residence in Kentucky would "countervail the fact that he voluntarily domiciled his servants here for two years or upwards." But the time of domicile was not important, for if "they had remained but a day, the circumstance of his having transferred their domicil from Kentucky, and fixed it in Illinois, would have produced the same result." Wilson declared that "by bringing Jane" into Illinois "and domiciling" her there, Mateson had lost all claim to her.[19]

It is unclear from Wilson's opinion if "bringing" but not "domiciling" a slave in Illinois would also result in freedom. The dissent in *Eells*, in which Wilson concurred, suggests that it would. *In re Jane* was not appealed to the full Illinois Supreme Court, because Mateson was "an extremely kind and indulgent master," who at the

---

claimant it was not contrary to the Fugitive Slave Clause of the Constitution, as interpreted in *Prigg* v. *Pennsylvania*. In this case the Supreme Court did not get to the issue of slave transit. By the time of the appeal Eells, a well-known antislavery proponent, had died and his executor appealed in an attempt to relieve the estate of Eells's fine. It is also possible that Eells's executor had the same antislavery sentiments as Eells and wished to win a favorable precedent. Senator Salmon P. Chase, who was associated with the appeal, wrote Gerrit Smith asking for his assistance. This suggests the antislavery movement wished to make this case another forum for antislavery. Chase to Gerrit Smith, 11 Dec. 1852, Salmon P. Chase Papers, LC.

17. *Willard* v. *The People*, 4 Scam. (Ill.) 461 (1843), discussed in chap. 3.
18. *In re Jane, A Woman of Color*, 5 Western L. J. (Ill.) 202 (1848).
19. Ibid.; see n. 8 above.

circuit court "showed every disposition to submit to the result of an adjudication upon his claim." It is of course impossible to tell how Mateson would have fared before the full court, but one clue may be found in Justice Treat's acquiescence to Wilson's opinion. Treat had previously been a "proslavery" justice, dissenting in *Jarrot* v. *Jarrot*.[20] His silent concurrence in *In re Jane* may have been indicative of a shift toward freedom on the Illinois court.

The suspicion of this shift was confirmed four years later in *Hone* v. *Ammons* (1852).[21] An alleged fugitive slave was fraudulently sold to Ammons by Hone. Hone sued Ammons for payment on the promissory note and, after losing in the circuit court, appealed to the state supreme court. In the circuit court the jury decided the black was not a slave and therefore the sale was void. Speaking for the court, Justice John Caton declared that in Illinois "the presumption of law was that he was a free man." Only if the man in question could be proved to be a fugitive might he be claimed as a slave. This had not been done, so the presumption of freedom prevailed, and the note was void for lack of a sufficient consideration. Thus the court finally accepted the argument first made by Lockwood, in *Eells*, that a slave brought into Illinois could not be claimed as a fugitive slave. In upholding the circuit court, however, the supreme court could offer no new definition of the status of slaves in Illinois, because the lower court had determined that the black had never been a slave. Justice Lyman Trumbull understood this point, but did not want to miss an opportunity to attack slavery.[22]

Although too ill to meet with his fellow justices and about to leave the court for a career in the United States Senate, Trumbull was concerned enough about this case and its implications to write letters to Caton and Chief Justice Treat. He also wrote a concurring opinion that went to the critical questions implied by the case—could a slave, fugitive or otherwise, be sold in Illinois? In doing so he accepted the contention that the slave was in fact a fugitive who owed service in Missouri when he was captured by Hone. Trumbull argued that when "the master sold the negro if the sale was valid, he ceased to owe service or labor in the State of Missouri, under the laws thereof." If the slave "owed service anywhere, it was in the State of Illinois, to one of its citizens, under its laws." However, Illinois had "no law authorizing the holding of persons in slavery." Thus, "[t]he moment the master sold the slave in" Illinois, "to one of its citizens, he ceased to be a fugitive from any other, and . . . by the very act of selling the slave here, his master must be considered as having

20. *Jarrot* v. *Jarrot* 2 Gil. 1, 32 (1845).
21. *Hone* v. *Ammons*, 14 Ill. 29 (1852).
22. Ibid. 29, 31–32.

consented to his coming and remaining here; and this made him free." Again, it is difficult to determine whether the act of consenting to the slave *coming* to Illinois, or to his *remaining* in Illinois, or both, worked to free the slave. Nevertheless, the direction of Trumbull's thinking is clear.[23]

Whatever the justices of the Illinois Supreme Court may have intended, the state legislature attempted to resolve the entire matter in 1853 with the passage of a comprehensive anti-Negro statute. This law prohibited bringing any slave into the state "for any purpose," including manumission. It also prohibited free blacks from entering the state. Those who did come to Illinois could be fined or sold "at public auction" for a limited period of time to pay the fine. Masters claiming fugitive slaves fined under the law had to pay the fines and any other costs before they could remove their slave. The one major exception to this procedure was that the statute should "not be construed so as to affect persons or slaves *bona fide* traveling through this state from and to any other state in the United States."[24]

The prohibition against blacks entering the state was upheld in 1855 and again in 1864. During the Civil War, however, thousands of blacks actually entered the state, and although much protest and some riots resulted, few prosecutions occurred.[25] Despite the act of 1853, in *Rodney* v. *Illinois Central Railroad* (1857),[26] the Illinois court asserted that "negroes within our jurisdiction are presumed to be free." This case involved a suit to recover the value of a fugitive slave who successfully eluded his master by boarding an Illinois Central Railroad train at Cairo. In rejecting the master's claim, the Illinois court declared that the "plaintiff, under the local law, where the alleged conversion occurred, had no property in the negro" because "property in persons" was "repugnant" to the "laws and genius" of Illinois. The decision implied that a slave gained freedom under Illinois law by entering the state. Nevertheless, the 1853 law allowing masters transit across the state remained in force until 1865. In "The Land of Lincoln," comity between the states was clearly more important than any antislavery ideology. In addition, antiblack sentiment was much stronger in Illinois during this period

23. Ibid. 31–32; Lyman Trumbull to John D. Caton, 29 June 1853, John D. Caton Papers, box 5, (LC).

24. *Illinois Session Laws, 1853*, Act of February 12, 1853, 57.

25. *Glenn et al.* v. *The People*, 17 Ill. 104 (1855); in upholding the statute the court nevertheless freed Glenn. *Nelson (a mulatto)* v. *The People*, 33 Ill. 390 (1864); Voegeli, *Free But Not Equal* 17–18, 88–89. Leon F. Litwack, *North of Slavery: The Negro in the Free States, 1790–1860* (Chicago: University of Chicago Press, 1961) 67–71.

26. *Rodney* v. *Illinois Central Railroad Company*, 19 Ill. 42 (1857).

than antislavery sentiment. The South's fears of Lincoln were certainly not justified by the legislation of his adopted home state, which was more hostile to free blacks than slavery.[27]

Ohio

Ohio, more than any other state, faced the problems and dilemmas of slave transit. What was for Massachusetts almost an academic problem, and for Illinois and Indiana an occasional incident, was for Ohio nearly a day-to-day occurrence. Three aspects of the state's geography led to this situation. First, the Cumberland, or National, Road, crossed Ohio, providing the main land route west for many slaveowners from Virginia, Maryland, and Delaware. More important than the road was the state's long river border with Virginia and Kentucky. The Ohio River was one of the main "highways" for all Americans traveling west. Finally, in the antebellum period Cincinnati was the most important city west of the Atlantic coast; by 1850 it was the fifth largest in the nation. As the nation's fourth largest manufacturing city, Cincinnati was a major trading center for southerners. When not coming to Cincinnati for industrial goods, some slaveowners from as far away as Louisiana came to "Porkopolis" to buy meat for their chattels. As early as 1826 one resident asserted, with some justification, that the city's trade was "co-extensive with steamboat navigation on the western waters." Virtually all river traffic stopped at the "Queen City of the West," and even the most scrupulous master might be unable to avoid bringing his "servant" into Ohio. Thus, a great number of slaves, both in transit and fugitive, entered Ohio during the antebellum period. Their presence aroused hostility, sometimes led to violence, and eventually became a major political and legal issue in the Buckeye State.[28]

Ohio's early concerns were not with slaves, but with blacks in general. The 1803 state constitution permitted blacks no political rights (including denial of the franchise) but left them with no other special disabilities either. This "omission" was soon rectified. In 1804 the legislature passed an act "to regulate black and mulatto

27. Ibid. 45–46; Voegeli, *Free But Not Equal, passim*; Litwack, *North of Slavery, passim*.

28. Richard Wade, *The Urban Frontier* (Cambridge: Harvard University Press, 1967) 196–97, 220–21; Zane L. Miller, *Boss Cox's Cincinnati: Urban Politics in the Progressive Era* (New York: Oxford University Press, 1968) 5; Sam Bowes Hilliard, *Hog Meat and Hoecake: Food Supply in the Old South, 1840–1860* (Carbondale: Southern Illinois University Press, 1972) 14, 23–25, 106–8.

persons." It required that blacks migrating to the state show proof of their freedom and register with the county clerk where they settled. Whites hiring blacks without such certificates could be fined from ten to fifty dollars. In 1807 the maximum fine was raised to a hundred dollars. This act also required blacks entering the state to post a five-hundred-dollar bond, signed by two bondsmen, and prohibited blacks from testifying against whites in court cases. In 1831 blacks were denied the right to serve on juries, and in 1837 a public school system was created "for the education of the white youth" in the state. In 1849 a combination of Free Soilers, old-line Whigs, Democrats, and two independents who held the balance of power in the state legislature, repealed all of Ohio's Black Laws except those relating to juries and poor relief. The constitutional restriction on voting also remained in effect. Although limited, the 1849 repeal was the only one of its type in the three free states on the northern bank of the Ohio River.[29]

Ohio's Black Laws, and their repeal, reflect the diverse patterns of settlement in the state. Like other midwestern states, Ohio was partially settled by southerners who disliked slavery but hated blacks. A large number of Pennsylvania farmers who shared the sentiments of their southern neighbors were also among its pioneers. Thus slavery was outlawed in the state and free blacks were discouraged from coming.[30]

At the same time, however, a number of southern Quakers came to Ohio, where they liberated their slaves and fought for the rights of free blacks. They were joined by New Englanders and other northerners who would become sympathetic to abolition and even some type of racial equality. Although weak at the time of the state's founding, this group eventually came to compete on equal terms with less egalitarian Ohioans. As Gilbert Barnes has shown in his classic study, *The Anti-Slavery Impulse*, by the 1840s much of Ohio had been "converted" to abolition. Indeed, if Illinois was the home of the moderate republicanism symbolized by Abraham Lincoln and

29. Litwack, *North of Slavery* 74; Hurd, 2 *Law of Freedom and Bondage* 191; *Ohio Laws, 1804*, 356. Frank U. Quillin, *The Color Line in Ohio: A History of Race Prejudice in a Typical Northern State* (Ann Arbor: George Wahr, 1913) 13–43.

30. Quillin, *The Color Line in Ohio* 13–43; Robert E. Chaddock, *Ohio before 1850: A Study of the Early Influence of Pennsylvania and Southern Populations in Ohio* (New York: Columbia University Press, 1908) 33–35, 40. According to Chaddock, about 43 percent of Ohio's early population came from Pennsylvania, many of whom were poor farmers who tended to be both antiblack and antislavery. About 25 percent of the population came from the South. See also C. P. Galbreath, "Anti-Slavery Movement in Columbiana County," 30 *Ohio Archaeological and Historical Quarterly* 355–57 (1921). By close votes Ohio outlawed slavery and discriminated against free blacks.

the "Conservative Radical" Lyman Trumbull, then Ohio was the home of the "radical" radicals of the Republican party. In 1838 Joshua Reed Giddings of Ohio's Western Reserve district became one of the first radical antislavery congressmen. In the next twenty-five years Thomas Morris, Benjamin Wade, Edward Wade, Jacob Brinkerhoff, James Ashley, and most important of all, Salmon Portland Chase, followed Giddings to Washington.[31]

As a lawyer and politician, Chase was a major figure in converting the antislavery movement from a quasireligious crusade to a successful political force. In his study of the ideology of the Republican party Eric Foner concluded, "No anti-slavery leader was more responsible for the success of this transformation, and none did more to formulate an anti-slavery program in political terms" than Chase.[32] In addition to his political activities, Chase argued so many cases involving slaves that he became known as the "Attorney General for Fugitive Slaves." He constantly challenged the federal fugitive slave acts in valiant, but usually futile, attempts to protect fugitives or to defend those who aided and abetted runaway slaves. Chase's arguments in these cases were as much political and philosophical as they were legal. Although most of his legal work involved fugitives, the theories he worked out and some of the cases were directly relevant to the problem of slave transit. Indeed, while his demand for "the absolute and unconditional divorce of the [federal] Government from slavery"[33] had no impact on the enforcement of the

31. Thomas Morris actually entered the U.S. Senate before Giddings went to the House. Morris served one term, 1833–39, during which he was a leading critic of slavery. His performance was too radical for the Ohio Democratic party, which refused to reelect him in 1840, even though the party dominated the state legislature. In 1844 Morris was the Liberty party candidate for vice-president. Although Ohio as a whole was not sufficiently antislavery to elect men like Morris (after his views became known), some districts—those in the Western Reserve, for example—could easily elect radicals like Giddings. Only after a decade of antislavery activities was Ohio ready for antislavery senators such as Chase and Wade; Hans L. Trefousse, *The Radical Republicans: Lincoln's Vanguard for Racial Justice* (New York: Alfred A. Knopf, 1969) 11; Gilbert Hobbs Barnes, *The Anti-Slavery Impulse: 1830–1844* (reprint of 1933 ed. New York: Harcourt, Brace, and World, 1964); Eric Foner, *Free Soil, Free Labor, Free Men: The Ideology of the Republican Party before the Civil War* (New York: Oxford University Press, 1970) 73–75 and *passim*; Mark Krug, *Lyman Trumbull: Conservative Radical* (New York: A. S. Barnes, 1965).

32. Foner, *Free Soil, Free Labor, Free Men* 73. On Chase see also Louis S. Gerteis, "Salmon P. Chase, Radicalism, and the Politics of Emancipation, 1861–1864."

33. Chase coined this phrase in 1841 and repeated it consistently until the Civil War. In 1849 he wrote to Charles Sumner, "Nothing less than the Divorce of the General Government from slavery will satisfy me. I originated this expression in 1841 in the first Liberty Address published in Ohio . . . and I mean to be faithful to its entire import"; Chase to Charles Sumner, 15 Sept. 1849, Charles Sumner Papers, v. 1.19:11, Houghton Library, Harvard University, Cambridge, Massachusetts. See also

federal fugitive slave laws, it did provide some of the legal and political arguments necessary to end slave transit in Ohio.

Chase began his adult life as a Whig, but soon became an anti-slavery Democrat, a member of the Liberty party, a Free Soiler, and a Republican. Throughout his political career he advocated the Democratic philosophy of limited national government and state sovereignty. Even his service in Lincoln's cabinet and his appointment by Lincoln as chief justice of the United States Supreme Court did not lead Chase to give up his Democratic party leanings. As late as 1868 he told Horace Greeley, "I believe myself to be, as you say, 'a thorough democrat according to the true definition of that much-abused term'; and nothing would more rejoice my heart than to see the Democratic party conforming its policy to democratic ideas and principles."[34]

Chase rigorously applied these "democratic ideas and principles" to political antislavery in the antebellum period. Under his theory of states rights the federal government had absolutely no jurisdiction over slavery within the states or territories. Slavery was strictly a local issue, to be governed by local law. He argued that the national government "cannot under the constitution, create, continue, or enforce any such relation as that of owner and property, or,—what is, under the slave codes the same thing,—of master and slave." He thought that "[t]he Constitution found slavery and left it a state institution—creature and dependent of State law—wholly local in its existence and character. It did not make it a national institution."[35] Thus, while morally committed to abolition, Chase made his political attacks on slavery within the framework of constitutional law, rather than natural law. He concentrated most of his legal and political attacks on slavery where it could be most easily reached—in the North. While demanding the "divorce of the [national] Government from slavery," he was also protecting the right of the free states totally to exclude any form of slavery from within their borders.

Foner, *Free Soil, Free Labor, Free Men* 79, and Gerteis, "Salmon P. Chase, Radicalism, and the Politics of Emancipation, 1861–1864" for a discussion of Chase's application of these principles during the Civil War.

34. Chase to Horace Greeley, 19 May 1868, in Robert B. Warden, *An Account of the Private Life and Public Services of Salmon Portland Chase* (Cincinnati: Wilstach, Baldwin, 1874) 696–97. On Chase's Democratic political leanings and his antislavery activity in Lincoln's cabinet, see Louis S. Gerteis, "Salmon P. Chase, Radicalism, and the Politics of Emancipation, 1861–1864."

35. From Chase's address to the Liberty Party Convention of 1841, as excerpted in J. W. Schuckers, *The Life and Public Services of Salmon Portland Chase* (New York: D. Appleton and Company, 1874) 49.

Chase argued numerous cases involving fugitive slaves and slaves in transit. Although he recognized the legal distinctions between the two, his arguments on behalf of fugitive slaves, those charged with aiding fugitive slaves, and slaves in transit are all quite similar. They all revolve around the notion that slavery was limited to the jurisdictional boundaries of the slave states. In his most famous and complete attack on the Fugitive Slave Law of 1793, in *Jones* v. *Van Zandt* (1847),[36] Chase asserted, "The very moment a slave passes beyond the jurisdiction of the state in which he is held as such, he ceases to be a slave: not because any law or regulation of the state which he enters confers freedom upon him, but because he *continues* to be a man and *leaves behind* him the law of force, which made him a slave."[37] Such arguments held little sway before the proslavery Taney court.[38] But before the courts of Ohio and within the Republican party, Chase's theories were ultimately persuasive.

Chase thought antislavery politicians should place themselves "on the ground of the separation of the Genl. Government from slavery, leaving all questions of slavery within states to the states themselves."[39] His battle plan for this project was simple: "[L]et us free the slave here under our own laws—let us establish liberty & justice as the basis of legislation & executive action & judicial administration in our own states & in the nation."[40] As a lawyer, United States senator, and two-term governor of Ohio, Chase tried, with varying degrees of success, to implement this program.

Before 1861 Chase was most successful at the state level, but invariably failed before the federal courts and in the Senate. Ultimately, as a member of Lincoln's cabinet and then chief justice, Chase made important contributions to a total divorce of the federal government from slavery.[41]

Chase's constitutional theory developed out of his democratic poli-

36. *Jones* v. *Van Zandt*, 5 Howard (U.S.) 215 (1847).

37. Salmon Portland Chase, *Reclamation of Fugitives from Service* (Cincinnati: R. P. Donogh and Company, 1847) 84–86.

38. On the proslavery nature of the Taney court, see William M. Wiecek, "Slavery and Abolition before the United States Supreme Court, 1820–1860," 68 *Journal of American History* 34–59 (1978). Also see Don E. Fehrenbacher, *The Dred Scott Case: Its Significance in American Law and Politics* (New York: Oxford University Press, 1978). Fehrenbacher rejects the traditional view of Taney as conservative and proper, and forcefully argues him to be vindictive and proslavery in the extreme. "Behind the mask of judicial propriety, the Chief Justice had become a bitter sectionalist, seething with anger at 'Northern insult and Northern aggression'" (at 311).

39. Chase to Charles Sumner, 26 Feb. 1851, Sumner Papers, v. 16:36, Houghton Library, Harvard University.

40. Chase to Charles Dexter Cleveland, 28 May 1843, Chase Papers, HSP.

41. Gerteis, "Salmon P. Chase, Radicalism, and the Politics of Emancipation."

tical ideology, which stressed, among other things, state sovereignty. But this ideology was formulated and refined through legal cases and the necessity of creating arguments that might aid fugitive slaves, slaves in transit, and abolitionists. Until 1836 Chase was "opposed . . . to the views of the abolitionists," although through his sister and his brother-in-law, Dr. Isaac Colby, Chase knew many of the antislavery activists in Cincinnati. In 1836 an organized anti-abolition "mob" attacked the offices of the antislavery newspaper, *The Philanthropist.* Chase's sister fled her own house and took refuge in his. Chase viewed this riot "with disgust and horror" and he actively opposed mob violence; indeed, his first act as a "political abolitionist" was to organize a mass meeting in favor of law and order. Later Chase helped initiate a damage suit that ultimately brought in more than fifteen hundred dollars for the owners and printers of *The Philanthropist,* and its editor, James Gillespie Birney. This suit marked the beginning of a long and fruitful coalition between the two men.[42]

In March 1837 Chase became involved in another case with Birney. Birney had hired a black woman named Matilda who was later claimed as a fugitive slave. Chase obtained a writ of habeas corpus for Matilda in a futile attempt to prevent her rendition. Later he was more successful in defending Birney against a prosecution for harboring a fugitive slave.[43]

Matilda was owned by Larkin Lawrence, who was returning to Missouri with her after they had visited Virginia. In May 1836 they landed in Cincinnati to wait for another steamboat, which would take them directly to St. Louis. While in Cincinnati Matilda left her hotel room and made her way to the city's black neighborhood, where she was hidden for a few days. When Lawrence continued west without attempting to find her, Matilda came out of hiding and was soon employed by Birney as a maid in his house. In the meantime, Lawrence hired James M. Riley, a reputed slave catcher living in Cincinnati, to recover Matilda. In March 1837, nearly a year after she had been brought to Cincinnati, Riley and his cohorts obtained warrants from a state judge and arrested her as a fugitive from labor under the federal Act of 1793.[44]

42. Chase, "Autobiographical Sketch," in Chase to "My dear Sir," 10 July 1853, Chase Papers, box 9 (LC). See also Betty Fladeland, *James Gillespie Birney: Slaveholder to Abolitionist* (Ithaca: Cornell University Press, 1955) 142–44; Schuckers, *Life* and *Public Services of Salmon Portland Chase* 74. On antiabolitionist riots, including the ones in Cincinnati, see Richards, *"Gentlemen of Property and Standing."*

43. *Birney* v. *The State of Ohio,* 8 Ohio St. 230 (1837).

44. Fladeland, *James Gillespie Birney* 150–51; Salmon Portland Chase, *Speech of Salmon Portland Chase in the Case of the Colored Woman Matilda* (Cincinnati: Pugh and Dodd, 1837) 4.

Before the Hamilton County Court of Common Pleas, Chase argued that only a federal officer could enforce the Fugitive Slave Law of 1793. Thus he viewed the warrants issued by state officials and the proceedings in the state court as void. These arguments were "treated with ridicule or disregard" during the hearing over Matilda's status, and later before the Ohio Supreme Court. However, within five years they would be partially adopted by the United States Supreme Court in *Prigg* v. *Pennsylvania* and applied in the free states to liberate some slaves. Besides denying Ohio's jurisdiction in the case, Chase argued that the law of 1793 was unconstitutional and that even if it was constitutional, it did not apply to Ohio.[45]

Curiously, Chase made only passing reference to the facts that Matilda had been brought to Ohio by her master and that she did not run away to Ohio. He reminded the court that the Act of 1793 authorized "arrest or seizure in those cases only, where a person held to service in one state escapes thence to another." This, he told the court, was not the case here, for there was nothing to show "when, where, or how the escape was effected." In surprisingly tentative language, Chase argued that Matilda "may have escaped from the service of the claimant during a journey through this state; after being brought into the state as an attendant, during a visit; or after being sent into the state to labor. . . . There is nothing which shows, that the petitioner was held to labor in one state and escaped into another."[46]

Chase had already argued that slavery ceased to exist "when the

45. Foner, *Free Soil, Free Labor, Free Men* 74; Chase, *Matilda*, passim. As he would do in 1847 in the Van Zandt case, Chase sent copies of his *Matilda* argument to lawyers, politicians, and abolitionists. Isaac Blackford, the Indiana lawyer and supreme court reporter for that state, returned the favor by sending Chase a recent copy of the Indiana Supreme Court Reports. Blackford said of the Matilda argument, "It certainly does you great credit." His comment perhaps indicates that the arguments presented there were not treated universally with "ridicule or disregard"; Isaac Blackford to Chase, 5 July 1837, Chase Papers, box 5 (LC).

46. Chase, *Matilda* 13. William M. Wiecek, *The Sources of Antislavery Constitutionalism in America, 1760–1848* (Ithaca and London: Cornell University Press, 1977) 192, argues that in Matilda's case Chase was quite creative in his use of the transit-sojourn argument. However, I believe this was not the case. In subsequent legal battles Chase did creatively use the transit-sojourn argument, but in Matilda's case he unfortunately argued only that the Fugitive Slave Law of 1793 was unconstitutional and did not apply to Ohio because of the Northwest Ordinance. This last argument was based on the Fugitive Slave Clause of the Northwest Ordinance, which applied only to states that existed in 1787. Chase thus argued that this clause in the ordinance was inapplicable to the newer states, such as Kentucky and Missouri. He also claimed that the ordinance could not be superseded by the Constitution of the United States or the Fugitive Slave Law of 1793.

master and the slave meet together in a state where positive law interdicts slavery. The moment the slave comes within such a state he acquires a legal right to freedom." But inexplicably Chase failed to tie this point to the circumstances of Matilda's entering Ohio. This failure might be explained by Chase's deference to Shaw's opinion in *Aves*. Matilda and her master were clearly in transit from one state to another when they stopped in Cincinnati to change boats. This was the one exception found in Shaw's opinion. Although this exception was dictum, Chase may have been reluctant to challenge any part of Shaw's opinion, especially since Chase later used the *Aves* precedent to support his contention that the Fugitive Slave Law of 1793 could not be enforced by the states.[47]

Chase chose to attack the Fugitive Slave Law, rather than argue that Matilda was not a fugitive slave. This tactical error may have been the result of either Birney's abolitionist doctrine, which influenced Chase, or Chase's inexperience in dealing with slavery in a legal setting. Chase had but twenty-four hours to prepare for the case, and he spent the time with Birney, getting a "concentrated lesson on the legal and constitutional aspects of the fugitive slave law as it applied in Ohio."[48] But, as Chase should have realized, the Hamilton County Court was not about to declare an act of Congress unconstitutional. To the extent that Chase actually wanted to free Matilda, his argument was an utter failure. As part of a political test case, it was not much more successful, since no one was convinced and the case was lost. Matilda was remanded to Riley and returned to slavery. In future cases Chase would be less ideological and more pragmatic, perhaps having learned from this failure. While never missing an opportunity to denounce the Fugitive Slave Law, after Matilda's case Chase exploited arguments based on slave transit in fugitive slave cases, such as *Jones* v. *Van Zandt*.[49]

Lawrence's agent, Riley, was not satisfied with simply returning Matilda to slavery. He immediately secured an indictment of Birney for harboring a fugitive slave in violation of the Ohio law of 1804. The prosecution of this case was conducted by the same three lawyers who had argued for Matilda's rendition. In the county court Birney was convicted and fined fifty dollars. Unlike Matilda, who was forcibly removed from the state as soon as her trial had ended, Birney remained in the state and was able to appeal the conviction. The case was argued before the Ohio Supreme Court in January 1838, which gave Chase plenty of time to prepare his case. He apparently had learned from his past mistakes, for his argument was

---

47. Chase, *Matilda* 8, 19–20.
48. Fladeland, *James Gillespie Birney* 152.
49. *Jones* v. *Van Zandt*, 5 Howard (U.S.) 215 (1847).

much stronger and more coherent than it had been at Matilda's trial.

Chase argued that it was impossible to harbor "a person *being the property* of another person" because no such property relationship could exist in Ohio. He argued that although a fugitive slave might be delivered to an owner under the Constitution, this did not mean that the fugitive was in fact a slave while in Ohio. For the federal Constitution declared only that fugitives could not, under the laws of the state into which they escaped, be discharged of the labor they owed in the state from which they escaped. And, because slavery could not exist in Ohio under its constitution, a fugitive slave could not be considered property while in Ohio. By this logic, any slave coming into a free state became immediately free, although fugitive slaves might still owe service in the state from which they escaped.[50] For this reason, he felt the 1804 statute was unconstitutional.

Chase did not base the entire case on this rather precarious argument of unconstitutionality. After arguing against the validity of the statute, he demurred on the entire question. Even if the statute were constitutional, he felt it could not be applied to this case, for it could apply only to fugitive slaves. But was Matilda "a person of this class?" he asked the court. "Was she held to service in one state, and did she escape into another? Plainly not." The tentative nature of his earlier discussion of this point had now completely vanished. Chase asserted, "At the time she left the individual who claimed to be her master, she was within the territorial limits of Ohio, by the consent of that individual. If she had ever been a slave she had ceased to be such that moment when she was brought by Lawrence within these limits, and she had power to go whithersoever she chose." Matilda's going to Birney "was in no just sense of the term, an escape." Rather, "It was the first exercise of that freedom, which the constitution of Ohio had conferred upon her."[51]

Chase still had to deal with the dictum in *Aves* that transit across a free state ought to be allowed. He did this by ignoring the Massachusetts case altogether. He noted "that some decisions can be found which maintain that slaves, traveling with their masters through free states, will not become free." But these decisions, he asserted, "were made by the courts of slaveholding states" and had no authority in Ohio. The only authority for allowing the rendition of fugitive slaves was the United States Constitution, which said nothing about slaves in transit, leaving that question to the states. "Plain common sense, fortified by every principle of sound construction," re-

50. *Birney* v. *The State of Ohio*, 8 Ohio 230, 232 (1837).
51. Ibid. 236–38.

quired Ohio not to grant comity to masters in transit. Thus Matilda had not been a slave in Ohio, and Birney had committed no offense.[52]

The state offered no argument in the case, perhaps because by this time no one was interested in prosecuting Birney. It is also possible that growing antislavery sentiment made further prosecution unpopular or counterproductive.

The Ohio Supreme Court, after listening to Chase's subtle and comprehensive arguments, completely ignored them. Justice Reuben Wood, in the opinion of the court, concluded that Birney could not possibly have known that Matilda was a slave when he hired her. Therefore, he did not knowingly commit a crime. Nor was knowledge of Matilda's status alleged in the indictment. The court asserted that no "positive action is held criminal, unless the intention accompanies the act, either expressly or necessarily inferred from the act itself." Wood thus reversed Birney's conviction and it became "unnecessary to decide upon the other points, so laboriously argued for the plaintiff in error, and of a character too important in their bearing upon the whole country to be adjudicated upon without necessity." Although this was not the victory Birney and Chase had hoped for, it was not a defeat. In fact, Birney was vindicated on the important point that in Ohio "the presumption is in favor of freedom." Indeed, the recognition of that presumption allowed Wood to conclude that Birney could not have known that Matilda was a slave unless he was specifically informed of it.[53] More important, however, these two cases had brought Chase's powerful legal mind to the antislavery movement. In tacit recognition of the force of Chase's arguments, the court departed from its usual policy and ordered the arguments of counsel printed with the court report. The report was slightly over nine pages long, but eight of these pages were devoted to Chase's arguments.[54]

In two separate cases in 1841 Chase's arguments were implicitly accepted by the Ohio Supreme Court and the Hamilton County Court of Common Pleas. In November 1839 a group of Virginians with their slaves passed through Ohio en route to Missouri. In Clinton County a group of abolitionists heard of this party and pursued

---

52. Ibid. 238–39.
53. Ibid. 237–38.
54. Ibid., *passim*; Schuckers, *Life and Public Service of Salmon Portland Chase* 44. Albert Bushnell Hart, *Salmon P. Chase: The Political Abolitionist* (Boston and New York: Houghton Mifflin and Company, 1899) 74. Hart notes that the state supreme court's reversal "was based on a technicality which Chase had carefully avoided raising, and not on the bold principle of freedom under the laws of Ohio." The court "took the unusual step" of ordering Chase's arguments printed "in order to bring his point to the attention of the profession."

the travelers, overtaking them twenty miles away, outside Lebanon, Ohio. The abolitionists acted on the assumption "that by the laws of Ohio, every person claimed as a slave, becomes free upon entering her territory with the consent of his owner."[55] The slaves were informed of their rights and immediately fled. Seventeen Ohioans were subsequently indicted on various charges of larceny, abduction, riot, and miscellaneous misdemeanors. They were convicted of riot but acquitted on all other charges.[56] These convictions were appealed to the Ohio Supreme Court in *State* v. *Farr*.[57] According to newspaper accounts of the case, the Ohio Supreme Court overturned the conviction because of an erroneous charge to the jury. The *Cincinnati Gazette* reported that the supreme court "did not decide the question of whether a servant could be taken through the State with his master, or whether the master removing from one slave State to another, could pass through Ohio with his slaves, retaining his property in them." This question was not raised in the oral arguments before the supreme court, and the conviction was overturned on the jury charge question. However, the bill of exceptions presented by Farr did claim that the trial judge ought to have informed the jury that proof of slavery in Virginia was immaterial to the question of whether the defendants had a right to inform the slaves of their freedom while in Ohio. Having already overturned the conviction, the chief justice went out of his way to declare that even if he were a slave in Virginia "he became free when brought to this State by his master, since the Constitution and the act of Congress, under which alone the state of slavery subsists in Ohio, applies to *fugitives* only."[58] Although this last statement is only dictum, the case at least indicated where the chief justice stood on this question. In just three years Chase's arguments had gone from ridicule to supreme court dictum.

Under this ruling it appeared to many that slave transit would no longer be allowed in Ohio. *Niles Weekly Register* reported the case under the title "NO SLAVERY IN OHIO," declaring it an "interesting and important decision." The *Register* was careful to point out that fugitive slaves were unaffected by *State* v. *Farr* and could be recaptured in Ohio. But traveling masters could lose their slaves and might in fact be prosecuted for attempting to recover them.[59]

At almost the same time *State* v. *Farr* was argued before the

55. Letter of Dr. Abraham Brooke, *The Philanthropist*, 16 Dec. 1840.
56. Ibid., 16 June 1841; *Cincinnati Gazette*, 21 May and 1 June 1841.
57. Ibid. The case was not reported in any law reports or journals.
58. Ibid.
59. *Niles Weekly Register*, 29 May 1841.

Ohio Supreme Court, Salmon Chase was arguing before the Hamilton County Court of Common Pleas on behalf of Mary Towns. The judge in this case was Nathaniel C. Read, who as an attorney three years earlier had opposed Chase in the cases involving Matilda and James G. Birney. In this case, however, Judge Read found the arguments of his former adversary persuasive. Mary Towns was a Kentucky slave who came to Cincinnati in 1831, married, and lived there unmolested for ten years. In 1841 her former master seized her as a fugitive and she was brought before a local judge. At the end of this trial the judge ruled that the putative master had not proved Towns was his slave. However, instead of freeing the alleged slave, the judge jailed her and gave the claimant a second chance to prove his title to Towns. At this point Chase secured a writ of habeas corpus from Judge Read.[60]

As usual, Chase argued against the unconstitutionality of an Ohio judge's issuing a certificate of removal under the federal Fugitive Slave Law. He also argued that the proposed second trial was double jeopardy and that the first trial should have been before a jury. But the most important part of his case rested on the fact that the slaveowner's affidavit "does not state that she had escaped from his service *in* Kentucky, *into the State of Ohio*," and thus she was not technically a fugitive slave. It was this argument that Judge Read found persuasive. Read observed that "[s]he might have escaped from his place of residence and then been licensed to come to Ohio," in which case she would be free. This was not dictum, but an important part of the opinion that concluded Mary was not a fugitive slave—and therefore not a slave at all—because in Ohio "liberty is the rule, involuntary servitude the exception."[61] The writ of habeas corpus was granted and Mary went free.

After these two cases it was clear that Ohio had joined Massachusetts on the forefront of antislavery decision making. In the future numerous attempts would be made to change Ohio's position. But in general slave transit was no longer possible in the Buckeye State after 1841.

The Philanthropist was elated with these two decisions. However, the paper did complain that the excitement over the cases "only shows that for 39 years the clause of the Constitution excluding slavery has been in part a dead letter." This abolitionist paper also noted a "scurrilous handbill" printed across the river in Covington, Kentucky, which complained bitterly about the "total insecurity of our property" and asked if the "harmony of our Union can last much

60. *Cincinnati Gazette*, 21 May and 1 June 1841.
61. Ibid.

longer." Furthermore, the handbill threatened "if retribution is inflicted woe betide the wretches who provoke it." *The Philanthropist* sarcastically proclaimed, "Alas for Cincinnati! Who will come to her help against the great city of Covington?" Other papers were less sanguine. Cincinnati's democratic press feared the decision would disrupt the trade and commerce upon which the city depended, and in Kentucky the *Louisville Journal* warned that the decision would cause difficulty for travelers passing through Ohio.[62]

These two cases also led to a series of letters in the *Cincinnati Daily Gazette* between "Author of Federalism" and "Sherman." "Author of Federalism" felt that slave property was the same as any other type of property and should not be interfered with when passing through the state. As the writer's nom de plume implied, he thought that federalism and interstate harmony were much more important than the freedom of any particular slave. "Sherman" wrote three letters citing numerous English, northern, and southern cases on why slaves in transit should be freed when brought to free states. These letters reveal that the transit question was more than simply an academic legal one. The exchange between the two letter writers brought the problem of slave transit directly to the public, who could read about the issue in great detail. The final word on the debate at this time was claimed by the *New Orleans Bulletin.* The *Cincinnati Daily Gazette* reprinted an editorial from the New Orleans paper declaring that the recent decision in Ohio "by which the freedom of a slave (voluntarily taken there by his master) was recognized" was "not only in accordance with equity and justice," but with the decisions of the Louisiana Supreme Court as well.[63] Although the New Orleans paper accurately described the law of Louisiana and some of the rest of the South at that time, it may not have reflected the feeling of most southerners. In any event, within the next decade the law in the South would go through a major change. By 1852 most courts and legislatures in the slave states would reject the principles of *Somerset* and cease to recognize the free status of slaves who visited or resided in free states.[64]

In 1845 Chase again argued the case of a slave in transit before Judge Read. By this time Read had been elevated to the Ohio Supreme Court, and his decision carried much greater weight. The case, *State* v. *Hoppess* (1845),[65] involved Henry Hoppess, who was

62. *The Philanthropist*, 16 and 30 June 1841.

63. *Cincinnati Gazette*, 22, 27, 29 May and 1, 2, 3 June 1841.

64. This line of development in the South will be examined in chap. 7 of this volume.

65. *State* v. *Hoppess*, 2 Western L. J. (Ohio) 279 (1845); case was not reported in any official reports. Apparently some other cases involving slaves in transit also were

returning to Virginia from Arkansas with his slave Watson. The trip was made on a steamboat that stopped at Cincinnati. When the ship prepared to dock at Cincinnati, Hoppess attempted to transfer to another boat because he "did not intend to permit Watson to land on the Ohio shore." This information suggests that Hoppess understood that a slave voluntarily brought into Ohio might become free. In any event, Hoppess was unable to change boats without landing, and the steamship docked with Hoppess and Watson still aboard. Sometime between the morning docking and sundown Watson left the boat. He was found by Hoppess "leaning quietly against a post at the landing, not a hundred yards from the boat." Hoppess nevertheless assumed Watson was attempting to escape and had the slave brought before a justice of the peace "for the purpose of proving his right to his [Watson's] services." Here again Hoppess failed to accomplish his goal, because a writ of habeas corpus was secured by the omnipresent Salmon Chase. The next day argument on the writ was heard by Judge Read.[66]

Having learned from past mistakes, Chase concentrated most of his arguments on the facts of the case, although this did not stop him completely from attacking the Fugitive Slave Law. As far as Chase was concerned, the only point in question was whether Watson was in Ohio when he left the boat. Chase cited numerous Kentucky, Virginia, and federal statutes and cases to show "that the true boundary between Ohio, Indiana[,] and Illinois, upon one side of the river, and Kentucky on the other side, was the middle of the stream." But he was willing to concede the point, "for argument's sake" that the boundary was the low-water mark on the north shore.

---

not reported. Chase noted in his diary on 30 April 1843, "Friend Reynolds called about obtaining process to prevent a woman from taking away a colored child whose mother, brought here by her mistress has escaped from her. Gave him necessary instructions"; Chase Diary, 1829–54, Chase Papers, box 1, (LC).

66. *State* v. *Hoppess* 279–80. Hoppess was apparently not the only master who feared bringing his slaves into Ohio. In 1840 one Chilton was returning to Missouri after a visit to Virginia. When he reached Cincinnati he contracted with Lepper, "the master of a steamboat then lying at the wharf," for passage to St. Louis. Lepper "agreed and promised that his boat should leave the port of Cincinnati that evening, Chilton having represented to him, that upon no other terms would he consent to ship his slaves on the said boat." The slaves were transferred to the boat only after the fires were started and the steam raised. However, the boat was delayed and one of the slaves escaped. Eventually Chilton sued and won a judgment, which Lepper appealed. *Lepper* v. *Chilton*, 7 Mo. 21 (1841). The reasons for Chilton's reluctance to have his slaves in Cincinnati are unclear—perhaps he feared they would run away (as one of them did) or possibly he thought keeping them in Ohio overnight would free them. In any event, he did not want to bring them into a free state or keep them there any longer than necessary.

For Chase to concede this point was not damaging to his case, because evidence showed that the boat was actually tied to the Ohio shore, and therefore, under standard rules of riparian law, within the jurisdiction of Ohio. Citing the recent case of *State* v. *Farr,* as well as other American cases, Chase argued that the moment a slave entered Ohio he "was a man, under protection of the Constitution and the laws of Ohio, and beyond the reach of the fugitive slave law." In making this argument Chase stressed the local nature of slavery, arguing that a man could be held as a slave only by the force of local law; once the slave was brought beyond the jurisdiction of that law he became free, because there was no law enslaving him.[67]

Judge Read began his opinion with a detailed explanation of the dilemma facing Ohio and the rest of the nation, with regard to black slavery. "Slavery is wrong inflicted by force" and "opposed to the principles of natural right and justice." It was "the only blot upon the white pennant of universal liberty" that Americans had "flung upon the free air, for the admiration and imitation of the world." No one could "defend it" or "support it" and "it was only tolerated" because of "circumstances, which appeared to rise above our control." The greatest of these circumstances was "the peculiar characteristics of the race enslaved." Read asked, "[I]f free what will you do with him?" "No one scarcely would wish to confer upon him equal political rights," much less "social equality and the amalgamation of the races." The presence of the Negro was "a vast evil" and the judge had no real solution to the problem, except to condemn the abolitionists and declare that the problem was one that the individual states had to solve. But it was with a view to these conflicting problems—the immorality of slavery versus the problem of the free Negro—that Read would "approach the legal questions directly under consideration." As a further admonition to himself, and perhaps for the benefit of future historians who might doubt the importance of slave transit, Read added, "Questions of higher moment could not be presented to the consideration of a court."[68]

After discussing the history of the Northwest, Read concluded that slavery had existed there until at least 1787 and that fugitive slave rendition was an organic part of the law of that area, as well as of the rest of the nation. He then came to the "great question" before him: "the effect of coming within the Ohio side of the middle of the stream, or touching upon our shore in the navigation of the river, upon the right of the master to his slave."[69]

67. *State* v. *Hoppess* 280–81.
68. Ibid. 285–87.
69. Ibid. 287–88, 290.

Here Chase won a moral victory, only to lose the case in the end. Read began with an admission of some importance, which was a great compliment to Chase's legal forensics. "At one time," Read said, "I was of the opinion he [the master] had the right of passage through a free State with his slave." This "would harmonize with the spirit of the Compromise upon this subject." But, after "more careful examination" Read was "satisfied the master must lose his slave, if he brings him into a free State, unless the slave voluntarily returns to a state of slavery; because the master loses all power over the slave by the law of the State to which he has brought his slave; and there is no other law authorizing him to remove him." The Fugitive Slave Law did not apply here because "[i]f the master bring his slave into Ohio, and the slave refuse to go any further or to return into a state of slavery, there is no escape from the State where he owed service."[70] This interpretation of law and policy placed Ohio in the forefront of those states ready to challenge the right to bring slavery, in any shape or form, into the North. It certainly removed any taint of slavery from both Ohio and Read. It also answered the first part of Read's dilemma—that of the immorality of slavery.

But the second part of the dilemma remained—what to do with the freed slave. The implied third part was how to balance Ohio's moral outrage with the needs of the Union. In an exercise of hairsplitting worthy of the proverbial Talmudic scholar, Read set out to resolve these questions.

According to Read's interpretation of the law, if Hoppess brought Watson into Ohio, he had "no authority to detain him in custody, or to remove him from the State." This was so, even though Hoppess had tried to be landed in Kentucky or to change boats in midstream. Watson had clearly debarked from the boat into the state of Ohio. Thus "if the steamboat was within the sole jurisdiction of the State of Ohio," Watson was free. This led "to the important question of the jurisdiction over the Ohio River."[71]

Read examined the deed of cession given to the national government by Virginia for the lands "northwest of the Ohio River." He concluded that the purpose behind this phrase "unquestionably was to secure the full and free use of navigating the river, without hazarding any interference with her slaves navigating the river, by extending her jurisdiction over the water in the bed of the stream." He was unwilling to extend this principle to property rights in-

70. Ibid. 290.
71. Ibid. 290–91.

volving land bordering on the river or islands in it. He asserted only that a "concurrent jurisdiction over the water within its banks" existed and Ohio could not unilaterally deny passage to slaveowners or any other group. This interpretation of the law was also based on comity and it had to extend to the Ohio shore itself. Otherwise, Ohio would be saying, "If you land upon our shore, or are driven there by any cause, your slaves are free." But this was "strange language to the people of a sister state," and its effect would be "to deny the right to navigate the Ohio with a slave." Such an interpretation, Read felt, "would be lamentable," since it "would make the Ohio river in truth what it has been said that its name signifies, the river of strife—the war-river—the river of blood. The people on the one side would attempt to free the slaves on the river—the people on the other would regard it as mere robbery, and would defend their property." Fortunately, these horrors would not occur. For on the question of slave transit, Read found that masters navigating the river were "within the jurisdiction of Virginia or Kentucky." Thus, "if the slave escape from the boat, it is an escape from the jurisdiction of one State into another, within the meaning of the Constitution and the act of Congress." This interpretation also allowed a boat to "be made fast to the Ohio shore," since tying up a boat was "incident to the right to navigate. . . ."[72]

Read's opinion left many important questions unanswered. It did not, for example, indicate the status of a slave who left a ship, with the permission of his master, to spend the night in a Cincinnati hotel, or merely to eat a meal. Would the slave have to be confined to a ship, without actually coming on land? The opinion was also extraordinary for its disregard for riparian law. Read acknowledged that it had "been decided if a boat was attached to either shore, for the purpose of civil or criminal process, the jurisdiction was exclusive in the State to which it was attached."[73] Somehow, this rule did not apply if there were slaves on the boat. Perhaps the only logical explanation could be that the "peculiar institution" led to peculiar lawmaking. Read was trying to balance freedom and slavery, and to an extent he succeeded. He maintained the integrity of Ohio's "free-state" status without actually offending the citizens of any neighboring states. The only ones who were offended by his decision were the abolitionists—whom he singled out for their "commission of acts which annoy, excite, and awaken the passions, without at all promoting their design"—and the slave, who really didn't matter much,

72. Ibid. 291–92.
73. Ibid. 292.

since as a Negro, he stood "out just as distinct from our race when free, as a slave"—and in Read's view was probably no worse off as the latter.[74]

Chase and other abolitionists were naturally unhappy with this decision. Judge William Jay wrote Chase that Judge Read "most certainly erred" and his interpretation of riparian law was "fallacious." But this case could also be seen as a partial victory for antislavery. Although Watson was remanded to his master, Judge Read had clearly stated that slave transit through Ohio would usually result in the emancipation of the slave. Only boats docked along the Ohio would be exempt from these rules. So important was this ruling that antislavery proponents in Cincinnati printed a pamphlet about the case. The black community of Cincinnati was especially grateful to Chase for his service on behalf of Watson and presented him with an engraved silver pitcher.[75]

In 1846 Governor Mordecai Bartley used the power of his office in an attempt to support the free status of a slave brought to Ohio. Jerry Phinney was a slave in Kentucky who was hired out to a gambler named Allgaier. Allgaier told Phinney's owner he would not take the slave out of Kentucky, but in fact he took Phinney to Cincinnati and kept him there six months. When Phinney's owner discovered her slave was not in Kentucky, she wrote to Allgaier, threatening to sue him if he did not bring Phinney back. Phinney was then returned to Kentucky. Phinney next asked for, and received, permission to return to Cincinnati to get his clothes and personal effects. Phinney's owner gave him permission to enter Ohio.

---

74. Ibid. 286–87.

75. William Jay to Chase, 22 May 1845, Chase Papers, HSP; Schuckers, *The Life and Public Services of Salmon Portland Chase* 78. The Ohio antislavery community remembered Read's adverse decisions and later made Read pay for them. In 1849 a small group of antislavery politicians who held the balance of power in the Ohio legislature used their leverage to secure Chase's election to the United States Senate and the repeal of Ohio's black laws. In return, they agreed to support Democrats for other offices. However, when the Democratic party offered Read as their candidate for state supreme court, the antislavery legislators found him unacceptable. Negotiations on the election of U.S. senator, the repeal of the black laws, and the organization of the state legislature with a Democratic speaker were held up for a number of days because of Read. Chase's ally wrote: "The principal difficulty is this. The Democrats are anxious . . . to secure Judge Read's election to the Supreme Bench. I told [them] on this point that I did not believe any of our members could conscientiously vote for Judge Read," but that they would support "any competent & reputable men for judges whom the Democrats would name." Ultimately his party abandoned him, and Read left the state. A nonabolitionist paper noted, "The people will rejoice that Judge Read no longer disgraces the Supreme Bench." Stanley Mathews to Chase, 11 and 24 Jan. 1849, Chase Papers, LC; *The* [Painesville, Ohio] *Telegraph*, 7 Mar. 1849.

Upon reaching Cincinnati Phinney disappeared and refused to return to Kentucky and slavery. Sixteen years later two Ohioans, A. C. Forbes and Jacob Armitage, seized Phinney and without any legal proceedings took him to Kentucky. Forbes and Armitage were then indicted for kidnapping and Governor Bartley asked his Kentucky counterpart to assist in their arrest and extradition. After their arrest, the two slave catchers petitioned the Franklin County Circuit Court in Kentucky for their release on the grounds that Phinney was a slave and thus they had not kidnapped anyone. The state of Ohio responded by sending an attorney, William Johnston, to argue for the extradition.[76]

Johnston argued that twice Phinney had been allowed to enter a free state. The first time he had entered Ohio in the company of a man legally responsible for him. The second time "he went by permission of his mistress; as much so as if she had come herself, with Jerry attending on her as a servant." Johnston believed that Phinney had gained his freedom during his first trip to Ohio, but "if, indeed, we can suppose he was a slave after his return with Allgaier, this last act made him free." This was supported by the recent Ohio decision in *State* v. *Hoppess*, by *Commonwealth* v. *Aves* in Massachusetts, and by federal court decisions in *Butler* v. *Hopper*, *Ex parte Simmons*, and *Jones* v. *Van Zandt*.[77]

Despite the Ohio and other precedents, which showed Phinney was in fact free, the Kentucky court decided he was still a slave. Because of this decision, Judge Mason Brown refused to allow the extradition of Forbes and Armitage. Brown did not view them as the kidnappers of a free black, who were thus fugitives from justice. Rather, he saw them as the captors of a fugitive slave.[78] What is important about this case is not only how Kentucky viewed the law of Ohio. As the discussion of Kentucky law in chapter 7 will show, this decision was not entirely inconsistent with the law of that state.

76. *The State of Ohio vs. Forbes and Armitage, Arrested upon the Requisition of the Government of Ohio on charge of Kidnapping Jerry Phinney, and tried before the Franklin Circuit Court of Kentucky, April 10, 1846* (N.p., 1846) 8–9.

77. Ibid. 30–32. These federal cases will be discussed in chap. 8.

78. Ibid. 8–14. Part of the argument against extradicting Forbes and Armitage rested on the notion that Allgaier did not have a legal right to take Phinney out of Kentucky, and thus Phinney's owner should not suffer the loss of her property because of his improper actions. However, as the renter of Phinney, Allgaier in fact had legal authority over him. Allgaier might have been successfully sued by Phinney's mistress for losing her slave, but that could not have affected the fact that Phinney gained his freedom through the voluntary action of his owner or her agent. For a striking case on the rights of renters and other agents of a master, see *State* v. *Mann*, 2 Devereux (N.C.) 263 (1829).

This case is useful primarily as an indication of how the executive and the judiciary in Ohio viewed the question of slave transit. The governor of Ohio believed that residence in that state, with the master's consent, had freed Phinney. The governor was willing to support Phinney's claim to freedom by seeking the arrest and trial of his kidnappers, and perhaps subsequent to that, seeking the return of Phinney. However negrophobic the state had once been, by 1846 the executive and the judiciary accepted the doctrine that Ohio's free soil could free slaves, and the members of both branches were willing to act to support that theory of law.

In August 1854 a group of abolitionists at Salem, Ohio, stopped a passing train and removed a slave girl from it. The incident was reported in Ohio's newspapers but did not lead to any legal actions. By that time it was clear that under Ohio law any slave brought into the state, except aboard a docking ship, became instantly free.[79]

The importance of Ohio's geography to slave transit was underscored in the spring of 1855, when heavy ice interrupted traffic on the Ohio River. At its annual meeting the Western Anti-Slavery Society noted that because of this condition many slaves were taken through Ohio by train. The society was pleased that two children had been freed during such a transit, without any major court action. In two other cases, however, the masters successfully eluded abolitionists.[80] That same spring two slaves were removed from a mail boat that was docked at Cincinnati. A number of leading attorneys, including Chase and two former judges, assisted John Jolliffe in arguing for the freedom of these slaves. One local abolitionist thought it "a fine case of Habeas Corpus" and would "hardly entertain a doubt of the men being pronounced free." But he did not count on the will of the slaves. Midway through the proceedings they demanded "to be permitted the liberty of going with their master." After making sure "that the request was perfectly sincere, and made with a full knowledge of its consequences, they were discharged from the custody of the Court" and continued on with their master to Kentucky. The *Cincinnati Daily Commercial* regretted that "the interesting and important question raised in the case had ceased to be practical," and thus there was no decision in the case.[81] That the Superior Court granted the writ of habeas corpus and was willing to hear the case suggests a willingness to overturn the prece-

79. Galbreath, "Anti-Slavery Movement in Columbiana County" 380–87.

80. Minutes, Minutebook of Western Anti-Slavery Society, Western Anti-Slavery Society, 13th annual meeting, 1855, LC.

81. C. Donaldson to My dear Sir [George Julian], 19 Mar. 1855, Giddings-Julian Papers, v. 2, LC, *Cincinnati Daily Commercial*, 17 & 21 Mar. 1855.

dent set in Watson's case. These slaves were on board a ship docked at Cincinnati, the one exception to the right of transit allowed in *State* v. *Hoppess.* Had the slaves desired their freedom they might have gained it, and in the process Ohio would have closed all loopholes to slave transit. These minor cases, were, however, overshadowed by the extensive litigation and controversy surrounding a sixteen-year-old slave girl named Rosetta. The Rosetta case was complicated by the attempt of her master to apply the Fugitive Slave Law of 1850 to slave transit. This in turn led to a major conflict between the federal and state courts. In this case the federal courts successfully asserted their supremacy over the state courts. Nevertheless, Rosetta ultimately gained her freedom.[82]

Rosetta was the slave of the Reverend Henry Dennison of Kentucky. Dennison was the son-in-law of former president John Tyler, and that connection perhaps increased the importance of the case. In March 1855 Dennison sent Rosetta to Virginia in the care of his friend, Dr. Miller. Miller left the Ohio River at Cincinnati and traveled on by rail. At Columbus Miller was served with a writ of habeas corpus, and at a hearing before Judge Garrison of the county probate court Rosetta was declared free because she had been voluntarily brought into Ohio by her master's agent. Dennison then went to Cincinnati and obtained from United States Commissioner John L. Pendery a warrant for Rosetta's arrest as a fugitive slave. Armed with this warrant, he proceeded to Columbus where he attempted to convince Rosetta that she ought to return voluntarily to Kentucky. When she refused to give up her freedom, Rosetta was arrested under the warrant from Commissioner Pendery and forcibly taken to Cincinnati. Before Pendery could hold a hearing on her status, Salmon P. Chase obtained a writ of habeas corpus to have her brought before Judge Parker of the Hamilton County Court of Common Pleas. The writ was served on Federal Marshal H. H. Robinson, who brought her before Judge Parker. There she was declared free and returned to her guardian, Louis Van Slyke. After this hearing Marshal Robinson again seized Rosetta, and she remained in custody until her hearing before Commissioner Pendery. In the meantime, Marshal Robinson was arrested by state officials for contempt of court in rearresting Rosetta after Judge Parker had freed her.

---

82. Rosetta's case was never actually reported. See ibid.; *Ex parte Robinson*, 20 F. Cas. 296 (1855), involving the federal marshal who seized Rosetta; Levi Coffin, *Reminiscences* (Cincinnati: Western Tract Society, 1876) 554–57; Eugene H. Roseboom, *The Civil War Era: 1850–1873* (Columbus: Ohio State Archaeological and Historical Society, 1944) 344–45. Campbell, *Slave Catchers* 141–42, mistakenly states that Rosetta was returned to slavery.

Rosetta remained in federal custody as an alleged fugitive slave and Federal Marshal Robinson remained in state custody for contempt of state court.[83]

Flamen Ball, Salmon P. Chase's law partner, represented Rosetta before Commissioner Pendery. Ball argued that Rosetta became free the moment her master's agent brought her into the state. He further argued that Dennison acknowledged her freedom when he asked her to return to Kentucky with him. Hundreds of people attended the hearing and anxiously awaited its outcome. Commissioner Pendery deferred his decision for four days. When announcing his decision, Pendery "contented himself with asserting his Commissioner's Court as superior to all the Courts of Ohio, and then gravely but singularly deciding that Rosetta was free." Although entitled to a five-dollar fee, Pendery generously waived it, and Rosetta left the courtroom a free woman.[84]

While the hearing over Rosetta's status was proceeding before the commissioner, Marshal Robinson remained in jail under the state contempt citation. In order to extricate himself from this situation, he applied to United States Supreme Court Justice John McLean for a writ of habeas corpus. McLean quickly granted the writ, held a hearing, and ordered Robinson released. McLean asserted that state officials could not interfere with federal officials who were performing their federal duties.[85] This interpretation of the Supremacy Clause of the Constitution and of the nature of a federal union is, of course, reasonable. But McLean's opinion left some unanswered questions, for as it ultimately turned out, Robinson had had no legitimate jurisdiction or right to arrest Rosetta because she was not a fugitive. While Commissioner Pendery accepted the distinction between fugitive slaves and sojourning slaves, not all federal officials did so. Only a few months after this case, for example, Passmore Williamson was imprisoned by Federal Judge John Kane for helping slaves in transit gain their freedom in Pennsylvania. Indeed, in both Williamson's and Rosetta's cases the question of federal jurisdiction over slaves in transit appeared to be claimed by the federal courts and denied by the state courts. And even though Rosetta gained her freedom, abolitionists in Ohio were not entirely pleased with the outcome. It was not enough for them that Commissioner Pendery accepted the legal theory that slaves brought into Ohio were not fugitives and therefore could be freed by state courts. The executive committee of the Western Anti-Slavery Society

83. Minutes, Minutebook of Western Anti-Slavery Society, Western Anti-Slavery Society, 13th annual meeting, 1855, LC.
84. Ibid.; Coffin, *Reminiscences* 554–57.
85. *Ex parte Robinson.*

thought Justice McLean was "the slaveholder's agent for the interpretation and execution of the slaveholder's constitution." Between the actions of McLean and Commissioner Pendery, Ohio "was disgraced and subdued, and she quietly submitted."[86]

In 1856, a year after the Rosetta case, the Ohio Supreme Court gave its last decision on the transit question. It was a total victory for the antislavery cause. John Anderson, a Kentucky slaveowner, had for a number of years allowed his slave Henry Poindexter to come in and out of Ohio, often hiring himself out as a laborer. Eventually Anderson agreed to allow Poindexter to purchase himself. Poindexter signed a number of notes, which were cosigned by his white friends in Ohio. But after Poindexter went to Ohio, he and his sureties refused to honor the notes. In *Anderson v. Poindexter et al.* (1856),[87] the master sued for the value of the notes. In a very short opinion, Justice Ozias Bowen found that Poindexter had become free the moment he landed in Ohio and "his subsequent return to" Kentucky did not make him a slave again. Thus he was free at the time he made the contract to buy his freedom. There was no valid consideration for which Poindexter could pay money and therefore the contract was considered void by the court. Bowen also noted, with a touch of irony, that in Kentucky a contract between a slave and a master was void, and therefore, even if he enforced Kentucky rules, rather than those of Ohio, there would still be no reason to pay on the notes. Justice Joseph Swan made up for Bowen's brevity with a concurring opinion of more than twenty-five pages. He quoted extensively from *Aves*, *Butler* v. *Hopper*, and a number of southern cases, as well as repeating the entire *Somerset* decision. While offering no new ideas or theories, Swan wrote an excellent summary of previous decisions on the subject.[88]

In 1857 the Ohio legislature was temporarily dominated by an antislavery majority, which created criminal penalties for anyone entering the state with an intent "to hold or control . . . any other person as a slave." The law further declared that "every person coming within this State," other than a fugitive slave, "shall be deemed and held in all courts as absolutely free." In 1858 the Ohio legislature was dominated by "administration democrats," who repealed this punitive law. The Ohio Supreme Court, however, re-

86. Minutes, Western Anti-Slavery Society, 13th annual meeting, 1855, and Report of the Executive Committee, 14th annual meeting, 1856, Minutebook of Western Anti-Slavery Society, LC.

87. *Anderson* v. *Poindexter et al.*, 6 Ohio St. 622 (1856).

88. Ibid.; for a discussion of Justice Swan, see Robert M. Cover, *Justice Accused: Antislavery and the Judicial Process* (New Haven: Yale University Press, 1975) 252–56.

mained antislavery until the Civil War, and its decision in *Anderson
v. Poindexter* remained the law of the state. Although the Democratic legislature repealed the 1857 statute, it did not pass any law
allowing transit.[89]

After *Anderson* the Ohio court faced the fugitive slave issue in *Ex
parte Bushnell, Ex parte Langston* (1859),[90] in which the Ohio court
initially challenged federal authority and the constitutionality of
the fugitive slave laws. Langston and Bushnell were abolitionists
accused of aiding fugitive slaves in the famous Oberlin-Wellington
rescue. After issuing writs of habeas corpus, the Ohio court concluded that the federal law was constitutional and the men remained
in federal custody. The Ohio court respected federal authority in this
area of law. Although Ohio would not help a master capture and
return a fugitive slave, the state's courts would not interfere with
that process, unless there was reason to believe the black was not
in fact a fugitive slave. By the time the Civil War began, Ohio's
highways and railroads were closed to slaveowners in transit. Only
the United States Constitution prevented the state from freeing
fugitive slaves as well.[91]

Northern Comity Ends

The Ohio court's decisions in *Anderson v. Poindexter* and *Ex parte
Bushnell, Ex parte Langston* were not the last such cases to reach
northern state courts, but they do represent the line of development
of the comity question in the North. The United States Constitution
demanded that fugitive slaves be remanded. Many northerners disliked this and some northern courts fought against it. But, the power
of the federal government, the moral force of the Constitution—
which was viewed as almost a sacred document—and the fear of
civil war all coalesced to support the Fugitive Slave Law in form if
not in fact. The northern courts often attempted to ignore the law
and sometimes hindered its enforcement, but they were never able
to stop its enforcement. Only in Wisconsin did they ever really try.

89. *Ohio Acts of 1857*, 186; *Ohio Acts of 1858*, 19.

90. *Ex parte Bushnell, Ex parte Langston*, 9 Ohio St. 77 (1859).

91. Ibid.; Morris, *Free Men All* 180–88; Cover, *Justice Accused* 252–56. Other Ohio
courts were equally unwilling to challenge the authority of the federal government.
In *Ex parte Early*, 3 Weekly Law Gazette (Ohio) 234 (1858), the Hamilton County
Common Pleas Court refused to issue a writ on a federal marshal who held a black
under a warrant by the U.S. fugitive slave commissioner. An attorney for Early
argued "that if Early left the state of Virginia and came into Ohio alone or in
company . . . by the consent of . . . his master, he was a free man." The court acquiesced in this proposition, but nevertheless refused to issue the writ.

Only "the people" could stop its enforcement—often at the high cost of fine and imprisonment.[92] Slaves in transit, however, were another matter. Here the Constitution was silent. True, comity was built into the Constitution; it demanded that "Full Faith and Credit" be given by one state to the laws of another and it guaranteed privileges and immunities for citizens of one state visiting others. But these were vague, broad demands: Full faith and credit, but to whose laws? Those of the slave states or those of the free states? Privileges and immunities—to the master or the slave or both?

At the Founding this question had not been extremely significant. Comity was freely given to slave owners, because, if for no other reason, slaveowners were not confined to the South. But as slavery disappeared in the North, the people of that section grew less and less tolerant of the institution in any form. Starting in the 1830s northern courts began to strike at slavery whenever they could. The rights of masters in transit were most vulnerable, and in the twenty-five years before the Civil War these rights were denied in all but a few states. Only New Jersey and Illinois gave any statutory protection to masters in transit. California offered some limited rights of transit through the state if dicta from earlier decisions had been applied.[93] In Ohio masters might still use the Ohio River but could claim no protection if they strayed from its banks. This was of course consistent with the one exception first enunciated by Chief Justice Shaw in the *Aves* case. But, as discussion of the *Lemmon* case will show, even this right was under serious attack by 1860.

The South responded to this denial of comity with two legal counterattacks. First, southern courts, gradually at first and then almost in unison, began to deny comity to blacks who had lived in the North, where they had gained their liberty. Also, individual southerners, and eventually entire states, began to seek new remedies when northern state courts denied them comity. As early as 1806 Pierce Butler had sought protection in a federal court from the juris-

---

92. On Wisconsin's refusal to enforce the Fugitive Slave Law of 1850 and the judiciary's challenge to that law and the federal courts, see *Ex parte Booth*, 3 Wis. 145 (1854); *In re Booth and Rycraft*, 3 Wis. 157 (1857); *Arnold* v. *Booth*, 14 Wis. 180 (1861); and *Ableman* v. *Booth* and *United States* v. *Booth*, 18 Howard (U.S.) 479 (1856) and 21 Howard (U.S.) 506 (1859); James I. Clark, *Wisconsin Defies the Fugitive Slave Law: The Case of Sherman M. Booth* (Madison: The State Historical Society of Wisconsin, 1955).

93. On California decisions, see n. 1 above. While no statutes gave explicit protection for masters traveling through Indiana, it is likely that the courts of that state would not have interfered with such transit. In 1851 Iowa prohibited the immigration of Negroes into the state; *Iowa Laws of 1851*, chap. 72. This negrophobic act may indicate that Iowa's earlier proclivity to free blacks brought into the state may have changed.

diction of state courts. By the 1840s and 1850s this course of action became more common. Slaveowners asked federal courts to interpret the Fugitive Slave Clause in the broadest possible terms, to protect their property while in transit through free states. Some masters were quite successful. In 1860 the state of Virginia was preparing to appeal the *Lemmon* case to the United States Supreme Court, where there was a high probability that the right of a master in transit would have been affirmed by the nation's highest tribunal.[94]

Before the transit problem can be viewed as a federal question, it must first be examined from the southern point of view, through the prism of southern court decisions.

94. This issue will be discussed in chaps. 9 and 10.

Chapter 7

The South and Comity: The Rejection and Adoption of *The Slave, Grace* Doctrine

At first glance it would appear that southern courts and jurists would have no direct concern with the issues of slave transit and comity. Slaves freed while in the North were unlikely to return to the South, where their new status might be jeopardized; and if the newly freed slaves remained in the North a southern court would have no way to interfere with their status. Southern newspapers, politicians, and jurists might complain about the lack of comity between the two sections, but short of federal intervention or civil war, they could do little to change northern legislation and judicial action.

Nevertheless, in two significant ways southern courts faced the problem of slave transit with some frequency. First, a number of slaves lived or visited in the North and then returned to the South. Later they sued for freedom in slave-state courts on the grounds that they had become free while living in the North and, once free, they could not be reenslaved without specific legislation for that purpose. Second, some slaves were voluntarily manumitted in the North by their masters and later returned south. Often these slaves were the children or paramours of their former masters. In some cases these slaves returned to live with their former masters; in others they visited and then went north again. Usually these slaves did not have to sue for their freedom in slave-state courts. Rather, they became involved in suits over property bequeathed to them by their former owners.

The holdings in these cases varied a great deal from state to state and, more importantly, they changed quite dramatically between 1810 and 1860. A surprising number of slaves were freed by courts in slave states, especially in the period before 1840. Several factors led to these decisions: in some states the adherence to common-law principles favored freedom; in others it was the notion that no one could be enslaved without positive law. Thus a person could be born a slave under the positive law of a slave state, but once that person gained freedom he could not be reenslaved without specific legislation. Other decisions were based primarily on comity and a desire to maintain good relations with the North. Thus, while Illinois and Indiana were reluctant to free slaves in transit or even sojourning slaves, Missouri and Kentucky would often free such slaves out of respect to the laws of the free states. In Louisiana, on the other hand, the maxims of French law led to the freedom of any slave whose foot had touched free soil.

In all of these cases, southern judges (before the 1840s and 1850s) showed a remarkable tendency to free slaves whom they believed had gained their freedom under the laws of the North. The best statement on the reasons for such decisions is found in the early Kentucky case of *Rankin* v. *Lydia* (1820).[1] In freeing the slave Lydia, Justice Benjamin Mills asserted that if by the

> positive provisions in our code, we can and must hold
> our slaves in the one case, and statutory provisions equally
> positive decide against that right in the other, and liberate the
> slave, he must, by an authority equally imperious, be declared
> free. Every argument which supports the right of the master on
> one side, based upon the force of written law, must be equally
> conclusive in favor of the slave when he can point out in
> the statute the clause which secures his freedom.[2]

This fidelity to the law itself may go a long way in explaining why the courts in a number of southern states were willing to liberate slaves who had lived in free states. It was not sympathy for blacks nor a desire to end slavery that led to these decisions. These state courts saw themselves not as enforcing vaguely defined general principles of liberty, but as preserving the integrity of the law. And until the higher-law principles of the positive good of slavery and of abolition intervened, the integrity of the courts and laws was much more important than any individual claims to liberty *or* property.

This fidelity to law—this impartiality of decision making—began to fade in the 1830s and disappeared throughout most of the South before 1860. By then fidelity to the institution of slavery was more important than fidelity to abstract concepts of law. The process of change was gradual across the slave South, but it was often quite dramatic and abrupt in particular states.

It would be convenient and tidy to argue that southern courts

---

1. *Rankin* v. *Lydia*, 2 A. K. Marsh. (Ky.) 467 (1820).
2. Ibid. 470.

ceased granting comity to the North—that is, ceased to free slaves who had visited, worked, or resided in the North—in response to northern decisions denying comity to slaveowners in transit. Some legal historians have in fact argued this.[3] But it is not at all clear that the change came about in this way. A number of distinct problems emerge from such an analysis.

First, southern courts freed slaves who had spent time in the North well *before* northern courts freed slaves in transit. It surely would be absurd to argue that southern jurists reversed their own precedents because northern jurists had endorsed them. Second, there is little evidence that southern jurists or legislatures were responding to specific northern decisions when they altered their decision making in favor of slavery. A great deal of evidence, however, suggests that southern lawmakers were responding to national events, particularly the antislavery movement, when this change occurred.

By 1860 the courts of the North and South had diverged to such an extent that a judicial secession had taken place. In Mississippi judicial civil war was being advocated.[4] This divergence was in part the result of radical changes in decision making and the willingness to grant comity on both sides of the Mason-Dixon line. But, as decisions discussed in this chapter reveal, it was not simply a judicial quid pro quo with the South reacting to unwarranted denials of comity initiated by the North.

Nor can the change in southern judicial behavior be explained by claiming that the late antebellum cases were substantively different from earlier ones. Don E. Fehrenbacher has recently argued, "There was no general southern repudiation of the earlier" precedents. Rather he maintains, "Scholars have fallen into error by failing to keep an eye on the difference between sojourning and domicile." Fehrenbacher argues, "In the decades after 1830, however, fewer slaveholders risked losing their slaves by holding them on free soil for extended lengths of time. Most of the cases arising in the later antebellum period therefore involved sojourning or transit, rather than domicile. In short, what had changed on the eve of the Civil War was not so much the quality of southern justice as the nature of the demands laid upon it."[5] This analysis overstates

3. Don E. Fehrenbacher, *The Dred Scott Case: Its Significance in American Law and Politics* (New York: Oxford University Press, 1978) 55–56.

4. *Mitchell* v. *Wells*, 37 Miss. 235 (1859). This case is discussed at length in chap. 9.

5. Fehrenbacher, *Dred Scott Case* 56. Fehrenbacher's view of slave transit and sojourn is too narrow for a critical understanding of what was going on in southern courts. Cases involving inheritances are also important. If slave-state courts refused to allow an emancipated slave to inherit property, the slave state was in effect saying

the distinctions between sojourn and domicile and misconstrues the change in southern decision making. It may be true, as Fehrenbacher argues, that most southern states never freed slaves simply on the basis of transit across a free state. But Fehrenbacher is wrong in arguing that southern courts *only* freed slaves who had been domiciled in the North. Some slaves who had sojourned in the North were freed. Indeed, sojourn, or brief transit, when accompanied by additional factors—such as the slave's being hired out in a free state—led to the liberation of slaves in a number of southern courts. Nor is it correct to assert that cases in the late antebellum period were substantively different from those of the earlier period. It is true that most masters no longer took their slaves into free states. But many freedom suits were based on dormant claims arising from earlier trips to the North. Dred Scott, for example, sued for his freedom ten years after he had first resided in a free jurisdiction. Finally, we must reject the contention that most of the South continued to recognize the freedom of slaves who were domiciled in the North. Had the Missouri courts continued to follow their own precedents *Scott* v. *Emerson* (1852)[6] would simply be another case in a long line of successful freedom suits based on residence in a free state; and in *Mitchell* v. *Wells* (1859)[7] the free black Nancy Wells

---

that the emancipated slave was still a slave. Fehrenbacher correctly notes that *Cleland* v. *Waters*, 19 Ga. 35 (1855) confirmed the right of a master to free his slaves in Africa. He then goes on, "The court did denounce northern withdrawal of sojourners' rights, but it declared that slaves sent to live permanently in a free country became free"; *Dred Scott Case* 612 n. 21. Even under *Cleland* v. *Waters*, however, the permanency of residence was the critical issue. As long as the slave or master resided in the free state it could be asserted that domicile had changed. But if the slave ever returned to the slave state, then the permanency of the original domicile would be in question. For a number of states, particularly in the Deep South, the rejection of freedom based on northern laws was not merely a question of time spent in the North. In 1846 a Louisiana statute declared that "no slave shall be entitled to his freedom under the pretence that he has been with or without the consent of his owner in a country where slavery does not exist, or in any of the States where slavery is prohibited"; *Louisiana Acts of 1846*, chap. 189. Similarly, a Georgia statute of 1859 prevents the manumission of slaves "within or without the State" through a will. This law would counter any pro-freedom aspects of *Cleland* v. *Waters*, which apparently stimulated passage of the act; John Codman Hurd, 2 *The Law of Freedom and Bondage in the United States* (2 vols. Boston: Little, Brown, 1862) 109. Of more than tangential importance to this question is the hostility toward free blacks in most of the South. Free blacks were prohibited from migrating into many slave states. Thus, blacks who had perhaps gained a right to freedom in the North were not likely to be able to test that right in some Deep South states by 1860. By returning to the South they were themselves prima facie evidence that their domicile had not been permanently changed to a free state.

6. *Scott* v. *Emerson*, 15 Mo. 577 (1852).

7. *Mitchell* v. *Wells*, 37 Miss. 235 (1859).

would have quietly obtained the legacy her father and former owner had bequeathed to her.

What does emerge from an examination of the southern cases dealing with slave transit is a distinct change in the jurisprudence of most slave states. Not surprisingly, the greatest change came in a Deep South state, Mississippi, while the border state of Kentucky remained most consistent when dealing with the problem.

The Slave, Grace and the South

In freeing the slave girl Med, Chief Justice Shaw relied on the absence of positive law and the subsequent lack of "authority on the part of the master" to restrain Med or forcibly remove her from the state. In a rejection of Lord Mansfield's expansive doctrine in *Somerset*, Shaw specifically disclaimed any extraordinary qualities of his state, such as "breathing our air, or treading on our soil," that could free the slave or alter his status under "the law of his domicil." This reasoning suggested that if a slave voluntarily returned to the slave state, or was forced there before the Massachusetts authorities could intervene, the *status* of slavery might reattach. Shaw acknowledged as much by citing the British case, *The Slave, Grace* (1826), which upheld Grace's slave status after she voluntarily left England for a slaveholding colony in the West Indies. Shaw also noted, "A different decision . . . has been made of the question in some of the United States." But this was not the question before him in *Commonwealth* v. *Aves* and indeed would be an unlikely question for a Massachusetts judge ever to face. So, Shaw did not "consider it further."[8]

While the problem of a returning slave was not critical or even a relevant question for the judges of the free states, it was an important one for jurists in the slave states. Many slaves were brought into free states at various times, by the design of their master, by the exigencies of interstate travel, or simply by accident. Some of these slaves later sued for their freedom, in a slave state, on the basis of transit, sojourn, or residence in a free state.

The Slave, Grace (1826)[9] was Britain's corollary to *Somerset*. In 1822 Grace was brought to England by her mistress. A year later she voluntarily returned to Antigua, where she was treated as a slave. In 1826 Grace sued for freedom, claiming that the residence in England had emancipated her, and that once free she could not then be reenslaved. In the High Court of Admiralty, Justice William

8. *Commonwealth* v. *Aves*, 18 Pick. (Mass.) 193, 208, 218 (1836).
9. *The Slave, Grace*, 2 Hagg. Adm. (G.B.) 94 (1827).

Scott, Lord Stowell, found Grace was still a slave. Stowell admitted that Grace had a right to freedom while in England, but determined this right "totally expired when that residence ceased and she was imported into *Antigua*." Stowell thought the "sole question" decided in *Somerset* was "whether a slave could be taken from this country in irons and carried back to the *West Indies*, to be restored to the dominion of his master." This, Stowell agreed, could not be done. But he found that Mansfield's other "observations to the foundation of the whole system of slavery" were obiter dicta. Stowell accepted the doctrine of "once a freeman ever a freeman" but was willing to apply it only to England; and when Grace returned to Antigua she resumed her status as a slave. "The temporary freedom" acquired in Britain was "superseded upon the return of the slave."[10]

Essentially, *The Slave, Grace* reaffirmed the *Somerset* doctrine that a slave brought to England was entitled to freedom. But if the slave did not establish that claim while in England and if he or she returned to a slave jurisdiction, then, under *The Slave, Grace*, he or she could not later sue for freedom on the basis of the English residence. While this may have been a sufficient discussion of the problem as it applied to Britain, it left many questions unanswered if *The Slave, Grace* were to be applied to the United States. For example, what was the status of a slave who lived in a free jurisdiction and was forced to return to a slave jurisdiction before establishing a claim to freedom in a court? Similarly, there was the possibility that a slave could be brought to a free state, establish a claim to freedom, and return to the slave state. Could the slave state then reenslave the black? Finally, in some states (such as New York and Pennsylvania) freedom was established by statute and no *Somerset*-type decision was required to secure it. After residence in such a state was the slave then free for life, even if he or she returned to a slave state?

These unanswered questions were part of the reason that *The Slave, Grace* was not immediately incorporated into American law. Three other factors, however, were even more important. First, unlike *Somerset*, *The Slave, Grace* occurred half a century *after* American independence was declared and was not part of the nation's common law heritage at the Founding. Second, England's relationship to her colonies was clearly different from that between one American state and another. Imperial law and policy had always differed from that of the metropolis, because different parts of the empire had different needs. Thus, while slavery was prohibited in

10. Ibid. 94, 98–99, 106–7, 127, 124.

England, in the colonies it had "an almost unbounded protection."[11] Most important, *The Slave, Grace* was not applied to American law because it ran contrary to a number of American court decisions that had been decided before Grace was even taken to England. In all of these early cases, slaves who had resided in free states or territories were liberated when they sued for freedom in slave-state courts.

"In favorem vitae et libertatis"

The development of "*The Slave, Grace*" doctrine in the American South is best illustrated by an examination of the case law in four slave states: Kentucky, Louisiana, Missouri, and Mississippi. In each state cases were decided before *The Slave, Grace*, in which slaves who had lived in a free state and returned to a slave state were freed by the slave-state court. These decisions were based on a combination of comity, fear of free-state retaliation, and three complementary legal doctrines: that residence, or even presence in a free jurisdiction could immediately free a slave; that a person once free was always free; and that only positive law could make someone a slave, and thus until a slave state passed legislation reenslaving former slaves they would remain free. No court relied on all of these reasons, and some courts used different combinations of them for different cases. Comity, for example, was more useful when the slave relied on specific free-state statutes or an act of manumission than when a slave relied on the rather broad principles of freedom contained in many state constitutions and the Northwest Ordinance. Simple presence in a free state, however, could be used in those cases where comity was less helpful.[12]

In all four states the amount of time spent in a free territory was often the critical difference between slavery and freedom. The longer a slave resided outside a slave state, the better were his chances of being freed by a slave-state court. But specific state policy was perhaps the most important factor. As the Kentucky Court of Appeals explained:

11. Ibid. 128–29.

12. For another view of how southern courts dealt with slaves, see A. E. Keir Nash, "A More Equitable Past? Southern Supreme Courts and the Protection of the Antebellum Negro," 48 *North Carolina Law Review* 197–242 (1970); A. E. Keir Nash, "Fairness and Formalism in the Trials of Blacks in the State Supreme Courts of the Old South," 56 *Virginia Law Review* 64–100 (1970); A. E. Keir Nash, "Reason of Slavery: Understanding the Judicial Role in the Peculiar Institution," 32 *Vanderbilt Law Review* 8–218 (1979).

> [T]he laws of no State have, by their own force, any
> operation beyond the territorial or jurisdictional limits of
> that State; that it pertains to the sovereignty of every
> independent State, to determine for itself, and according to its
> own interests and policy, in what cases and to what extent the
> foreign law shall be adopted as part of its own, and operate upon
> persons and things within its territory. And that it is an
> essential principle of the law of comity which, in the absence of
> any municipal law upon the subject regulates, upon grounds of
> reason and practice, the admissibility of the foreign law, that no
> State is bound to admit, or give effect to, a foreign law which
> violates its own rights or policy, and is destructive of
> the rights and interest of its own citizens.[13]

What is striking, however, is that in numerous cases the courts of
the slave states respected the power of free states to liberate slaves.
This was true even where masters took their slaves to free states for
the purpose of evading slave-state laws prohibiting manumissions.
In such instances slave-state courts might have rejected claims of
freedom, but they often enforced them. Indeed, since slave-state
policy discouraged the growth of a free black population and encouraged masters to control their slave property, slave-state courts
might have rejected all freedom claims based on northern residence,
laws, or court decrees. To do otherwise would have violated stated
public policy. Instead, at least until the 1830s, slaves often won suits
for freedom based on free-state laws.

These early liberating decisions suggest that an ambivalence existed within slave-state judiciaries on the question of freedom and
bondage. In 1818, for example, Mississippi's highest court asserted
that slavery could "only exist through municipal regulations, and in
matters of doubt, is it not an unquestioned rule, that courts must
lean 'in favorem vitae et libertatis.'"[14] Although such emphatic language was not adopted by all states, it does indicate that at least
for a time some southern courts were willing to give an honest and
fair hearing to those slaves who might have a bona fide claim to
freedom.[15] Indeed, in many ways the South was more liberal toward

13. *Collins* v. *America, a woman of color,* 9 B. Mon. (Ky.) 565, 571 (1849).

14. *Harry* v. *Decker & Hopkins,* Walker (Miss.) 36, 42 (1818).

15. For a discussion of how southern courts dealt with slaves charged with crimes,
see Nash, "A More Equitable Past?" "Fairness and Formalism," and "Reason of Slavery"; Mark Tushnet, "The American Law of Slavery, 1810–1860," 10 *Law and Society
Review* 119 (1975); Michael Hindus, "Black Justice under White Law: Criminal
Prosecutions of Blacks in Antebellum South Carolina," 63 *Journal of American History* 575 (1976); Daniel Flanigan, "Criminal Procedure in Slave Trials in the Antebellum South," 40 *Journal of Southern History* 537 (1974).

freedom claims than the North. With not unjustified pride, Missouri Senator Thomas Hart Benton claimed that slaves suing for freedom were "always preferring to try their case in a slave State, where they found most favor." During the Oregon debates of 1848, Illinois Senator Sidney Breese candidly admitted that in transit cases "the courts of the slave States have been more liberal . . . than the courts of the free States." Courts in Illinois had "uniformly decided against the right of freedom," while "in precisely similar cases" courts in Kentucky and Missouri freed slaves who had lived in the North. Breese found it "a remarkable fact" that in the slave states "where there was any doubt about the right to hold the person in slavery, the decision had been invariably in favor of the right to freedom."[16]

Yet, even as Breese was piling accolades on his slave-state neighbors, the pattern of their laws and decisions was changing. As early as 1837 Mississippi reversed its earlier policy of liberality and refused to recognize a manumission certified by an Ohio court. In 1845 Kentucky indicated that slaves might be introduced to a free state for a short period of time without any change of status. (Until the end of the Civil War, however, Kentucky continued to free slaves who had actually become residents of free states.) An 1846 Louisiana statute specifically eliminated free-state transit or residence as a basis for freedom. Finally, in 1852 Missouri reversed nearly three decades of decision making by declaring that a long-term residence in a free state would not make a slave free. Kentucky and a few other slave states continued to recognize freedom claims based on the laws of other states throughout the antebellum period. But even in these liberal states the trend was moving away from decisions in favor of liberty.[17] By the 1850s most of the South had, to one degree

---

16. Thomas Hart Benton, *Historical and Legal Examination of that part of the Decision of the Supreme Court of the United States in the Dred Scott Case* . . . (New York: D. Appleton and Company, 1857) 44–45n.

17. See the following cases for other states. Tennessee: *Blackmore and Hadley* v. *Negro Phill,* 7 Yeager 452 (1835); *Laura Jane* v. *Hagen, Admir.,* 10 Humphrey 332 (1849); Texas: *Moore's Adm'r* v. *Mary Minerva and Her Children,* 17 Tex. 20 (1856); Virginia: *Griffith* v. *Fanny,* Gil. 143 (1820); *Spotts* v. *Gillaspie,* 6 Rand. 566 (1828); *Hunter* v. *Fulcher,* 1 Leigh 172 (1829); *Betty and others* v. *Horton,* 5 Leigh 615 (1833); *Foster's Adm'r* v. *Fosters,* 10 Grat. 485 (1853). Virginia's relatively liberal attitude toward comity and free state residence may have been changing by the end of the 1850s. From the beginning some countervailing trends had always been apparent in Virginia. See, for example, *Lewis* v. *Fullerton,* 1 Rand. 15 (1821); *Charlton* v. *Unis,* 4 Grat. 58 (1847); *Unis & als.* v. *Charlton's adm'r & als.–Four Cases,* 12 Grat. 484 (1855); *Morris ex Parte,* 11 Grat. 292 (1854); *Virginia, Laws of 1834,* chap. 68. Also, *Richmond Enquirer,* 21 Feb. 1855, reported that one William Cranch was arrested for bringing a free Negro into the state when he returned to Virginia with his slave after they had been in New York for a year. Although under New York law the black was

or another, decided that interstate comity could not extend to cases involving slaves who claimed to be free.[18]

Kentucky

In 1806 a slave named Joseph sued for his freedom in Kentucky. In rejecting Joseph's plea, the Kentucky Court of Appeals noted that Joseph had never been "out of the limits of" Kentucky or Virginia. This decision seems to imply that had Joseph been outside Kentucky, and in a free state, he might have been entitled to his liberty.[19]

In 1808 the state legislature eliminated one type of freedom claim based on an out-of-state residence, which had apparently created problems for Kentucky masters. Pennsylvania's 1780 and 1788 statutes required that all masters register their slaves and indentured Negroes. Virginia required all masters bringing slaves into the state to record them and take an oath of intention to become citizens of the state. In both states the statutes freed slaves when masters failed to comply with the law.[20] These statutes also led to freedom

---

free, a judge in Richmond ruled that the black was still a slave and that Cranch had violated no law. Cited in Hurd, 2 *Law of Freedom and Bondage* 9.

18. See, for example, Georgia: *The State ex rel. Turner* v. *Lavinia, A Person of Color*, 25 Ga. 311 (1858); North Carolina: *Green & al.* v. *Lane & al.*, 8 Ired. Eq. 70 (1858); *Green & al.* v. *Lane & al.*, Busb. Eq. 102 (1852); *White* v. *Cline and White*, 7 Jones 174 (1859); Alabama: *Glover* v. *Millings*, 2 Stew. & P. 28 (1832). In Maryland, compare *Negro David* v. *Porter*, 4 Harr. & McH. 418 (1799), in which a slave hired out in Pennsylvania was freed, to *Cross* v. *Black*, 9 Gill. & J. 198 (1837), in which a manumission in Ohio was not enforced by the Maryland court. Also *Porter* v. *Butler*, 3 Harr. & McH. 168 (1795); *Davis* v. *Jacquin & Pomerait*, 5 Harr. & J. 100 (1820); Arkansas: *Rheubottom et al.* v. *Sadler Exr.*, 19 Ark. 491 (1858); South Carolina: *Guillemette* v. *Harper*, 4 Rich. 186 (1850), upheld the freedom of a black specifically emancipated in Ireland and then brought back to South Carolina as a slave. While taking note of *Somerset*, Justice John Belton O'Neall did not base his opinion on it, stating that "[T]hat case carries the law further than I should willingly acknowledge. . . ." Instead, he simply upheld the right of a master to free his slave in a free country. This right, which was not based on comity, was reaffirmed in *Willis et al.* v. *Jolliffe et al.*, 11 Rich. 447 (1860), which held that a master could take his slaves to Ohio and free them, as long as they did not return to South Carolina. The court there specifically rejected the idea that the Northwest Ordinance or the Ohio Constitution could "reach cases of persons passing through Ohio with slaves, or where a slave accompanies his master or mistress on a temporary sojourn for business or pleasure. For, in point of fact, the master, and the slave, as his property, are entitled by the comity of States, and also by the Constitution of the United States, to be protected"; *Willis* v. *Jolliffe* 513.

19. *Beall* v. *Joseph*, Hardin (Ky.) 51, 52 (1806).

20. For example, *Wilson* v. *Isbell*, 5 Call (Va.) 425 (1805); *Henderson* v. *Allens*, 1

suits in Kentucky. The preamble to Kentucky's 1808 statute noted that "creditors, purchasers and others are exposed to great injustice, by the assertion, by persons held in slavery, of dormant claims to their freedom, founded upon certain acts of the legislatures of Virginia and Pennsylvania." In "the interest and peace of society," the Kentucky legislature set a two-year limit on such claims. The constitutionality of this law was upheld in 1822, long after the two years had passed: a slave's claim to freedom was denied because it was based solely on the failure of her master to comply with registration laws in Pennsylvania and Virginia.[21]

The 1808 law was not, however, designed to enslave blacks who were born in Pennsylvania after 1780, or whose masters sojourned there longer than six months. In 1812 the slaves Violet and William sued for freedom on the ground that they were born in Pennsylvania after 1780. Their owner argued that the slaves could not "maintain their action under the act of Pennsylvania," because "its penalties and forfeitures" could not be enforced in Kentucky. But the Court of Appeals disagreed. "To admit" that the laws were enforceable only in Pennsylvania "would place it in the power of the master, at all times to evade the forfeitures of the act, and to keep in bondage and slavery those entitled to their freedom. It would only require a coercive transportation of a free man from the state of Pennsylvania to this state, to reduce him to a state of abject slavery." The court would not tolerate "[s]uch a construction," and held that the "coercive act" of the master "cannot alter their rights; cannot make them slaves, if they were free."[22]

The Kentucky court's early commitment to justice and freedom seems to have transcended technical rules. Violet and William had appealed in a joint action after their master had received a favorable verdict from the trial court. The master correctly argued that this was an improper appeal, because the "plaintiffs' right to freedom is not joint but several." The court might have simply denied the appeal on these technical grounds and left the blacks enslaved. In-

---

Hen. & M. (Va.) 235 (1807); *Murray* v. *M'Carty*, 2 Mumf. (Va.) 393 (1811); *Montgomery* v. *Fletcher*, 6 Rand. (Va.) 612 (1828); *Pennsylvania* v. *Blackmore*, Addison (Pa.) 284 (1797); *Lucy (a negro woman)* v. *Pumfrey*, Addison (Pa.) 380 (1799); *Giles (a negro man)* v. *Meeks*, Addison (Pa.) 384 (1799).

21. *Amy (a woman of colour)* v. *Smith*, 1 Lit. (Ky.) 326 (1822); see also *Frank* v. *Milam's ex'r*; *Tom* v. *Smith*; *Mary* v. *Shannon*; *Betsy* v. *Shannon*, 1 Bibb (Ky.) 615 (1809). For an attempt to enforce the Pennsylvania act in Kentucky, see John Rowan and Richard Johnson to Samuel McKean, 15 Aug. 1806, Pennsylvania Abolition Society Papers, reel 3, p. 141, HSP.

22. *Violet and William* v. *Stephens*, Lit. Sel. Ca. (Ky.) 147 (1812).

stead, the court dismissed the appeal and remanded the case for a new trial.[23]

The most important early Kentucky case to deal with slave transit was *Rankin* v. *Lydia* (1820).[24] In a comparatively long opinion[25] Judge Benjamin Mills thoroughly examined the problem of slaves who were brought into the Northwest Territory after the Ordinance of 1787 outlawed slavery there. The decision set a precedent that Kentucky would adhere to for the next forty-five years and that both northern and southern courts would often cite.[26]

Lydia was born a slave, in Kentucky, in 1805. In 1807 she was brought to Indiana and registered as an indentured servant. Lydia's indenture, which was for twenty years, would expire in 1827, when she was twenty-two years old. But in 1814 she was sold to Rankin, who removed her to Kentucky. In 1820 she sued for, and won, her freedom in the Shelby County Circuit Court. Rankin appealed to the Court of Appeals.

Judge Mills was unwilling to condemn slavery, or to be swayed by "appeals to morality." "In deciding this question," he declared, "we disclaim the influence of the general principles of liberty, which we all admire, and conceive it ought to be decided by the law as it is, and not as it ought to be." He reminded anyone who might disagree with this lack of idealism that "[s]lavery is sanctioned by the laws of this state." But he was quick to acknowledge that this was only "a right existing by positive law of a municipal character, without foundation in the law of nature, or the unwritten and common law." Although the Kentucky court would not base its decision on a theory of "in favorem vitae et libertatis," as its Mississippi counterpart had done, the court did feel an obligation to interpret and enforce the law with complete impartiality. And, if the law in one case made a man a slave, then the law in another might "by an authority equally imperious" free a slave: "Every argument which supports the right of the master on one side, based upon the force of written law, must be equally conclusive in favor of the slave when he can point out in the statute the clause which secures his freedom."[27]

---

23. Ibid. 147–49. See also *Barringtons (coloured persons)* v. *Logan's Administrators*, 2 Dana (Ky.) 432 (1834); *Gentry* v. *Polly McMinnis*, 3 Dana (Ky.) 382 (1835).

24. *Rankin* v. *Lydia*, 2 A. K. Marsh. (Ky.) 467 (1820).

25. The opinion was over twelve pages long in an era when many opinions were less than one page long. One interesting aspect of this study is the ever-increasing size of opinions throughout the period.

26. For example, *Commonwealth* v. *Aves*, 18 Pick. (Mass.) 193, 217 (1836); *Jackson* v. *Bulloch*, 12 Day (Conn.) 38, 41 (1837); *Lemmon* v. *The People*, 20 N.Y. 562, 587 (1860); *Scott* v. *Emerson*, 15 Mo. 577, 591 (1852); *Marie Louise, f.w.c.* v. *Marot et al.*, 9 La. 473, 475 (1836).

27. *Rankin* v. *Lydia*, 2 A. K. Marsh. (Ky.) 467–70 (1820).

In determining Lydia's status, Judge Mills examined the Indiana territorial statutes and the Northwest Ordinance. He concluded that their purpose was to proclaim "that every inhabitant *shall be free.*" Therefore, if a slave "could exist and reside in the territory, and be there a slave, the ordinance could not be true—for slavery existed, the ordinance notwithstanding." Mills could not "recognize the logic that will prove a man free and a slave at the same time—or that slavery can exist without a right or power in some one existing over the slave at the same moment." And if Lydia was a slave in Indiana, then "[w]here, or in who, did the right to the servitude or slavery" exist? It clearly was "[n]ot in any resident of Kentucky; for no citizen in this state had then any claim to her"; and it could not exist in Indiana. Thus Lydia could not have been a slave while in Indiana.[28]

But there remained the question of her status after returning to Kentucky. This was not a problem for Violet and William, because they had *never* been slaves. Lydia, however, was born a slave. Rankin's counsel argued that although "the compact vested a right to freedom, yet, as it was never acknowledged, and as Lydia was never in its actual enjoyment, the right cannot be coerced." This proposition, the Kentucky court pointed out, had no analogy in law. Citing the law of inheritance, Judge Mills pointed out that an heir could gain "the vested right of inheritance" even though the claim had been dormant for many years. As to the suggestion that Lydia's freedom was temporary and existed only while she was in Indiana, the court felt that the slave status "was not only suspended, but ceased to exist," and the court was "not aware of any law of the state which can or does bring into operation the right of slavery when once destroyed." Indeed, such a presumption cast an aspersion on the very honor of the state. In an oblique acknowledgment of *Somerset*, Mills asked: "Is it to be seriously contended that so soon as he transported her to the Kentucky shore, the noxious atmosphere of this state, without any express law for the purpose, clamped upon her newly forged chains of slavery, after the old ones were destroyed! For the honor of our country, we cannot for a moment admit, that the bare treading of its soil is thus dangerous, even to the degraded African."[29]

Rankin's counsel also argued that freeing Lydia would be an act "of a penal character"; and because this penalty "accrued by the laws of another government," it could not, or at least should not, be enforced in Kentucky. Here for the first time, Mills suggested natural rights arguments might have some force in Kentucky. Mills

28. Ibid. 471–72.
29. Ibid. 471.

thought that if some other white person had disputed Rankin's title to Lydia, by claiming her as a slave under some Indiana law that was unknown in Kentucky, Rankin's argument based on "a penal character" of the law *might* have some force. But in this case it was of no value, because it was Lydia herself who disputed Rankin's claim to her services. Mills declared that "freedom is the natural right of man, although it may not be his birth right." Thus, the Kentucky court was not really freeing Lydia, and thereby enforcing some Indiana statute, but was merely acknowledging that her residence in Indiana had already freed her.[30]

After easily disposing of these complex legal propositions, Mills came to Rankin's simplest and yet "most formidable" argument: "that arising *ab inconvenienti* [from hardship]." Rankin contended that "there is no difference between a transient passing or sojourning in Indiana, under the ordinance in question, and a residence there." If a slave was "there an hour" he "would be as much under the influence of the ordinance as the one who resided ten years." Just as his abolitionist counterparts would do a few years later, trying to prove the opposite point, Rankin's counsel offered a list of horrible consequences if his position were not accepted by the court: "[I]f the ordinance could give freedom at all, it could and would do it in a moment when the slave touched the enchanted shore, and that the consequence would be, that the slave of the traveller who attended his master—the slave of the officer who marched in the late armies of the United States—those sent of [*sic*] errands to the opposite shore—or attending their masters while removing beyond the Mississippi through the territory, would all have an equal right to freedom with Lydia; and that, by a decision in her favor, the right to such property would be much jeopardized."[31]

Mills considered this argument with great care. Using extensive quotes from Emmerich de Vattel's *Law of Nations*, Mills proved to his own satisfaction that there was a substantive difference between transit and residence. One important difference was that property in transit was exempt from municipal regulations, while property of a domiciled individual was not. Clearly Lydia's original master had become domiciled and, indeed, was still domiciled in Indiana. Thus, she became subject to the laws of that state. Had it been a case of transit, a different result would have been called for. He noted that Vattel's rules applied to international conflicts, and if "nations, amidst all their jealousies and thirst for power, could adopt such rules to govern themselves, . . . how much stronger is the reason and

---

30. Ibid. 475–76.
31. Ibid. 476–77.

propriety of the rule, when applied between the different branches of the American family?" Unable to appreciate the implicit moral questions of slavery that would soon threaten comity on both sides of the Ohio River, Mills asked, "Can it be for a moment supposed that any one of them [the states] would reject a principle so strongly based in reason, propriety, and the nature of things?" Curiously, at no point in this discussion did he mention any of the northern decisions and statutes that supported the right of transit, although he had already cited Pennsylvania's gradual emancipation statute.[32]

Mills ended his opinion by further suggesting that the ab inconvenienti argument might backfire. Indiana had passed laws "prohibiting the removal of their domiciled negroes." If Kentucky ignored these laws and blacks were illegally removed and enslaved in Kentucky, it would "produce retaliatory measures." The free states would "detain and refuse our transient slaves" a right of uninterrupted movement. Such a response was, of course, comity at its most basic level. Kentucky would enforce Indiana's laws in the hope that Indiana would enforce Kentucky's laws. Kentucky would take property away from its own citizens if they flagrantly violated Indiana's law, in order to preserve the property of Kentucky citizens who did not violate the law of the free state. When northern states changed their laws, however, Kentucky would reevaluate its position. For the moment, the court upheld Lydia's claim to freedom, which was "equally as precious, valuable and sacred, as if it commenced with her existence."[33]

Although this case might have been viewed as one of simple comity—shall Kentucky enforce the freedom granted under Indiana's statute—the Kentucky court went far beyond the comity issue. Only at the very end of the decision, in the answer to Rankin's ab inconvenienti argument, was the comity question seriously considered. For the most part, Lydia's freedom claim was sustained on the basis of her long residence in a place where there were no laws allowing slavery to exist and where there were constitutional prohibitions against it. Even without her formal emancipation and indenture under Indiana law, Lydia's claim would probably have been upheld, because in the view of the Kentucky court, her very residence in a nonslave jurisdiction made her a free woman for life.

Following Lydia's case, the Kentucky Court of Appeals heard a number of cases in which slaves claimed their freedom on the basis of northern residence or birth. In these cases the court maintained its policy of freeing those slaves who had resided or been born in free

32. Ibid. 477–78, 474.
33. Ibid. 479.

jurisdictions. The problem of transit was not involved in any of the cases, because the residence or birth was clearly established. Until 1844 Kentucky's policy underwent no changes.[34]

In 1844 the court of appeals heard the dual case of *Graham* v. *Strader and Strader* v. *Graham.* It was heard again in 1847 and went to the United States Supreme Court in 1850.[35] The case provided the Kentucky court with an opportunity to apply the limiting dictum in *Rankin* v. *Lydia* concerning slave transit and the short-term use of a slave in free states. As such, it became the first major slave-state opinion to support the right of a master voluntarily to employ his slaves in a free state for a short time, and then return to a slave state, where they would remain slaves. As a federal case, *Strader* was used, or perhaps misused, by the United States Supreme Court as a precedent for its decision in *Dred Scott* v. *Sandford* (1857).[36]

Although it became a major precedent for denying freedom, *Strader* was not brought as a freedom suit. Rather, Graham brought suit to recover damages for three slaves who had traveled "by steamboat from Louisville to Cincinnati" and then escaped to Canada. Graham sued Strader and others connected with the steamboat for the value of the slaves.[37]

Graham's three slaves, Reuben, Henry, and George, were trained "scientific musicians" valued at fifteen hundred dollars each. In 1837 Graham allowed Reuben and Henry to study music in Louisville with a free black named Williams. Graham authorized Williams "to take them to Cincinnati, New Albany [Indiana] or to any part of the South, even so far as New Orleans." Williams had full control over the slaves until Graham might "wish to call them home." Graham relinquished any claim to money the slaves might earn under Williams's tutelage, it being his "object . . . to have them well trained in music."[38]

In his letter authorizing Williams to teach and govern the slaves, Graham revealed a naiveté about the fidelity of slaves shared by many other masters. Graham told Williams that the slaves "have

34. *Bush's Representatives* v. *White*, 3 T. B. Mon. (Ky.) 100 (1825); *Carney, a coloured man* v. *Hampton*, 3 T. B. Mon. (Ky.) 228 (1826); *Barringtons (coloured persons)* v. *Logan's Administrators*, 2 Dana (Ky.) 432 (1834); *Gentry* v. *Polly McMinnis*, 3 Dana (Ky.) 382 (1835); *Amy (a woman of color)* v. *Smith*, 1 Lit. (Ky.) 326 (1822).
35. *Strader et al.* v. *Graham*, 5 B. Mon. (Ky.) 173 (1844); 7 B. Mon. 637 (1847); *Strader et al.* v. *Graham*, 10 Howard (U.S.) 82 (1850).
36. *Dred Scott* v. *Sandford*, 19 Howard (U.S.) 393 (1857). For a discussion of *Strader* v. *Graham* and *Dred Scott* v. *Sandford* as federal cases, see chap. 8.
37. *Strader* v. *Graham*, 5 B. Mon. 173.
38. Ibid. 173–74.

been faithful hardworking servants, and I have no fear but that they will always be true to their duty, no matter in what situation they may be placed." He had "no fear" they would "ever act knowingly wrong, or put me in trouble." In the next four years the slaves traveled in Ohio, Indiana, and Kentucky, with and without Williams, and always returned to Louisville. Ultimately Graham's faith proved ill-founded. In January 1841 both slaves, together with a third, boarded Strader's steamboat for Ohio and absconded for freedom, taking clothes, books, and musical instruments with them.[39]

Graham sued under a Kentucky statute that made shipowners and captains responsible for slaves who escaped by boarding their ships. The defendants asserted that the blacks were not "slaves" because they had been allowed "to travel about as free negroes" and had received "their wages earned by them." Furthermore, they were "frequently" allowed to leave Kentucky "as if they were free." The defendants also claimed that the "written permission" to go to Ohio and Indiana had freed them. They were sent to the free states "to perform service as slaves," and thus "they acquired a right to freedom" because slavery could not exist in the free states.[40] If the slaves were indeed free, then they were not owned by Graham and he could not recover for their loss.

Strader also argued that even if the blacks were still slaves, the letter of 1837 gave them blanket permission to travel across the river. At the initial hearing before the Louisville Chancery Court, the chancellor agreed that the letter "was a sufficient license" to take Henry and Reuben out of the state and he dismissed the suit for the value of those two slaves. The question of liability for George was put to the jury, which awarded Graham a thousand dollars. Neither side was happy with the result and both appealed.[41]

The Kentucky Court of Appeals reversed the decision to dismiss the claim for the value of Henry and Reuben and remanded the entire case for further proceedings. The court held that the 1837 letter allowed the slaves to leave the state only if they were accompanied by Williams. In addition, there was no pretense that the ship captain had any knowledge of the letter when he allowed the slaves to board the steamboat.[42]

In order to reverse the lower court decision, the court of appeals had to reject the defense's claim that the blacks became free by visiting and working in Ohio and Indiana. Graham argued that

39. Ibid.
40. Ibid. 176, 173–74.
41. Ibid. 175–76, 187.
42. Ibid. 176–78, 184.

Strader could not "assert a right to freedom in Henry and Reuben, under the laws of Ohio and Indiana, which they did not themselves assert, and thus try the question of their freedom in this collateral way." This reasoning implied that if Henry and Reuben had sued for freedom they might have won. Speaking for the court, Justice Thomas A. Marshall was not ready to concede even this.[43]

Marshall acknowledged that the Northwest Ordinance and the Indiana and Ohio constitutions ended slavery for citizens and residents in those states. He "conceded" that either state might "not only refuse their aid to a master voluntarily bringing his slave within its territory, even for a temporary purpose" but might also "aid the slave in resisting that claim, and thus enable him, if he will, to remain there a freeman." This right the free states had, but it was not a right that Marshall thought they should exercise.[44]

Marshall saw a clear distinction between submitting to the laws of a state while temporarily under its jurisdiction and enforcing them in the courts of another state. While a master risked losing his slave by entering the free state, "[h]e certainly" was "not to be understood as renouncing it when he takes the slave with him as a slave, with the intention of bringing him back immediately as such." And if the slave willingly returned to the slave state, without resorting to the rights accorded him in the free state, the court could "perceive no principle which would afterwards entitle him to claim his freedom in the domestic forum, on the ground that he might have asserted it in the foreign State, and could not have been compelled to return." Under this reasoning, freedom was not gained "instantaneously and forever, by the mere force of this general principle" that no slavery could exist north of the Ohio River. Judge Marshall thought that even when slaves were hired out in the free states, they were "still sojourners for a transient purpose, not inhabitants nor residents." In the logic of the Kentucky court it followed:

> If a master may take his slave into one of these States,
> he may surely receive and direct his services while they
> are voluntarily rendered: his charging and receiving pay for
> those services when directed to the benefit or amusement of
> others, is itself an assertion of right and dominion over them,
> which cannot operate either as a renunciation or a forfeiture,
> and as he might in this State, give or allow them a part of what
> was earned, without affecting his right of dominion over
> them, he might do it there.[45]

43. Ibid. 179–80.
44. Ibid. 180–81.
45. Ibid. 180–81, 183–84.

Had the Kentucky court acted any other way, it would be placing its "laws and policy in subordination to those of a foreign State," which "would be carrying the principle of comity to a most unwarrantable length. . . ." This was especially so since Kentucky's law had met "with so little respect" in the free states. The principle "that a slave returning voluntarily with his master from a free State, is still a slave by the laws of his own country" was supported by citations from Story's *Commentaries on the Conflict of Laws*, *Commonwealth* v. *Aves*, and *The Slave, Grace*.[46]

While denying that Reuben or Henry might be free, the court reaffirmed the position, first outlined in *Rankin* v. *Lydia*, that a slave taken to reside in a free state would be free. But, if the "master and slave, having gone from their own country, not with a view of becoming domiciled in another, but for a merely transient purpose, and having in accordance with their intention, returned without any visible change in their relations, their relative condition under their own laws, will remain the same as [if] they had never gone."[47]

On remand Strader was found liable for the slaves. He again appealed to the court of appeals, where Marshall, now chief justice, again wrote the opinion of the court. Marshall found no errors in the second trial and affirmed its result. He did, however, "take this opportunity of relieving" the earlier opinion of some "misconstruction" that had been associated with it. This problem centered on "the effect of a transient visit made by master and slave to a State in which slavery is prohibited by the fundamental law," which was "supposed to involve the principle or inference . . . that the slave though once free by reason of such visit, becomes a slave again by a voluntary return to Kentucky. . . . " The court had not held this in its first opinion in *Strader*, and Marshall wanted to reaffirm that. Neither opinion contained any

> concession either express or implied, that the slaves in
> question were ever free, or could properly have become so
> by being temporarily in a free State with their master or other
> citizen of this State, having control over them. On the contrary,
> it is clearly and repeatedly stated, that the Court does not
> admit that in consequence of such a fact, and by force of
> the mere general prohibition of slavery in the fundamental or
> declaratory law of the State, which might be thus visited,
> the relation of master and slave, as existing under the laws of
> their own State, would be affected. And a question is made
> even as to the effect to be given here, to the decision of a

46. Ibid. 182–83.
47. Ibid. 181–82.

tribunal in the free State, which upon the appeal of the
slave there, should have declared him free.[48]

In 1850 Strader appealed to the United States Supreme Court,
claiming that the Kentucky decision violated the Northwest Ordinance. Speaking for a unanimous court, Chief Justice Taney declared that "[e]very State has an undoubted right to determine the
status, or domestic and social condition, of the persons domiciled
within its territory," unless specifically restrained by the United
States Constitution. Thus, Kentucky had the right to decide who
was a slave and who was not, and the United States Supreme Court
could not impose the laws of Ohio on the state of Kentucky. The
Supreme Court dismissed Strader's appeal for want of jurisdiction
based on its determination that the Northwest Ordinance was no
longer in effect in Ohio and Indiana and could not be enforced in
Kentucky.[49]

Although the United States Supreme Court decision in *Strader* v.
Graham upheld the right of a state to ignore the laws of other states
in determining the status of blacks, the Kentucky Court of Appeals
was not ready to go that far. In 1848 the court freed Tom Davis, who
had lived in Ohio for two years. The court felt that by this "residence in Ohio, the plaintiff became free, and being once free, his
return to this State did not make him again a slave." This freedom was secured "by virtue of the ordinance of 1787" as decided in
Rankin v. *Lydia* and other cases. Thus, before the United States Supreme Court could declare the ordinance inoperative in its opinion
in *Strader*, the Kentucky court again asserted its viability. The Kentucky court found no conflict "between these views and the doctrine
and principles asserted in" *Strader* v. *Graham*:

> There the reasoning all applies to a case where the slave
> is taken, for a temporary purpose, to a State where slavery
> is prohibited, with an intention not of residence, but to bring
> him back again as a slave in this State. In such a case it was
> held, even if the slave by appealing to the laws of the foreign
> State, while within its jurisdiction, could release himself from
> the control of his master, and become free, yet if he failed to
> do so, and returned voluntarily, his condition would be
> unchanged, and he would still remain a slave.

Here, however, the slave had lived in Ohio "a sufficient length of
time to make that the place of his domicil" and, accordingly, he

48. *Strader* v. *Graham*, 7 B. Mon. 633, 635 (1847).
49. *Strader et al.* v. *Graham*, 10 Howard (U.S.) 82, 93, 99 (1850).

was free.[50] In a number of subsequent cases, the principles laid down in *Lydia* and *Strader* and reaffirmed in Tom Davis's case were applied. Freedom depended on the length of time and the nature of the residence in a free jurisdiction.[51]

Until 1851 all of Kentucky's transit cases involved visits or residences in the Northwest Territory or the states created from it.[52] In that year, however, the court of appeals heard *Maria* v. *Kirby* (1851),[53] a freedom suit based on a sojourn in Pennsylvania. Two years later *Ferry* v. *Street* (1853)[54] raised a similar claim. Although both suits were based on time spent in Pennsylvania and on the laws of that state, the specific facts of the cases differed and the resulting decisions created a startling contrast. Both cases are distinguishable from *Strader* v. *Graham* and *Rankin* v. *Lydia*, although the court rested its decisions primarily on those two precedents.

Mrs. Rebecca Kirby had taken her slave Maria to Pennsylvania in 1848, and "during a delay of three or four days in Washington County" a free black petitioned for a writ of habeas corpus. Maria was brought before a Pennsylvania judge who "discharged" her

50. *Tom Davis of color* v. *Tingle et al.*, 8 B. Mon. (Ky.) 539, 545–46 (1848).

51. In the following cases slaves were not freed, even though they spent time and may have worked in free states: *Collins* v. *America, a woman of color*, 9 B. Mon. 565 (1849); *Ben Mercer (of color)* v. *Gilman*, 11 B. Mon. 210 (1850); *Maria* v. *Kirby*, 12 B. Mon. 542 (1851); *Norris (of color)* v. *Patton's Administrator*, 15 B. Mon. 575 (1855); *Winn* v. *Sam Martin (of color)*, 4 Metc. 231 (1862). In 1846 the Franklin County Circuit Court refused to allow the extradition of two whites accused of kidnapping a free black from Ohio. The black man, Jerry Phinney, was born a slave in Kentucky, but was hired out to a gambler who took him to Cincinnati for six months. He was later allowed to return to Cincinnati to obtain his belongings. On this trip he remained in Cincinnati until he was forcibly brought back to Kentucky. In the circuit court Judge Mason Brown ruled that Phinney had not gained his freedom in the six-months residence in Cincinnati, and thus no kidnapping took place. Judge Mason cited *Strader* v. *Graham* in support of this decision. *The State of Ohio vs. Forbes and Armitage, Arrested Upon the Requisition of the Government of Ohio, On Charge of Kidnapping Jerry Phinney, and Tried Before the Franklin Circuit Court of Kentucky, April 10, 1846* (N.p., 1846); slaves gained their freedom after long-term sojourn or residence in *Ferry* v. *Street*, 14 B. Mon. 355 (1853); and *Joe Henry (of color)* v. *Graves*, 2 Duv. 259 (1865). Many of the slaves who did not win their freedom in Kentucky might have been able to do so in Missouri, before the *Dred Scott* case, since in Missouri slaves were sometimes freed if they worked in a free state for a very short period of time, even if they did not live there.

52. Four Kentucky cases involved birth in Pennsylvania and two involved birth in New York: *Violet and William* v. *Stephens*, Lit. Sel. Ca. 147 (1812); *Frank* v. *Milam's ex'r et al.*, 1 Bibb 615 (1809); *Barringtons (coloured persons)* v. *Logan's Administrators*, 2 Dana 432 (1834); *Gentry* v. *Polly McMinnis*, 3 Dana 382 (1835); *Carney (a coloured man)* v. *Hampton*, 3 T. B. Mon. 228 (1826); and *Commonwealth* v. *Van Tuyl*, 1 Metc. 1 (1858).

53. *Maria* v. *Kirby*, 12 B. Mon. 542 (1851).

54. *Ferry* v. *Street*, 14 B. Mon. 355 (1853).

from "custody and restraint" and declared her free "to go where she pleases without coercion or restraint from any one." Maria returned to Kentucky where she remained a slave until 1850, when she sued for her freedom.[55]

Maria's claim can be distinguished from *Strader* in two important ways. First, Maria did not claim freedom under some "general principle" of a constitutional provision. Rather, she relied on the Pennsylvania statutes of 1780, 1788, and 1847. Second, she relied on a specific judicial decree that had freed her in Pennsylvania. Thus she could argue that after the decree she was free, and as the Kentucky court had previously declared, once a person was free, returning to Kentucky did not re-create the status of slave. Unlike the blacks in *Strader*, Maria had "asserted it [the right to freedom] in the foreign State" when her freedom was decreed by the Pennsylvania judge.

Speaking for the court, Judge Marshall acknowledged the right of Pennsylvania "to determine by her laws, what shall be the condition of all persons within her limits." But he would "not admit that, as to strangers, this right exists any longer than while they are within her [Pennsylvania's] limits, or that on the ground of a transient entry, or momentary sojourn, upon her territory for a temporary and lawful purpose, a new and permanent condition or *status* can by her laws be stamped [*sic*] upon strangers so as that it shall adhere to them and determine their condition on their return to their own domicil."[56] This position was essentially the same as that taken in *Strader*. Unlike the slaves in *Strader*, or *The Slave, Grace*, however, Maria had been brought before a judicial authority in the free state, where her new status was affirmed. Had Marshall acknowledged that the status was changed by the Pennsylvania law or the habeas corpus action, then he would have been violating the precedents and maxims that held that slavery could not reattach itself once it had been legally dissolved.

But Marshall did not acknowledge that Maria had ever been free. He agreed only that while in Pennsylvania she was discharged from her "restraint" and had been declared "a free woman to go where she pleases, etc." This wording, Marshall thought, conceded "her right of choice between freedom and slavery." And because she returned to Kentucky with her owner, Marshall concluded that she thus chose to remain a slave. Marshall felt that this position was strengthened by the fact that Maria had not sued for freedom in Pennsylvania, but that a free black had obtained the writ of habeas corpus on her behalf, without her knowledge.[57] This position was

55. *Maria* v. *Kirby* 542.
56. Ibid. 542, 545.
57. Ibid. 542–43, 545.

somewhat problematic, in legal terms, since it implied that Maria had made a legal choice, whether to be free or not. Because slaves could rarely make legal decisions about anything,[58] Maria must have been a free person when she chose to return to slavery. But no Kentucky law would make Maria a slave when she returned to that state, even if she wanted to be one. In any event, she had not formally requested to become a slave; she had merely returned to Kentucky.

Although Marshall did not deal with this problem, he did suggest another reason for the decision: simply that the case in Pennsylvania was not conclusive because it had been heard by only a circuit court judge, and there "was no regular litigation between Mrs. Kirby and Maria, and therefore no final determination of their respective rights."[59]

All of Marshall's reasons appear simply to be rationalizations for the real basis of the decision: the Kentucky court was unwilling to enforce or recognize statutes and judicial acts of Pennsylvania that freed slaves in transit. Marshall, after all his attempts to explain himself around this, finally admitted, "[S]uch a statute would not . . . operate of itself to make Maria free according to our laws, so neither can the proceedings upon the *habeas corpus* have that effect" in the Kentucky court. As far as granting comity to Pennsylvania's laws, Kentucky was willing to do so only if those laws were of the type that would be enforced in Kentucky.[60]

Similarly, Kentucky was unwilling to give "Full Faith and Credit" to Pennsylvania's judicial proceedings. Marshall found the proceedings in this case to be "conclusive as to nothing except that such proceedings were had." Thus "there was nothing decided by the Judge, but that the slave became free by being brought into that State, and as the question is now to be decided by our laws, we say that according to our laws, the transitory ingress of Mrs. Kirby and her slave into the State of Pennsylvania did not make the slave absolutely free, notwithstanding the statute and the decision under it."[61]

Thus comity was denied to the statutes and proceedings of a neighboring state. Kentucky could not have reenslaved Maria if she had remained in Pennsylvania, but since she chose to return to Kentucky the proceedings in Pennsylvania could be ignored. The Kentucky court did not speculate on why Maria might have returned to

---

58. See *Thomas* v. *Generis*, 16 La. Ann. 483 (1849) below. Also, *Bailey & als.* v. *Poindexter's ex'or*, 14 Grat. (Va.) 132 (1858).

59. *Maria* v. *Kirby* 542, 551, 543.

60. Ibid. 550.

61. Ibid. 551.

Kentucky: on the assumption that she was a free woman; under coercion; or on the assumption she might later claim her freedom. Nor did the court suggest what would have happened if Maria had returned to Kentucky and immediately claimed her freedom. All the court did was to assert that the Pennsylvania law and court decision would be ignored in Kentucky.

Maria v. *Kirby* might have signaled the end of comity in Kentucky but, like *Strader* v. *Graham,* it only limited the freeing of slaves. The Kentucky court objected to the immediate freeing of Maria and, in effect, to the denial of comity *by Pennsylvania* toward Kentuckians traveling in that free state. In his opinion Marshall stated that the 1847 repeal of the six-months law "does not seem to refer itself to any view of internal policy, but results apparently from a disregard or denial of rights of property established by our laws, and which on principles of comity, should be at least passively respected in other States so far as their exercise in those States would not disturb the peace and order of society, or violate its internal policy." Indeed, Marshall suggested that if a State passed a law freeing a slave after "six months, or three months, or even one, . . . there might be some reasons for saying that such a law should operate permanently, even upon the rights of strangers, because they would have an opportunity of knowing its provisions and avoiding its consequences."[62]

This dictum was tested two years later in *Ferry* v. *Street* (1853). In 1838 the slave Clarissa Street was sent to Pennsylvania by her owner, Mrs. Trigg, to nurse Trigg's relative. Before sending Street to Pennsylvania, Trigg consulted a friend, who "informed her that he was no lawyer, but his impression was, that if Clarissa should remain in Pennsylvania as long as six months, she would be entitled to her freedom." Trigg thought the slave would be there for at least a year, but "she did not believe Clarissa would avail herself of the laws of Pennsylvania, because she had a husband and children in Kentucky, and because Clarissa knew she was to be free at her (Mrs. Trigg's) death."[63]

Clarissa returned to Kentucky after more than six months in Pennsylvania. She remained a slave there for the next fifteen years. In the meantime, Trigg went into debt and sold Clarissa to her stepdaughter, Mrs. Ferry, with the understanding that Clarissa could be repurchased at a later date. But Trigg died before she repurchased Clarissa. By the terms of Trigg's will, all her remaining slaves were freed, but Clarissa remained in bondage and sued for freedom.

The Kentucky court noted that this case was the first in which it had had to adjudicate a case involving Pennsylvania's six-months

62. Ibid. 547–48.
63. *Ferry* v. *Street* 355, 356.

law, although the law had been repealed six years earlier. The court asserted the right of transit and short sojourn with a slave in a free state, but it also cited the dictum in *Maria* v. *Kirby* that reasonable free-state policy ought to be enforced. The court noted that Trigg knew Pennsylvania's laws before she sent Clarissa there, and "in such a case" it concluded "the condition of Clarissa in that state, after remaining in that state longer than six months, should follow her to Kentucky, and be her condition here." "Under these circumstances" the court found "she was free there, and should be free here."[64]

Since Mrs. Ferry knew the facts of Clarissa's residence in Pennsylvania, she had no reason to claim that the sale had been a fraud, especially since Ferry was also Trigg's executor and knew that Trigg wanted the estate to purchase Clarissa and then free her with the rest of Trigg's slaves. But as executor Ferry had prevented this. The ironic justice was that Ferry lost the money she gave to Trigg as well as the right to Clarissa's labor. Clarissa was freed and the Kentucky court showed that when a free state was reasonable in its antislavery legislation, at least this one slave state would continue to free slaves by enforcing such legislation. Indeed, as late as 1865 the Kentucky Court of Appeals would free a slave whose master had kept him in Illinois for six months.[65] In suits based on short-term transit, however, the Kentucky court remained firm in its opinion that slaves were not entitled to their freedom.

Throughout the antebellum period the Kentucky court remained, with respect to comity, one of the most consistent and fair-minded of any of the slave-state courts. Unlike most other slave states, neither the courts nor the legislature in Kentucky succumbed to the pressures of the era to the point of denying freedom to slaves who had lived in free states. As will be seen below, such moderate states as Louisiana and Missouri, as well as a fire-eater like Mississippi, were unable or unwilling to prevent the passions of the day from being incorporated into their legal systems. This is particularly striking since all three states began as being *more* liberal toward the claims of slaves than Kentucky. While Kentucky remained on an even keel throughout the period, these other states changed quite dramatically.[66]

---

64. Ibid. 360.

65. *Joe Henry (of color)* v. *Graves*, 2 Duv. 259 (1865).

66. See above, n. 17. Especially see Virginia and Tennessee cases, which indicate that those states remained almost as consistent as Kentucky. Perhaps it is significant that in the election of 1860 these three states remained moderate, voting for the compromise ticket of Bell-Everett under the Constitutional-Union party. Yet, these moderate states showed some change away from comity. Tennessee's cases do not

Louisiana

Louisiana was unique among the slave states in its tolerance for free blacks. Some free blacks became quite wealthy, owning plantations and slaves. Some had white husbands or wives. Others lived openly with their white paramours. Free blacks attended school with whites, were members of slave patrols, and joined the militia. Indeed, three regiments of free blacks offered to join the Confederate army.[67] Although Louisiana was no paradise for free blacks, they probably enjoyed greater social and legal protections than those in the other southern, and most northern, states.

The tolerance of free blacks in Louisiana was probably due to that state's French and Spanish background. The French influence was particularly strong in the state's legal system. As one expert recently noted, "The law of slavery, based on the French *Code Noir*, was unique in some respects. . . ." The *Code Noir*, along with French precedents, regulated the freeing of blacks who had lived or traveled in free jurisdictions. From 1791 on, the law of France proclaimed, "Tout individu est libre aussitôt qu'il est en France." In the Louisiana courts this law was applied not only to France, but to all free jurisdictions. Even after 1846, when the legislature specifically banned judicial emancipations based on free-state residence, the Louisiana court freed some slaves who had lived in free jurisdictions. By the beginning of the Civil War, however, the liberating aspects of the *Code Noir* were rejected, as Louisiana brought the code "into harmony with the slave codes in the other southern states."[68]

---

provide a large enough sample to draw any clear conclusions, but the evidence from Virginia indicates that that state was no longer willing to free slaves who had lived in the North. In addition, in Kentucky most of the late antebellum cases were decided against the slave petitioners. Fehrenbacher argues that this outcome resulted because the nature of the cases had changed from long-term sojourn to short-term transit; Fehrenbacher, *Dred Scott Case* 55–56. However, it is also possible to view these later cases as a gradual movement away from freedom. Many of the slaves involved had worked in the North; see n. 51 above. Working in a free state had often been a reason for freeing a slave in Missouri and in some of the free states. Yet, Kentucky rejected this test in favor of a strict time-limit approach.

67. John W. Blassingame, *Black New Orleans: 1860–1880* (Chicago: University of Chicago Press, 1973) 1–47; Ira Berlin, *Slaves without Masters: The Free Negro in the Antebellum South* (New York: Pantheon Books, 1974) 108–32. The free "blacks" in Louisiana were usually mulattoes, known as *libre gens du couleur*. The fact that Louisiana made any distinctions between Negroes and mulattoes underscores the state's unique race relations.

68. George Dargo, *Jefferson's Louisiana: Politics and the Clash of Legal Traditions* (Cambridge: Harvard University Press, 1975) 171–73. Helen Tunnicliff Catterall, 3 *Judicial Cases Concerning American Slavery and the Negro* (5 vols. Washington: Carnegie Institution, 1926–37) 389; *Louisiana Laws of 1846*, chap. 189.

In 1810 Adelle, "a woman of color," sued for her freedom. She had been brought from the West Indies and enrolled in a New York boarding school before being taken to New Orleans. Although these facts would have freed Adelle under New York law, the territorial court freed her because she was mulatto and her alleged owner could produce no "written title" to her. The presumption was that "negroes brought to this country" were slaves, but "[p]ersons of color may have descended from Indians on both sides, from a white parent, or mulatto parents in possession of their freedom."[69]

Six years later, in *Forsyth* v. *Nash* (1816)[70] the Louisiana Supreme Court suggested that residence in a free state might free a slave. In 1803 Forsyth purchased Nash in the Michigan Territory, where a deed of sale was recorded. He was later taken to Illinois. Nash eventually escaped and was captured in New Orleans, where Forsyth sued to establish his claim as Nash's owner. The Louisiana court concluded there was "no evidence of any residence of the defendant [Nash], in any country in which slavery is lawful." Therefore, the court had to examine the Northwest Ordinance, which was the law of Nash's domicile. Servitude under the ordinance was allowed only "for conviction of a crime by which freedom was *forfeited*" or for the capture and rendition of fugitive slaves. Neither of these applied to Nash, and the court accordingly released him. Whether Nash had ever been a slave remained in doubt. His freedom was affirmed, not solely because he lived in free territories, but also because Forsyth "failed in a very essential point, proof of the alleged slavery of the defendant." This failure was of course mainly attributable to Nash's lifetime residence in the Northwest Territory. But had Nash been born of a slave mother in a slave jurisdiction, and proof of that been established, he still might have been free because of his residence in the Northwest Territory.[71] Ironically, Nash gained his freedom by running away to a slave state. It is impossible to know if Nash purposely ran to Louisiana because he felt a free black would fare better there or simply ended up there in his efforts to elude Forsyth. But his case underscores the pro-freedom inclination of some southern courts in this early period.

While *Forsyth* v. *Nash* did not turn entirely on free-state residence, the court's opinion suggested that such residence might work to free a slave. This was affirmed in *Lunsford* v. *Coquillon* (1824).[72] Lunsford, unlike Nash (but like Lydia in Kentucky), did "not pretend that she was born free," but claimed her freedom on the basis of

69. *Adelle* v. *Beauregard*, 1 Mart. O.S. (La.) 183 (1810).
70. *Forsyth* v. *Nash*, 4 Mart. O.S. (La.) 385 (1816).
71. Ibid. 385, 388–90.
72. *Lunsford* v. *Coquillon*, 2 Mart. N.S. (La.) 401 (1824).

several years' residence in Ohio. She alleged that her former master had taken her from Kentucky to Ohio "with the intention of residing there. . . ." When she attempted to assert her freedom "he defeated it by her forcible removal into Kentucky." Later she was brought back to Ohio and then sold to Louisiana. Lunsford's counsel argued that "she was a free woman" in Ohio and "she must be held so every where."[73]

Speaking for the Louisiana court, Justice François-Xavier Martin went to first principles, citing *Somerset* to prove that slavery was "a creature of the municipal law" and could not exist without it. *Somerset* had been much criticized on this point, since Lord Mansfield had argued that positive law was necessary to establish slavery, when in fact positive law had rarely been used to establish slavery. Martin deftly handled this criticism. He agreed that "perhaps, in none of them [the American colonies and states] a statute introducing it as to the blacks can be produced," but this was unimportant, for "in all" slave states "statutes were passed for regulating" slavery. Without such legislation, Martin was convinced slavery could not exist. And this was the situation in the Northwest Territory, just as it had been in England.[74]

Martin also adopted an interpretation of the Fugitive Slave Clause of the United States Constitution that permitted a state to free all slaves within its jurisdiction, except fugitives. The clause included "a very forcible implication . . . that such persons, who do not escape, but whose owners voluntarily bring, may be discharged by the laws or regulations of the state, in which they are so brought. For if this could not be, to what use would be prohibition?"[75]

Finally, Martin concluded that Ohio's constitution "emancipates, *ipso facto*," the slaves of owners moving to Ohio "with the intention of residing there." Thus Lunsford was "as effectually emancipated, by the operation of the constitution, as if by the act and deed of her former owner." Since "she could not be free in one state, and a slave in another" the court declared "her freedom was not impaired" by the forcible removal into Kentucky, or the subsequent removal to Louisiana, whether it was "voluntary or forced."[76]

The court fully understood the implications of this decision and ended by explicitly stating that the outcome was based entirely "on the former owner of the plaintiff removing into Ohio, with the intention of settling" there. But, unlike judges Mills and Marshall in Kentucky, Martin refused to offer dictum on whether "slaves

73. Ibid. 401–2.
74. Ibid. 403–4.
75. Ibid.
76. Ibid. 408.

attending their masters sojourning in, or traveling to Ohio, are not thereby emancipated"; that question was not before him.[77]

Lunsford v. *Coquillon* acknowledged the right of a state to abolish or prohibit slavery, as it chose. It also supported the principle that freedom once attained could not be forfeited, even if the slave voluntarily moved back to a slave state. This aspect of the decision was particularly important because Judge Martin recognized that slaves taken to a free state might not voluntarily return to a slave state but could be forced to do so. By declaring that freedom once attained could not be forfeited by a return to a slave state—whether the return was voluntary or involuntary—Martin obviated the difficult evidentiary task for a black of proving that his or her return had been forced. The principles laid down by Martin were supported by English law and the United States Constitution but their spirit was influenced by the more liberal French laws and ideology. The principles—that a slave who gained freedom could not later be reenslaved—were not based on comity. Rather, Martin accepted them as the rule for all jurisdictions, which could be contravened only by specific, positive law.

In his decision Martin implied that the intention of the master to reside in a free state was critical in determining the status of a slave brought into that state. This criterion had also been adopted by Kentucky. But while Kentucky never moved very far from this position, Louisiana modified its rule making in a number of cases in which the slave had only sojourned, with no intention to reside. Martin also left open the question of transit through a free state, indicating that it was not as settled as the Kentucky court supposed.

Before the Louisiana court could explain itself further on such questions as residence and transit, it was faced with the problem of the children of slaves who were born in free states or territories. In *Merry* v. *Chexnaider* (1803),[78] the court freed the plaintiff because he had been born in the Northwest Territory after the Ordinance of 1787. While this was not a particularly creative interpretation of the ordinance, it should be remembered that the "free" state of Illinois did not reach this conclusion until 1845.[79] The court faced a more complicated birth question in *Frank, f.m.c. [free man of color]* v. *Powell* (1838).[80] Frank, the child of a slave, was born while his master and mother were traveling through Pennsylvania. The transit had been interrupted by illness and the "inclemency of the weather," as well as by the birth. Since Pennsylvania had not re-

77. Ibid. 409.
78. *Merry* v. *Chexnaider*, 8 Mart. N.S. (La.) 699 (1830).
79. *Jarrot* v. *Jarrot*, 2 Gil. (Ill.) 1 (1845).
80. *Frank, f.m.c.* v. *Powell*, 11 La. 499 (1838).

pealed its six-months law, Frank's mother was clearly not free. And since she was not affected by Pennsylvania's "free air," it was at least arguable that her offspring should not be affected either. But a troublesome question arose of whether, under any circumstances, a slave could be born in Pennsylvania. The Louisiana court, with obvious relief, did not have to inquire whether the circumstances of Frank's birth while his mother was in transit formed "an exception to the general rule outlined in *Merry* v. *Chexnaider.*" The court was spared such an inquiry since Frank was later hired out in Ohio, which made him free.[81]

The Louisiana court heard a number of freedom suits based on visits to or residence in France. In *Marie Louise, f.w.c. [free woman of color]* v. *Marot et al.* (1835),[82] the court concluded that Marie's being taken to France "where slavery or involuntary servitude is not tolerated, operated on the condition of the slave, so as to produce an immediate emancipation." And, as in cases involving the United States, "[b]eing free for one moment in France, it was not in the power of her former owner to reduce her again to slavery." This decision was reaffirmed in a number of other cases until the law of 1846 was passed.[83] *Marie Louise* and its successors showed that intention to reside was not the only guideline in these cases. For in none of them was it ever claimed that the owner had intended to reside permanently in France. These cases also suggest that fidelity to the law, a law that favored freedom, rather than comity, guided the Louisiana court. Certainly, no "federalism" question was involved when freedom was based on transit in a foreign nation.

A very peculiar variant of the "intention to reside" problem was presented to the court in *Elizabeth Thomas, f.w.c.* v. *Generis* (1840).[84] Elizabeth Thomas was purchased as a slave in Virginia and brought to Kentucky. In 1833 she was taken to Illinois, where she lived for about three and a half years. Under *Lunsford* this should have been a simple case of freedom based on residence in a free state. However, Generis introduced evidence to show that Elizabeth had been sent to

81. Ibid. 499–503. See also *Phillis, f.w.c.* v. *Gentin,* 9 La. 208 (1836).

82. *Marie Louise, f.w.c.* v. *Marot et al.,* 8 La. 475 (1835), and *Marie Louise* v. *Marot et al.,* 9 La. 473 (1836).

83. *Marie Louise* v. *Marot,* 8 La. 475. See also *Pricilla Smith, f.w.c.* v. *Smith,* 13 La. 441 (1839); *Frank, f.m.c.* v. *Powell,* 11 La. 499 (1838); see also *Guillemette* v. *Harper,* 4 Rich. (S.C.) 186 (1850). And a series of cases in Missouri: *Chouteau* v. *Pierre (of color),* 9 Mo. 3 (1845); *Charlotte* v. *Chouteau,* 11 Mo. 193 (1847), reargued at 21 Mo. 590 (1855); 25 Mo. 465 (1857); 33 Mo. 194 (1862), all of which deal with freedom suits based on foreign residence. For a discussion of the Missouri cases, see Helen Tunnicliff Catterall, "Some Antecedents of the Dred Scott Case," 30 *American Historical Review* 56–71 (1924).

84. *Elizabeth Thomas, f.w.c.* v. *Generis et al.,* 16 La. 483 (1840).

Illinois at her own request, to be treated by "an eminent physician" living there. Testimony from Judge Walter B. Scates of the Illinois Supreme Court was also introduced by Generis. Scates felt that "residence by a slave from another state, in Illinois with the consent of the owner and slave, would never operate an emancipation of the slave, but if it were against the will and consent of the slave, she would become free *immediately*." Scates asserted that if the slave voluntarily came to Illinois there could be no involuntary servitude. This rather bizarre bit of reasoning was politely ignored by the Louisiana court, which pointed out that "however respectable" his opinion might be, it "must yield to the principle so well recognized by our laws that a slave has no will, and cannot give any consent. . . ." Thus, the court relied on the precedents of *Lunsford* and *Marie Louise* v. *Marot* to free Elizabeth. This decision contrasts sharply with *Maria* v. *Kirby* in which the Kentucky court implied a slave could give "consent" to being freed.[85]

In 1830 the Louisiana legislature moved to limit the growth of the state's free black population. The attitude of the legislature and the court toward free Negroes was intrinsically related to transit and comity questions. If the state policy opposed any emancipations, then the court might not allow blacks to be freed, no matter how long they might have lived in a free state or country. The 1830 act retroactively required all free blacks who had entered Louisiana since 1825 to leave within sixty days. In the future no free blacks were to enter the state. However, these provisions did not "extend to any free negro, . . . who may have been a slave in this State and who shall have, with the consent of his owner, been emancipated in any other State of the Union, and shall have after such emancipation, returned to this State." In 1842 the legislature further restricted the influx of free Negroes with "AN ACT more effectually to prevent free persons of color from entering into this state, and for other purposes." Most of the act centered on the policing of ports, harbors, and river landings. Free black seamen from other states were to be jailed until their ships left, while the captain of the ship had to post bond to insure that the blacks would be removed from the state. Free blacks entering the state would be expelled and could be sentenced to five years at hard labor if they returned. If the black remained in the state thirty days after the five-year sentence expired, a life sentence was mandated. Finally, the law prohibited masters from taking their slaves to free states or countries and then returning with them. Violation could lead to expelling the slaves and fining the master. This clause implicitly acknowledged that a

---

85. Ibid. 483, 487–89.

slave brought into a free state became free. No reported cases enforce the ban on bringing slaves into free states. And some indications suggest that Louisiana was not yet ready to exert much effort in ending the growth of the free black population. Throughout the 1840s and into the 1850s the legislature continued to approve special acts of manumission.[86]

Besides discouraging the increase of free blacks, the ban on travel to free states with slaves may have had two other objectives: to protect citizens from abuse and hostility in the North and to prevent slaves from bringing abolitionist ideas back with them. Curiously, the 1842 act did not reverse the policy of respecting the free status slaves acquired by residing in nonslave jurisdictions. But this fidelity to precedent and Louisiana's liberal heritage lasted only four more years. On 30 May 1846 the legislature passed an act declaring that "no slave shall be entitled to his or her freedom under the pretence that he or she has been, with or without the consent of his or her owner, in a country where slavery does not exist, or in any of the States where slavery is prohibited."[87] The state policy, as determined by the legislature, was to cease enforcing the freedom created by foreign and out-of-state laws. It was a rejection of precedent and comity.

Nine months after this new law was passed, in *Eugenie v. Preval* (1847),[88] the court acknowledged the new policy, but refused to enforce it. In 1830, long before the new law was passed, Eugenie had been taken to France by her owner. Citing the Louisiana Code, Chief Justice George Eustis declared, "A law can prescribe only for the future; it can have no retrospective operation, nor can it impair the obligation of contracts." Since Eugenie had been legally free since 1830, or at least entitled to her freedom, the new law could not affect her status. Eustis reaffirmed this result the same year, in the nearly identical case of *Arsene v. Pigneguy* (1847),[89] which is particularly interesting for its absolute rejection of the principles used by the Kentucky court in *Strader v. Graham*. Pigneguy claimed that although he spent two years in France he continued to own property and maintain his business in Louisiana; therefore, he claimed, he acquired no domicile in France and Arsene was not entitled to her freedom. The Louisiana court rejected his claim because it could

86. Hurd, 2 *Law of Freedom and Bondage* 164 contains the best summary of these statutes. On private manumissions, see Joe Gray Taylor, *Negro Slavery in Louisiana* (Baton Rouge: Louisiana Historical Association, 1963) 155–56.

87. *Louisiana, Act of 1846*, chap. 189.

88. *Eugenie v. Preval et al.*, 2 La. Ann. 180 (1847).

89. Ibid.; *Arsene v. Pigneguy*, 2 La. Ann. 620 (1847). Also see *Josephine v. Poultney*, 1 La. Ann. 42 (1846).

not "expect that foreign nations will consent to the suspension of the operation of their fundamental laws, as to persons voluntarily sojourning within their jurisdiction for such a length of time."[90] Although Kentucky would probably have freed a slave after a two-year sojourn in a free jurisdiction, it would not have accepted the Louisiana court's reasoning. Indeed, in *Strader*, the Kentucky court specifically allowed a master to take his slave into a free state and employ him there, which was clearly in violation of the fundamental laws of any free state.

In 1850 the new law was enforced for the first time, when a slave who had gone to France in 1847 sued for freedom. In his decision Chief Justice Eustis noted that the 1846 statute "merely enacts and established as law the rule laid down by Lord Stowell," in *The Slave, Grace*. He felt that "[t]here can be no question as to the legislative power to regulate the condition of this class of persons within its jurisdiction, and to prescribe in what form and by what facts such conditions shall be changed."[91]

Earlier that year Eustis wrote an opinion that indicated that the chief justice had moved away from his relatively liberal opinions in *Arsene* and *Eugenie. Mary, f.w.c.* v. *Brown* (1850)[92] was a very complicated freedom suit involving the conflict of laws. Mary's deceased owner had taken her from Mississippi to Ohio, where he had emancipated her under the laws of that state. They both then returned to Mississippi, where the master subsequently died, and Brown, the administrator of the estate, hired Mary and her children to someone in Louisiana. Thus, the Louisiana court had to decide whether it would enforce the laws of Mississippi or those of Ohio. In rejecting the claim of the slaves, Eustis cited a Mississippi precedent that "controls this case." Because the emancipation was considered a fraud against the laws of Mississippi, which prohibited manumissions, Eustis refused to free the slaves.[93] That the Louisiana court chose to enforce the laws of Mississippi, rather than those of Ohio, reveals that sectional and slaveholding ties had become more important to the court than freedom.

This suspicion is confirmed by *Liza, c.w. [colored woman]* v. *Puissant* (1852).[94] Liza had been taken to France in 1821, but had remained there only a short time. In language difficult to reconcile with earlier opinions, Eustis refused to free Liza. Eustis noted that under the long-standing precedent of *Marie Louise* v. *Marot* a slave

90. *Arsene* v. *Pigneguy* 620.

91. *Conant, Tutor of Mary, a negro woman* v. *Guesnard*, 5 La. Ann. 696, 697 (1850).

92. *Mary, f.w.c. et al.* v. *Brown*, 5 La. Ann. 269 (1850).

93. Ibid. Cf. *Barclay f.w.c.* v. *Sewell*, 12 La. Ann. 262 (1857), n. 102 below.

94. *Liza, c.w.* v. *Puissant et al.*, 7 La. Ann. 80 (1852).

brought to France would be free "and her return to Louisiana does not subject her to servitude." This precedent should have applied to Liza, because she had been in France, and thus gained her freedom, long before the new 1846 law. Since he was not applying the new law, because in fact he could not do so, Eustis felt it his "duty to state" why the *Marie Louise* v. *Marot* precedent did not free Liza.

> The court there [*Marie Louise* v. *Marot*] say, the plaintiff being free for one moment in France, it was not in the power of her former owner to reduce her again to slavery. That this is true, in France, there can be no question; the law of France recognizes no such relation as that of master and slave. But I do not concur in the opinion, that on the voluntary return of the slave to the country of his domicil, from one in which slavery does not exist, the dominion of the master can in no case be exercised.

Citing Chief Justice Taney's decision in *Strader* v. *Graham*, Eustis declared, "It rests with each State to establish and regulate the domestic relations of its inhabitants. A State may prohibit slavery within its limits, may abolish the paternal power; but this imposes no obligation on other States to hold the conditions of persons domiciled there, as extinguished by reason of a presence in the State to which the relation is not recognized."[95] Eustis's comparison of abolishing "the paternal power" to abolishing slavery indicates that the Louisiana court was overreacting, a not uncommon occurrence among southern judges dealing with slavery and comity in the 1850s. Eustis also managed to rewrite the history of his court in order to support this decision. Ignoring his opinions of five years earlier, he concluded, "This court has held the *status* of a slave to be changed by a residence in a country in which slavery did not exist, when the residence, with the consent of the master, had a character of permanency, but not that the *status* was affected by a transit for a temporary purpose." Eustis cited no case to support this assertion, because, of course, this was the first time the court had ever ruled thus. Perhaps if the court had always maintained this position, as the Kentucky court had, the Louisiana legislature would not have passed the 1846 law.[96] Given his earlier opinions, it is possible that Eustis was reading the law as the legislature wanted it read, rather than as it had always been interpreted.

Haynes v. *Forno* (1853)[97] also involved a Mississippi slave freed

---

95. Ibid. 81–83.
96. Ibid. This is suggested in *Barclay, f.w.c.* v. *Sewell*, 12 La. Ann. 262 (1857).
97. *Haynes* v. *Forno*, 8 La. Ann. 35 (1853).

in Ohio. Citing *Mary* v. *Brown*, Chief Justice Eustis found Haynes to be a slave under the laws of Mississippi. He also cited *Liza* v. *Puissant* to show that Haynes's short residence in Ohio would not have freed her under Louisiana law.[98] This interpretation of his own decision was of course questionable. For Liza had not been sent to France for the purpose of being freed, and thus claimed her freedom on the basis of French law, Louisiana precedent, and comity. But in this case the slave claimed her freedom by virtue of a legal manumission in Ohio. By applying Mississippi law she was still a slave, but to claim that she was also a slave under Louisiana law was to stretch the new precedent of *Liza* v. *Puissant* far beyond what the case actually held.

A month later Eustis wrote his last decision on slave transit. In this case the slave had lived in New York for about five years between 1823 and 1832. Her master then migrated to Maryland. Eustis concluded that the "purpose and intention of removing to New York and to reside there" was "unquestionable." Under New York law the slave was free and the removal to Maryland could not reenslave her. This decision was consistent with the restrictive dictum found in *Liza* v. *Puissant* and should not be considered as a softening of the court's attitude toward freeing slaves.[99]

By 1855, however, in *Virginia and Celesie, f.p.c.* [*free persons of color*] v. *Himel*,[100] the court's position had again changed. Virginia and Celesie had been taken to Cincinnati in 1835 and manumitted. This act was "acknowledged, first before the Mayor of that city" and later before the circuit court of St. Louis, Missouri. They then returned to Louisiana with their master, who died in 1842. The slaves were freed by a lower court and this decision was upheld by the supreme court. In his decision Justice A. N. Ogden noted that in *Mary* v. *Brown* the emancipation was a fraud against the laws of Mississippi. But Ogden said that the laws of Mississippi "are entirely different from our own." Under Mississippi law a slave could be freed only by a legislative act "permitting his emancipation." Louisiana law allowed "a slave to make a contract with his master for his freedom." He pointed out that before the passage of the 1846 statute "the removal of the master with the slave to a free State had the effect *ipso facto* of setting the slave free, and that the right to freedom was not forfeited by the return of the slave to Louisiana."[101] Thus, the harsh dictum of two years earlier was replaced by a more liberal interpretation of the state's statutes.

98. Ibid.
99. *Lucy Brown, f.w.c.* v. *Smith*, 8 La. Ann. 59 (1853).
100. *Virginia and Celesie, f.p.c.* v. *Himel*, 10 La. Ann. 185 (1855).
101. Ibid. 185–87.

In 1857 the Louisiana court offered what would be its final interpretation of the law of slave transit. *Barclay, f.w.c.* v. *Sewell* (1857)[102] upheld the freedom of a woman emancipated in Ohio in 1839. The court noted that in 1839 such an emancipation was legal and so it should be upheld. After quickly reaching that conclusion, Justice H. M. Spofford turned to "the general policy of the Louisiana Legislature." The legislature had always been "adverse to the indiscriminate manumission of slaves and now [1857] it has become altogether prohibitive of emancipations in the State." This new policy, Spofford thought, was "probably in consequence of injudicious and impertinent assaults from without upon an institution thoroughly interwoven with our interior lives." In 1830, before the abolitionist assaults, "the Legislature recognized the validity of such emancipations as the one under consideration." Not until 1842 did the legislature prohibit taking Louisiana slaves into free states; but even this law recognized that such slaves would be free. Only the 1846 act prohibited the court from freeing slaves who had resided in free states. Spofford thought this act was a necessary corrective "probably called out by a series of decisions in the Supreme Court of this State, which were incorrect in principle, because they held that the status of a slave whose master resided in Louisiana, could be changed by even a transient presence upon free territory." Spofford thought that this act did not "prohibit an *express* emancipation of a slave in a foreign State by a master resident in Louisiana. It only guards against manumission being implied from the mere fact that the slave, whether with or without the consent of the master, has been upon the soil of a territory where slavery is prohibited."[103] However, since free blacks could not enter the state, it is questionable whether an owner could take a slave to a free state, free him or her, and return with the ex-slave to Louisiana. Given Spofford's dictum, however, that might have been acceptable to the court.

When the Civil War began, Louisiana was not a "liberator" of slaves as it had once been. Transit in a free area after 1846 would not free a slave. It was illegal to free slaves in the state and probably illegal to take them to free states, free them there, and return to Louisiana. But slaves who had lived in free states before 1846 might still sue successfully for their freedom. This made Louisiana less pro-freedom than Kentucky but, as will be shown, much more liberal than either Missouri or Mississippi.

102. *Barclay, f.w.c.* v. *Sewell,* 12 La. Ann. 262 (1857).
103. Ibid. 264–65.

Missouri

Missouri's early decision making on slave transit resembled that of Kentucky and Louisiana. *Winny* v. *Whitesides* (1824)[104] was the first in a long series of cases freeing slaves who had lived or worked in free states. About the year 1799 Whitesides and her husband brought the slave Winny from one of the Carolinas to Illinois. Later all three moved to Missouri, where in 1822 Winny sued for her freedom. The St. Louis Circuit Court judge instructed the jurors that "if they believed the defendant and her then husband, resided in Illinois, with an intention to make that place the home of themselves and of the said Winny," they should find in Winny's favor. The jury did so find and Whitesides appealed to the Missouri Supreme Court.[105]

Whitesides argued: (1) Under the Articles of Confederation Congress lacked power either to purchase the Northwest Territory "or to forbid, by law, that slaves should be held in that Territory." (2) If Congress did have power to buy the Northwest Territory and govern it, nevertheless, whatever claim to freedom Winny might have had while there had no force in Missouri. Because Winny had failed to assert her freedom while in Illinois, "the master's right revived, so soon as he found the slave in Missouri." (3) The Northwest Ordinance did not in and of itself declare that "the slave of a person settling in that Territory, becomes thereby free," but some type of legislation was needed to enforce the antislavery clause in the ordinance. By 1860 the last two arguments would be successful in Missouri in defense of slave property; the first argument would be applied to the territory west of the Mississippi, rather than to the Northwest Territory. However, in 1824 the Missouri court, like its counterparts in Louisiana and Kentucky, was inclined to favor freedom where possible.[106]

The court asserted that Congress did have the right both to obtain and to govern various territories. The antislavery clause in the Northwest Ordinance was thus both legal and appropriate. As to Whitesides's third point, the clause was held to be self-enforcing. In a surprising statement for a slave-state institution, the Missouri Supreme Court declared: "When the States assumed the right of self-government, they found their citizens claiming a right of property in a miserable portion of the human race. Sound national policy

104. *Winny* v. *Whitesides*, 1 Mo. 472 (1824).
105. Ibid.
106. Ibid.

required that the evil should be restricted as much as possible. What they could, they did."[107]

To answer Whitesides's second point, that a return to Missouri re-created Winny's slave status, the court relied on Huberus's conflict of laws theory, concluding that "personal rights or disabilities, obtained or communicated by the laws of any particular place, are of a nature which accompany the person wherever he goes." The court declared, "[I]f, by a residence in Illinois the plaintiff in error [Whitesides] lost her right to the property in the defendant [Winny], that right was not revived by a removal of the parties to Missouri."[108]

The court concluded that when a person takes a slave into a free jurisdiction "and by the length of his residence there indicates an intention of making that place his residence and that of his slave, and thereby induces a jury to believe that fact, [he] does, by such residence, declare his slave to have become a free man." The court emphatically asserted that this would not affect "every person travelling through the territory" with a slave. Only those intending to take up residence with a slave need be concerned.[109]

Thus "intention to reside with a slave" became a critical test in determining the status of slaves who had spent time in the old Northwest and were later brought to Missouri. This understanding of the meaning of the ordinance and free-state constitutions was far more limited than had been determined in either Kentucky or Louisiana. Presumably, long-term transit or sojourn with a slave might be permissible under this test, as long as there was no "intention to reside."

In 1827 the court added birth in a free jurisdiction as another ground for freedom in Missouri. Thus, a child born to a slave mother in Illinois was free, even though the mother was a slave in Illinois because she had been living there as such before the Northwest Ordinance was passed. While this determination was not particularly striking, even for a slave-state court, it came eighteen years before the Illinois Supreme Court reached a similar decision. Like Illinois, however, the Missouri court refused to free slaves who were living in the Northwest Territory before the ordinance and remained under its jurisdiction. Thus, although the court had previously said that the ordinance was meant to restrict "the evil . . . as much as possible," this apparently did not mean that slaves living under it, even for more than twenty years, were entitled to their freedom.[110]

107. Ibid. 474–75.
108. Ibid. 475.
109. Ibid. 476.
110. *Merry* v. *Tiffin and Menard*, 1 Mo. 725 (1827); *Theoteste (alias Catiche)* v.

In 1828 the Missouri court heard the first of at least seven successor cases to *Winny*, in which the meaning of "intention to reside with a slave" was reinterpreted. In *La Grange* v. *Chouteau* (1828)[111] the court held that a resident of Illinois might own a slave as long as that slave did not reside in Illinois. The slave La Grange was owned by Pierre Menard, a resident of Kaskaskia, but worked in Missouri. Eventually, however, Menard sent him to Kaskaskia "where he was put on a keel-boat, and after remaining about two days, went on said boat as a working hand to New Orleans." When the boat returned to Kaskaskia, La Grange "remained a few days, (one witness stated eight or nine,) assisting to unload" the boat. He later spent two or three more days in Illinois, after which he returned permanently to Missouri. Menard also testified he did not buy La Grange "with the intention of keeping him, or making Kaskaskia his place of residence." Rather, he bought La Grange for Pierre Chouteau, who took possession of him a few months later.[112]

The supreme court felt that "[a]ny sort of residence contrived or permitted by the legal owner, upon the faith of secret trusts or contracts, in order to defeat or evade the ordinance, and thereby introduce slavery de facto" would free the slave. But the court would also look at the "spirit and object" of the ordinance. An owner moving to Illinois "and carrying his slave along with him to reside there permanently" would introduce slavery "against the express terms of the ordinance." But

> the owner of a slave who is merely passing through the country with him, or who may be resident in Illinois and may choose to employ him in Missouri in mining, or as a sailor, or boat hand, upon the river or high seas, in boats or vessels that occasionally lade and unlade their cargoes at some port or place within the State, though he may not do much in "extending the fundamental principles of civil and religious liberty" certainly, does nothing towards engrafting slavery upon the social system of the State.[113]

Slavery, and not the slave, had to be introduced into a free territory or state before the Missouri court would free a slave.

In the same term in which La Grange was denied his freedom, two

---

Chouteau, 2 Mo. 144 (1829); see also *Nancy* v. *Trammel*, 3 Mo. 306 (1834); *Chouteau and Keizer* v. *Hope*, 7 Mo. 428 (1842), and n. 83 above.
111. *La Grange* v. *Chouteau*, 2 Mo. 19 (1828).
112. Ibid. 21–22.
113. Ibid. 22.

other slaves were freed on the basis of previous residence in Illinois. These cases reaffirmed the *Winny* precedent.[114] In *Vincent* v. *Duncan* (1830)[115] the court expanded the "intention to reside with a slave" test to free a slave hired out in Illinois. The Illinois Constitution allowed slaves to be hired out at the Shawnee Town saltworks for terms of up to one year until 1825. Vincent worked there in 1817, the year before the constitution was adopted, and thus the Missouri court found him free under the Northwest Ordinance. In *Ralph* v. *Duncan* (1833)[116] the court freed Ralph because he was allowed to hire his own time in Illinois after legally working a year at the saltworks. In both cases the actual introduction of slavery into the state, not the abstract test of "intention to reside with a slave," freed the slave. This was modified by *Nat* v. *Ruddle* (1834),[117] in which the court ruled that the hiring out in a free state had to be with the master's consent. Ruddle, an Illinois farmer, hired out Nat in Missouri, but Nat preferred to be with his master and ran away to Illinois. It was planting season and Ruddle could not return Nat to Missouri. In the meantime Nat worked on Ruddle's farm and hired his own time. Three years later Nat sued for his freedom on the basis of his working in Illinois. In a swipe at *Somerset*, the court declared, "[T]here was nothing in the soil of Illinois as in England, that would work the emancipation of a slave by mere setting foot thereon." Since Nat ran away to Illinois against his master's wishes, he was not entitled to his freedom.[118]

By the time *Nat* v. *Ruddle* was decided the Missouri court had already rejected the "intention to reside with a slave" test in favor of a factual determination: "Did the master actually introduce slavery into a free state?" This rejection was the basis for the decision in *Julia* v. *McKinney* (1833)[119] freeing Julia. In 1829 Julia's owner, Mrs. Lucinda Carrington, moved from Kentucky to Illinois. Carrington "intended to hire" Julia out in Missouri; but she kept Julia in Illinois for almost three months, "exercising the ordinary acts of ownership and dominion over her" and in the process hired her out for two days. "Some time" later Julia returned to Illinois for a few weeks, after which she was sent back to St. Louis and sold to McKinney.[120]

---

114. *Milly* v. *Smith*, 2 Mo. 36 (1828); *Trammel* v. *Adam*, 2 Mo. 155 (1828).
115. *Vincent* v. *Duncan*, 2 Mo. 214 (1830).
116. *Ralph* v. *Duncan*, 3 Mo. 194 (1833).
117. *Nat (a man of color)* v. *Ruddle*, 3 Mo. 400 (1834).
118. Ibid. 401; see also *Hay* v. *Dunky*, 3 Mo. 588 (1834); *Wilson* v. *Melvin*, 4 Mo. 592 (1837).
119. *Julia* v. *McKinney*, 3 Mo. 270 (1833).
120. Ibid. 271–72.

In deciding this case the Missouri court strenuously defended the right to cross Illinois with a slave. "The object" of that state's constitution "was not to prevent persons owning slaves in Kentucky, from passing through Illinois with their slave property" to Missouri, but rather "to prevent the relation of master and slave from existing in that State by an inhabitant and resident thereof." The court further asserted that under the Privileges and Immunities Clause of the United States Constitution it was "the undoubted right of every citizen of the United States to pass freely through every other State with his property of every description, including negro slaves, without being in any way subject to forfeit his property for" this act. But in Julia's case her owner "was not an emigrant" passing through Illinois. She was there "with an avowed view to make that State her home." Thus bringing Julia into Illinois "surely amounted to the introduction of slavery." The objection that it was difficult or impossible for Carrington to take Julia to Missouri before residing in Illinois was totally rejected. The court answered that an "excuse to raise an exception, must be something more than the mere convenience or inconvenience of the owner." Similarly, the "intention to reside with a slave" test was rejected, as the court asked if it were "true that if a person says he does not intend to do an act and yet does it, that the act is not done?" The Illinois Constitution did not "regard the intention to introduce or not to introduce slavery," but prohibited "the act." With this reasoning Julia was freed.[121]

In *Rachael* v. *Walker* (1836)[122] the Missouri court dealt with a variant of the residence question that would have far-reaching consequences. Rachael was the slave of an army officer stationed at Fort Snelling, in what became Minnesota. She later accompanied him to Prairie du Chien, Michigan. After returning to Missouri, Rachael sued for freedom on the basis of her residences in these free territories. The trial court ruled that an army officer was exempt from the principles first stated in *Winny* v. *Whitesides* and thus Rachael was still a slave. But the Missouri Supreme Court rejected the notion that military officers might have rights that civilians did not have:

> Shall it be said, that because an officer of the army owns slaves in Virginia, that when as officer and soldier, he is required to take command of a post in the non slave holding States or territories, he thereby has a right to take with him as many slaves, as will suit his interests or convenience? It surely cannot be the law . . . that the convenience or supposed convenience of

121. Ibid. 272–77.
122. *Rachael* v. *Walker*, 4 Mo. 350 (1836).

the officer, repeals as to him and others who have the same character, the ordinance and the act of 1821 admitting Missouri into the Union, and also the prohibitions of the several laws and constitutions of the non slave holding States.

Although army officers were allowed to have servants, the court was "yet to learn that the law which gives to officers servants of a certain sort, authorise such officers to hold slaves in lieu of such servants, and in places forbidden by the ordinance." But the Northwest Ordinance and the Missouri Compromise dictated that Rachael was free, and thus the circuit court judgment was reversed.[123] The facts of Rachael's case were almost identical to those in Dred Scott's case, in which the Missouri court would reject nearly three decades of liberal decision making.

Between 1837 and 1852 the Missouri Supreme Court heard no significant freedom suits based on prior residence or sojourn in a free jurisdiction.[124] The earlier cases "seem to have so fully settled that quetion [sic]" that no one asked for a reconsideration of the principles first laid down in *Winny* v. *Whitesides* until *Scott* v. *Emerson* (1852)[125] reached the court.

Dred Scott was the slave of John Emerson, an army surgeon. Between 1834 and 1838 Emerson was stationed at Rock Island in Illinois and at Fort Snelling, in what would soon be Minnesota. One was a free state, the other a free territory under the Missouri Compromise of 1820. Scott accompanied Emerson to both posts. After Emerson died, Scott offered to purchase his freedom but Mrs. Emerson refused the offer. So, in 1846 Scott petitioned the St. Louis Circuit Court for permission to sue for his freedom. The facts of his case were almost identical to those in *Rachael* v. *Walker*. Thus it came as somewhat of a shock when a jury, in 1847, returned a verdict in favor of Mrs. Emerson's right to own Scott. This result came about largely because of the lack of a key witness and the eloquence of Emerson's lawyer. Scott won the right to a new trial, and in 1850 a jury declared him free. At this point Mrs. Emerson appealed to the Missouri Supreme Court. If the Missouri court followed its precedents the appeal would be hopeless. However, a changing political scene in Missouri, combined with new laws and precedents in Kentucky, Louisiana, and other southern states, as well as the United States Supreme Court decision in *Strader* v. *Graham*, made the appeal seem viable. For Mrs. Emerson this was an auspicious

123. Ibid. 354.
124. *Randolph* v. *Alsey*, 8 Mo. 656 (1844); *Robert* v. *Melugen*, 9 Mo. 170 (1845), and "Chouteau" cases cited above created no new precedents.
125. *Scott* v. *Emerson*, 15 Mo. 576 (1852).

moment to test the Missouri precedents.[126] The appeal was to result in one of those rare instances in which a court would explicitly overturn long-standing precedents.

Speaking for the court, Justice William Scott acknowledged that in past cases of this nature the slave had usually been freed. This, he claimed, had been done because "it is the duty of the courts of this State to carry into effect the constitution and laws of other States and territories, regardless of the rights, the policy or the institutions of the people of this State."[127] This characterization of previous Missouri decisions seems exaggerated. In *Winny* v. *Whitesides* the court had determined that the owner, by taking a slave with him to reside in a free state "does . . . declare his slave to have become a free man." This language indicates that the Missouri court was inclined to ascribe the result in this case not to their own actions, but to the act of the slaveowner. This was not a conscious rejection of Missouri policies and law, but rather a recognition of the fact that once a slave became free, under the law of some other jurisdiction, there was no Missouri law that could make that person a slave. In *Winny* and subsequent decisions, the Missouri court recognized the power of Congress to ban slavery from the Northwest Territory and other territories and acknowledged its obligation to obey that congressional power because it was the law of the nation. By 1852 the Missouri court was no longer willing to recognize the authority of Congress to legislate for the territories and indeed went so far as to deny that Congress had such power. Thus, Dred Scott's claim to freedom, based on a long residence in that territory designated "free" by the Missouri Compromise, was totally rejected by the Missouri court. This rejection of federal power was consistent with the "states' rights" arguments being made throughout the nation whenever slavery was discussed. In previous decisions the Missouri court had

126. The best discussion of the circumstances surrounding the appeal by Mrs. Emerson is Fehrenbacher, *Dred Scott Case* 250–65. Fehrenbacher corrects many errors made in such earlier, but still useful, works as Vincent C. Hopkins, *Dred Scott's Case* (New York: Fordham University Press, 1951) 4–20. Fehrenbacher and Walter Ehrlich, *They Have No Rights: Dred Scott's Struggle for Freedom* (Westport, Conn.: Greenwood Press, 1979), successfully demolish any notion that Mrs. Emerson's appeal was part of either a proslavery or an antislavery conspiracy. Ehrlich persuasively argues that Mrs. Emerson appealed for practical reasons: she did not want to lose Scott and his family and, perhaps more important, she did not want to lose the money Dred Scott had earned since 1846, which was held in escrow throughout the suit. When Scott sued for his freedom he was hired out by the court. By the time the case was finally decided in 1857, almost eleven years of income had accrued. This factor alone made the appeal by Mrs. Emerson worthwhile. For early litigation, see also *Emmerson* [sic] v. *Harriet (of color)–Emmerson* [sic] v. *Dred Scott (of color)*, 11 Mo. 413 (1848).

127. *Scott* v. *Emerson* 582.

supported national policies and interstate harmony. But by 1852, when slavery was at issue, the Missouri court was prepared to place a higher value on local policy than on national policy.

The court did not openly declare that it was nullifying federal law. Instead, Scott based his opinion on the power of the states to enforce laws within their jurisdictions: "Every State has the right of determining how far, in a spirit of comity, it will respect the laws of other States. Those laws have no intrinsic right to be enforced beyond the limits of the State for which they were enacted. The respect allowed them will depend altogether on their conformity to the policy of our institutions. No State is bound to carry into effect enactments conceived in a spirit hostile to that which pervades her own laws."[128]

Judge Scott found it "a humiliating spectacle, to see the courts of a State confiscating the property of her own citizens by the command of a foreign law." That the "foreign law" was in fact a federal law or the constitution of a sister state, was immaterial to Scott. He asked, if Dred Scott were free, was it "by the constitution of the State of Illinois or the territorial laws of the United States?" In either case, he wished to know, "Are not those governments capable of enforcing their own laws?" And, "if they were not" Scott asked why he should enforce them, especially "at the cost to our own citizens?"[129] One wonders if Scott would have approved of Illinois or the federal government sending marshals or soldiers into Missouri to enforce Dred Scott's freedom.

Scott's histrionics were only a prelude to his real complaints: that the free states "maintain that if a slave, with the consent of his master, touch the soil he thereby becomes free." But this too was an exaggeration. Both Illinois and Indiana allowed slave transit. Indeed, the Missouri courts had been consistently more liberal in freeing slaves than the courts of Illinois or Indiana, and neither Illinois nor Missouri had freed slaves in transit. Although no federal cases on this subject exist for the Minnesota Territory, in the neighboring Iowa Territory a judge had specifically declared that masters with slaves could cross that free territory without interference.[130] And, although Missouri freed slaves hired out in Illinois, the Illinois courts and legislature seemed reluctant to do so. Yet, now Judge Scott argued: "Some of our old cases say, that a hiring for two days would be a violation of the constitution of Illinois and entitle the slave to his freedom. If two days would do, why not one? Is there any difference in principle or morality between holding a slave in a free territory two days more than one day? And if one day, why not six

128. Ibid. 583.
129. Ibid. 584.
130. See *Daggs* v. *Frazer*, 6 F. Cas. 1112 (1849); also 9 Am. Law Journal 73 (1849).

hours?"[131] Significantly, Scott did not cite any of these extreme "old cases" because there were none to cite. They did not exist. Scott may have had *Julia* v. *McKinney* (1833) in mind because Julia had been hired out in Illinois for two days. But she had also lived in Illinois for nearly three months with her owner and had later returned to Illinois. In other cases, like *La Grange* v. *Chouteau* (1828) and *Nat* v. *Ruddle* (1834), the Missouri court refused to free slaves who worked in Illinois under certain circumstances. Indeed, the courts of Missouri, Kentucky, Louisiana, and Illinois had always been able to distinguish between residence or long-term sojourn, which led to freedom, and transit or short sojourns and visits, which did not.

Scott next asserted, "Laws operate only within the territory of the State for which they are made, and by enforcing them here, we, contrary to all principle, give them an extra territorial effect." This ignored the fact that federal law, in the Missouri Compromise and the Northwest Ordinance, was theoretically in force everywhere in the United States. Instead of facing this question, Scott simply asserted that Emerson had been "ordered by superior authority to the posts where his slave was detained in servitude" and he had "naturally supposed" this was legal.[132] This position was in direct conflict with the 1836 decision in *Rachael* v. *Walker*, which Judge Scott completely ignored. More important than the rejection of this earlier precedent was the argument that implied that Emerson had a *right* to take Dred Scott into Illinois and Missouri. Since those places had no laws enforcing Dred Scott's slave status, it must be assumed the status was derived from Missouri law. Thus, while Scott was denying "an extra territorial effect" of the Missouri Compromise, the Northwest Ordinance, and the Illinois Constitution, he was demanding that effect for the Missouri slave code.

If Judge Scott found it convenient to ignore *Rachael* v. *Walker*, he had no difficulty remembering *Strader* v. *Graham* and *The Slave, Grace*. Scott cited both, along with selections from Shaw's opinion in *Commonwealth* v. *Aves* to support the position "that if a slave accompanies his master to a country in which slavery is prohibited, and remains there a length of time, if during his continuance in such country there is no act of manumission decreed by its courts, and he afterwards returns to his master's domicile, where slavery prevails, he has no right to maintain a suit founded upon a claim of permanent freedom."[133] This had not been the holding in *Strader* v. *Graham*, which the Missouri court used to support this conclusion. All the Kentucky court in *Strader* had decided was that a short-

131. *Scott* v. *Emerson* 584.
132. Ibid. 585.
133. Ibid.

term sojourn would not free a slave. The United States Supreme Court had merely upheld the legal theory of *lex fori*—and asserted that it was up to the court of the state in which the slave sued to determine the status of the slave. The United States Supreme Court did not say a state *could not* free a slave after a residence in a free state, but only that the federal courts lacked jurisdiction to *compel* a state to do so. Scott's interpretation of *The Slave, Grace* was correct, but he did not indicate that the relationship between Britain and her colonies was quite different from that between one state and another or between a state and the United States government.

All these inconsistencies could be ignored because the granting of comity, even in the Union, was "a matter of discretion," which "must be controlled by circumstances."[134] At last Scott came to the critical issue at hand—the circumstances and politics of the 1850s. Judge Scott, "an ardent proslavery Democrat," had only recently gained his seat on the state supreme court after a successful battle against the more moderate Missouri Democrats led by the aging Thomas Hart Benton.[135] His political beliefs, and those of his constituents, are clearly reflected in the conclusion of his opinion:

> Times are not as they were when the former decisions
> on this subject were made. Since then not only individuals
> but States have been possessed with a dark and fell spirit in
> relation to slavery, whose gratification is sought in the pursuit
> of measures, whose inevitable consequence must be the
> overthrow and destruction of our government. Under such
> circumstances it does not behoove the State of Missouri to
> show the least countenance to any measure which might
> gratify this spirit.[136]

It was not the abstract principles of law nor the enactments of the legislature that led to this decision. Rather it was the growth of the antislavery sentiment and the specter of abolition that compelled the decision. Judge Scott thought that these developments were leading the nation toward civil war and that his decision might avert the crisis by protecting southern interests. Ironically, his decision and that of the United States Supreme Court upholding it would be more direct causes of the eventual war than the acts of most abolitionists and northern states.[137] By denying any comity

134. Ibid. 586.
135. Fehrenbacher, *Dred Scott Case* 262.
136. *Scott* v. *Emerson* 586.
137. See Carl B. Swisher, *History of the Supreme Court of the United States: The Taney Period, 1836–1864* (New York: Macmillan Company, 1974) 528–29, 592–630, and Hopkins, *Dred Scott's Case* 241 n. 1.

for free-state interests, and at the same time demanding extraterritorial protection for slavery, Judge Scott was only exacerbating the very conditions he lamented.

The decision in this critical case was not unanimous. In a stinging dissent, Chief Justice Hamilton R. Gamble reprimanded the two majority judges: "[I]n the midst of all such excitement, it is proper that the judicial mind, calm and self balanced, should adhere to principles established when there was no feeling to disturb the view of the legal questions upon which the rights of parties depend." Gamble did not attempt to distinguish this case from *Strader* or *The Slave, Grace*. Nor did he argue that Missouri could be compelled to grant comity in cases like *Dred Scott*. He simply recited the major cases from other slave states, and nearly all of Missouri's earlier cases, to show that Missouri had always granted comity in the past, that this policy was in line with that of other states, and that there should be no change at this time. His emphasis was on precedent and an impartial judiciary. "Times may have changed, public feeling may have changed, but," he stated, "principles have not and do not change; and . . . there can be no safe basis for judicial decisions, but in those principles, which are immutable."[138]

Scott v. *Emerson* was not an absolute rejection of all freedom claims. The decision did imply that Missouri would recognize a claim to freedom based on an "act of manumission by" a free-state court. However, since 1847 it had been illegal for free Negroes to migrate to the state. Presumably a slave actually manumitted in a free state could not then return to Missouri. Enforcement of laws prohibiting the immigration of free blacks was often lax, however, especially if a former master protected the newly freed slave; and even if newly manumitted slaves could not return to Missouri, it would be possible for them to inherit or own property in the state. But, if *Scott* v. *Emerson* did not close all doors to freedom in Missouri, it did close a major one. Unlike Louisiana, which upheld freedom claims based on free jurisdiction residence before 1846, Missouri's change was immediate and covered all cases—past, present, and future.[139]

Scott v. *Emerson* would soon be taken to the United States Su-

138. *Scott* v. *Emerson* 590–91.
139. Ibid. 586; Missouri, *Annual Laws, 1847*, 103; see 3 Western Law Journal 477–78 (1845) for enforcement of an earlier law requiring free black settlers to obtain licenses to stay in the state. Missouri continued to allow masters voluntarily to manumit their slaves in the state. Unlike the laws in most other slaves states, Missouri law permitted such newly free blacks to remain in the state; Berlin, *Slaves without Masters* 138–39, 139n. However, a slave who gained freedom by court order or manumission in another state would not be allowed to return to Missouri. For subsequent Missouri cases reaffirming *Scott* v. *Emerson*, see *Calvert* v. *Steamboat Timoleon*, 15 Mo. 595 (1852), and *Sylvia* v. *Kirby*, 17 Mo. 434 (1853).

preme Court, where as *Dred Scott* v. *Sandford* it would become the nation's most important and controversial case. That decision would be an open invitation for slave-state courts to reject all freedom cases based on northern residence, even where specific acts of manumission had been granted by free-state courts. Mississippi would ultimately apply the United States Supreme Court's ruling in that way. However, long before Dred Scott's case reached any court, the courts in Mississippi began to decide cases against freedom.

Mississippi

In 1818 Mississippi became the first southern state to free a slave solely on the basis of residence in a free jurisdiction. The case, *Harry* v. *Decker & Hopkins* (1818),[140] also resulted in one of the strongest condemnations of slavery in any of the slave states. The reasoning of the Mississippi court in 1818 made it the most liberal of any slave-state court to adjudicate transit and residence cases.

In 1784 John Decker, a Virginian, brought Harry and two other slaves to Vincennes in the Northwest Territory, where they lived until July 1816, when they all migrated to Mississippi. Although the point was not discussed by the court, this move was probably made to avoid the antislavery provisions of the Indiana state constitution, which was ratified on 29 June 1816 and went into effect in July. Whatever Decker's motives were, after arriving in Mississippi the three slaves sued for freedom. They relied on the antislavery provisions of the Northwest Ordinance and the Indiana Constitution. Decker claimed that the treaty of cession between Virginia and the United States protected slave property in the territory. Such a position would eventually be upheld in Missouri. Decker also asserted that the Indiana Constitution could not end slavery there, because that would violate the treaty of cession. The liberating aspects of the Northwest Ordinance were, in Decker's opinion, only applicable to slaves brought into the territory after 1787. This indeed would be the position of the Illinois Supreme Court until 1845.[141]

These arguments were quickly disposed of by the Mississippi court. The court agreed that the treaty of cession protected the property of the settlers living there at the time, but this treaty was superseded by the Ordinance of 1787. Any other interpretation of the ordinance would, in the court's opinion, "defeat the great object of the general government" and be "inadmissible upon every principle of legal construction." The court firmly believed that the

140. *Harry* v. *Decker & Hopkins*, Walk. (Miss.) 36 (1818).
141. Ibid. 36–39.

Indiana constitution makers had every legal right to abolish slavery. Furthermore, the court argued that Decker had been "a party to the articles of the compact" for the treaty of cession, the Northwest Ordinance, and the Indiana Constitution. As a Virginian Decker had been represented when the treaty of cession was signed by his state government; as a United States citizen Decker had apparently some type of virtual, if not actual, representation in the Congress when the Ordinance of 1787 was enacted; and as a citizen of the territory, Decker was represented when his neighbors and fellow settlers drew up and ratified the Indiana Constitution. Thus, he could not "claim a particular exemption from the operation of the constitution."[142]

The court concluded that if slavery existed in Indiana, after 1787, "language loses its force, and a constitution intended to protect rights, would be condemned by reason and the laws of nature," and could exist only "through municipal regulations." If the construction was doubtful, the judge asked, "How should the Court decide? . . . I presume it would be in favour of liberty." Indeed, the Mississippi court thought it "an unquestioned rule, that courts must lean '*in favorem vitae et libertatis*.'" Thus, Harry and the other slaves were freed.[143]

The opinion in *Harry* v. *Decker* was extraordinary for its explicit condemnation of slavery and its interpretation of the Northwest Ordinance. The Mississippi court's understanding in 1818 "that courts must lean '*in favorem vitae et libertatis*,'" is especially striking when compared to the 1820 Kentucky opinion in *Rankin* v. *Lydia*. There Judge Mills would specifically "disclaim the influence of the general principles of liberty" and reject "appeals to morality."

Unfortunately for Mississippi's slaves, *Harry* v. *Decker* was the first and the last case of this type to free slaves in the state. For two decades no cases were brought in which the questions of free-state residence or transit were raised. In the meantime the legislature passed a number of statutes designed to discourage the growth, or even continuance, of a free Negro population. Manumission was allowed only for "meritorious or distinguished services" and had to be ratified by the state legislature. Free blacks were not allowed to immigrate to the state after 1819 and an 1831 law allowed for their expulsion from the state, even if they were born there. Short of appealing to the legislature, the only way a master might voluntarily free his slaves was to take them to a free state. But under the law prohibiting the migration of free Negroes into the state, such an out-of-state emancipation would not allow the ex-slave to return to

142. Ibid. 36, 39, 40, 42.
143. Ibid. 42–43.

Mississippi. Twenty years after *Harry* v. *Decker* this question was decided by the Mississippi High Court of Errors and Appeals in the case of *Hinds* v. *Brazealle* (1838).[144]

In 1826 Elisha Brazealle took a slave woman and her son John Munroe Brazealle to Ohio where "he executed a deed of emancipation of said slaves and then returned with them to his residence" in Mississippi. The three continued to live together, in Mississippi, until Elisha died. In his will he "recited the fact" of the emancipation and "devised his property to the said John Munroe, acknowledging him to be his son." Elisha Brazealle's executors "took charge of the estate," which prompted Brazealle's relatives to contest the will. Their suit was based on the fact that slaves could not inherit property. They claimed that John Munroe Brazealle was still a slave, and it was to that question that the court turned.[145]

In this, as in all other Mississippi cases, *Harry* v. *Decker* and its pro-freedom rhetoric were conveniently ignored. Speaking for the court, Chief Justice William Sharkey framed the question before him in terms of the enforcement, in one state, of a contract made in another. He saw the deed of manumission simply as a contract made in Ohio. Its enforcement in Mississippi was governed solely by the rules of comity, under which no state was "bound to recognize or enforce a contract made elsewhere, which would injure the state or its citizens; or which would exhibit to the citizens an example pernicious and detestable." In addition, it was "a settled and sound principle that no state will enforce a contract made by its citizens elsewhere in violation and fraud of its own laws." In applying these principles to the emancipation Sharkey found, "To give it validity would be, in the first place, a violation of the declared policy, and contrary to the positive law of the state." Mississippi's policy was "indicated by the general course of legislation" under which "free negroes are deemed offensive, because they are not permitted to emigrate to, or remain in the state" and "are allowed few privileges, and subject to heavy penalties for offences." In addition there was positive law prohibiting the manumission of slaves within the state except with the consent of the legislature for meritorious or distinguished service. Sharkey concluded:

> The state of the case shows conclusively, that the contract had its origin in an offence against morality, pernicious and detestable as an example. But above all, it seems to have been planned and executed with a fixed design to evade the rigor of the laws of this state. The acts of the party in going to

144. *Hinds et al.* v. *Brazealle et al.*, 2 Howard (Miss.) 837 (1838).
145. Ibid. 841.

Ohio with the slaves, and there executing the deed, and his immediate return with them to this state, point with unerring certainty to his purpose and object. The laws of this state cannot be thus defrauded of their operation by one of our own citizens.

Thus, John Munroe Brazealle was declared to be a slave and the original plaintiffs gained possession of the estate.[146]

The reasoning in this case indicates that Mississippi would not tolerate any casual growth of a free black population. Only through an act of the legislature might a master free slaves in the state and keep them there. This case did imply, however, that a master could take his slaves out of the state and free them, as long as he did not bring them back into the state. This was confirmed two years later in *Ross* v. *Vertner* (1840),[147] which also involved a contested will. In this case the master bequeathed that some of his slaves be sent to Liberia to be freed. In upholding the will, the court there explained how Brazealle might have successfully freed his son:

It will not be contended, however, that the testator had not a right to take the slaves to Ohio, and leave them there in the enjoyment of freedom, according to the constitution of that state. Placed thus beyond our limits, their freedom could not be the subject of animadversions by the municipal laws of Mississippi, whose rigorous police regulations on this subject, were designed for the security of slave owners in the state, against the dangers of too great an increase of free negroes, whose example and whose means of sowing the seeds of mischief, of insubordination, perhaps of revolt, amongst the slaves in their neighborhood, was very justly to be apprehended and guarded.[148]

The holdings in these two cases were reaffirmed by an 1842 law prohibiting slaves who had been taken out of the state and emancipated from returning.[149]

The dictum in *Ross* v. *Vertner* was specifically affirmed and applied in *Leiper* v. *Hoffman* (1853).[150] Although Leiper was not formally emancipated, her "former owner asserted no claim upon her, and expressly recognized her as a free person," and she ultimately went to Ohio where she lived at the time of the suit. Before going to

146. Ibid. 841–44.
147. *Ross et al.* v. *Vertner et al.*, 5 Howard (Miss.) 305 (1840).
148. Ibid. 360.
149. *Mississippi Laws of 1842*, 66.
150. *Leiper* v. *Hoffman et al.*, 26 Miss. 615 (1853).

Ohio she had purchased property in Mississippi, which was the object of her suit against Hoffman. Hoffman claimed that Leiper was a slave when she purchased the land and as such was debarred from property ownership. Hoffman bought the property from Leiper's white guardian in what appeared to be a collusive effort by the two to defraud Leiper after she moved to Ohio. Speaking for the court, Justice Alexander Handy cited both *Ross* and *Hinds*. He thought that Leiper's "change of residence appears to be *bona fide*" because she continued to live in Ohio. Rather than deciding if Leiper could win the property outright as a resident of Mississippi, Handy suggested that the guardian held it for her in trust while she was a slave "until that disability was removed by her admission to the rights of a free person." Thus "she would be entitled to enforce them [her rights] against the trustee" after becoming a free citizen of Ohio. After a vigorous condemnation of both whites, Handy ordered the title to the property and the rents due to be given to Leiper.[151]

Five years later, in *Shaw* v. *Brown* (1858),[152] Handy again upheld an out-of-state manumission. In 1850 James Brown took two of his slaves, who were also his sons, to Ohio where he freed them and then purchased land for them in Indiana. After this, Brown returned to Mississippi alone. In 1852 Brown's sons (ex-slaves) visited their father in Mississippi but returned to Indiana in the spring of 1853. The elder son also visited Brown in 1854, but again returned to the North and was "never since that time" in Mississippi. Brown also visited his sons, and it was on such a visit to Indiana in 1856 that he died at the home of the mother of his two sons, whom Brown had also taken to Indiana and freed. Brown's will "directed the executor to sell the land and slaves of the testator" and after the payment of debts, "to deposit the residue of the proceeds of the sale in the Bank of Louisiana" subject to the draft of his elder son, or, in the case of his death, the next son. Brown's "next of kin," John Brown, contested the will, claiming that the emancipation had been a fraud against the laws of Mississippi. Shaw, the executor, denied this, and after losing in chancery court, appealed to the Mississippi High Court of Errors and Appeals.[153]

John Brown proved that the ex-slaves had returned to Mississippi after being manumitted in Ohio. He offered evidence that the deceased had made statements "to the effect, that their residence in Indiana was temporary; that their permanent residence was at" his home, and he had also purchased land for them in Mississippi. These facts and statements, the "next of kin" argued, proved that his rela-

151. Ibid. 615, 618, 621–24.
152. *Shaw* v. *Brown*, 35 Miss. 246 (1858).
153. Ibid. 303–7.

tive had attempted fraudulently to evade the law of the state. This evidence did not convince Handy. The judge thought that Brown had been "infatuated or debased" with love for his mulatto children and that these declarations were made only "after he had separated the children from him, showing that it was his intention, as it certainly was his desire, to have them with him, if it could have been done consistently with his paramount object of setting them free." Handy did not think that the emancipation was a fraud, although he made no attempt to hide his disgust for Brown's "debased" affection for his children.[154]

Even if the manumission was not a fraud, Brown's kin argued that a free black could not inherit property in Mississippi. This argument was based in part on the recent United States Supreme Court decision in *Dred Scott*, which held that blacks were not citizens. Handy agreed that the two ex-slaves were not citizens of the state they resided in, but he did think that they were *"inhabitants and subjects* of the State, owing allegiance to it, and entitled to protection by its laws and those of the United States." Although they were indeed members of "a subordinate and inferior class of beings," a state could "grant them certain rights of person and property; and they would be entitled to the enjoyment of those rights in any other State of this Union" unless prohibited by positive law of the other states. Although Mississippi had laws hostile to free blacks, Justice Handy did not think it against state policy for free Negroes from other states to have some rights in Mississippi. Handy did not think that the free Negro was "an outlaw, a banished person, or natural enemy of our people, against whom any man's hand may be raised with impunity, and as wholly without the protection of our laws." Therefore the bequest was not void and the will was upheld.[155]

Handy's "enlightened" rhetoric should not be misunderstood. He was willing to grant only the most minimal application of comity. Where Mississippi law did not interfere, he was willing to allow free blacks from other states a few basic rights in Mississippi. They could recover stolen property; if kidnapped they could sue for freedom; they could not be attacked or killed as outlaws; and they could, under this decision, inherit property. Slaves in Mississippi could not sue for freedom on the basis of free-state residence because the very act of returning to Mississippi violated that state's law. Nor could they be emancipated in the state without a special act of the legislature. Emancipations in other states were valid only if the slave did not return to Mississippi. Yet even the few rights that Handy conceded to Mississippi slaves who had been freed in the North would

154. Ibid. 307–8.
155. Ibid. 315–21.

not be upheld for long. A year later, in *Mitchell* v. *Wells* (1859),[156] the decision in *Shaw* v. *Brown* would be reversed. By 1859 Mississippi would be unwilling to grant *any* comity to the North when considering the status of a slave. But, *Mitchell* v. *Wells* is best understood in the context of *Dred Scott* and the *Lemmon* case. Thus, a discussion of it will be deferred until chapter 9.

In Favor of Slavery

Before 1830 nearly every slave state recognized the power of a free-state constitution, the Northwest Ordinance, or the Missouri Compromise to emancipate slaves who had resided in nonslave jurisdictions. Some slave states were willing to free slaves who had merely traveled through, or spent a few days in, a free state. Yet before the 1830s, the northern free states were reluctant to free slaves in transit or after short residences. As the northern states began to free slaves in transit, the slave states began to reject similar claims to freedom. No immediate causal relationship between these changes existed. Southern courts did not reject freedom claims because northern courts were becoming more emancipationist. Indeed, it would be absurd to argue that the South rejected its own precedents because the North adopted them. Rather, sectionalism was simply becoming more uncompromising, and on the issue of slavery, states were less willing to grant comity.

The slave-state courts reflected the attitudes of the people they served, and beginning in the 1830s those people became more and more sensitive about slavery and race. In 1818 Mississippi judges could condemn slavery as an evil. By the mid-1830s Mississippi politicians were suggesting that slavery was a positive good. By the 1850s the court openly debated whether free blacks were "outlaws" or if they had any rights at all. In 1860 the Mississippi legislature considered a measure that would have enslaved all free blacks who did not leave the state; in the same year such a law was actually passed in Arkansas.[157]

These decisions, laws, and legislative deliberations reflected the hardening of racial attitudes in the South as well as the growing sectional conflict. As never before, southerners believed that Negroes were suited to be slaves and nothing else. Thus, southern

---

156. Ibid. 320–21; *Mitchell* v. *Wells*, 37 Miss. 235 (1859); *Hearn* v. *Bridault*, 37 Miss. 209 (1859). For a brief, and not very analytical, discussion of these and other Mississippi cases, see Meredith Lang, *Defender of the Faith: The High Court of Mississippi, 1817–1875* (Jackson, Miss.: University Press of Mississippi, 1977) 69–93.

157. Berlin, *Slaves without Masters* 373–80.

courts and legislatures looked for ways to stop the growth of a free black population. The refusal to grant comity to northern states on the issue of freedom through transit, sojourn, or residence reflected this attitude. The attitude was also a function of the sectionalism that was leading southerners toward secession. By the eve of the Civil War most of the slave South was unwilling to grant comity to northern laws that interfered with their peculiar institution. This increasingly intransigent position was supported by the state legislatures, the state courts, and by 1860, the federal courts as well.

Chapter 8

Comity and the Federal Courts: The Constitution as a Proslavery Compact

No study of slave transit and comity would be complete without a thorough examination of the federal cases on the subject. While few in number, the federal cases, even more than the state cases, reveal the inadequacies of the Constitution's comity provisions. One of the major purposes of the federal court system was to arbitrate interstate legal conflicts. Given the prevailing ideology of states' rights and the limitations on federal interference with the states, however, satisfactory solutions to interstate problems caused by slave transit would have been difficult. These existing conditions were exacerbated by a proslavery bias on the part of some federal jurists. The perception of this bias, particularly in the 1840s and 1850s, led many northerners to believe that the federal courts could not be trusted to arbitrate fairly between the two sections.

The importance of the federal courts on interstate relations is underscored by the fact that nine major federal cases dealing with slavery and comity began as state cases and were later appealed to, or retried in, the federal courts. Moreover, many federal decisions were influenced by the opinions of state jurists. Similarly, federal decisions were often cited in state courts. Indeed, the distinctions between state and federal law (and between legal history and constitutional history) are not always precise.

Finally, the most important United States Supreme Court case of the antebellum period was *Dred Scott* v. *Sandford* (1857).[1] While the most prominent political issues surrounding *Dred Scott* centered on slavery in the territories, the case arose because Scott had lived in a free state and a free territory. Indeed, if the Missouri Supreme Court had followed thirty years of precedents and held Scott to be free, the case would never have been brought into the federal courts.

The development of a law of slave transit at the federal level

1. *Dred Scott* v. *Sandford*, 19 Howard (U.S.) 393 (1857).

was somewhat haphazard. Judges in different circuits sometimes reached conflicting positions on similar issues. In addition, important statements on transit and comity often came as dicta or in concurring or dissenting opinions in the United States Supreme Court. Nevertheless, certain trends and developments can be identified and explained. Between 1805 and 1847 five lower court decisions supported the right of free states to liberate slaves within their borders. The one Supreme Court case touching on this issue offered conflicting concurrences. After 1847 both lower federal courts and the Supreme Court generally protected slave transit and even long-term sojourn at the expense of pro-freedom results.

Slavery and Federal Jurisdiction

From the Constitutional Convention until the Civil War an accepted maxim of American legal theory stated that the states had virtually total authority to determine the status of persons living in them,[2] with only two major exceptions. Under the Constitution, Congress had the power to regulate the naturalization of immigrants. In 1790 the first of many laws enforcing this provision was passed. The Constitution also decreed that slaves could not gain their freedom—that is, acquire a new legal status—by escaping from one state into another. This was enforced by the Fugitive Slave Law of 1793 and that of 1850. The federal compact also declared that "[t]he Citizens of each State shall be entitled to all Privileges and Immunities of Citizens in the several States." The clause was never enforced by congressional legislation, however. Indeed, its very wording seems to confirm the states' inherent power to determine the status of all people within their jurisdictions.[3]

Because the status of slaves in transit was basically the province of the states, few federal cases on the subject came before the courts. Slaveowners who lost their human chattel under the laws of the free states had three main avenues into the federal courts. First, they could attempt to reclaim their slave under the Fugitive Slave Law and in so doing test the right of the free state to free slaves in transit. If the slave successfully eluded recaption, the master might sue those individuals who aided the slave for the value of the slave under the private right of action in the Fugitive Slave Law. This course of action would also have allowed the federal court to exam-

2. This changed after the Civil War with the addition of the Thirteenth, Fourteenth, and Fifteenth amendments to the Constitution.
3. U.S., *Constitution*, art. IV, sec. 2.

ine the status of the alleged slave. Second, they could bring suit in
federal court against some individual within the free state either to
gain monetary recompense for the loss of their slave property, or to
regain custody of the slave. Federal jurisdiction in this case would
be based on a diversity of state citizenship between the slaveowner
and the free-state resident being sued. Finally, it was possible to
appeal directly to the United States Supreme Court if a federal
statute or a provision of the United States Constitution were at
issue and if that issue had been properly raised in the state court.
Most masters in fact claimed a federal right to travel with their
slaves (under the Privileges and Immunities Clause, the Fugitive
Slave Clause, the Full Faith and Credit Clause, or the Commerce
Clause) at the state court level, and might have appealed to the
nation's highest court from the state courts.[4] But for a number of
reasons masters rarely used any of these avenues to bring their
cases into the federal courts, either at the lower levels or at the
United States Supreme Court level.

The use of federal courts by masters in transit would have been
costly, difficult, and perhaps futile. A master who lost his slave
while traveling through a free state and wished to sue for monetary
compensation, might find it impossible to wait until a federal court
was in session. Until the passage of the Fugitive Slave Law of 1850
there were no regular federal commissioners, sitting full-time in
convenient places, to whom slaveowners might appeal. The cost of
suit in federal court might be more than the slave was worth, and
applying the Fugitive Slave Law to recover a liberated slave was
complicated by factors of time and distance. By the time a master
could reach a federal court (or even a fugitive slave commissioner),
the now-free black would most likely be out of reach of the master or
even the federal courts.[5] Appeals to the United States Supreme
Court from the lower federal courts were even more difficult and
costly. Under the Judiciary Act of 1789, appeals from the lower
federal courts to the Supreme Court were possible only if the value
of the property at issue was greater than two thousand dollars; this
jurisdictional requirement could be circumvented only if the two
judges at the circuit court level could not agree on the questions of
law in a specific case.[6]

4. An example of this last point would be the Fugitive Slave Clause of the Constitution. See especially *Prigg* v. *Pennsylvania*, 16 Peters (U.S.) 539 (1842).

5. See, for example, the discussion of Passmore Williamson's case in chap. 5 and in this chapter.

6. I *U.S. Statutes* 73. The jurisdictional requirement did not apply to cases involving a federal statute or law or to cases appealed from state supreme courts directly to the U.S. Supreme Court.

Because of these jurisdictional limitations there are not many federal cases involving slave transit; only a very few of those reached the United States Supreme Court. Indeed, not until 1850 did the United States Supreme Court hear a case in which the effect of transit on a slave's status was at issue.[7] And not until *Dred Scott*, in 1857, did the court decide a case in which a slave's status was itself before the court.

Despite the small number of them, the federal court decisions were important to the development of the law of slave transit. More critical was their effect on the politics of the antebellum period. *Dred Scott* is, of course, the most famous example of this. But other Supreme Court and lower court decisions were also responsible for creating political storms. By the end of the period they also created the impression in the minds of many northerners that the entire federal court system was a tool of the "slaveocracy." As early as 1845 Salmon P. Chase decried that "[i]n the Judiciary, the very balance wheel of our government, and which has continually before it the most important questions ... that are to decide the LIBERTY OR SLAVERY OF MAN; here, we say, the preponderance of the Slave power is still more alarming." The preponderance of slave-state presidents or their northern "doughface" allies had also led to lower court judges throughout the nation who sympathized with the South and were hostile to antislavery. By the 1850s there was reason to believe that the federal courts were intent on protecting slavery, even in the free states. Thus, the philosophy of states' rights or state sovereignty was adopted by many northerners who sought the right to free all slaves brought into their states.[8]

Butler v. *Hopper*

In 1806 Pierce Butler became the first slaveowner to ask the federal courts to protect his claim to a slave. Butler had been a delegate to the Constitutional Convention in 1787 and was later elected to the United States Senate from South Carolina. But even when not holding that office he maintained a house in Philadelphia, where he

7. *Strader et al.* v. *Graham*, 10 Howard (U.S.) 82 (1850).

8. Salmon P. Chase and Charles Dexter Cleveland, *Anti-Slavery Addresses of 1844 and 1845* (Philadelphia: J. A. Bancroft, 1867) 24–25, 138, 148. The most important states' rights claim in North was made in *Ableman* v. *Booth*, 21 Howard (U.S.) 506 (1859). See also Thomas D. Morris, *Free Men All: The Personal Liberty Laws of the North, 1780–1861* (Baltimore: Johns Hopkins University Press, 1974), and William M. Wiecek, "Slavery and Abolition before the United States Supreme Court, 1820–1860," 65 *Journal of American History* 34–59 (June 1978).

kept his slave Ben. In September 1805 Ben won his freedom in a habeas corpus proceeding before the Philadelphia Court of Common Pleas. As a slave retained in the Keystone State for more than six months, Ben had become free.

In October 1806 Butler sued in federal court to regain custody of Ben. That Butler had to wait over a year to gain a hearing between the two cases indicates the difficulty of using the federal courts in cases of transit or sojourn. Ben's continued presence in Philadelphia suggests he had no fear of losing his freedom, for in the intervening period he could certainly have moved very far away from Butler. In the future, other slaves who were unwilling to test their freedom in appellate courts would often move to Canada or cities in the far north as soon as they gained their freedom.

Butler first obtained a writ *de homine replegiando* (personal replevin), which was served on Ben's employer, a man named Isaac Morris. This writ was obtained from United States Supreme Court Justice Bushrod Washington and was served by a United States marshal. Butler demanded a two-thousand-dollar bail, probably in hopes that Ben could not raise such a sum and therefore could be more easily enslaved. However, two members of the Pennsylvania Abolition Society, Isaac T. Hopper and Thomas Harrison, signed the bail bond and Ben remained free. Hopper had originally served a state writ of habeas corpus on Butler, which had led to Ben's freedom in 1805. Perhaps because of this earlier relationship with Ben, Butler directed his suit at Hopper.[9]

Butler v. *Hopper* (1806) was tried before a jury with Judge Richard Peters and Justice Bushrod Washington presiding. Washington's opinion does not give the exact nature of the suit, but it does indicate Butler's major agruments. Butler based his claim to Ben on three separate assertions: (1) The Pennsylvania law freeing Ben violated the Slave Importation Clause of the United States Constitution. (2) As a sojourner he was exempt from state interference with his property. (3) The law had been wrongly applied, because as a member of Congress he was exempt from it. Although Butler cited the Fugitive Slave Law to support his cause, he does not seem to have brought the case into federal court under the Act of 1793. Rather, it appears that Butler relied on his South Carolina citizenship to assert a diversity of citizenship between the parties, thus giving the federal court jurisdiction. This was in fact the only reasonable basis for bringing his case before Justice Washington. Unfortunately the exact arguments made on behalf of Butler have not survived, and

9. *Butler* v. *Hopper*, 4 F. Cas. 904 (1806); Lydia Marie Child, *Isaac T. Hopper: A True Life* (2d ed. New York: Dodd, Mead, and Company, 1881) 98–103; for a discussion of this case in the state courts, see chap. 2.

they must be pieced together through inferences based on Justice Washington's opinion.[10]

Justice Washington first disposed of Butler's claim that the 1780 law violated the Slave Importation Clause (article I, section 9) of the United States Constitution. That prohibition on legislation against the importation of slaves was directed solely at Congress and did "not in words or meaning, apply to the state governments."[11] Butler had been at the Constitutional Convention and was an active participant in the debate over the Slave Importation Clause. That his attorney would make such arguments on Butler's behalf is nothing short of incredible. It indicates that where slaves were concerned, even at this early date, theories of state sovereignty were strictly one-sided. Butler was willing to grant South Carolina complete autonomy in regulating the ingress of slaves, but he was unwilling to grant the same right to a free state such as Pennsylvania.

Justice Washington next turned to Butler's contention that he could recover his slave under the Fugitive Slave Law of 1793. Washington, himself a slaveowner and nephew of the first president, had little sympathy for this interpretation of the federal law or the Constitution. Washington found that the Fugitive Slave Clause did not "extend to the case of a slave voluntarily carried by his master into another state, and there leaving him under the protection of some law declaring him free." Washington noted that Pennsylvania was not unique in prohibiting the importation of slaves. "Laws of this nature, but less rigid, exist in most of the states where slavery is tolerated."[12] Washington's interpretation of the Fugitive Slave Clause was clearly the correct one. Butler's attempt to apply the clause to a slave voluntarily brought into a free state was just as fantastic as his attempt to apply the Slave Importation Clause to prove that Pennsylvania could not prohibit the importation of slaves before 1808. Butler knew perfectly well that no one at the federal convention believed that either of these clauses protected slaves voluntarily brought into free states.

With these questions out of the way, Justice Washington turned to Butler's claim that the Pennsylvania law had been wrongly applied. Had this been an appeal from the Pennsylvania court, this question would not have been open for Justice Washington to examine. But this case was essentially a new one, involving new parties. Thus Justice Washington could not simply reject Butler's arguments as res judicata. Butler claimed that as a United States senator he was exempt from the operation of the 1780 law. The Pennsylvania stat-

10. Ibid. 904–5.
11. Ibid. 905.
12. Ibid.

ute did in fact exempt congressmen and senators from the law. However, Butler's absence from the national legislature for more than six months while Ben was kept in Philadelphia made the claim of congressional immunity untenable. Justice Washington declared that the exemption for congressmen could not apply to Butler because for a two-year period he had not been in the Congress or the Senate.

Butler's only remaining claim was that as a sojourner in Pennsylvania he was exempt from that state's laws. This was not based on the six months allowed to visiting masters. Rather, Butler appears to have based his claim on the Privileges and Immunities Clause of the Constitution. Unfortunately, at this critical point Washington gives no indication of the reasoning behind Butler's claim. Instead, the justice noted that the jury found "that the plaintiff was a resident" of the state from 1794 on, which destroyed any claims under the comity clauses of the Constitution. There were conflicting facts on just where Butler maintained his permanent residence, since he served as the United States senator from South Carolina and was also elected to the legislature of that state. Nevertheless, Washington accepted the jury's conclusion that Butler was really a resident of Pennsylvania. Justice Washington would not order Ben turned over to Butler, and the case ended.[13]

Butler v. *Hopper* was significant as a federal case for a number of reasons. First, it showed that some federal courts, at least in this early period, would enforce free-state laws emancipating slaves in transit. Indeed, Justice Washington specifically acknowledged that the states had a right to pass legislation freeing slaves (except fugitives) within their jurisdiction. More important, it allowed the state law, and a jury, to determine who was a resident and who was not. Taken to its logical end, this decision meant that states could free any nonfugitive slave who entered their jurisdiction. Finally, the case made a clear distinction between fugitive slaves and slaves in transit.

Seventeen years later, in *Ex parte Simmons* (1823)[14] Justice Washington was directly confronted with a sojourning master who claimed his slave under the Fugitive Slave Law of 1793. Simmons, like Butler, was a South Carolinian and lived in Pennsylvania for about eleven months with his slave. At that point Simmons attempted to return to South Carolina with the slave and applied to Washington for a certificate of removal under the Act of 1793. It is unclear if Simmons applied for the certificate because his slave had

13. Ibid.
14. *Ex parte Simmons*, 22 F. Cas. 151 (1823).

been freed by a state court or because he wished to avoid any possible legal problems from state officials. Washington refused to grant the certificate, because Simmons's claim was not "within either the words or the intention" of the Fugitive Slave Law. Washington asserted that the Fugitive Slave Law did "not extend to the case of a slave voluntarily carried by his master into another state, and there leaving him under the protection of some law of the state declaring him free." Rather, the Fugitive Slave Law extended only "to slaves escaping from one state to another."[15]

Because Simmons voluntarily brought his slave to Pennsylvania, Washington could take "no cognizance of the case" and directed Simmons to seek a remedy in the state courts. In a bit of obiter dictum that could not have pleased the South Carolinian, Washington added that he was "of opinion that the alleged slave is free under the act of the assembly" of Pennsylvania because he had been kept there more than six months.[16]

It would be twenty-six years before another slave transit case reached the federal courts in Pennsylvania. In the meantime, antislavery would become a major social and political force that would lead to the repeal of the six-months law, thereby denying slaveowners any right of transit in Pennsylvania. In the intervening period three cases reaffirming Washington's position reached federal courts outside Pennsylvania. The first, *Polydore* v. *Prince* (1837)[17] was heard by the United States District Court for Maine. The other two, from Ohio and Indiana, were brought before the United States Seventh Circuit Court.[18]

Freedom through the Lower Federal Courts

Polydore v. *Prince* was a suit against the ship *Prince* by Polydore, a slave traveling with his master from Guadeloupe to Portland, Maine. During the voyage the ship's captain ordered Polydore to "clean out a hen-coop" and do other tasks. When Polydore failed to carry out these orders and "behaved otherwise insolently," the captain beat him severely. Later there were other beatings. When the vessel reached Maine, Polydore sued "a libel for an assault and battery" against the ship. Evidence showed Polydore did in fact fail

15. Ibid. 151–52.
16. Ibid. 152.
17. *Polydore* v. *Prince*, 19 F. Cas. 950 (1837).
18. *Jones* v. *Van Zandt*, 13 F. Cas. 1040 (1843) and 5 Howard (U.S.) 215 (1847); *Vaughn* v. *Williams*, 28 F. Cas. 1115 (1845).

244 An Imperfect Union

to obey the captain, partly because Polydore "did not understand a word of English" and the captain knew almost no French.[19]

The main defense of the ship's captain was that as a slave Polydore was barred from maintaining a suit. It was to this point that District Judge Ashure Ware directed most of his opinion. Ware concluded Polydore's civil incapacity—his status as a slave in Guadeloupe—was based on the law of a foreign country, which did not follow him to the United States. Ware declared that while in the United States Polydore was a free man and could sue in court. He could also choose to remain in the United States as a free man or return to Guadeloupe if he wished. This opinion was similar to Justice Lemuel Shaw's in the Massachusetts case *In re Francisco* (1832), which Ware cited to support his opinion. Ware also cited Justice Bushrod Washington's federal court opinions in *Butler* v. *Hopper* and *Ex parte Simmons*, as well as two important slave-state cases, *Lunsford* v. *Coquillon* and *Rankin* v. *Lydia*. Greatest stress was laid on Shaw's opinion in *Commonwealth* v. *Aves*. Citing this case, Ware asserted: "[A]ll the civil incapacities which are peculiar to that servile state, depend entirely on the local law. It follows of course that when a slave passes into a country, by whose laws slavery is not recognized, his civil condition is changed from a state of servitude, to that of freedom, and he becomes invested with those civil capacities which the law of the place imparts to all who stand in the same category."[20]

Ware did not deny Polydore might be reenslaved if he returned to his native land. Nor would the judge speculate on what would have happened if Polydore's ship had landed in a slave state and he had attempted to bring suit there. But, "sitting as this court does, in a place where slavery by the local law is prohibited," he felt "called upon" to ignore "the laws of a foreign power" that made Polydore a slave.[21]

Such an understanding of federal law and slavery implied that the federal courts ought to follow local law when dealing with slavery. Had this reasoning been adopted nationally, it would have given federal support to slavery in the slave states and federal support to freedom in the free states. Essentially this would have been applying the *lex fori* in cases involving the conflict of laws. This application of the *lex fori* would in fact be followed in some federal courts. But with the exception of one obscure federal case in Iowa,[22] after

19. *Polydore* v. *Prince* 950–51.
20. Ibid. 950–55. For the Massachusetts cases see chap. 4; for the slave-state cases, see chap. 7.
21. Ibid. 956.
22. *Daggs* v. *Frazer*, 6 F. Cas. 1112 (1849); see chap. 6 n. 3.

1847 the principle of *lex fori* was applied only when it benefited the slaveowner. *Polydore* v. *Prince* was never cited in a federal case dealing with slavery, probably partly because it was an admiralty case involving slaves from a foreign nation. The omission of *Polydore* is particularly striking in the *Dred Scott* case, where Chief Justice Roger B. Taney denied that blacks had ever had the right to sue in federal courts. None of the justices noted the precedent of *Polydore*, even though many cited admiralty cases, such as *The Slave, Grace*, and the two dissenters, justices Benjamin R. Curtis and John McLean, sought to disprove Taney's contention that blacks never had the right to sue in federal courts.[23]

The last two important federal court cases to support freedom through transit were heard by Supreme Court Justice John McLean in 1843 and 1845.[24] Like *Ex parte Simmons* in Pennsylvania, these cases reached the circuit court as claims under the Fugitive Slave Law of 1793. Unlike *Simmons*, however, in both cases slaves had actually run away from their masters into a free state. The first case, *Jones* v. *Van Zandt*, proved to be a bona fide claim under the Act of 1793 and on its face should not be part of an examination of slaves in transit. However, the circumstances of the case, combined with McLean's charge to the jury, illustrate the close connection between fugitive slaves and slaves in transit. The second case, *Vaughn* v. *Williams*, also appears at first glance to be a legitimate claim under the Fugitive Slave Act. Its ultimate result, however, was a refinement of the distinction between fugitive slaves and slaves in transit. *Vaughn* v. *Williams* reached McLean's court in 1845, two years after *Jones* v. *Van Zandt*, and must be understood in the context of the former case.

Wharton Jones owned nine slaves who escaped from his home in Kentucky. After reaching Ohio the slaves encountered John Van Zandt, who was driving his wagon down the same road on which the fugitives were walking. Although Van Zandt, "an old man, of limited education and slender means, but distinguished by an unquestioned integrity and benevolence of heart," believed the blacks were probably runaways, he nevertheless offered them a ride. After about four hours of travel they were "arrested by two bold villains, who, without any legal process, without any authority or request from the claimant [Wharton Jones] or any other person . . . in open breach of the laws of Ohio, undertook to seize the blacks and carry them out of the state by force, on suspicion that they were fugitive slaves." These men were professional slave catchers who, upon hearing of the escape, simply crossed the river into Ohio and started searching for

23. *Dred Scott* v. *Sandford*, 19 Howard (U.S.) 393, 499, 534–35 (1857).
24. The only exception to this is *Daggs* v. *Frazer*, 6 F. Cas. 1112 (1849).

the slaves. After stopping Van Zandt, they successfully captured eight of the nine runaways and took them back to Kentucky. Van Zandt's resistance did enable one of the slaves, Andrew, to escape.[25]

Upon returning the slaves to Jones the manhunters were paid a mandatory $450 reward under a Kentucky statute. Jones then sued Van Zandt for that sum, the value of Andrew, and additional costs, all of which totaled $1,200. A suit was also begun to recover a $500 penalty under the Fugitive Slave Law. These suits were first heard in July 1843, but the case continued for another eight years, being heard by the United States Circuit Court five times and by the United States Supreme Court once.[26]

The review of the case by the United States Supreme Court sustained the original conviction and Justice McLean's charge to the jury. Justice McLean and District Judge H. H. Leavitt had recorded a difference of opinion in interpreting the Fugitive Slave Law so the case could be brought to the United States Supreme Court, even though the amount in controversy was less than two thousand dollars. This procedure was "in conformity to what is understood to have been the usage in the circuits, they accommodated the parties by letting a division *pro forma* be entered on all the points present."[27] In the nation's highest court the case was an important cause célèbre for the antislavery movement. Van Zandt was represented by Salmon P. Chase of Ohio and William H. Seward of New York, who were undoubtedly the most distinguished antislavery lawyers west of Boston.[28]

However important the Supreme Court case was for the antislavery movement, it was in the circuit court, where Van Zandt was also represented by Chase, that the fundamental questions were raised and discussed. Justice Levi Woodbury's opinion in the United States Supreme Court added nothing to McLean's decision, indicating at least a tacit acceptance of his reasoning by the high court.

In the circuit court Chase argued that Van Zandt could not have known that the blacks he encountered were fugitives, since no one informed him of that fact. He asserted that a presumption of freedom existed in Ohio, where giving someone a ride was not a crime. These arguments had major implications for slaves in transit, since they

25. Salmon Portland Chase, *Reclamation of Fugitives from Service* (Cincinnati: R. P. Donogh and Company, 1847) 6–7.

26. *Jones* v. *Van Zandt*, 13 F. Cas. 1040 (1843); at 1047 (1843); at 1054 (1849); at 1056 (1849); at 1057 (1851) and 5 Howard (U.S.) 215 (1847).

27. *Jones* v. *Van Zandt*, 5 Howard (U.S.) 215, 223 (1847).

28. See, for example, Henry Wilson, 1 *History of the Rise and Fall of the Slave Power in America* (2 vols. Boston: James R. Osgood and Company, 1872), 475–77. Chase did not actually argue the case before the Supreme Court, but rather sent printed briefs. Seward did appear before the court.

implied that any slave voluntarily brought into the state might be presumed free.

In charging the jury McLean accepted much of Chase's argument. The justice told the jury: "[I]f the slaves left the service of the plaintiff [Jones] with his consent, or in any other mode, except as fugitives from labor, and came into the possession of the defendant [Van Zandt], as alleged, the plaintiff has no right to their services, and still less to recover from the defendant their value." He also endorsed the proposition that "every person in Ohio, or in any other free state, without regard to color, is presumed to be free." Therefore, the color of the fugitives could not lead to the "presumption" that Van Zandt "had notice they were slaves."[29]

But McLean also told the jury that formal notice was not necessary for Van Zandt to know he was harboring fugitives. If Van Zandt "had a full knowledge of the fact, however acquired, that they were slaves and fugitives from labor, it is enough to charge him with notice." Such notice, combined with the act to help the slaves escape, made Van Zandt liable under the statute.[30]

It remained only to determine "[w]hat shall constitute a harboring or concealing within the statute?" McLean told the jury: "This offence is not committed, in my judgment, by treating the fugitive on the ordinary principles of humanity. You may converse with him, relieve his hunger and thirst, without violating the law. In short, you may do any act which does not show an intent to defeat the claims of the master. But any overt act which shall be so marked in its character, as not only to show an intention to elude the vigilance of the master, but is calculated to attain such an object, is harboring of the fugitive in violation of the statute." On the strength of this charge, the jury found in Jones's favor and awarded him the twelve hundred dollars he asked for. The suit for the five-hundred-dollar penalty was also successful. Van Zandt, however, died during the appeals, and while his estate was eventually charged with the seventeen-hundred-dollar judgment, two more appeals to the circuit court were necessary before Jones actually obtained the money.[31]

Jones v. *Van Zandt* had two implications for slave transit. McLean's charge to the jury supported the proposition that a slave voluntarily brought into a free state was not recoverable under the Fugitive Slave Law. He asserted that only if the blacks were truly fugitives could they be claimed. If they "left the service" of a master "with his consent, or in any other mode" they would not be fugi-

29. *Jones* v. *Van Zandt*, 13 F. Cas., 1040, 1044 (1843).
30. Ibid.
31. Ibid. 1044, 1046.

tives. This view would certainly preclude any type of hiring out in a free state and might possibly have been applied to transit. McLean further asserted that if anyone "should attempt to subvert the law, by a clandestine introduction of slavery into the state, every good citizen would say they should suffer the penalties for such an offence." Finally, McLean endorsed the proposition that "every person in Ohio, or any other free state, without regard to color, is presumed to be free." The pro-freedom implications of McLean's charge were tempered by his interpretation of what official "notice" meant under the law.[32] Had the trend of federal court decisions been to support freedom, it is likely that McLean's charge would be seen today as essentially pro-freedom. Although it certainly had many pro-freedom implications, the federal courts were not moving in that direction. Thus *Jones* v. *Van Zandt* is remembered chiefly as a Supreme Court decision in which a harsh interpretation of the Fugitive Slave Law was sustained.

The dilemmas implicit in *Jones* v. *Van Zandt* were again brought before Justice McLean in *Vaughn* v. *Williams* (1845).[33] Like Wharton Jones, Livingston Vaughn was the owner of slaves who ran away, this time from Missouri to Indiana. Like John Van Zandt, Owen Williams was sued after he helped the fugitives. But in this case all the slaves successfully gained their freedom, while the slaveowner was unable to win recompense for his loss.

Vaughn purchased three slaves, Sam, Marian, and their child, in Missouri. They subsequently escaped, and he traced them to Hamilton County, Indiana. There Vaughn obtained an arrest warrant from a local judge and, accompanied by "a constable to execute the process," and some others "to render assistance that might be necessary," he went to Sam's cabin before daybreak. When these predawn raiders were refused admission to the house, they "pried the door from its hinges, and threw down the chimney." At this point the blacks surrendered. Sam appeared willing to go peacefully with his master, but first he asked permission to put his affairs in order. Sam claimed he owed a neighbor some money and wished to repay this before he left. Vaughn agreed to wait while the neighbor was summoned. This tactic proved successful, for in a short time a number of whites arrived "who expressed strong interest in behalf of the slaves." Outnumbered, Vaughn agreed to allow the slaves to be brought before a magistrate before returning south with them, and the party set out for a nearby village. Over Vaughn's objections the entire group stopped for breakfast at a farmhouse, and by the time travel was resumed "the company had increased to about one hun-

32. Ibid.
33. *Vaughn* v. *Williams*, 28 F. Cas. 1115 (1845).

dred and fifty," most of whom opposed Sam's return to slavery. At a crucial fork in the road the wagon with the blacks in it turned west instead of east and Vaughn was unable to stop it. The blacks escaped and were not heard from again. Vaughn later sued Williams and some other individuals for the value of his slaves under the Fugitive Slave Law of 1793.[34]

Williams never denied his actions in helping the slaves. Instead, he attacked the constitutionality of the Fugitive Slave Law of 1793 and at the same time proved that Sam and his family had a legitimate claim to freedom. Both arguments reflect the strategies of Salmon P. Chase, who had been refining his tactics in the courts of Ohio for a number of years. Although Chase declined to argue this case himself, he did advise those managing it. Chase's advice may have resulted in Williams's rather bizarre argument that Indiana was obligated only to return fugitive slaves who fled from the original thirteen states, because that was all the Northwest Ordinance of 1787 required. Just as Ohio judges had rejected this argument when made by Chase in the state courts, United States Supreme Court Justice John McLean rejected it in his court. McLean gave a long explanation for the Fugitive Slave Clause and why it applied to all the states. Although McLean thought the clause made the Constitution "less perfect" than it might have been, he told the jury that "while it remains the fundamental law of the Union, no good citizen will disregard its provisions."[35]

Williams was apparently prepared to lose on the constitutional issue, because at some expense witnesses had been brought from a "remote part of Illinois" to give testimony on behalf of Williams. These witnesses proved that Vaughn had purchased the slaves from an unnamed Missourian who had obtained them from one Tipton, a Kentuckian, who had taken the slaves to Illinois in 1835. Tipton and the slaves had lived in Illinois for six months, after which he had moved to Missouri and sold them. Tipton then returned to Illinois, where he lived and voted for at least the next two years. Before he took the slaves out of Illinois "there was much conversation in the neighborhood as to the right of the colored persons to their freedom." The fact that Tipton left Illinois with the slaves sometime before sunrise suggests that he feared the slaves would be rescued if he tried to remove them when his neighbors were awake.[36] On the advice of Salmon P. Chase, Williams's attorneys argued that this

34. Ibid. 1116–17.
35. Ibid.; Benjamin Stanton to Salmon P. Chase, 10 Oct. 1844; M. C. White to Chase, 11 May 1845; H. W. DePay to H.B. [Henry B. Stanton?], 26 Nov. 1844; all in Chase Papers, box 6, LC.
36. *Vaughn* v. *Williams* 1117–18.

residence in Illinois had freed Sam and his family. Thus Williams could not be held liable for the value of the slaves, because they were not in fact slaves.[37]

In charging the jury, Justice McLean made a blistering attack on Williams's conduct. He thought Williams had incited a mob, which "was unlawful, as its object was to defeat a legal investigation of an asserted right." But McLean was also certain that Sam and his family were not in fact slaves. "Having been brought to the state of Illinois, which prohibits slavery, by their master . . . and kept at labor for six months, under a declaration of the master that he intended to become a citizen of that state, and who actually exercised the rights of a citizen by voting, there can be no doubt that the slaves were, thereby, entitled to their freedom." Citing the "decisions repeatedly made by the supreme court of Missouri," McLean concluded that the blacks were free. It was "clear that the plaintiff had no knowledge whatever of the removal and employment of the slaves in Illinois," when he purchased them, and McLean thought "a gross fraud was practiced on him by the person of whom he purchased the slaves, and against him or Tipton he may have recourse." If the blacks were not slaves, though, he had no recourse against Williams.[38]

McLean noted that it was argued that "if the colored persons voluntarily returned into slavery" the title would be good. This question was moot since there was "no evidence that they went voluntarily to Missouri." On the contrary, there could be "no doubt that they were forcibly abducted by Tipton." McLean concluded by telling the jury: "[I]f you believe the evidence, which is not contradicted, you will find for the defendant, however improper his conduct may have been. If the fugitives were free, he is not subject to the penalty claimed of him." It took the jury only a few minutes to find Williams innocent.[39]

Vaughn v. *Williams* was the last major federal decision to support the concept of freedom through transit or residence. It is particularly interesting when compared with *Strader* v. *Graham*, which had been decided a few months earlier in Kentucky. In that case the Kentucky Court of Appeals refused to try the status of slaves who were no

37. Stanton to Chase, 10 Oct. 1844; White to Chase, 11 May 1845; DePay to H.B., 26 Nov. 1844, in Chase Papers, box 6, LC.

38. *Vaughn* v. *Williams* 1117–18.

39. Ibid. When it became obvious that Vaughn would lose his case, he and his fellow Missourians "were bound in $1000 bond to appear at the next court for an assault upon the persons and injury done to the dwelling of a *free citizen* of *Indiana*." There is no record that anything came of this case, but it does indicate the hostility toward slavery that could exist, even in a state like Indiana, which was noted for its negrophobia; H. W. DePay to H.B., 26 Nov. 1844, in Chase Papers, box 6, LC.

longer in the state. Strader was eventually required to pay for the slaves who escaped on board his steamship, although two of them had previously spent time in Ohio and Indiana. While the Kentucky court doubted that their short transits would have freed them, the court refused even to consider their status as long as they were outside its jurisdiction. Yet in *Vaughn* McLean did exactly that. He declared the slaves free in absentia, even though he strongly disapproved of the methods Williams and his cohorts had used to secure their freedom. In this sense the decision was the strongest support for freedom of any federal case.

Federal Courts Support Slavery

Five years later, in *Oliver* v. *Kauffman et al.* (1850),[40] a federal circuit court jury in Pennsylvania faced a case similar to *Vaughn*. In March 1847, Pennsylvania repealed its six-months law, which meant that slaveowners had no right of transit through the state with their human chattels. Two months later Mrs. Cecilia Oliver crossed the Keystone State with twelve slaves, while returning to Maryland from Arkansas. In October the slaves ran back to Pennsylvania, where they were aided by Daniel Kauffman. Mrs. Oliver failed to capture them and sued Kauffman for their value in a state court. Although she won her initial suit, the decision was overturned by the Pennsylvania Supreme Court on the ground that the state court had no jurisdiction.[41]

Oliver then initiated a suit in the United States Circuit Court under the Fugitive Slave Law of 1793. The case was tried before Supreme Court Justice Robert Grier, a Pennsylvania Democrat sympathetic to slaveowners. Oliver claimed that Daniel Kauffman, Philip Breckbill, and Stephen Weakley "did tortuously and illegally *harbor and conceal*" Oliver's twelve slaves after "illegally enticing, persuading, procuring, aiding and assisting" the slaves to run away. She asked for damages amounting to $26,000. Thaddeus Stevens defended Kauffman and his friends with three arguments. First, that the slaves had been illegally imported into Maryland and were thus free under that state's laws. Second, that Oliver had previously brought the slaves into Pennsylvania and they were thus free under Pennsylvania laws because the six-months law had been repealed. Finally, that the defendants had no "notice" that the blacks they

40. *Oliver* v. *Kauffman et al.*, 18 F. Cas. 657 (1850).
41. *Kauffman* v. *Oliver*, 10 Pa. St. 514 (1849). For a discussion of this case in the state courts, see chap. 5.

gave shelter to were in fact fugitives and thus they were not responsible for their escape.[42]

In his charge to the jury Grier said that the questions of law concerning the status of Oliver's slaves after she brought them to Pennsylvania and Maryland should be left to the court to decide. The jury should only decide if Kauffman had reason to believe that the blacks he aided were fugitive slaves. In his charge Grier gave a long explanation of what "to harbor" or "help" meant. Like Justice McLean in *Jones* v. *Van Zandt*, Grier noted that the Fugitive Slave Law did "not intend to make common charity a crime, or treat that man as guilty of an offense against his neighbor who merely furnishes food, lodging, or raiment to the hungry, weary or naked wanderer, though he be an apprentice or a slave." The "harboring made criminal by" the law required "some other ingredient besides a mere kindness or charity rendered to the fugitive." To win her case Oliver had to prove that Kauffman acted with "[t]he intention or purpose to encourage the fugitive in his desertion of his master; to further his escape and impede and frustrate his reclamation." Finally, Grier urged the jury to ignore the political and antislavery arguments made by Stevens. Grier noted "[m]uch has been said during the discussion of this case by learned counsel, on this unfortunate subject of slavery, as one which has perverted the moral sentiments of many of our citizens, both North and South, and originated *peculiar notions* hostile to the stability of this Union." Grier reminded the twelve citizens deliberating in this case that "you have sworn to perform of rendering a true verdict on the issue presented to you. . . . No theories or opinions which you or we may entertain with regard to liberty or human rights, or the policy or justice of a system of domestic slavery, can have a place on the bench or in the jury box." Ten of the jurors believed Kauffman had knowingly violated the Fugitive Slave Law and held him liable for Mrs. Oliver's losses. But two did not, and the case was dismissed.[43]

42. *Oliver* v. *Kauffman et al.*, 18 F. Cas. 657, 658; Charge of Judge Grier [in *Oliver* v. *Kauffman*], 10 *American Law J.* 160, 161 (1850); *The Liberator*, 1 Nov. 1850. This case was reargued and decided in Oct. 1852 and is reported in the Federal Cases as *Oliver* v. *Weakley*, 18 F. Cas. 657 (1853). *Both* of the official reports of these cases in the *Federal Cases* are inaccurate. The second case, *Oliver* v. *Weakley*, is reported as having taken place in October 1853 when in fact it took place in October *1852*. The report of the first case is even more confusing. It contains most of Justice Grier's charge to the jury from the 1850 case, but it also contains a good portion of his charge from the 1852 trial. This leads to a charge to the jury which the official reports claim took place in 1850 but which includes information from an 1851 case! For this discussion of these cases I have supplemented the official reports with reports of the cases from newspapers and contemporary law journals.

43. 10 *American Law J.* 166, 168, 169.

Two years later Oliver again sued the same defendants. By this time, however, the legal issues in the case were overshadowed by events which had occurred throughout the nation. The Fugitive Slave Law of 1850 was passed a month before Grier heard Oliver's case for the first time, in October 1850. In his 1850 charge to the jury Grier had obliquely referred to the protests against the new statute. By the time the case was retried in 1852, Grier could no longer avoid confronting directly the new law and the protests it had stimulated. Various state legislatures had condemned the law or considered resolutions to that effect. The Chicago Common Council passed a resolution of nullification, while throughout the North blacks and their white allies had organized for defense against the law. Rescues of alleged fugitive slaves in Boston and Syracuse gave the appearance of a strong national movement to oppose the law and the federal government. Addressing the National Free Soil Convention in Pittsburgh, Frederick Douglass suggested that the best way to deal with the law was "to make a dozen or more dead kidnappers . . . [for] dead kidnappers carried down South could cool the ardor of Southern gentlemen, and keep their rapacity in check." In the year between Oliver's first suit and this second trial blacks in Pennsylvania followed Douglass's advice. At Christiana, Pennsylvania, a Marylander attempted to seize his runaway slaves. The slaves resisted and, by the time the smoke cleared, the owner was dead and two of his relatives were severely wounded. The fugitive slaves escaped, but more than forty whites and blacks living in the area were indicted for treason. Only one man, Castner Hanway, was tried (before Justice Grier) and he was acquitted.[44]

During Kauffman's second trial "allusion was made, on both sides, to the late trials in this Court for treason, arising out of the riot and homicide at Christiana," and to the "Report of the Attorney General of Maryland, made to the Executive of that State." The Maryland attorney general's report had condemned the people of Pennsylvania for their refusal to support the Fugitive Slave Law. In his charge to the jury Grier began by urging the jurors to allow "no prejudice to affect your minds, either for or against either of the parties to this suit. The odium attached to the name 'abolitionist' (whether justly

44. Philip S. Foner, 2 *The Life and Writings of Frederick Douglass* (4 vols. New York: International Publishers, 1950–55) 207; Stanley W. Campbell, *The Slave Catchers: Enforcement of the Fugitive Slave Law, 1850–1860* (Chapel Hill: University of North Carolina Press, 1970) 50–79; Jonathan Katz, *Resistance at Christiana: The Fugitive Slave Rebellion, Christiana, Pennsylvania, September 11, 1851. A Documentary Account* (New York: Thomas T. Crowell, 1974); Paul Finkelman, "The Treason Trial of Castner Hanway," in Michal R. Belknap, ed., *American Political Trials: The Role of Politicized Justice in United States History* (Westport, Conn.: Greenwood Press, forthcoming).

or unjustly, it matters not), should not be suffered to supply any want of proof of the guilty participation of the defendants in the offence charged. . . . [t]he defendants are on trial for their *acts*, not for their *opinions*." He urged the jurors to ignore "the occasional insolence and violent denunciation of the South" by the defendants. Although appearing to charge the jury to ignore the political issues in the trial, Grier went on to discuss the Christiana Riot which he said was "the legitimate result of the seditious and treasonable doctrines diligently taught by a few vagrant and insane fanatics. . . ." But Grier also urged the jurors to ignore "certain official statements" from Maryland "reflecting injuriously upon the people of Pennsylvania and this Court." The duty of the jury was "to treat with utter disregard ignorant and malicious vituperation of fanatics and demagogues, whether it come from North or South" and instead to follow the obligations of the Constitution.[45]

On the legal questions before the jury Grier changed his charge from the 1850 case in one critically important way. In 1850 he had said that the status of the slave under Pennsylvania law was a question for the court to determine. Thus, only if there was a verdict against Kauffman would he have to answer that question. In 1852, however, Grier stated quite clearly that the status of the slaves "depends on the law of Maryland, and not of Pennsylvania. This Court cannot go behind the *status* of these people where they escaped." Thus, Grier asserted that, despite "some very pretty things (in the case of Somerset), which are often quoted as principles of common law," the slaves were not free when they left Maryland. He referred to *Strader* v. *Graham*, which had been decided after the first trial in this case, to support this position. On the basis of this charge the jury found Kauffman liable for Oliver's slaves and fixed a judgment against him of $2,800. The other defendants were acquitted.[46]

Grier's charge was a new and striking development in the federal adjudication of comity cases. In Pennsylvania the law specifically declared that slaves brought into the state became free the moment they came under Pennsylvania jurisdiction. No court action or other procedure was required to free a slave. Yet Grier declared that this law would not be recognized by a federal court sitting in a free state. The implications of this decision were frightening. Slaves could be brought into Pennsylvania by a master and, if they refused to leave, the master could simply seize them and bring them back to the slave state. If they later escaped into Pennsylvania, where they

---

45. *Oliver* v. *Kauffman*, 1 *American Law Register* 142, 144–45 (decided, October, 1852; reported, January 1853).

46. Ibid., 148–49; *Oliver* v. *Weakley*, 18 F. Cas. 657 (1853). This case is also reported in *The Liberator*, 19 Oct. 1852 and 19 Nov. 1852.

were legally entitled to freedom, the federal courts would not protect them. Rather, the federal courts would protect the master's right to seize them. The court would not "go behind the *status* of these people where they escaped" even if they had a legitimate claim to freedom when they escaped.

Passmore Williamson's Case

Five years after *Oliver* v. *Kauffman* the laws of Pennsylvania were again at issue in the federal courts. United States District Judge John K. Kane presided over a series of hearings involving the slaves of John H. Wheeler and a Quaker abolitionist named Passmore Williamson. Like Justice Grier, Judge Kane was a Pennsylvania Democrat who usually sided with slaveholders when they came before his bench. Henry Wilson, the antislavery senator and later vice-president, characterized Kane as "a judge who more than once disgraced both himself and the judiciary by his cruel renderings of the law."[47] His conduct in Williamson's case was by far his most notorious.

Passmore Williamson was secretary of the Acting Committee of the Pennsylvania Abolition Society. One of his duties was to aid slaves brought into Pennsylvania or captured there. In July 1855 he organized the escape of three slaves owned by John H. Wheeler, a native of North Carolina. Wheeler, the United States minister to Nicaragua, had stopped in Philadelphia to pick up personal possessions stored at the home of his wife's parents. Wheeler arrived in Philadelphia on the morning of 18 July and planned to take a two o'clock ship to New York. He missed that boat and was forced to wait three hours for the next one. In the meantime Wheeler and his slaves went to a nearby restaurant. There Jane, the mother of the two other slaves, told a black waitress that she (Jane) wished to be free.[48]

47. Wilson, 2 *Rise and Fall of Slave Power in America* 235. *United States ex rel. Wheeler* v. *Williamson*, 28 F. Cas. 682, 686 (1855). The American edition of Lord John Campbell, *Lives of Atrocious Judges: Lives of Judges Infamous As Tools of Tyrants and Instruments of Oppression*, Edited by Richard Hildreth (New York and Auburn: Miller, Orton & Mulligan, 1856), contains a full account of Williamson's case. Hildreth, like Wilson and others, considered Judge Kane's actions "atrocious." See also George Frisbie Hoar, ed., 5 *Charles Sumner: His Complete Works* (20 vols. New York: Negro Universities Press, 1969) 52–57. See also Ralph Lowell Eckert, "The Ordeal of Passmore Williamson," 100 *Pennsylvania Magazine of History and Biography* 521–38 (1976). Randall O. Hudson and James Durham, *The New York Daily Tribune and Passmore Williamson's Case: A Study in the Use of Northern States' Rights* (Wichita, Kansas: Wichita State University, 1974).

48. *United States ex rel. Wheeler* v. *Williamson*, 28 F. Cas. 682, 686–87 (1855);

Williamson was soon informed of Jane's situation and he immediately contacted William Still, the "conductor" of the underground railroad in Philadelphia. Williamson then went to the wharf and boarded Wheeler's ship just before it was to leave. A number of blacks followed Williamson onto the ship. Williamson believed that "the persons thus held as slaves were entitled to their freedom by reason of their having been so brought by their master voluntarily into" Pennsylvania. He explained this to Wheeler, then forced his way to the slaves and helped the slaves leave the ship. Williamson claimed the slaves voluntarily left with him, and this was later affirmed by Jane in an affidavit. Other witnesses claimed the slaves were dragged off by the blacks accompanying Williamson and driven away in carriages. After the slaves were safely away from the area, Williamson told Wheeler his name, where he could be reached, and "that he would be responsible for any legal claim" Wheeler "might have to the slaves."[49]

Wheeler immediately secured a writ of habeas corpus, which he attempted to serve on Williamson the next day. Williamson was conveniently out of town and did not return until two days after the rescue when a second writ was served on him. The writ commanded Williamson to bring the three slaves before District Judge Kane.[50]

In his return to the writ Williamson stated that the slaves "are not now, nor was [*sic*] at the time of the issuing of the said writ, or at any other time, in the custody, power or possession of, nor confined, nor restrained their [*sic*] liberty by him. . . ." Williamson could not "have the bodies of said Jane, Daniel and Isaiah" brought before the court because he had no power over them. Williamson asked for a continuance "to prepare testimony to prove the truth of the return," but Kane denied the request and testimony was taken that day.[51]

Various witnesses for Wheeler placed Williamson at the scene of the abduction and as the ringleader of it. At the end of this testimony Wheeler's counsel, who was also the United States district attorney, moved to charge Williamson "for contempt in making a false return to the writ," and "[t]hat he be held to bail in $5,000 to answer the charge of perjury."[52]

Narrative of the Facts in the Case of Passmore Williamson (Philadelphia: Pennsylvania Anti-Slavery Society, 1855) 3–5; John K. Kane, *Case of Passmore Williamson* (Philadelphia: Uriah Hunt and Son, 1856) 3–9. For a discussion of this case in the state courts of Pennsylvania, see chap. 5 of this volume.

49. Campbell, *Lives of Atrocious Judges* 389; *United States ex rel. Wheeler* v. *Williamson* 682–83.

50. *United States ex rel. Wheeler* v. *Williamson* 682.

51. Ibid.

52. Ibid. 683.

Although surprised by this tactic, Williamson nevertheless took the stand in his own defense. He again denied responsibility for the blacks. He claimed that he went to the wharf only to inform the slaves of their rights. When asked by the United States attorney if it was his intention "to take them from Mr. Wheeler," Williamson answered, "It was, if they desired." Williamson denied that he brought any help with him or that he hired the carriage that took the slaves away. He said that he would have sought a writ of habeas corpus to free the slaves but there was neither time nor an available judge.[53]

At no time did Williamson assert that the slaves were free under Pennsylvania law and he had thus committed no crime. However, this defense may have been sidetracked by the threatened contempt and perjury proceedings. Williamson was not being prosecuted under the Fugitive Slave Law, but for failing to respond to the writ of habeas corpus.

Judge Kane was not impressed with Williamson's defense. He thought the abolitionist "made it plain that he had been an advisor to the project, and given to his confederates sanction throughout." Kane could not "look upon this return otherwise than as illusory—in legal phrase as evasive, if not false."[54] Indeed, by asserting that the slaves were never "within his power, custody or possession at any time whatever" Williamson had overstated his innocence. Kane thought "[i]t would be futile, and worse, to argue that he who has organized, and guided, and headed a mob to effect the abduction and imprisonment of others—he in whose presence and by whose active influence the abduction and imprisonment have been brought about—might excuse himself from responsibility by the assertion that it was not his hand that made the unlawful assault, or that he never acted as the gaoler." In ignoring the writ, Williamson had "chosen to decide for himself upon the lawfulness as well as the moral propriety of this act . . . [and] put himself in contempt of the process of this court. . . ."[55]

Kane concluded by noting that Williamson had offered no legal justifications for his acts. One possibility occurred to Kane "as perhaps" within Williamson's view, and the judge thought "it right to express" his opinion on it. He also agreed that he would "frankly reconsider" this issue if raised in any future proceedings. Kane thought Williamson might have acted because he felt the blacks "were not legally slaves inasmuch as they were in the territory of Pennsylvania when they were abducted." Kane knew "of no statute of Pennsylvania, which affects to divest the rights of property of citi-

53. Ibid. 684.
54. Ibid. 685.
55. Ibid.

zens of North Carolina, acquired and asserted under the laws of that state, because he has found it needful or convenient to pass through the territory of Pennsylvania." And, without giving any reasons, Kane further asserted that such a statute could not "be recognized as valid in a court of the United States." In any event, Kane thought it "altogether unimportant whether they were slaves or not." For "[i]t would be the mockery of philanthropy to assert, that because men had become free, they might therefore be forcibly abducted."[56] Kane thereby ignored the existence of the 1847 repeal of the six-months law, denied its constitutionality, and declared that it could not be used to protect slaves from their former owners. Having reached these conclusions, Kane determined that Williamson's answer to the writ was both evasive and insufficient. Kane found Williamson in contempt of court and sent him to Moyamensing Prison.

Kane's use of the writ of habeas corpus was truly ironic. Had the blacks been claimed as fugitive slaves by the alleged master and applied for a writ of habeas corpus to prove their status as free men, it is doubtful that Kane would have issued the writ. Kane's commitment to slavery precluded his issuing the "Great Writ" to support liberty. But to protect a slaveowner and punish an abolitionist, Kane willingly granted a writ of habeas corpus on behalf of the blacks. Had the writ been carried out, the blacks would have been "liberated" from Williamson, only to be reenslaved by Wheeler.

Williamson applied to the Pennsylvania Supreme Court for a writ of habeas corpus that would release him from prison. The Pennsylvania court agreed that "unless they were fugitives" the blacks "could not be slaves at all" and the federal court had no jurisdiction over the case. But the state court also refused to order Williamson's release because it was Williamson who "stopped the investigation *in limine*." Only when Williamson gave a proper return to the federal court could the status of the blacks be determined. Until then the state court, with one justice dissenting, was willing to allow Williamson to remain in prison.[57]

---

56. Ibid. 686.

57. *Passmore Williamson's Case*, 26 Pa. St. 9 (1855). The federal prosecutors in Pennsylvania carefully watched this case. James Van Dyke feared the Pennsylvania court would find in favor of Williamson and "[i]n such an event important questions involving the conflict of authority between the powers of the U.S. and the States courts will doubtless arise." Van Dyke felt the U.S. marshal should resist any order to release Williamson, and "[h]e will then be attached by the S[tate] Court and taken into custody of the sheriff—I would then apply for a writ of Habeas Corpus from the Circuit Court of the U.S." Van Dyke hoped Attorney General Caleb Cushing could come to Philadelphia to discuss the issue with him. On 7 September Van Dyke telegraphed Cushing to let him know that nothing had been decided. However, on 8 September a relieved U.S. Marshal F. W. Wynkoop telegraphed Cushing, "Habeas

Williamson then returned to Judge Kane with a new plan of action. By this time the blacks were in Boston. Williamson secured from Jane, who now used the last name of Johnson, a petition requesting that the contempt charge be dropped. Jane Johnson stated that "she was not at the time of her leaving Mr. Wheeler . . . or any time since, in any way or manner in the custody, power, possession or control" of Williamson. This deposition was sworn before C. W. Loring, the commissioner for the United States District Court in Massachusetts.[58]

Kane responded to this petition with a disquisition on the rights of slaveowners in Pennsylvania and an elaborate discussion of the 1847 repeal of the six-months law. Kane felt that "it did not effect to vary or rescind the rights of slave owners passing through" Pennsylvania. Rather, it applied only "to persons resident" or "sojourning" who "sought to retain their slaves" in the state. Over these persons Kane acknowledged that Pennsylvania had jurisdiction. But the state legislature, under his interpretation of the repeal, "left the right of transit for property and person, over which it had no jurisdiction, just as it was before, and as it stood under the constitution of the United States and the law of nations."[59]

Kane "affirmed . . . the right of a citizen of one state to pass freely with his slaves through the territory of another state, in which the institution of slavery is not recognized." This opinion was based on the "law of nations" and the United States Constitution. All experts, Kane observed, regarded "the right of transit for person and property through the territory of a friendly state, as among those which cannot, under ordinary circumstances, be denied." He acknowledged that it was not "an unqualified" right, since states might "impose reasonable conditions" on transit. But Kane would not admit that a state might interfere with the passage of any types of property. He sought to defend all property in transit, a position that would by inclusion protect slave property in transit. Kane found the right of transit to be the same "as to person and to property." For "the same argument, that denies the right of peacefully transmitting one's property through the territories of a state, refuses the right of passage of its owners." This was a dubious proposition, since certain types of property, such as liquor, explosives, and even slaves, had

Corpus is refused by vote of four to one"; James C. Van Dyke to Caleb Cushing, 6 Sept. 1855; Van Dyke to Cushing (by telegram), 7 Sept. 1855; F. W. Wynkoop to Cushing (by telegram), 8 Sept. 1855; Van Dyke to Cushing, 10 Sept. 1855; all in Attorney General's Papers, Letters Received, Pennsylvania, box 1, 1813–55, National Archives, Washington, D.C.

58. *United States ex rel. Wheeler* v. *Williamson* 687.
59. Ibid. 692.

often been prohibited from passing through a given state or nation. But Judge Kane saw the question only in the most simplistic terms. He asserted that if one state decreed that there was "no property, no right of ownership in human beings," then "another, in a spirit of practical philanthropy only a little more energetic" might ban "the products of slave labor." And a third could "outlaw against all intoxicating liquids." That some states had successfully accomplished this apparently eluded Kane. Kane envisioned states banning "the sugar of New Orleans, the cotton of Carolina, the wines of Ohio, and rum of New England." He predicted that New Jersey would refuse "to citizens of Pennsylvania the right of passing along her railroads to New York." With unintentional irony, he admitted the imperialistic demands of slavery by noting that this right of one state to exclude the commerce of another "was exploded in Europe more than four hundred and fifty years ago, and finds now, or found very lately, its parting illustration in the politics of Japan."[60] Japan had only recently been "opened" to trade and travelers by the unanswerable extralegal argument of Commodore Matthew Perry's gunboats.

Kane had just created a new constitutional right—"transit for property and person"—based on a Constitution written "to establish a more perfect union."[61] This understanding of the Constitution as it applied to persons was probably correct, although, as has been seen here, the South was not willing to extend that constitutional right to the free black citizens of the North. Kane's attempt to give abso-

60. Ibid.; by 1855 all of New England, New York, Michigan, and Iowa were "dry." In 1851 Maine became the first state to ban "all intoxicating liquids." As early as 1847, in the *License Cases*, 5 Howard (U.S.) 504, the Supreme Court upheld local laws prohibiting or taxing the transportation or sale of liquor. Earlier, in *Cohens* v. *Virginia*, 6 Wheaton (U.S.) 264 (1821), the court had upheld a Virginia prohibition on the sale of lottery tickets, even though the lottery had been authorized by Congress. In *Groves et al.* v. *Slaughter*, 15 Peters (U.S.) 449 (1841) [see below, at n. 91 and *passim*], both Chief Justice Taney and Justice McLean declared in concurrences that all states had the right to prohibit slave importation, the Commerce Clause notwithstanding. Although Congress had exclusive power over commerce under art. I, sec. 8 of the Constitution, the states could prohibit at least some products (such as liquor, explosives, lottery tickets, and slaves) from sale within their jurisdiction, under their domestic police powers, powers of inspection, and residual powers guaranteed by the Tenth Amendment. Chancellor James Kent, who usually supported an expansion of the power of the federal government, nevertheless argued, "Inspection laws are not, strictly speaking regulations of commerce. . . . The laws act upon the subject before it becomes an article of commerce. Inspection laws, quarantine laws and health laws, as well as laws for regulating the internal commerce of a state, are component parts of the immense mass of residuary state legislation, and over which congress have no direct power, though it may be controlled when it directly interferes with their acknowledged powers"; James Kent, 1 *Commentaries on American Law* (4 vols. 5th ed. New York, 1844) 339.

61. *United States ex rel. Wheeler* v. *Williamson*, 28 F. Cas. 686, 692 (1855).

lute constitutional protection to all property in transit was clearly an overextended interpretation of the Constitution.

Kane again overextended the logic of his argument with a discussion of what would happen if a slave escaped from a master while in transit through a free state. Kane doubted that redress could be found in Pennsylvania law and was certain that the Constitution did not cover such a case, for the Fugitive Slave Clause dealt only with people escaping *into* another state. But Kane thought a master could resort to the ancient common law rights of manucaption and detainer. He did "not suppose that the employment of such reasonable force could be regarded as a breach of the peace," if used only to recapture a slave. Rather, he felt it was "incident to his character of master."[62] Such reasoning was logical, if the master had a right to take his slave into Pennsylvania. But as so many northern attorneys had pointed out in cases since *Aves*, this meant that some type of slavery would be forced on the North. Kane, in a judicial sleight of hand, had first discovered the constitutional right to bring property (including slaves) into all the states and then turned to the common law of the free states to protect that property. Thus a master in transit could govern his slave and capture the slave if he escaped, since one had a common law right to protect his property. Incredibly, Kane had now imposed slavery onto the common law of Pennsylvania by asserting that the Constitution allowed masters to bring their "property" into the free states.

After this long defense of slaveowners' rights, Kane returned to Williamson's petition and Jane Johnson's affidavit. He refused to allow the affidavit on the pretext that the name of the person signing it was new to him. This was not entirely true, for the case clearly concerned a black woman, Jane, and her children. Only the last name, Johnson, was new to Kane. But Kane asserted that Jane Johnson could have no status before his court unless she appeared in person. Kane also rejected the affidavit because it came from outside his district "in the name of the party who is alleged to be under constraint, and whose very denial that she is so [constrained] may be only a proof that the constraint is effectual."[63] This statement implied that the name of the person signing the affidavit was not "a stranger to any proceeding" before Kane but that she was indeed the person in question. More important, it raised the serious question of *who* was still restraining Jane Johnson and her family. Williamson was in prison at this time, so it was clear he was not restraining her. The affidavit had been sworn before United States Commissioner C. W. Loring, who had affixed his seal to it. Thus,

62. Ibid. 693.
63. Ibid. 695.

Kane's opinion implied that Jane Johnson was being denied her liberty by the United States commissioner for the District Court of Massachusetts. This was of course absurd.

With the affidavit refused, Williamson had no other basis for his appeal, and he remained in prison. In November 1855 he again returned to Kane's court. By this time Kane was under great public pressure to release Williamson. He had already indicated his willingness to do so if Williamson would admit his error. Williamson refused to do so until November, when a compromise of sorts was reached. Williamson this time claimed that he had meant no contempt of court and had not tried to evade the writ. Rather, he said that he did not produce the slaves because they were no longer in the state. Williamson refused to admit, as Kane wished him to do, that the slaves were the legal property of Wheeler. Nevertheless, Kane granted the petition, which differed from the others in tone and form, although not in substance.[64]

Passmore Williamson's Case and the Proslavery Argument

Judge Kane's defense of slaveholders' rights were not new. As early as *Commonwealth* v. *Aves*, in 1836, attorneys had made similar arguments in favor of slave property in transit. Indeed, by 1855 these proslavery arguments were part of a larger discussion of the overall position of slavery in American politics. Similarly, Williamson's action was based on the free-state notion that states' rights was a two-edged sword, to be used by those opposed to slavery as well as those in favor of it. And Williamson's imprisonment fit nicely into the antislavery movement's need to expose the cruelty of slavery and its threat to whites as well as blacks.

Kane's assertion that Wheeler had a right to bring his slaves into Pennsylvania and capture them there if they escaped was more than simply an interpretation of the comity clauses by a federal judge. The position was consistent with a series of arguments that Arthur Bestor has accurately called the "extraterritorial implications of slavery," which were being taken seriously by some politicians and judges. One of these arguments asserted that the western territories belonged to the whole nation and ought to be open equally to slavery and freedom. The high-water mark of this position would emerge in the *Dred Scott* case,[65] a year after Kane's opinion.

64. Eckert, "The Ordeal of Passmore Williamson" 533–37.
65. Arthur Bestor, "State Sovereignty and Slavery—A Reinterpretation of Pro-

A second argument centered on the Fugitive Slave Clause of the Constitution. Slaveowners asserted an absolute right to recover their slaves, wherever they might be. Kane's opinion affirmed this position, declaring that such a right existed for masters in transit whose slaves might leave them. In 1843 this right was asserted in the international sphere. When the independent Texas government refused to allow the reclamation of fugitive slaves, Secretary of State Abel P. Upshur of Virginia suggested that southerners "would assume the right to reclaim their slaves by force" if necessary. Bestor sees this as "an extreme statement of the view that the slaveholding states were justified in attempting to control the internal policies of other states whenever those policies threatened, even indirectly, to affect the institution of slavery adversely."[66] Southern newspapers applauded Kane's opinion, since it defended the rights of slaveholders to bring their human property into the North. Indeed, Wheeler's main argument was that he owned Jane and her children "under the laws of the state of N[orth] Carolina, and of my own country."[67] This argument implied that the laws of his home state of North Carolina followed Wheeler into Pennsylvania.

Five years later, in congressional debate, Senator James S. Green of Missouri would assert that "the prohibition of slavery in the United States is local, and that the right to hold slave property wherever there is no prohibition is national." But Green's pronouncement only restated John C. Calhoun's declaration that "[s]lavery is national, freedom sectional."[68] Such statements from slave-state senators were not surprising and certainly could not threaten the North. But Judge Kane was a federal jurist living and deciding cases in a free state. And his decision was even more extreme. He did not acknowledge that freedom could even be sectional. Rather, he asserted Wheeler's right to bring slavery into Pennsylvania, despite state law explicitly prohibiting it.

Kane's proslavery opinion and his arbitrary incarceration of Williamson made the case an instant cause célèbre for the antislavery movement and, more important, to the emerging Republican party. While in prison Williamson was nominated for the post of canal commissioner. Although conservative pressure forced his name off the ticket, he nevertheless received over seven thousand votes. News-

slavery Constitutional Doctrine, 1846–1860," 54 *Journal of the Illinois State Historical Society* 117–80 (1961).

66. Ibid. 129.
67. Kane, *Case of Passmore Williamson* 6.
68. Bestor, "State Sovereignty and Slavery" 165; Fawn M. Brodie, *Thaddeus Stevens: Scourge of the South* (New York: W. W. Norton and Company, 1959) 111.

papers throughout the North discussed his plight. Petitions were circulated protesting his imprisonment and printed sermons appeared, praising the martyr Williamson and condemning Kane.[69] Senator Charles Sumner wrote Williamson congratulating "the portion of responsibility and dignity which is yours." He told the imprisoned abolitionist, that "[i]t is a privilege to suffer for truth," and that he (Sumner) would "prefer your place within the stone walls of a prison to the cushioned bench of the magistrate by whose irrational and tyrannical edict you have been condemned."[70] Gerrit Smith , the New York abolitionist, thanked Sumner for his "timely" letter, which particularly raised Williamson's spirits.[71]

More important than Williamson's martyrdom, however, was the precedent set in the federal and state courts by this case. While in prison, Williamson appealed to the Pennsylvania Supreme Court for a writ of habeas corpus. But that court determined that it had no jurisdiction over the case. A leading New York Republican told his associate in Pennsylvania that the state court should free Williamson because Kane had "no *jurisdiction* . . . except in the precise mode pointed out in the [fugitive slave] act of 1850." He thought "the Federal Courts have no common law duty or power in asserting the *liberty* of a citizen—that it is none of their business. . . . " This Republican vainly hoped that the state court would free Williamson to test the question "has *Pennsylvania* the pluck to take Williamson by *Military force* and to fight the federal government in doing it." The political implications for all this were clear, as such a decision would "drive [President Franklin] Pierce to make his election between war with Penn. & the abandonment of the South and his decision either way is fatal." What Pennsylvania needed was a Republican governor, for "if Thad Stevens was Governor, he would not shrink from trying the virtue of buckshot." But this Republican's fantasy could not materialize, for there were not "enough Republicans to take this ground" on the court and he saw that in Pennsylvania "the mercantile spirit cares as little for liberty of a white Quaker or of *all* white Quakers as it does for that of a black cotton

69. Eckert, "The Ordeal of Passmore Williamson"; there was also talk of trying to have Judge Kane impeached. See Minutes of Western Anti-Slavery Society, 13th annual meeting, 1855, Western Anti-Slavery Society minutebook, LC. This society sent Williamson a long letter, praising his courage and his actions, while thrilling at his martyrdom. The society told Williamson, "Sooner or later an impartial verdict will be rendered, which shall be as terrible as that which caused the power to pass from the hands of Balshazzar. For that verdict, and for that time, you can well afford to wait."

70. Hoar, 5 *Charles Sumner* 57.

71. Gerrit Smith to Charles Sumner, 31 Aug. 1855, Sumner Papers, v. 19:28, Houghton Library.

picker."⁷² And, as predicted, the state court rejected Williamson's plea. The rejection meant, for Republicans at least, that slavery had corrupted yet another area of the nation—the judiciary in Pennsylvania. The liberties of all white men were once again threatened by the slave power.

Charles Sumner was even more fearful of the acts of Federal Judge Kane. He found the whole incident "a clear indubitable, and utterly unmitigated outrage." Sumner was particularly disturbed by the "new fangled doctrine, that a master can *voluntarily* import his alleged slave—of course with all the revolting incidents of Slavery—into the Free States. . . . " This was "odious," "preposterous," and "disowned by universal jurisprudence." He warned a Faneuil Hall audience that decisions like Kane's would lead to "the actual introduction of Slavery into the Free States."⁷³

Comity in the Supreme Court

Theories of the extraterritoriality of slavery and the rights of masters in transit were supported by the United States Supreme Court in a number of decisions. *Prigg* v. *Pennsylvania* and *Jones* v. *Van Zandt* affirmed the right of a master to recapture a fugitive slave without state interference. This position was subsequently given statutory force by the Fugitive Slave Law of 1850. With the exception of fugitive slave cases, where the transit was a tangential question,⁷⁴ the high court discussed slave transit in only three major

72. Erasmus Pershire Smith to Henry C. Carey, 22 Aug. 1855, Edward Carey Gardiner Collection, box 77, HSP. *Passmore Williamson's Case*, 26 Pa. St. 9 (1855); Campbell, *Slave Catchers* 144. The state court opinion was written by Jeremiah S. Black, a Democrat who would later serve as Buchanan's attorney general. George Hoar later asserted that the Pennsylvania court "was in obvious sympathy with the National Court, and both were sympathetic with Slavery"; Hoar, 5 *Charles Sumner* 54. Hoar's statement and E. P. Smith's are a bit extreme. The Democratic majority on the state court was obviously sympathetic to the national administration, but it is questionable whether these free-state jurists were proslavery or "sympathetic with Slavery." It is likely they honestly believed that they had no jurisdiction on the contempt citation issued by a federal court.

73. Hoar, 5 *Charles Sumner* 55 and 71.

74. In *Prigg* v. *Pennsylvania*, 16 Peters (U.S.) 539 (1842), one of the blacks seized as a fugitive slave had actually been conceived and born in Pennsylvania and thus ought to have been free. This fact was conveniently ignored by Story but his opinion was probably not meant to enslave the children of slaves born in free states. That the federal judiciary generally accepted the maxim that free-state birth made the child of a slave free is indicated by an 1851 fugitive slave case before Judge John K. Kane in Philadelphia. The woman before Kane was about to give birth. Kane thus "prolonged the session of the court into the night" so she could be returned to Maryland before the child was born, thus assuring that the child would be born a slave. This doughface

cases: *Groves* v. *Slaughter* (1841),[75] *Strader* v. *Graham* (1850),[76] and *Dred Scott* v. *Sandford* (1857).[77] Careful analysis shows a general bias on the part of the Taney court in favor of slavery. This is particularly true of Chief Justice Taney's own "opinion of the Court" in *Dred Scott* v. *Sandford*. As Don E. Fehrenbacher has persuasively argued, this opinion, "carefully read, proves to be a work of unmitigated partisanship, polemical in spirit though judicial in its language, and more like an ultimatum than a formula for sectional accommodation."[78] This case was the culmination of the transit issue for the federal courts. But *Dred Scott* v. *Sandford* must be understood in the light of the earlier Supreme Court decisions bearing on the subject.

Groves v. Slaughter

On its face, *Groves* v. *Slaughter* had nothing to do with slave transit. In 1836 Groves, a Mississippian, purchased slaves from Slaughter of Louisiana. Groves signed a note for seven thousand dollars, but when the note came due he refused to pay it. Groves argued that the note was void under the Mississippi Constitution of 1832, which prohibited the importation of slaves "as merchandise, or for sale" after 1 May 1833. Slaughter then brought suit in federal court. The diversity of citizenship between the two parties gave the federal courts jurisdiction, and the amount involved more than met the requirement necessary for an appeal to the United States Supreme Court. When Groves lost his case in the federal circuit court he appealed to the United States Supreme Court.[79]

Statutes similar to this constitutional provision existed at various times in a number of states. Unlike the constitutional provision, however, these statutes did provide mechanisms for enforcing their policy. Most of these statutes were passed to regulate or discourage

---

judge understood that if the child was born in Pennsylvania it would be free; Wilson, 2 *Rise and Fall of the Slave Power* 325. Questions of slave transit were also raised in a number of cases involving the African slave trade and the international movement of slaves. These cases have not been discussed here because they had little significance for federalism and interstate comity. Particularly, see *United States* v. *The Garonne*, 11 Peters (U.S.) 73 (1837) and *United States* v. *The . . . Amistad*, 15 Peters (U.S.) 518 (1841). See also Wiecek, "Slavery and Abolition" 34–38.

75. *Groves et al.* v. *Slaughter*, 15 Peters (U.S.) 449 (1841).

76. *Strader et al.* v. *Graham*, 10 Howard (U.S.) 82 (1850).

77. *Dred Scott* v. *Sandford*, 19 Howard (U.S.) 393 (1857).

78. Don E. Fehrenbacher, *The Dred Scott Case: Its Significance in American Law and Politics* (New York: Oxford University Press, 1978) 3.

79. *Groves et al.* v. *Slaughter* 449, 497.

the growth of slave populations. The Mississippi provision, on the other hand, was designed to limit the amount of capital and cash flowing out of the state by prohibiting the importation of slaves as merchandise. Since no enforcement mechanisms were provided, this provision was ignored and many Mississippians continued to purchase slaves from other states. Indeed, Slaughter's counsel argued that over three million dollars owed to sellers in Virginia, Maryland, Kentucky, and other slave states would be affected by the outcome of the case. The importance of the case was further underscored by the seven days devoted to oral argument and the quality of Slaughter's counsel: Slaughter retained "the Ajax and Achilles of the bar," Henry Clay and Daniel Webster.[80]

In a straightforward opinion, Justice Smith Thompson concluded that a statute was necessary before Mississippi's constitutional provision would take effect, thus affirming the lower court ruling. In reaching this decision Justice Thompson avoided the more difficult question of whether this clause of the Mississippi Constitution violated the United States Constitution by infringing on the power of Congress to regulate interstate commerce.[81]

Although it was unnecessary for Thompson to reach this last issue, three concurring justices thought it vital to do so. Justices McLean, Taney, and Baldwin realized that the far-reaching implications of this question ought to be clarified for the nation. Although the case was decided in 1841, before slavery became *the* political issue in the nation, the concurrences anticipated the arguments and problems of the coming decades.

Justice John McLean of Ohio spoke for the emerging free-state, antislavery position. He also represented the nationalist tradition of the Federalists, Whigs, and future Republicans. McLean strongly endorsed the power of Congress to control all interstate commerce. He thought the "necessity of a uniform commercial regulation, more than any other consideration, led to the adoption of the federal Constitution." This power had to "be not only paramount, but exclusive" if the Constitution was to function as it should. McLean denied that the states had concurrent jurisdiction over the "commercial power" if Congress did not act. Indeed, all regulations of commerce were "exclusively vested in Congress," as the Supreme Court had determined in numerous other cases.[82]

Under such a construction McLean might have concluded the Mississippi ban on importing slaves as merchandise infringed on the

---

80. Ibid. 481–82, 477; Charles Warren, 2 *The Supreme Court in United States History* (2 vols. Boston: Little, Brown and Company, 1922) 678.

81. *Groves* v. *Slaughter* 496–503.

82. Ibid. 505–6.

law-making powers of Congress. Instead he asked, "Can the transfer and sale of slaves from one state to another, be regulated by Congress, under the commercial power?" If it could, then a Pandora's box would be flung wide open. McLean had no intention of opening that box. Rather, he concluded that under the Constitution slaves were "persons" and not "merchandise." He admitted slaves were considered as merchandise in some states, but this status could not "divest them of the leading and controlling quality of persons by which they are designated in the Constitution." Their "character" as property was "given them by the local law." And while this local law "is respected, and all rights under it are protected by the federal authorities," slaves were nevertheless, in McLean's reading of the Constitution, persons and therefore could not be controlled by the Commerce Clause.[83]

McLean pointed out that his home state, Ohio, as well as others, prohibited the introduction of slaves for any purpose whatsoever. If some states could take such a position, then certainly Mississippi could "regulate their admission." He noted that Ohio could not have prohibited the importation "of the cotton of the south, or the manufactured articles of the north." For if a state could "exercise this power, it may establish a non-intercourse with the other states. This, no one will pretend, is within the power of a state." But, while "Ohio could not proscribe the productions of the south, nor the fabrics of the north, no one doubts its power to prohibit slavery."[84]

McLean then asserted a principle with which nearly all slave-state politicians could agree: "The power over slavery belongs to the states respectively. It is local in its character, and in its effects; and the transfer or sale of slaves cannot be separated from this power. It is, indeed, an essential part of it."[85] It would be another decade before the most adamant proslavery partisans would reject this idea in favor of the extraterritorial effect of slavery.

McLean's concurrent opinion was not designed to please slaveowners; it was only a coincidence if it did. His purpose was to protect the right of Ohio and the rest of the North to exclude slaves and slavery. This right was central to the transit question, although McLean did not mention transit. In concluding his opinion, McLean invoked a "higher law" principle with regard to slavery in general: "The right to exercise this power [to exclude slaves], by a state, is higher and deeper than the Constitution. The evil involves the prosperity, and may endanger the existence of a state. Its power to guard against, or to remedy the evil, rests upon the law of self-

83. Ibid. 506–7.
84. Ibid. 507–8.
85. Ibid. 508.

preservation; a law vital to every community, and especially to a sovereign state."[86] The sectional interests that Justice McLean represented demanded this inalienable right to exclude slavery from their midst.

From a different perspective, the interests Chief Justice Roger B. Taney represented made many of the same demands as the North. Taney was also convinced that "the power over this subject is exclusively with the several states; and each of them has a right to decide for itself whether it will or will not allow persons of this description to be brought within its limits, from another state, either for sale, or for any other purpose." The power over slavery could not "be controlled by Congress, either by virtue of its power to regulate commerce, or by virtue of any other power conferred by the Constitution of the United States." Taney wrote this separate opinion "on account of the interest which a large portion of the Union naturally feel in this matter, and from an apprehension that . . . [his] silence," in light of McLean's opinion, "might be misconstrued."[87]

Taney thus reassured the South that the chief justice would still staunchly protect slavery from federal interference. His opinion supported McLean's, although the purposes of the two were quite different. McLean was protecting the free states from slavery and Taney was protecting the slave states from any outside powers. Justices Story, Wayne, and McKinley joined Taney and McLean in concluding that the Constitution's Commerce Clause did not interfere with the right of the states to prohibit slaves as merchandise. While holding this, McKinley and Story nonetheless dissented from the court's decision, because they considered the notes sued upon void.[88]

Justice Henry Baldwin concurred in the opinion and decision of the court. He felt it covered "every point directly involved" and was thus reluctant to write any opinion at all. He thought the questions concerning slavery and commerce were too important to be considered indirectly. But after McLean and Taney gave their opinions on the subject, Baldwin felt obliged to abandon this position of judicial restraint, "lest it be inferred" that his opinion coincided with that of the other justices.[89]

Baldwin rejected Taney's classical states' rights position that "the action of the several states upon this subject [slavery] cannot be controlled by Congress. . . . "[90] While Taney warned Congress not to

86. Ibid.
87. Ibid. 508–9.
88. Justice Philip P. Barbour died before the case was decided; John Catron was ill and did not participate in the decision.
89. *Groves* v. *Slaughter* 510.
90. Ibid. 508.

interfere with the slave trade (an unlikely prospect), Baldwin challenged the assumptions inherent in McLean's (and perhaps Taney's) opinion that the free states could ban all slaves from their jurisdiction. Perhaps because he was a Pennsylvania Democrat, Baldwin understood the slave transit problem more keenly than could a Marylander like Taney. In any event, this northern "Doughface" was more shrewd and realistic than Taney in his defense of slave property. While Taney was protecting slavery in the South, where it was already secure, Baldwin was protecting the rights of masters who might travel to free states.

Responding to Justice McLean, Baldwin acknowledged that Ohio could ban the slave trade as well as slavery itself. But he added:

> If, however, the owner of slaves in Maryland, in transporting them to Kentucky, or Missouri, should pass through Pennsylvania, or Ohio, no law of either state could take away or affect his right of property; nor, if passing from one slave state to another, accident or distress should compel him to touch at any place within a state, where slavery did not exist. Such transit of property, whether of slaves or bales of goods, is lawful commerce among the several states, which none can prohibit or regulate, which the constitution protects, and Congress may, and ought to preserve from violation. Any reasoning or principle which would authorize any state to interfere with such transit of a slave, would equally apply to a bale of cotton, or cotton goods; and thus leave the whole commercial intercourse between the states liable to interruption or extinction by state laws, or constitutions.

Baldwin thought any state could "entirely prohibit the importation of slaves" by virtue of its legitimate state police power. But prohibiting transit would be "partial, anti-national, subversive of the harmony which should exist among the states, as well as inconsistent with the most sacred principles of the constitution."[91]

Baldwin predicated this defense of slave transit on the assumption "that wherever slavery exists by the laws of a state, slaves are property in every constitutional sense, and for every purpose, whether as subjects of taxation, as the basis of representation, as articles of commerce, or fugitives from service. To consider them as persons merely, and not as property" was "the first step towards a state of things to be avoided . . . in relation to this species of property." While McLean looked to the Constitution to prove that slaves were "persons," Baldwin looked to "the law of the states before the adoption of

91. Ibid. 516.

the Constitution, and from the first settlement of the colonies" to show that they were property. He also found support for this principle "in our diplomatic relations . . . and in the most solemn international acts, from 1782 to 1815." That he might "stand alone" on the court did "not deter" him from declaring that slaves should be considered property and thus be protected while in transit.[92]

Baldwin's opinion, written five years after the decision in *Commonwealth* v. *Aves*, may have been an attack on that decision. It was certainly a direct attack on the decision's principles, before they were implemented throughout the North. It also anticipated by fifteen years the strong defense of slavery that Taney would offer in *Dred Scott*. Indeed, without citing Baldwin's opinion, Taney would use similar arguments in *Dred Scott* to show that slaves were property and as such were protected by the Constitution. In 1841 Baldwin stood alone in his defense of slave transit, but jurists in the lower federal courts and the United States Supreme Court would soon adopt his position.[93]

Strader v. *Graham*

Nine years after *Groves* v. *Slaughter* the United States Supreme Court heard an appeal in *Strader* v. *Graham*. By this time the case had been twice before the Kentucky Court of Appeals. Christopher Graham was the owner of three slaves who had performed as musicians in free states and then returned to Kentucky. In 1841 the slaves boarded Jacob Strader's steamboat and went to Ohio. They soon made their way to Canada and freedom. Graham sued Strader for the value of the slaves and his costs in attempting to recover them. This suit was brought under a Kentucky statute that made the owners and officers of steamboats liable for any slaves escaping on their vessels. Graham was successful and was ultimately awarded three thousand dollars. Throughout the case Strader maintained that the blacks were not slaves, because they gained their freedom when Graham allowed them to work in free states. When this argument failed before the Kentucky court, Strader appealed to the United States Supreme Court.

Strader's appeal was based on two separate contentions. He argued first that the slaves became free when Graham allowed them to travel and work in Ohio and Indiana. Thus the Supreme Court

92. Ibid. 516–17, 513.

93. *Groves* v. *Slaughter* was followed by the previously discussed lower federal cases of *Oliver* v. *Kauffman* and *Passmore Williamson's Case*, as well as the Supreme Court decisions in *Strader* v. *Graham* and *Dred Scott* v. *Sandford*.

should enforce the laws of the free states, determine the slaves to have been free, and reverse the judgment against Strader. Second, Strader argued that under the Northwest Ordinance the slaves became free and the high court should vacate the judgment on that ground. The second contention was perhaps the stronger of the two, since the ordinance was an act of the national government and presumably applied to all states.

Chief Justice Taney refused to consider the status of the blacks under Indiana or Ohio law. Instead, he affirmed that "[e]very State has an undoubted right to determine the *status* or domestic condition, of the persons domiciled within its territory" except as "restrained" by the United States Constitution. He emphatically declared, "It was exclusively in the power of Kentucky to determine for itself whether their employment in another State should or should not make them free on their return." If Kentucky chose not to enforce the laws of Ohio and Indiana, the United States Supreme Court would not intervene. Indeed, Taney thought that even if he wanted to overrule the Kentucky court, the question was not within his jurisdiction.[94]

The second question was more complex. If the ordinance was still viable then presumably the court would have jurisdiction because federal law would be at issue. This did not mean, of course, that the court *had* to find in favor of Strader. The court might have determined that the slaves were not freed by the ordinance, because they had not actually become residents of the states carved out of the Northwest Territory, or the court might have concluded that when a slave worked in any free state or territory, the slave became free. Useful state precedents were available on both sides of this issue. But *if* the court held that the ordinance was in effect, it would have to accept jurisdiction, interpret the ordinance, and rule on the merits of Strader's appeal.

The way around this sticky issue was to determine that the ordinance was no longer in force. Chief Justice Taney held precisely that, and his brethren on the court unanimously supported him. But Taney did not stop with this easy, simple, and apparently constitutionally correct interpretation of the case and laws before him. Instead, he unnecessarily gave his opinion on what would be the status of the case if the ordinance *were* in force. Here he argued that "the regulations of Congress . . . for the government of a particular territory, could have no force beyond its limits." Such federal legislation "could not restrict the States within their respective territories" and thus even if the ordinance were in force, it "could have no more operation than the laws of Ohio" did in Kentucky. The ordi-

94. *Strader et al.* v. *Graham*, 10 Howard (U.S.) 82 (1850). See chapter 7 for a discussion of this case in the state courts.

nance, Taney asserted, could neither "influence the decision upon the rights of the master or the slave" nor give the Supreme Court jurisdiction.[95] This curious interpretation of congressional power over slavery would arise six years later in *Dred Scott v. Sandford*. What was given as dictum in *Strader* would be restated as settled law in *Dred Scott*.[96]

Although the court was unanimous in holding that it lacked jurisdiction in *Strader*, two judges objected to Taney's sweeping statements about the Northwest Ordinance. John McLean asserted that the only question before the court was the jurisdictional issue and anything else "in the opinion of the court, in relation to the Ordinance, beyond this, is not in the case, and is consequently extrajudicial."[97] With the question of slavery in the territories being debated in Congress, McLean was unwilling to allow Taney's dictum on the subject to go unchallenged. Justice John Catron, a slaveholder from Tennessee, was concerned that Taney's sweeping rejection of the Northwest Ordinance might interfere with the right of transit along the Ohio and Mississippi rivers. Although not specifically mentioning slave transit, Catron's opinion may have in part been motivated by the knowledge that if any of the free states north of the Ohio River chose to interrupt transit, their statutes and decisions would have been directed against slavery.[98]

Strader v. Graham affirmed the proposition that the states had the sole power to determine who was a slave and who was not. Such a conclusion could work for the benefit of free states as well as slave states. Under it Ohio would have had the right to declare blacks free, just as Kentucky could consider them slaves. But Taney's opinion and Catron's concurrence included hints that this might not be the case. Taney noted that states could decide the status of persons within their jurisdiction, "except in so far as the powers of the States in this respect are restrained, or duties and obligations imposed upon them, by the Constitution of the United States."[99] At minimum this referred to the Fugitive Slave Clause of the Constitution. But Taney and Catron may also have had the right of transit in mind. The "duties and obligations" imposed by the Constitution may have included the granting of privileges and immunities to slaveowners. If so, then Taney's opinion takes on even more of a proslavery cast. After unnecessarily suggesting that Congress had no power to im-

95. Ibid. 94–95.
96. Fehrenbacher, *Dred Scott Case* 385–87, discusses Taney's application and misuse of *Strader* in *Dred Scott v. Sandford*.
97. *Strader v. Graham* 97.
98. Ibid. 98–99.
99. Ibid. 93, 99.

pose its territorial regulations involving slavery on the states, Taney seems to have been hinting that the free states might be unable to interfere with slaves brought into their states. The implications of Taney's logic would become much more clear in *Dred Scott.*

Dred Scott v. *Sandford*

Groves v. *Slaughter* and *Strader* v. *Graham* were important to the development of the law of slaves in transit and the law of slavery in general. But they were really only preludes to *the* case of the antebellum period: *Dred Scott* v. *Sandford* (1857).[100] This case was undoubtedly the most controversial and complex to come before the Taney court. Taney's "Opinion of the Court"[101] became one of the most important political issues of the congressional elections of 1858 and the presidential contest of 1860. The decision was hailed in the South and vilified in the North. Lincoln's election and Republican congressional success were in part related to the decision. So was the nearly total rejection of comity by some northern and southern state courts. Indeed, for these and other reasons, Stanley Kutler is correct in asserting that "the Dred Scott decision bears directly upon the coming of the Civil War." To the extent that the Civil War was, in Arthur Bestor's words, a "Constitutional Crisis," *Dred Scott* was a factor in causing the war.[102]

The route that the case took in getting to the Supreme Court was almost as complicated as the case itself. As the slave of Dr. John Emerson, an army surgeon, Dred Scott had lived with his wife Harriet in Illinois and in the Missouri Territory north of the compromise line, in what later became Minnesota. In 1846, on the basis of those residences, Scott sued Emerson's widow to gain freedom for himself and his family. In 1850 Scott won in the state circuit court, but the Missouri Supreme Court overturned the decision in 1852. By this time Mrs. Emerson had remarried, and the administration of her husband's estate passed to John Sanford,[103] who had recently moved from Missouri to New York. This providential change of resi-

---

100. *Dred Scott* v. *Sandford,* 19 Howard (U.S.) 393 (1857).

101. Nine separate opinions were written, but Taney's has traditionally been regarded as the opinion of the court and the holding of the court. See Fehrenbacher, *Dred Scott Case* 333–34.

102. Stanley I. Kutler, ed., *The Dred Scott Decision: Law or Politics?* (Boston: Houghton Mifflin Company, 1967) xviii; Arthur E. Bestor, "The American Civil War as a Constitutional Crisis," in Stanley N. Katz and Stanley I. Kutler, eds., 1 *New Perspectives on the American Past* (2 vols. Boston: Little, Brown, 1969) 283–309.

103. John F. A. Sanford's last name was misspelled in the court documents as Sandford.

dence allowed Scott to sue Sanford in federal court on the grounds of a diversity of citizenship between the two parties. Claiming to be a citizen of Missouri, Scott sued for nine thousand dollars damages for assault, battery, and illegal confinement on behalf of himself and his family. The suit was initiated in November 1853 and argued the following April.[104]

Before United States District Judge Robert Wells, John Sanford entered a plea in abatement. In this plea Sanford denied that a federal court could take jurisdiction over the case because Scott was not a citizen of any state. Sanford argued that Scott was "a negro of African descent; his ancestors were of pure African blood" and as such he was not a citizen of Missouri or of the United States and could not sue in federal court.[105] Curiously, Sanford did not argue that the court had no jurisdiction because Scott was a slave and thus could not be a citizen and sue in federal court. This tactic was certainly the most obvious. Two logical explanations for this strategy can be presented. First, as Professor Fehrenbacher has argued, "This, to be sure, would have had the bizarre effect of raising as a jurisdictional question the very substance of the cause brought before the court."[106] Sanford would in effect be arguing that Scott could not sue for his freedom because he was a slave. Thus a second reason is raised for the plea in abatement's being based on race, rather than Scott's status. If Sanford had used Scott's status as a basis for the jurisdictional argument, he would have had a difficult time defending the suit on the merits if he lost on the jurisdictional question. However, by basing his jurisdictional argument on race, Sanford would still be in a strong legal position later to defend his claim to Scott on substantive grounds. And this is precisely what happened. Judge Wells overruled the plea in abatement on the grounds that if a black were free, then he could sue in federal court.

In May 1854 the case was finally heard by a jury, with Judge Wells presiding. The only evidence was a statement of facts, agreed to by both sides, that detailed Scott's past residences in free jurisdictions. Scott's attorney asked Wells to instruct the jurors that on the basis of the evidence they ought to declare Scott a free man. Wells admitted that Scott had been free, or at least entitled to his freedom, while in Illinois and the Missouri Territory north of the compromise line. But he also told the jury that upon voluntarily returning to Missouri, Scott's slave status reattached to him. The jury then returned a verdict in favor of Sanford. Scott asked for a new trial

104. *Dred Scott* v. *Sandford*, 13 American State Trials 242 (1854); for a discussion of this case in the state courts, see chap. 7.

105. *Dred Scott* v. *Sandford*, 19 Howard 393, 396–97.

106. Fehrenbacher, *Dred Scott Case* 278.

and was refused. He then appealed to the United States Supreme Court.[107]

The case was first argued before the Supreme Court in February 1856. Reargument was begun 15 December 1856. The decision was finally announced in March 1857, seven years after Scott's initial victory in the Missouri Circuit Court. During that interval slavery had become the most important issue in American politics. The Compromise of 1850 avoided one crisis, only to precipitate others because of the obnoxious provisions of the Fugitive Slave Law, which was part of the compromise package. In the North United States marshals were assaulted by mobs and arrested by state officials when they tried to enforce the new law. The South meanwhile demanded greater access to the territories and greater protection for its "peculiar institution." The Compromise of 1850 did not work, and the Compromise of 1854 followed—the Kansas-Nebraska Act—allowing slavery in areas that had been closed to slavery by the Missouri Compromise in 1820. This in turn led to the creation of the truly sectional Republican party, which showed impressive strength in the election of 1856. Earlier that year Senator Charles Sumner of Massachusetts was beaten unconscious while sitting at his desk on the Senate floor. His assailant, Congressman Preston Brooks of South Carolina, was enraged at Sumner's "Crime against Kansas" speech. In Kansas itself the first skirmishes of the coming war were fought at Hickory Point, Lawrence, Pottawatomie, and other previously obscure places. In Kansas the question of slavery in the territories had gone beyond a conflict over legislative enactment and legal theory. The *Dred Scott* decision would help push the rest of the nation to that point.

It was in this atmosphere that Chief Justice Taney read his "Opinion of the Court" on 6 March 1857, just two days after the inauguration of James Buchanan. Justices Nelson and Catron read their concurrences the same day, while 7 March was devoted to five hours of dissent from McLean and Curtis. The remaining justices—Wayne, Grier, Campbell, and Daniel—simply submitted their concurrences without presenting them orally. Taney would later expand his written opinion by nearly 50 percent to answer criticism from justices Curtis and McLean.[108] The entire report of the case, with its nine

---

107. *Dred Scott* v. *Sandford*, 13 American State Trials 242, 244.

108. See Kutler, *The Dred Scott Decision* ix–xviii, for a discussion of the importance of withholding the decision until after Buchanan's inauguration. Also see Fehrenbacher, *Dred Scott Case* 305–10 on this issue and on Taney's opinion at 319–21, and Lincoln's "House Divided Speech" in Paul M. Angle, ed., *Created Equal: The Complete Lincoln–Douglas Debates of 1858* (Chicago: University of Chicago Press, 1958) 1–9.

separate opinions, would eventually cover 248 pages in the United States Reports.

Taney's ultimate decision reached three conclusions, all of which pointed to the result that Dred Scott was still a slave and all of which had profound implications for the status of slaves in transit. For analytical purposes, Taney's holdings will be discussed in reverse of the order in which he delivered them.

Dred Scott's claim to freedom based on his residence in Illinois was the easiest for Taney to reject. He simply reaffirmed the holding in *Strader* v. *Graham* that the federal Constitution did not obligate one state to enforce a status acquired in another state and that in such cases the federal courts would not interfere. Taney declared, "As Scott was a slave when taken into the State of Illinois by his owner, and was there held as such, and brought back in that character, his *status*, as free or slave, depended on the laws of Missouri, and not of Illinois."[109] The material difference between the short transit of the slaves in *Strader* and the long residence of Scott did not affect Taney's reasoning because the consequences of that residence was an issue for the court of the forum state—in this case Missouri—to decide. This conclusion was the easiest to reach, and that which would have created few, if any, controversies. Indeed, Justice Samuel Nelson was originally assigned to write the "opinion of the court" and drafted an opinion based primarily on *Strader* v. *Graham*. Had the court stuck with this short, narrow, and diplomatic opinion, *Dred Scott* would have been a fairly minor case.[110]

One of the main reasons for moving away from this narrow opinion appears to have been proslavery pressure from within the court. James M. Wayne of Georgia, Taney, and to a lesser extent Campbell, Daniel, and Catron all wanted a stronger, proslavery decision.[111] In addition, *Strader* v. *Graham* was not a particularly good precedent for overruling Scott's freedom claim based on his residence in the territory north of Missouri. In *Strader* the antislavery provision of the Northwest Ordinance had been used to raise a federal claim that the slaves in question were really free. There the court declared the Northwest Ordinance was no longer in force, because the territories had become states. This determination was perfectly valid for Indiana, Ohio, or in Scott's case, Illinois. But it was not true for the area north of Missouri, which had been a territory when Scott was taken there, and which in fact was still a territory when the Supreme Court heard his case. Under the Missouri Compromise, slavery was

109. *Dred Scott* v. *Sandford*, 19 Howard 452–53; Kutler, *The Dred Scott Decision* xii.

110. Fehrenbacher, *Dred Scott Case* 306–8.

111. Ibid.

prohibited in this territory. Thus, if the compromise were still "good law," it was reasonable to argue that Scott had a valid claim to freedom. For, while Missouri might ignore Illinois law on the grounds that the two jurisdictions were equals and could not force their laws on each other, Missouri, as a member of the Union, was obligated to enforce, or at least respect, federal law. And even if Missouri chose not to enforce the federal law, the federal courts could certainly enforce the law and free Scott. In his opinion in *Strader* v. *Graham* Taney had argued that the states did not have to respect federal law that might free slaves in the territories. But this was not directly necessary for the holding in that case, and Justice McLean correctly labeled it dictum, and without legal force.[112] If Taney were to apply this reasoning to Dred Scott's case, he could not do it simply by restating or citing *Strader* v. *Graham.*

The inapplicability of *Strader* v. *Graham* led Taney to his second major conclusion, that the Missouri Compromise was unconstitutional. He reached this conclusion by a long, tedious, and inconclusive discussion of the relationships among Congress, the Constitution, the territories, and the people of the United States. He concluded that Congress could not pass legislation for the territories because that would be tantamount to treating the territories as colonies and the settlers as colonists. Congress could only make "rules and regulations" for the territories that were "needful" until the people settling them were in a position to assume control of their own political destiny and prepare for statehood. In this way Congress held the territories in a form of trust for all the people of the United States. It was "safely assumed that citizens of the United States who migrate to a Territory belonging to the people of the United States, cannot be ruled as mere colonists, dependent upon the will of the General Government, and to be governed by the laws it may think proper to impose." Congress could not, for example, "make any law in a Territory respecting the establishment of religion" or in any other way violate the Bill of Rights.[113]

Taney then argued that "the rights of property have been guarded with equal care" by the Constitution and were "united with the rights of person, and placed on the same ground by the fifth amendment. . . . " Thus Congress could not deprive a citizen "of his liberty or property, merely because he came himself or brought his property into a particular Territory of the United States. . . . " Such an act "could hardly be dignified with the name of due process of law."[114] This argument, combined with Taney's restrictive notion of con-

112. See nn. 96 and 97 above.
113. *Dred Scott* v. *Sandford*, 19 Howard 446, 447, 450.
114. Ibid. 450.

gressional power in the territories, led him to declare the Missouri Compromise unconstitutional.

Scott's lawyers had argued that the Missouri Compromise freed him. But if Congress had had no power to pass the compromise, then Scott had no basis on which to rest his claim that he was free.

Taney's third major conclusion (which was actually the first in his opinion) was that blacks had no right to sue in federal court. He reached this position by reexamining the original plea in abatement submitted to Judge Wells by Sanford. Taney concluded that no black, slave or free, had any rights under the Constitution or any standing to sue in federal court.

Blacks lacked standing to sue in federal courts because, in Taney's view, they were not and never had been citizens of the United States. "The question is simply this: Can a negro, whose ancestors were imported into this country, and sold as slaves, become a member of the political community formed and brought into existence by the Constitution of the United States, and as such become entitled to all the rights, privileges, and immunities guaranteed by that instrument to the citizens?" More simply put, Taney asked, are blacks "constituent members of this sovereignty?" His answer was concise and to the point: "We think they are not, and that they are not included, under the word 'citizen' in the Constitution, and therefore claim none of the rights and privileges which that instrument provides for and secures to the citizens of the United States."[115]

Taney acknowledged that some states had granted citizenship to blacks, but claimed

> We must not confound the rights of citizenship which
> a State may confer within its own limits, and the rights of
> citizenship as a member of the Union. It does not by any means
> follow, because he [is] . . . a citizen of a State, that he must be a
> citizen of the United States. He may have all the rights and
> privileges of a citizen of a State, and yet not be entitled to the
> rights and privileges of a citizen in any other State. . . . [Thus]
> he would not be a citizen in the sense in which that word is used
> in the Constitution of the United States, nor entitled to . . .
> the privileges and immunities of a citizen of the other
> States.[116]

Taney concluded that "when the Constitution was adopted," there were no black "citizens of the several States," because "a negro of the African race was regarded by them as an article of property" incapable of citizenship. While Taney was correct that most blacks

115. Ibid. 403–4.
116. Ibid. 405.

in 1787 were slaves, he was clearly wrong about black citizenship. As Justice Curtis correctly protested in dissent, "At the time of the ratification of the Articles of Confederation, all free native-born inhabitants of the States of New Hampshire, Massachusetts, New York, New Jersey, and North Carolina, though descended from African slaves, were not only citizens of those States, but such of them as had the other necessary qualifications possessed the franchise of electors on equal terms with other citizens."[117] Although his opinion was historically wrong, Taney was supported by a majority of his judicial brethren.

Taney seems to have been saying that for purposes of suing in federal court, it is up to the Supreme Court to determine who is a citizen and who is not. Thus, two types of citizenship really operated here—state and federal—and in 1787, or in 1857, the only type recognized by *all* the states and thus the only type that could be considered *federal* citizenship was that granted to whites.

By reaching this conclusion Taney eliminated all claims by blacks, slave and free, under the Privileges and Immunities Clause of the Constitution. This issue had been a thorny one for some time. Since 1822 South Carolina (and afterwards other southern states) had incarcerated or restricted free black seamen who came within their borders. Although United States Supreme Court Justice William Johnson ruled South Carolina's Black Seamen's Act of 1822 to be unconstitutional, such laws were enforced until the Civil War broke out. Commissioners sent by Massachusetts to Charleston and New Orleans were unable to settle the problem and in fact had been forced to leave both cities after their lives were threatened.[118] Ta-

---

117. Ibid. 407–8, 572–73. For a similar analysis of *Dred Scott*, and a superb study of citizenship in American law, see James Kettner, *The Development of American Citizenship, 1608–1807* (Chapel Hill: University of North Carolina Press, 1978) 324–33.

118. Two cases on the subject reached federal courts, first in South Carolina and later in Massachusetts. In both cases the discriminatory legislation was declared void; *Elkison* v. *Deliesseline*, 8 F. Cas. 493 (1823) and *The Cynosure*, 6 F. Cas. 1102 (1844). For litigation in the South Carolina courts see *Calder* v. *Deliesseline*, Harper (S.C.) 186 (1824), in which the South Carolina Supreme Court refused to enforce the law when British seamen were arrested under it, and *State* v. *Shaw*, 4 McCord (S.C.) 480 (1828), in which the state law was not enforced against a free black seaman from New Hampshire. In these cases the South Carolina court "used procedural technicalities to void convictions under the oppressive South Carolina Colored Seamen's Act"; A. E. Kier Nash, "Reason of Slavery: Understanding the Judicial Role in the Peculiar Institution," 32 *Vanderbilt Law Review* 78 (1979). See also A. E. Kier Nash, "Negro Rights, Unionism, and Greatness on the South Carolina Court of Appeals: The Extraordinary Chief Justice John Belton O'Neall," 21 *South Carolina Law Review* 141, 146–48 (1969); William M. Wiecek, *The Sources of Antislavery Constitutionalism in America, 1760–1848* (Ithaca and London: Cornell University Press, 1977) 132–40, and Wilson, 1 *Rise and Fall of the Slave Power* 576–86. Despite the two South

ney's decision implied that Justice Johnson's earlier rulings were erroneous, since no state was required to give any rights to blacks. Of course, in that case no slave state would have to recognize the free status a black acquired through transit, residence, express manumission, or even birth. Under Taney's fanciful reading of history and the Constitution, blacks were never entitled to any rights and that situation could not be changed by the action of one or more states. Ultimately Taney's decision would be reversed by the adoption of the Fourteenth Amendment to the Constitution. But, until then, Taney had ruled that under federal law and the Constitution blacks had no rights or privileges. They could, under *Dred Scott*, expect no legal protection from the federal government or the courts.

The Implications of *Dred Scott*

Although Taney's opinion is most remembered for its effect on slavery in the territories and its statement concerning black citizenship, the decision had profound implications for interstate comity and slave transit. Had the Civil War not occurred so soon after the decision, it is likely that these implications would be better remembered. Basically, *Dred Scott* told the slave states they could treat blacks however they pleased, without fearing action by the federal courts. In the extreme case, for example, a free black citizen of a northern state could be kidnapped and enslaved in a southern state, and the black would have no recourse to a federal court. While the slave states were not contemplating such extreme actions, many were already reconsidering the status of free blacks under their jurisdiction. A manumitted slave returning to his or her home state had no guarantee that the result of the journey would not be reenslavement. *Dred Scott* affirmed the right of states to treat blacks however they wished.

Dred Scott, did not, however, give free states the right to emancipate slaves passing through their territory. Under *Dred Scott* a black could not sue in federal court, but a master could. Thus, a master in transit could have asked that *Strader* v. *Graham*, *Dred Scott*, and Justice Baldwin's concurrence in *Groves* v. *Slaughter* be applied to protect slaves in transit. In Pennsylvania Federal Judge

---

Carolina cases cited above, the maltreatment of black seamen in South Carolina and elsewhere in the slave South and the maltreatment of the Massachusetts commissioners in Charleston and New Orleans undermined interstate comity. The memory of it influenced the drafting and passage of the Fourteenth Amendment after the Civil War.

John K. Kane had already declared that such protection existed, the Pennsylvania repeal of the six-months law notwithstanding. *Dred Scott* permitted slavery and slave transit in the territories. And if a slaveowner had a federal right to settle in Minnesota or Kansas with his human chattel, it would not have been difficult for the court to conclude that he had a right to cross Pennsylvania, Ohio, or other free states to get to those territories. Indeed, Justice Peter Daniel in his concurrence found slavery to have greater constitutional protection than any other form of property.[119] It would have been only a small step for Daniel, Taney, and the other proslavery judges to determine that this protection extended to the free states. Under this decision slave states were free to treat blacks however they wished, but the free states apparently did not have that right.

Taney's decision provoked dissents from justices John McLean and Benjamin Robbins Curtis. Both men came from states that, by 1857, were strongly antislavery. In both states slaves in transit had gained access to the courts and had been freed. Curtis's particularly potent dissent exposed the weakness of many of Taney's arguments, as well as the historical inaccuracies on which the opinion was based.[120] Taney's "Opinion of the Court" also provoked bitter denunciations in the North. Horace Greeley's *New York Tribune* was typical, saying that the decision had "just so much moral weight as . . . the judgment of the majority of those congregated in any Washington bar-room." The decision was debated in Congress and attacked both from the pulpit and the political stump. A number of northern states recognized its implications for slave transit and passed new statutes protecting free blacks and asserting the right to free slaves voluntarily brought into their states.[121]

Although two northern justices dissented, two others, Robert Grier and Samuel Nelson, concurred with the result and with the significant parts of Taney's opinion. The Nelson opinion, in which Grier specifically concurred, is particularly relevant to an under-

119. *Dred Scott* v. *Sandford*, 19 Howard 490.
120. Ibid. 564–633.
121. Fehrenbacher, *Dred Scott Case* 3, 431–37. For example, *Ohio Laws, 1857*, 186; *Vermont Laws of 1858*, chap. 37; *New Hampshire Laws of 1857*, chap. 1955; *Michigan Laws of 1859*, Act of 15 Feb.; *Maine Laws of 1857*, chap. 53. The New Hampshire statute specifically declared that "neither descent, near or remote, from a person of African blood, whether such person is or may have been a slave, nor color of skin, shall disqualify any person from becoming a citizen of this State, or deprive such person of the full rights and privileges of a citizen thereof." This was of course a direct rebuke and rejection of Taney's declaration that blacks could not be citizens of the United States. Vermont, New Hampshire, and Michigan made it a crime, punishable by fine or imprisonment, to hold any person as a slave within their jurisdiction.

standing of the importance of *Dred Scott* to the problem of slave transit and comity.

At the beginning of his opinion Nelson noted that "except as restrained by the Federal Constitution" every state had "complete and absolute power over the subject of slavery." This statement might have meant that Nelson thought free states were restrained only by the Fugitive Slave Clause. But it might also have meant there were other, hidden meanings in the Constitution, which would be found to protect slavery everywhere in the Union. Nelson's equivocal assurances worried many northerners. Most important, Nelson's position disturbed the Republican candidate for the United States Senate seat in Illinois, Abraham Lincoln. Lincoln and his opponent Stephen A. Douglas carefully scrutinized and analyzed the case in their 1858 debates. In the opening statement of his campaign, the "House Divided Speech," Lincoln singled out Nelson's phrase "except as restrained by the Federal Constitution":

> In what *cases* the power of the *states is* so restrained by the U.S. Constitution, is left an *open* question, precisely as the same question, as to the restraint on the power of the *territories* was left open in the Nebraska Act. Put *that* and *that* together, and we have another nice little niche, which we may, ere long, see filled with another Supreme Court decision, declaring that the Constitution of the United States does not permit a *state* to exclude slavery from its limits.[122]

Lincoln, and other northerners, saw the *Dred Scott* decision as a first step toward a judicial nationalization of slavery. Such a decision would probably have come through cases involving slave transit or sojourn. If this were to transpire, the Nelson opinion was potentially even more dangerous than Lincoln realized. Nelson was from New York and Grier from Pennsylvania. Both regularly heard federal circuit court cases in the free states, where such cases would arise. Thus, Nelson's view of slave transit, with Grier specifically concurring, is critically important for understanding how *Dred Scott* affected this issue. Nelson's concluding paragraph was almost a request for a chance to decide a slave transit case. He wrote:

> A question has been alluded to, on the argument, namely: the right of the master with his slave of transit into or through a free State, on business or commercial pursuits, or in the exercise of a Federal right, or the discharge of a Federal duty, being a citizen of the United States, which is not before us. This

---

122. *Dred Scott* v. *Sandford*, 19 Howard 459, and Angle, *Created Equal?* 7.

question depends upon different considerations and principles from the one in hand, and turns upon the rights and privileges secured to a common citizen of the republic under the Constitution of the United States. When that question arises, we shall be prepared to decide it.[123]

123. *Dred Scott* v. *Sandford*, 19 Howard 468–69.

Chapter 9

The National Rejection of Comity: The Cases of Jonathan Lemmon and Nancy Wells

By the eve of the Civil War most of the North had strictly limited, if not abolished, any rights a visiting or traveling slaveowner might have. Only in New Jersey and Illinois could a master in transit find explicit statutory protection for his slave property.[1] A number of New England states had specifically barred all slave transit. In New York and Pennsylvania the repeal of protective legislation implied that slave transit was prohibited. In other states, court decisions offered little comfort to owners of slaves who might venture north, accompanied by their bondsmen.

In the South freedom suits based on previous free-state residence were, with a few exceptions, virtually impossible to win. Only in Kentucky were blacks still able to vindicate such claims with any degree of consistency. Free blacks were barred from most states in the South, and emancipation was unlawful in many. The rights of free blacks from the North were totally ignored by a number of southern states.

The decisions and statutes of northern and southern states indicate that, in some ways, a division of the Union took place before the secession winter of 1860–61. The legal institutions of the free states reflected an antislavery attitude as strong as, and sometimes stronger than, that attitude among the general populace. As such, the claims of visiting slaveowners were rejected by northern courts. In the South extreme proslavery advocates were leaders of the bar and bench. Southern courts were willing to give total protection to what would soon be "the cornerstone" of the Confederacy. This protection would be given at the expense of free-state laws, the rights of free-state citizens, and interstate comity.

The decisions of southern and northern courts also illustrate how law can become, or may be used as, a force for social change. In-

---

1. Indiana, California, and Oregon offered no explicit protection, but court decisions and the constitutions of these states imply such protection.

deed, for both anti- and proslavery forces, legal institutions provided forums for propagandizing and vehicles for policymaking. By the eve of secession, on the important issues of slavery, comity, and federalism, the most extreme courts in the North and those in the South acted as though they were in separate nations—and they soon would be.

Of course, many members of the legal profession in both the North and the South regretted this trend. But in both sections they were being pushed to extremes by the force of events. Professor Joel Parker of the Harvard Law School, for example, was, by his own admission "reasonably conservative, devotedly attached to the Constitution," and the Union.[2] Parker bitterly opposed the Massachusetts Personal Liberty Law of 1855, which he believed was unconstitutional and would exacerbate the political and legal crisis of the age. However, the violence in Kansas, the caning of Charles Sumner, and the *Dred Scott* decision led even Parker to denounce the South and offer his own blood for a new revolution, if one "shall prove necessary." As historian Phillip Paludan has noted, for a conservative legalist like Parker, civil war had always been "the worst possible calamity." But after the Kansas violence and other events, Parker "now understood that there was something worse— law which was designed to protect liberty but employed to destroy it."[3]

Many northern jurists who deplored disunion nevertheless found themselves contributing to the crisis. In 1860 Chief Justice Lemuel Shaw resigned from the Massachusetts Supreme Judicial Court, in part because of the growing national trend toward disunion. Shaw, a conservative and a staunch unionist, publicly attacked the personal liberty laws of Massachusetts as soon as he left the bench.[4] Similarly, Benjamin R. Curtis, a northern Democrat and a conservative unionist, denounced the Massachusetts laws. In 1861 in a speech at Faneuil Hall, he urged acceptance of the Crittenden Compromise.[5] But both Shaw and Curtis were major figures in helping to create the crisis in law, comity, and federalism. Shaw of course wrote the precedent-setting opinion in *Commonwealth* v. *Aves*, which denied comity to a slaveholder visiting Massachusetts. Curtis wrote the major dissent in *Dred Scott*, which supplied most of the intellectual

2. Phillip S. Paludan, *A Covenant with Death: The Constitution, Law, and Equality in the Civil War Era* (Urbana: University of Illinois Press, 1975) 124.

3. Ibid. 124, 121.

4. Leonard W. Levy, *The Law of the Commonwealth and Chief Justice Shaw* (Cambridge: Harvard University Press, 1957) 106–8.

5. Benjamin R. Curtis, ed., 1 *A Memoir of Benjamin Robbins Curtis* (2 vols. Boston: Little, Brown, 1879) 243–63, 327–47.

and legal arguments used to attack the case. Curtis then resigned his position on the United States Supreme Court, partly because of *Dred Scott.* Thus even conservative unionists such as Parker, Shaw, and Curtis helped lead the legal profession to its own civil war before the South actually left the Union. Less conservative jurists, or those more committed to antislavery, had, by 1860, come to dominate many courts in the North. In the South, less conservative jurists—those committed to southern nationalism rather than the Union—were also ascendant.

In terms of decision making, the two most radical states in the Union were Mississippi and New York. Undoubtedly courts in other northern and southern states would have reached similar decisions, had cases been brought before them. But the Civil War abruptly ended most litigation on this subject. Nevertheless, the analysis of one Mississippi case, *Mitchell* v. *Wells* (1859)[6] and one New York case, *Lemmon* v. *The People* (1860)[7] illustrates the vivid contrast between the legal values of the two sections.

Mitchell v. Wells

Nancy Wells was the daughter of her slave mother and her mother's white owner, Edward Wells. In 1846 her father, who was also her owner, took Nancy from Mississippi, where they lived, to Ohio and manumitted her. Edward Wells then returned to Mississippi, where he died two years later. To his daughter Nancy, Edward Wells bequeathed "a watch, bed, and three thousand dollars." When the will was probated, Nancy Wells was still a minor and the money was invested for her. In 1848 Nancy Wells returned to Mississippi for about two and a half years, after which she permanently resided in Ohio. By 1857 she had still not received her legacy, and through her lawyer in Mississippi she sued her father's executor, William Mitchell.[8]

Mitchell demurred to the suit by asserting that Nancy Wells was still a slave and as such could not own or inherit any property. He argued that her return to Mississippi for two and a half years proved the manumission was a fraudulent attempt to evade the Mississippi law prohibiting manumissions within the state. This demurrer was overruled by the Madison County Chancery Court, which decided Nancy Wells was a free person, living in Ohio, and as such she could hold and inherit property in Mississippi, even though she

6. *Mitchell* v. *Wells,* 37 Miss. 235 (1859).
7. *Lemmon* v. *The People,* 20 N.Y. 562 (1860).
8. *Mitchell* v. *Wells* 235.

could not live there. This decision was supported by earlier Mississippi decisions and a year after the decision in chancery court, the Mississippi High Court of Errors and Appeals, in *Shaw* v. *Brown* (1858), reached a similar decision. In that case the Mississippi court held that slaves emancipated in Ohio or Indiana could inherit property from their white father, even though they had returned to Mississippi for short visits after their emancipations. After losing in chancery court Mitchell appealed to the High Court of Errors and Appeals. The appeal was initiated in 1857, before the decision in *Shaw* v. *Brown*, but the case was not decided until a year after *Shaw* v. *Brown*.[9]

In 1859 Justice William Harris reversed the chancery court decision and overturned the year-old precedent in *Shaw* v. *Brown*. Harris recognized the "great delicacy and importance of the questions" he faced. He noted that authorities in other states supported the right of Nancy Wells to sue in the court of a slave state and to acquire property in such a state. Had this been an "ordinary" case involving individual rights Harris was willing at least tacitly to acquiesce in the precedents of other states, even if they conflicted with his "own convictions of right." But in this case Harris felt obligated to follow the dictates of his own conscience. He frankly asserted:

> [I]n great questions of public policy, interesting alike to
> our own as to the citizens of other slaveholding States,
> involving the security of our institutions and the safety of our
> people, I do not feel that I am at liberty, in deference to the
> opinions of others to yield my convictions of duty and official
> responsibility, upon motives of delicacy, however oppressive, or
> upon principles of ordinary judicial expediency, however
> well established in matters of private right.[10]

Indeed, on issues of slavery and comity Justice Harris would be indelicate, harsh, oppressive, and innovative. He was prepared to make Mississippi the *setter*, rather than the follower of precedents.

Harris then proceeded to show why Nancy Wells could not inherit property in Mississippi. He argued that "both upon principle and the weight of authority," a slave once domiciled in Mississippi could "acquire no right, civil or political, within her limits, by manumission elsewhere." He asserted that such an out-of-state manumission or citizenship could not "even upon principles of comity, under our laws and policy, vest any right *here*."[11]

9. Ibid. 237–38; *Shaw* v. *Brown*, 35 Miss. 246 (1858).
10. *Mitchell* v. *Wells* 237–38.
11. Ibid. 238–39.

Before demonstrating this, Harris detailed Mississippi's decisions and laws concerning manumission and the rights of free blacks, establishing that since the 1830s Mississippi had maintained a policy that opposed the growth of a free black population. By 1859 it was illegal for a master to emancipate a slave by will, even with explicit instructions to take the slave out of the state, or even the country. But as late as 1858 the Mississippi high court, in *Shaw* v. *Brown*, had upheld the right of a master, while living, to remove his slaves and free them in another state. Indeed, the court had felt a master's right to take his slaves to another state "necessarily resulted from his absolute right of disposition of them as his property." Thus, while Mississippi policy discouraged manumission, the state could not stop it altogether without interfering with the master-slave relationship in a manner that tended to undermine the whole system of slavery. In *Shaw* v. *Brown* the court also interpreted the "principles of comity" to require that a former slave living in a free state be granted the same rights to hold and inherit property as any free person in Mississippi.[12]

Justice Harris could not go along with this precedent. He felt that "comity is subordinate to sovereignty and cannot, therefore, contravene our public policy, or the rights, interests, or safety of our State or people." It was illegal to emancipate a slave in Mississippi because the state was opposed to the growth of a free Negro population, not only in Mississippi, but anywhere. Thus, the emancipation of a Mississippi slave, no matter where it was done, contravened the explicit policy of the state. "The status of a slave, in Mississippi," Harris concluded, "is fixed by our laws, and cannot be changed elsewhere, so as to give him a *new status in this State*, without our consent." In other words, whatever status Nancy might have had in Ohio, before a Mississippi court she was, and would always remain, a slave.[13]

Harris found support for this position in the very nature of Mississippi society. He could not doubt "that it now is and ever has been, the policy of Mississippi to protect, preserve, and perpetuate the institution of slavery as it exists amongst us, and to prevent emancipation generally of Mississippi slaves." This policy demanded that free blacks be given as few rights as possible and that their numbers be limited. A slave could neither be emancipated in the state nor own or inherit property. If Nancy Wells had any claims to the legacy, "she must have derived them from the law of her new domicile." But that law could have no effect on Mississippi "except by the comity or consent" of the state.[14]

12. Ibid. 248–49.
13. Ibid. 249.
14. Ibid. 258.

The critical question was whether Mississippi should grant comity to the law of Ohio, which freed Nancy Wells and gave her the capacity to hold property, and maintain a suit to recover her inheritance. Here Harris turned to Taney's decision in *Dred Scott* for support of his position. Quoting at length from Taney's opinion, Harris found that "neither the right to sue, nor the right to acquire or hold property," nor any other "privileges belonging to free white citizens, or inhabitants of other states or nations, accorded by comity" could "be conferred upon the African race, in the State of Mississippi, by the authority of another State or nation."[15]

Harris then began a provocative inquiry into the meaning of comity and citizenship. He noted that Chancellor James Kent had written: "The laws and usages of one State cannot be permitted to furnish qualifications for citizens, to be claimed and exercised in other States, in contravention to their local policy." This legal theory was reasonable for a free state. Under such doctrine, Kent's home state of New York did not have to recognize as citizens persons from other jurisdictions who could not be citizens in New York. Such was also the case for Mississippi and Nancy Wells. Harris did not believe Mississippi needed to recognize Wells's status in Ohio as a free person capable of owning property. Harris was not satisfied at this point, however, for Mississippi would thus bear the onus of denying comity. Instead, Harris turned Kent's argument inside out and declared it was a breach of comity for Ohio to give citizenship to a person who was not entitled to that status in Mississippi. Harris in essence claimed that Mississippi ought to be able to determine who should be a citizen in Ohio! The jurist wrote that "'comity' forbids that a sister State of this confederacy should seek to introduce into the family of States, as equals or associates, a caste of a different color, and of acknowledged inferiority, who, though existing among us at the time of our compact of Union, were excluded from the sisterhood of common consent."[16]

This argument indicates the extreme nature of Harris's opinion. First, Harris wanted Ohio to bow to Mississippi's notion of who could be a citizen in the United States. Second, Harris expressed the fear that Ohio would force free black citizens upon the state of Mississippi. But Harris failed to recognize that Ohio had not made Nancy Wells a full-fledged citizen. Nor was there any suggestion that Nancy Wells should have rights of citizenship in Mississippi. She asked only for the right to obtain a lawfully inherited property—a right granted to white noncitizens from other nations, a right granted to free blacks living in Mississippi, and a right that

15. Ibid. 249, 259–60.
16. Ibid. 260, citing 2 *Kent's Commentaries* 36 (9th ed.).

had been granted a year earlier by the same court to former slaves who had been born in servitude, in Mississippi, and had become free in other states where they continued to reside.[17]

Harris continued to analyze the meaning of comity within the Union. In doing so he revealed just how far apart the North and South were on very basic questions of law. Judge Harris saw Ohio's willingness to free Nancy Wells as an affront to Mississippi, even though she had been brought to Ohio for the specific purpose of manumitting her. But if Ohio's action was an attack on Mississippi policy, then no comity could be granted by the latter state. Comity between enemies was impossible.

Harris ended his opinion with an attack aimed, not only at Ohio, but at the entire North. In refusing to give legal recognition to Ohio's laws making Nancy Wells a free person, Harris blamed Ohio for the breakdown of comity. Comity was impossible because

> [t]he State of Ohio, forgetful of her constitutional obli-
> gations to the whole race, and afflicted with a *negro-mania*,
> which inclines her to descend, rather than elevate herself to the
> scale of humanity, chooses to take to her embrace, as citizens,
> the neglected race . . . incapable of the blessings of free gov-
> ernment, and occupying, in the order of nature, an intermediate
> state between the irrational animal and the white man.[18]

Since blacks in Ohio could not vote, hold office, or attend schools with whites, it is difficult to understand what type of "citizen" Nancy Wells had become.

Harris next claimed that Ohio "introduces slaves into her political organization. . . ." This statement was, of course, nonsense. Ohio only declared that no one could be a slave and that all free persons, whatever their race or previous condition of servitude, had certain minimal rights, including the right to sue in court and inherit prop- erty. These rights were the same as those that free blacks had in Mississippi. Harris also rejected comity because Ohio's "citizens ex- tend encouragement and inducement to the removal of slaves from Mississippi, and in violation of the laws of the United States in relation to the rendition of fugitive slaves, introduces them into her limits as citizens." This may have been true, to the extent that some Ohioans did harbor fugitive slaves and abolitionists encouraged masters (with virtually no success) to free their slaves. But what is critical here is that Harris saw no distinction between the state of Ohio and some of the people living in it. Furthermore, Harris was unwilling to grant comity to a state that allowed antislavery people

17. Ibid. 263.
18. Ibid.

to speak out and function politically. Indeed, by allowing abolitionists to live there and by allowing Mississippians to free their slaves in the state, Ohio, in Harris's view, had violated the "intimate relation of constitutional brotherhood" that allowed for comity between the states. Comity was terminated by Ohio, "in the very act of degrading herself and her sister States, by the offensive association"; thus "the rights of Mississippi are outraged, when Ohio ministers to emancipation and the abolition of our institution of slavery, by such unkind, disrespectful, lawless interference with our local rights."[19] This opinion leads one to think that Ohio had forced Edward Wells to take Nancy north and free her.

In allowing Edward Wells to free his slave, Harris thought that Ohio had violated all the sacred rights of Mississippi. Harris implied that the laws, customs, government structures, and indeed even the people of Ohio were alien to Mississippi.

Although he clearly overstated the case, Harris may not have been entirely wrong. For all its negrophobia, prejudice, and discrimination, Ohio stood basically for freedom. Mississippi, on the other hand, was boldly creating a society with freedom subordinated to slavery, and with a perverse and pervasive racism at its foundation. In Ohio the debate was over the place of free blacks in a white society. In Mississippi the only debate allowed presupposed that blacks were fit only for servitude. Mississippians debated whether such slavery was a positive good and what was the best way to maintain the system. Five years earlier, in 1854, Theodore Parker, a Boston abolitionist, had aptly described what was happening to the legal systems of the two sections. "The North," Parker wrote, "has organized Freedom, and seeks to extend it; the South, Bondage, and aims to spread that." Or, as the Indiana congressman, George Julian, saw the issue, "It was a struggle between two civilizations, between reason . . . and the creed of Absolutism." Judge Harris only confirmed what farsighted northerners had long known: slavery ultimately demanded absolute support by all factions and sections of the Union. Anything less would be an affront to the rights and needs of the South. In the emancipation of one slave, Harris perceived a threat to the entire civilization of Mississippi and the South. He could not force Ohio to reenslave Nancy Wells, but he could verbally assault that state and deny any application of comity to its "lawless interference with" Mississippi's "local rights."[20]

Harris felt it was "disrespectful" and "lawless" for Ohio to free

19. Ibid.

20. Ibid.; David Brion Davis, *The Slave Power Conspiracy and the Paranoid Style* (Baton Rouge: Louisiana State University Press, 1969) 60; George W. Julian, *Political Recollections, 1840 to 1872* (Chicago: Jansen, McClurg, 1884) 152.

Nancy Wells. The mere suggestion that Mississippi should recognize the act truly repulsed the judge:

> But, when I am told that Ohio has not only the right thus
> to degrade and disgrace herself, and wrong us, but also, that
> she has the right to force her new associates into the Mississippi
> branch of the American family, to claim and exercise rights
> *here*, which our laws have always denied to this inferior race,
> and that Mississippi is bound to yield obedience to such
> demand, I am at a loss to understand upon what *principles* of
> law or reason, or courtesy or justice such a claim can be
> founded.

Finally, Harris suggested what might happen if Mississippi granted comity to the laws of a state that allowed slaves to be freed. Just as antislavery lawyers had warned northern courts of the dangers of any concession to slavery, Harris had his own list of slave-state horrors:

> Suppose that Ohio, still further afflicted with her peculiar
> philanthropy, should determine to descend another grade in
> the scale of her peculiar humanity, and claim to confer citizen-
> ship on the chimpanzee or the ourang-outang (the most
> respectable of the monkey tribe), are we to be told that "comity"
> will require of the States not thus demented, to forget their own
> policy and self-respect, and lower their own citizens and
> institutions in the scale of being, to meet the necessities of the
> mongrel race thus attempted to be introduced into the family
> of sisters in this confederacy?[21]

Harris concluded that "Ohio, by allowing the manumission" of Nancy Wells "contrary to the known policy of Mississippi," could "neither confer freedom on a Mississippi slave, nor the right to acquire, hold, sue for, nor enjoy property in Mississippi." Thus, the original decision was reversed, the case was dismissed, and Nancy Wells was ordered to pay all court costs.[22]

The Southern Alternative

Justice Alexander Handy, who had written the earlier decision in *Shaw* v. *Brown*, which this case overruled, dissented with a twenty-three-page opinion. Handy's suggestion that his judicial brethren had overstepped their bounds appeared to be a voice of moderation

21. *Mitchell* v. *Wells* 263–64.
22. Ibid. 264–65.

on a court of fire-eaters. Actually, his "moderate" opinion contains hints of a far more radical approach to the problem of interstate relations than a mere denial of comity.

Handy felt "the private opinion of the most enlightened, if not of all, amongst us," which had his "full concurrence," was that "negro emancipation" anywhere was "an evil." But, he argued, Mississippi "had no power to interfere with the *status* of the free negro residing in another State, and legally emancipated" there. The Mississippi court's "opinion in relation to the impolicy of tolerating" free Negroes by other states was "a mere abstract opinion" that could not be enforced, just as another court's opinion about Mississippi law could not be enforced in Mississippi. Handy admonished the majority judges: "We have no control over, or right to complain of, the internal policy of a sovereign State of the confederacy . . . though we may and do think that that policy is wrong in principle and dangerous in practice." It was "a rare thing," Handy said, "for governments to attempt to interfere with the rights of the resident subjects of another government." Besides its being impolitic, Handy thought it unnecessary. Mississippi opposed the increase of free blacks within its jurisdiction, and Ohio had done nothing to violate that policy. Therefore Mississippi had no right to complain of Ohio's action.[23]

But, the question of comity remained. Handy thought comity should be granted, not for the sake of Nancy Wells, or any other specific individual, but out of "respect to the nation of which the person, whose individual right is involved, is a member." This point was particularly critical if Mississippi wished her citizens to receive comity in Ohio.[24]

Finally, Handy turned to the problem of fugitive slaves and Ohio's general disrespect for the interests and policies of the slave states. Harris thought this was one more reason for denying comity to a citizen of Ohio. Relying on the ideal of southern honor, Handy stood this retaliation argument on its head: "If their courts of justice have been prostituted to the purposes of fanaticism and lawlessness that is no reason why we should descend from our elevated position, which should be superior to such influences, follow their unworthy example, and make this court the medium of propagating our political theories upon the same subject." The dignity and honor of Mississippi precluded the kind of action Harris's opinion endorsed. However, Handy did see a dignified, honorable, and legally correct method of dealing with the problem of comity and the free states:

23. Ibid. 279–80.
24. Ibid. 282–83.

Whilst the confederacy continues, we cannot justify ourselves
as a State in violating its spirit and principles, because other
States have in some respects, been false to their duties and
obligations. It may justify us in dissolving the compact, but not
in violating our obligations under it whilst it continues.[25]

If the legal systems of the slave and free states could not safely
grant comity to each other, or if they refused to do so from ideological
differences, then the charade of union had no purpose. Secession,
not a denial of comity, would solve the problem.

Judicial Civil War

Mitchell v. *Wells* brought the problem of comity into sharp focus.
The extreme proslavery ideology of the late antebellum period required northern acquiescence in southern demands. The North had
to give complete respect to southern institutions; anything less
would threaten southern civilization. If the North threatened slavery, in even the most indirect way, the South would respond by
verbal attacks on the North and a rejection of comity when the
rights of northerners were before its courts. But this activity, as
Handy clearly saw, could not bring about the desired results. It only
degraded the South by placing it on the same level as the North.

By 1859 the Mississippi court acted as if Ohio were an alien and
hostile nation. The majority judges concluded that the laws of Ohio
were so inimical to Mississippi that they could not be enforced.
Secession, as far as judicial respect and comity were concerned, had
already taken place. Justice Handy dissented, not from this determination, but from the Mississippi court's response to it. If Mississippi
could not safely respect the laws of Ohio—and if Ohio refused to respect the laws and institutions of Mississippi and the rights of slaveowners guaranteed by the federal Constitution—then the Union
itself lacked any practical value or purpose. A denial of comity only
placed Mississippi on the same hypocritical level as Ohio. If comity
could not be given, then there was no need for the Union. Mississippi
should respond, not with a denial of comity within the Union, but
with a denial of the Union itself. In less than two years the government of Mississippi, and ten other southern states, would formally
adopt this position.

25. Ibid. 286. On the importance of honor in the South during this period, see John
Hope Franklin, *The Militant South* (Cambridge: Harvard University Press, 1956).

Lemmon v. *The People*

If the action of Ohio, in allowing the manumission of a slave, was an insult to Mississippi, then the action of New York, in *Lemmon* v. *The People*, was tantamount to an act of war. The *Lemmon* case showed that an absolute denial of comity was not the prerogative of only the fire-eating defenders of slavery.

In 1852 Jonathan Lemmon and his wife left their native Virginia for Texas. They brought their eight slaves with them. The fastest and most direct route at that time was to go first by boat from Virginia to New York and then by steamboat directly to New Orleans. There was no direct steamship service between any Virginia or Maryland port and the Gulf coast, and the overland route was difficult, costly, and time-consuming.[26]

When the Lemmons arrived in New York they were warned by the captain of their ship not to bring the slaves ashore. They ignored this advice and took the slaves to a hotel, where the party prepared to wait for three days until they could continue to their final destination. In the hotel "they were discovered by a colored man named Louis Napoleon." As he had in the case of George Kirk six years earlier, Napoleon petitioned for a writ of habeas corpus. The writ was granted by Judge Elijah Paine of the Superior Court of New York. It was served on Lemmon the day he arrived in the city, and by the end of the day, 6 November, the slaves had been brought before Judge Paine.[27]

In his return of the writ Lemmon claimed he was in New York "for the mere purpose of passage and transit from" Virginia to Texas "and for no other purpose, intention, object or design whatever. . . ." He specifically denied Napoleon's allegation that he was a slave trader. Instead, he claimed a federal right to travel from one state to another without losing his property in a third state. Lemmon secured the services of Henry D. Lapaugh for this hearing, while E. D. Culver argued for the writ. Culver was aided by John Jay, a leading abolitionist and grandson of the former chief justice. Preliminary arguments were made on Saturday, 6 November, but because "it was an important case to both parties, and one of considerable interest," Judge Paine adjourned the hearing until Monday. The blacks were placed in jail for the weekend while both sides prepared their cases. When the case resumed on 8 November, "the lobbies and passages in the Court, were crowded by colored persons anxious to

26. *Lemmon* v. *The People*, 20 N.Y. 562 (1860); *Richmond Daily Dispatch*, 15 Nov. 1852.

27. *New York Times*, 9 Nov. 1852; *Lemmon* v. *The People* 564–65. See also discussion of Kirk's case in chap. 5 of this book.

know the result." E. D. Culver asked for a larger room so "that the public should have more accommodation." This request was granted and the case was postponed until Tuesday. After hearing arguments on both sides, Paine called an adjournment for five more days, in order to ponder the issues for, as Lapaugh had noted in his opening remarks, "The case was entirely new, and one in which there was no previous adjudication."[28] Indeed, this was the first time a New York court had to interpret the 1841 repeal of the "nine-months law."

On 13 November 1852 Paine "discharged the colored Virginians." Paine felt that the repeal of the nine-months law freed all slaves (except fugitives) who touched the soil of New York. The legacy of Lord Mansfield had been adopted in its most extreme form. The air of New York was too pure for a slave to breathe. The ex-slaves were led from the courtroom by Louis Napoleon, with a crowd of blacks cheering them on. The Lemmons' request that their former slaves be retained in custody while an appeal was pending was impossible. The "colored Virginians" took no chances with the New York legal system and quickly fled north, where they became "colored Canadians."[29]

The Lemmons were particularly depressed by the outcome of the case because the slaves "were nearly all the property they owned in the world." The *New York Journal of Commerce* described them as "struggling with poverty." That paper, which spoke for the New York business community, immediately began a fund-raising effort to compensate the Lemmons for the loss of their slaves. New York commercial interests wanted to assure their southern clients and customers that all of the North was not dominated by abolitionists, negrophiles, and other fanatics. Five thousand dollars were quickly raised and given to the Lemmons, who then returned to Virginia. Before leaving they agreed to manumit the slaves formally after a final adjudication of the matter. This action would enable a higher court to vindicate the Lemmons' right of transit without having to reenslave the blacks.[30]

28. *New York Times*, 8, 9, 10 Nov. 1852; *Lemmon* v. *The People* 564–65.

29. *Lemmon* v. *The People* 564–65; *Richmond Daily Dispatch*, 15 Nov. 1852.

30. *Richmond Daily Dispatch*, 11, 15, 27 Nov. 1852. The list of contributors to the fund for the Lemmons was headed by Judge Elijah Paine, the man who had freed their slaves; Brainerd Dyer, *The Public Career of William M. Evarts* (Berkeley: University of California Press, 1933) 34–35. That Judge Paine contributed to the fund for the Lemmons indicates that the decision was neither vindictive nor the result of an abolitionist on the bench. An abolitionist, after all, would not have wanted the Lemmons to receive any compensation for the loss of their human chattel. Rather, Paine's action reflects the notion, held even by many conservatives such as justices Lemuel Shaw and Joseph Story, that the states had a legitimate constitutional right to free slaves in transit and that this right was consistent with proper free-state policy.

Virginia Responds

At this point the case might have been terminated. The Lemmons had no interest in pursuing the matter, since they had a substantial cash settlement and had agreed to free the slaves even if they did win an appeal. Under the circumstances the Lemmons had no reason to pay for an appeal to the New York Supreme Court, to the higher Court of Appeals, and perhaps eventually to the United States Supreme Court.

But if the decision went unchallenged it would create a dangerous precedent. As the *Journal of Commerce* noted, this was "not the ordinary case of a slave brought" to a free state "by his master with the intention to remain." In such cases it had "been decided that the slave *eo instante* becomes free." This had been an integral part of northern law since *Commonwealth* v. *Aves* in 1836. Illinois and New Jersey, which did not adopt the *Aves* precedent, felt the necessity of passing specific legislation allowing masters to visit or cross their jurisdictions with slaves. But even in *Aves* Chief Justice Shaw had "clearly" shown "that he thought there was a difference between" residence and mere transit, and "he pronounced no opinion" on the latter. However, he indicated that in a case of pure transit a master might have a right to cross a free state with his slaves. This, the *Journal of Commerce* declared, was the case at hand, and Judge Paine's ruling violated the guidelines set down in *Aves*.[31]

The *Journal of Commerce* saw clear implications for states such as Ohio and Illinois if Paine's ruling were allowed to stand and ominously warned that "embarrassments and disturbances" were "likely to result from such a rule hostile to the interests of the States of the Union." The "Slaveholding States" would "never learn to discriminate between the confiscation of slaves, and other descriptions of property." In the view set out by the paper, "The Court doubtless understands that a decision adverse to the rights of Southern citizens will be regarded as an unfriendly act, and as a ground that treats them rather as strangers than as brothers."[32]

The *Richmond Daily Dispatch* was more direct. For over two weeks the paper carried stories and editorials about the case, including extensive reprints from the *Journal of Commerce* and other papers. "The more we reflect upon the decision of Judge Paine," the Richmond paper declared, "the more extraordinary it appears to us."

> If it be true that the inhabitants of one State had not the right to pass with their property through the territory of

31. *Richmond Daily Dispatch*, 17 Nov. 1852.
32. Ibid., 11, 17 Nov. 1852.

another, without forfeiting it, then the Union no longer exists. The objects for which it was instituted, and for which the Constitution of the United States was established, have been rendered, in one respect, impossible of attainment. Fifteen States have been declared out of the pale of legal protection, so far as New York can effect it, and the citizens of these states cannot pass through New York with property of a certain kind, without losing it, though it is recognized by the Constitution of the United States.

If this were in fact the law, then there was "no other right of which" Virginians "may not be deprived. The Constitution, then, so far as the State of New York is concerned, has no binding force."[33]

The *Daily Dispatch* thought the case should be appealed all the way to the United States Supreme Court, but that in the meantime pressure should be applied to convince New York to change the law freeing slaves the moment they entered the state.

We can do New York an infinite deal more injury than she can do us. If she confiscates the property of our citizens, we must confiscate the property of hers. If she says that our negroes shall be free, if they pass through her territory, our legislature must pass a law rendering every vessel from the State of New York, that touches one of our ports, a lawful prize! No taxing, no half way measures—they destroy Southern property at a blow—Let us do the same with theirs.

In this war on New York, with its lawful prizes the paper felt "we must call on our Southern brethren, everywhere, to unite with us."[34]

A few days later, with a slightly calmer voice, the paper urged the upcoming session of the Virginia legislature to deal with the problem. "We hope there will be no excitements—no agonizing words— no threats." Time should be given for appeals to the New York courts and for the New York legislature to change the law. But if there were no change, "We should conclude that the States were no longer bound by the Federal compact . . . we should, therefore, recommend reprisals upon any and all property belonging to New York, within the jurisdiction of Virginia and we should call on all the slave States to stand by us."[35] If this act of war went unchallenged, the Richmond paper thought others would follow. It was better to meet the problem head on, with retaliatory acts of war by a united and resolute South.

33. Ibid., 19 Nov. 1852.
34. Ibid.
35. Ibid., 24 Nov. 1852. See also 14 *DeBow's Review* 90 (Jan. 1853); and 1 *American Law Register* 126 (1853).

This advice to the Virginia government was soon accepted. On 17 December Governor Joseph Johnson presented a copy of Paine's decision to the legislature. Johnson told the legislature that because the Lemmons had been reimbursed for their loss by the New York business community they had no personal interest in the case. But this fact "by no means diminishes the extent to which the decision affects the rights and interests of our citizens at large." Johnson doubted that the New York Supreme Court would uphold the statute repealing the nine-months law; because it was "so contrary to the spirit of all law . . . so much at war, with the relations that should subsist between the sister States of the Union," and he asked for an appropriation to pay for an appeal.[36]

By a unanimous vote the Virginia House of Delegates directed the state attorney general "together with such counsel as the executive may think proper to associate with him" to appeal the decision "by which Jonathan Lemmon, a citizen of Virginia, was deprived of his slaves." While the Virginia legislature provided money for the appeal, the governor of Georgia, Howell Cobb, offered moral support. In his annual message Cobb took note of the New York decision:

> If it be true that the citizens of the slaveholding States, who, by force of circumstances, or for convenience, seek a passage through the territory of a non-slaveholding State with their slaves, are thereby deprived of their property in them, and the slaves *ipso facto* become emancipated, it is time that we know the law as it is. No court in America has ever announced this to be law. It would be exceedingly strange if it should be. By the comity of nations the personal status of every man is determined by the law of his domicile. . . . This is but the courtesy of nation to nation founded not upon the statute, but is absolutely necessary for the peace and harmony of States and for the enforcement of private justice. A denial of this comity is unheard of among civilized nations, and if deliberately and wantonly persisted in, would be just cause of war.[37]

The New York State government responded to the case only when it became clear that there would be an appeal. The distance between Virginia and New York, the slow pace of the court system, the difficulty of one state's hiring lawyers to appeal a case in another state, and the importance of the case all tended to delay the appeal process. In March 1854, State Senator Andrew B. Dickenson "presented the petition of citizens of New-York [City], praying for the appointment

36. *Richmond Daily Dispatch,* 22 Dec. 1853.

37. *Journal of the Virginia House of Delegates, 1852–53,* 449–50; *Report of the Lemmon Slave Case* (New York: W. H. Tinson, 1860) 13.

of counsel to defend the appeal." This petition was referred to the judiciary committee on 30 March, but was rejected by the Senate on 1 April. However, the following year Governor Myron H. Clark devoted nearly three pages of his message to the legislature to the case. He asked for "a resolution directing the Attorney General together with such counsel as may be associated with him, to defend the rights and interests" of the state. This resolution was quickly passed. In his message of 1856 Governor Clark reported he had "appointed two associate counsel," E. D. Culver and Joseph Blunt, "to act with the Attorney General" in the case. And when the attorney general died, Governor Clark appointed William M. Evarts as chief counsel for the case.[38]

In April 1857 the New York legislature added more fuel to the smoldering question by passing three resolutions, which Governor John A. King signed. The first was aimed directly at the *Lemmon* case:

> *Resolved,* . . . That this state will not allow slavery within
> her borders, in any form, or under any pretence, or for any time
> however short.

The second was a response to the *Dred Scott* decision, announced the previous month, but it also had important implications for *Lemmon*:

> *Resolved,* . . . That the supreme court of the United States,
> by reason of a majority of the judges thereof having identified
> it with a sectional and aggressive party, has impaired the
> confidence and respect of the people of this state.

The third resolution directed the governor to transmit the other two resolutions to all other governors in the Union. These resolutions show that the advocates of human freedom could be just as aggressive as those who advocated bondage.[39]

In October 1857 the case was finally argued before the New York Supreme Court. By this time it had been noticed beyond the borders of New York and Virginia. It was clearly not yet as important as the recent *Dred Scott* decision. Nor did it produce headlines equal to those concerning the struggle over Kansas. But for perceptive newspaper editors and politicians, *Lemmon* was, in the words of the *Springfield Republican*, "second only to the Dred Scott case in the importance of the general principles involved." At least one

---

38. *New York Senate Journal, 1854,* 87th Sess., 525, 563; *New York Laws, 1857,* II:746; *New York Laws, 1858,* 548; *New York Laws, 1859,* 1145; *New York Laws, 1860,* 841, 884; Charles Z. Lincoln, ed., 4 *State of New York: Messages of the Governors* (11 vols.; Albany: J. P. Lyon Company, 1909) 808–18, 860.

39. *New York Laws, 1857,* II:797.

New York politician thought the case would provide "the material for agitation through the whole of the next Presidential campaign, from 1860 to 1864." The case, which had "already attained an extended notoriety," had the potential of becoming a major factor in the growing sectional conflict.[40]

Before the New York Supreme Court, Lemmon and the State of Virginia were still represented by Henry Lapaugh. In addition, Virginia retained Charles O'Conor, a leading unionist, Democrat, and one of the finest and most successful lawyers in the state. O'Conor had long been a rival of William Evarts; after many years of opposing each other, they had now come to their "greatest battle." The arguments of both Evarts and O'Conor centered on questions of comity. They added little to the debate first laid out in *Commonwealth* v. *Aves*, except for more reliance on the meaning of the Privileges and Immunities Clause of the United States Constitution and, of course, federal and state decisions made since *Aves* were cited on both sides. To a surprising extent Evarts and O'Conor relied on the same precedents. *Aves*, for example, was cited by O'Conor to show slave transit ought to be allowed as long as there was no attempt to stay in the free state any longer than necessary. Evarts, on the other hand, used the case to show that a state could prohibit all slavery within its jurisdiction. Similarly, O'Conor suggested that the "general doctrines of Dred Scott's case must be maintained," while Evarts thought the same decision supported the right of a state to free any person within its jurisdiction except a fugitive slave.[41]

In a surprisingly short opinion the New York Supreme Court, with one Democrat dissenting, upheld Paine's original decision. The court declared: "Comity does not require any state to extend any greater privilege to the citizens of another state than it grants to its own. As this state does not allow its own citizens to bring a slave here, *in transitu*, and to hold him as a slave for any portion of time, it cannot be expected to allow the citizens of another state to do so." The court thought the Commerce Clause of the United States Constitution conferred "no power on congress to declare the *status* which any person shall sustain while in any state in the union." Indeed, if it "did not prevent the state of Mississippi from prohibiting the importation of slaves into that state for the purposes of sale," which

40. *Springfield Republican*, 12 Oct. 1857; Eric Foner, *Free Soil, Free Labor, Free Men: The Ideology of the Republican Party before the Civil War* (New York: Oxford University Press, 1970) 98; *New York Times*, 2 Oct. 1857. Salmon P. Chase sent John Jay a "very friendly note" complimenting Jay on his argument in the case; John Jay to Chase, 7 Jan. 1858, Chase Papers, box 10, LC.

41. Chester L. Barrows, *William M. Evarts: Lawyer, Diplomat, Statesman* (Chapel Hill: University of North Carolina Press, 1941) 72–87; *Lemmon* v. *The People ex rel. Napoleon*, 26 Barbour (N.Y.) 270, 276–77 (1857).

the Supreme Court had affirmed in *Groves* v. *Slaughter*, then the Constitution could not interfere with New York's total ban on slaves. If the slave states could regard the ban on slaves as merchandise "as a police regulation" it should "be so regarded as to the free states." The legislature considered "that the holding of slaves in this state, for any purpose, is injurious to our condition and to the public peace, as it is opposed to the sentiment of the people of this state," and the state supreme court saw no reason to doubt the constitutionality of the statute repealing the nine-months law, or the interpretation of it by Judge Paine.[42]

New York Denies Comity

The state supreme court decision was warmly supported by Governor John King in his 1858 message to the legislature. King noted that the "counsel of the State of Virginia" planned to carry the case to the court of appeals, and the governor asked "the Legislature to make such provision for the further maintenance of the rights of the State, as the importance of the question requires." Appropriations for attorneys' fees had been authorized the previous year for the supreme court appeal and were continued annually until 1860. In 1859 Governor Edwin D. Morgan made a clear reference to the case, declaring: "The State of New York . . . insists on her right to maintain whenever the issue shall be legitimately presented, the superiority of liberty over slavery whether as a condition of personal enjoyment, intellectual and moral development, or of social and general well being." Morgan reiterated this position in his January 1860 message. He strongly condemned the recent raid by John Brown at Harper's Ferry. But he also condemned "the novel doctrines which affirm that slavery is no evil at all, but a positive good . . . which logically require the conversion of our present federal territories into new slave marts." Morgan proclaimed:

> New York yields to none of her sister States in her devotion to the Union. She reveres it as the fruit of a long protracted contest for liberty and independence, and she cherishes it for its present benefits and its guarantees for the future. Her citizens discovered at a very early period that slavery was an evil, and prompt and considerable provision was made for its extinction . . . but we never claimed that we had the right to interfere, directly or indirectly, with slavery as it existed in the other States of the Union. We were satisfied with the solemn and

42. *Lemmon* v. *The People ex rel. Napoleon* 287–89.

earnest declarations recorded upon our statute book that
we regarded slavery as a governmental and social evil, and
treated it accordingly. New York still maintains that
position.[43]

Three weeks after this defense of New York's right to exclude
slavery from within her borders, the *Lemmon* case was finally argued before the New York Court of Appeals. The case was heard at a
time when the nation was intensely preoccupied with the struggle
over slavery in the territories, John Brown's raid, and the upcoming
presidential campaign. The *Lemmon* case provided another battlefield where the forces of slavery and freedom could oppose each
other.

By this time Chester A. Arthur had replaced E. D. Culver on the
team of lawyers representing the state. The elimination of the abolitionist Culver was compensated for by an amicus curiae brief presented by John Jay. Jay argued that for three reasons the case was
moot and should be dismissed: first, Lemmon had been paid for the
value of the slaves and therefore had no legitimate cause of action;
second, the slaves were in Canada and therefore beyond the reach of
the court no matter what it decided; finally, the suit was really a test
case, prosecuted not by the plaintiff, or even on the plaintiff's behalf,
but by the State of Virginia merely to get a New York statute declared unconstitutional. This last assertion was supported by the
fact that Lemmon had agreed to emancipate the slaves formally.[44]
Coming from an abolitionist, this brief was quite peculiar. Jay may
have felt that the application of the law was not constitutional, or at
least would be declared so by a proslavery United States Supreme
Court. From this point of view it was better to let the law, and
Paine's interpretation of it, stand without any definitive interpretation by the New York Court of Appeals. Whatever his motives,
Jay's arguments were rejected by the court, which then heard oral
arguments on the case.

On behalf of Lemmon, and the State of Virginia, Charles O'Conor
presented a long and elaborate argument that attempted to prove
three points: Paine's interpretation of the 1841 repeal of the nine-
months law amounted to judge-made law; if the interpretation was
correct then the law itself violated the United States Constitution;
and whatever the law was meant to accomplish, New York ought to
give comity to laws of a sister state under which Lemmon claimed
his slaves. O'Conor's most persuasive arguments centered on the
theory and constitutional provisions concerning comity and inter-

43. Lincoln, 5 *Messages of the Governors* 196–97.
44. *New York Times*, 2 Oct. 1857; 23 *Monthly Law Reporter* 59 (1860).

state commerce. All of his assertions were ultimately based on the underlying principles of federalism.

O'Conor relied on a very broad interpretation of the rights guaranteed in article IV of the Constitution, while finding the commerce power exclusive in Congress. He felt the former article worked to protect the Lemmons "from such a disturbance as" they had suffered while "peacefully passing through one state on their way to another." It was designed "not to compel States to give strangers the same 'rights' which they award to their own citizens; but to exempt the stranger from burdens, or obstructions of any kind." Thus, "[t]o stop his vessel or his carriage *in transitu* and carry off his negro servant—recognized as his property by the laws of his own State and the Federal Constitution" was "a manifest invasion of his just 'privileges and immunities.'" Article IV was not meant merely to "secure to the non-resident citizen in traveling through a State only such 'rights' as such State may allow its own citizens. Its object was to exempt him from State power, not subject him to it."[45] This argument on behalf of the state of Virginia underscores the extraterritorial demands of slavery. Virginia wanted its statutes protecting slavery to be enforced in a free state and, concurrently, Virginia wanted its citizens to be exempt from the laws of a free state. Virginia was not of course ready to exempt the free black citizens of the North from the rigors of her statutes.

O'Conor found the commerce power "absolutely exclusive in Congress." Thus any state interference with commerce was unconstitutional. "Commerce," he thought, included "the transportation of persons and the whole subject of intercourse between our citizens of different States as well as between them and foreigners." O'Conor thought it logically followed that "no State can impose duties, imposts, or burdens of any kind, much less penal forfeitures, upon the citizens of other States for passing through her territories with their property nor can any State interrupt or disturb them in such passage."[46] Had this been a case in which a New York vessel with free black seamen on it was stopped in Virginia or South Carolina, it is unlikely that the counsel for the slave state would have made such a strong and absolute defense of the congressional power over commerce. But, before a New York court where the issue was slave transit, political philosophy was less important.

Ultimately O'Conor based his case on the special nature of comity that ought to, *indeed had to*, exist between states under the federal Constitution. Comity, even "in its simplest form, awards a free tran-

---

45. *Lemmon* v. *The People* 578, 580–82.
46. Ibid. 578–79.

sit to members of a friendly State with their families and rights of property, without disturbance of their domestic relations." And this comity was strengthened by the Constitution, which, among other things, protected slavery. Thus O'Conor claimed, "[W]hatever others may do, no American judge can pronounce slave property an exception to this rule upon the general ground that slavery is immoral or unjust." With what must have been unintentional irony, O'Conor warned that if Paine's decision were upheld, "the non-slaveholding States could pen up all slaveholders within their own States as effectually as the slave is himself confined by the rule applied in this case." Therefore, New York State could not "without violating" the United States Constitution "restrain a citizen of a sister State from peaceably passing through her territory with his slaves or other property on a lawful visit to a State where slavery is allowed by law."[47]

As he had in 1857, O'Conor ended his presentation by asserting that "[t]he general doctrines of the court in Dred Scott's case must be maintained, their alleged novelty notwithstanding."[48] Clearly O'Conor was reminding the New York judges that a higher authority would overturn Paine's decision if they failed to do so.

Joseph Blunt and William Evarts made four basic points on behalf of the state. First, they presented the old but still viable argument that as a purely local institution, slavery could exist only by positive law. Second, they argued that comity could not be applied to slavery because slavery so obviously violated natural and international law. They noted that the only part of the Constitution that forced all states to recognize the peculiar institution, the Fugitive Slave Clause, did not apply in this case. All other cases, they declared, were solely within the jurisdiction of the states to be decided as they saw fit. Third, they argued that the Commerce Clause allowed for concurrent power in certain areas, and in any event, slaves in transit were not covered by the Commerce Clause, because they ceased to be slaves when they entered a free state. Finally, Evarts offered a rather creative list of "horrors" that would occur if any slave status were allowed to exist in New York. Among other things, he suggested if the slave were jailed for committing a crime in the free state "the owner must have replevin for him or trover for his value," and "[i]f a creditor obtain a foreign attachment against the slave owner the sheriff must seize and sell the slave." He concluded, "Everything or nothing, is the demand from our comity; everything or nothing must be our answer."[49]

47. Ibid. 576, 578, 580.
48. Ibid. 597–98.
49. Ibid. 584–99.

To answer O'Conor's interpretations of article IV, Evarts simply inverted them. He declared that New York did give "full faith and credit to the act of Virginia, that made these persons slaves there." But the slaves were no longer *there*; they were in New York, where different rules applied. Similarly, the Virginians were allowed "all the privileges and immunities of a citizen" of New York and were "not deprived of property" while in New York because the slaves "ceased to be property when he brought them into the State of New York."[50] No matter what the law might be in Virginia, it could have no extraterritorial effect in New York.

In language similar to Shaw's in the *Aves* case, Evarts argued: "[T]he municipal law which makes men the subject of property, is limited with the power to enforce itself, that is by its territorial jurisdiction . . . the strangers stand upon our soil in their natural relations as men, their artificial relation being absolutely terminated." Using the states' rights doctrine with marvelous skill, Evarts closed by declaring that the "free and sovereign State" of New York could determine the status of all people under its jurisdiction. It did not have to grant comity, and "under the same impulse which has purged its own system of the odious and violent injustice of slavery" the state would "prefer the law of nations to the law of Virginia, and set the slave free."[51]

In a five-to-three decision the court of appeals upheld the law and Paine's interpretation of it. The opinion of the court was delivered by Justice Hiram Denio, the only Democrat in the majority. Four other justices concurred, with a separate opinion written by Justice William B. Wright. Justice Thomas W. Clerke wrote a long dissent, and two other justices wrote short paragraphs agreeing with his dissent. Clerke's dissent is particularly noteworthy, because he served on the state supreme court in 1857, where he had been in the majority *against* Lemmon. His changing sides over the three-year period is perhaps indicative of the complexity and importance of the case. As a unionist and a Democrat, Clerke may have had second thoughts about committing himself, and the court, to a position that would exacerbate the sectional crisis.

The main point of contention between the majority justices was the meaning of the Commerce Clause of the Constitution. Justice Denio conceded: "Congress has power to provide for precisely such a case as the present," but "the unexercised power to enact such a law, to regulate such a transit, would not affect the power of the States to deal with the status of all persons within their territory in the meantime, and before the existence of such a law." Speaking for

50. Ibid. 590.
51. Ibid. 598–99.

the four other majority justices, Wright denied that passengers in transit were in fact commerce, and "in no view can the provision empowering Congress to regulate commerce among the States affect the power of the respective States over the subject of slavery." Wright went on to warn the slave states if it was "conceded that, by the exercise of any powers granted in the Constitution to the Federal Government, it may rightly interfere in the regulation of the social and civil condition of any description of persons within the territorial limits of the respective States of the Union, it is not difficult to foresee the ultimate result."[52] The implications of Wright's warning were clear. If advocates of the slave states argued for an absolute power in Congress to regulate the "social and civil conditions" of people in the states, then eventually a northern congressional majority might regulate the "social and political" conditions of the slaves in the South.

On most other points the majority justices were in agreement. The statute did intend to cover the case under review, and the legislature did have the power to regulate status under it. *Lemmon* was not a fugitive slave case, and therefore was not covered by the United States Constitution. They agreed that were it not for the Fugitive Slave Clause in the Constitution, even runaways would be declared free when they reached New York. Thus, "*a fortiori* he would be free if the master voluntarily brought him into a free State for any purpose of his own." Since no other clauses of the Constitution applied to slavery, "it would naturally be supposed that if there were other cases in which the rights of slave owners ought to be protected in the States which should abolish slavery, they would be adjusted in connection with the provision [in the Constitution] looking specially to that case instead of being left to be deduced by construction from clauses intended primarily for cases to which slavery had no necessary relation." Specifically, comity was not denied, because "the meaning is, that in a given State, every citizen of every other State shall have the same privileges and immunities— that is, the same rights—which the citizens of that State possess. . . . They can hold property by the same titles by which every other citizen may hold it, and by no other."[53]

Justice Clerke, in dissent, agreed that "[i]f the slave were to remain here for any time, legislators may, indeed, fear some detriment, some demoralization from his presence." But he asked "what could the most nervous or fastidious guardians of the public interests apprehend from persons passing through the State?" He regretfully concluded the acts were passed in "a spirit of the most wanton

52. Ibid. 614, 625, 629.
53. Ibid. 605–6, 628.

aggression" for "mere propagandism." He did not doubt that the legislature "intended to declare that all slaves voluntarily brought into this State, under any circumstances whatever, should become instantly free."[54]

Understanding the statute in this manner left the "question of much greater difficulty, whether the Legislature had the constitutional power to do so." Clerke felt that New York, as "a member of a confederacy of free and sovereign States, united for certain specific and limited purposes, under a solemn written covenant," did not have such power. He felt the Constitution was devised "in order to form a more perfect union," which among other things meant that congressional power over interstate commerce was exclusive. Clerke found that under the Articles of Confederation such commerce had been impeded by local action. Therefore, it seemed obvious that a "more perfect union" would lessen or eliminate all such problems. "Most assuredly," the framers "did not intend that the intercourse between the people of the different States should be more limited or restricted than" under the articles. Clerke asked: "Is it consistent with this purpose of a perfect union, and perfect and unrestricted intercourse, that property which the citizen of one State brings into another State, for the purpose of passing through it to a State where he intends to take up his residence, shall be confiscated in the State through which he is passing, or shall be declared no property, and liberated from his control?"[55]

Clerke then drew a critical analogy between international and domestic travel. He acknowledged "that the privilege accorded to the citizens of one foreign nation to pass unmolested with their property through the territory of any other, is founded merely on comity." But if comity were not granted, then the nations could resort to "the only method by which nations can obtain redress after remonstrance or negotiation fails." But the "relations of the different States of this Union . . . are of a much closer and more positive nature . . . war between them is legally impossible." Thus, comity had a special meaning for the states of the Union. New York was in error

> in supposing, because the law of nations refused to recognize slaves as property, the several States of this Union were at liberty to do the same: forgetting that the compact, by which the latter are governed in their relation towards each other, modifies the law of nations in this respect . . . [so that a state is] not permitted in its dealings or intercourse with other States or

54. Ibid. 642.
55. Ibid. 635–36.

their inhabitants to ignore the right to property in the labor and service of persons *in transitu* from those States.[56]

Like Justice Handy in *Mitchell* v. *Wells*, Justice Clerke realized that the ultimate result of an extreme denial of comity would be disunion; and Clerke foresaw that disunion would lead to civil war. The important difference was that Handy saw disunion as a reasonable and perhaps desirable solution. Clerke did not. What both justices sensed, but could not admit, was that the legal systems of the North and South could no longer coexist. Indeed, the nation could not "endure, permanently half *slave* and half *free*."[57]

The End of Comity

The *Lemmon* case was more than simply a legal controversy over the status of "eight colored Virginians." It was the culmination of eighty-eight years of Anglo-American case law, which began with *Somerset* in 1772. Its companion at the terminus of this case line was *Mitchell* v. *Wells*. Within the realm of state action *Lemmon* represents the final development in the law of freedom, while *Mitchell* symbolized the ultimate logic of the law of bondage.

On one level *Lemmon* represented a legal problem that threatened to tear the Union apart, and eventually did so. To a large extent the Civil War was a crisis in law. Certainly many of the issues and arguments were framed in legal terms, although the underlying causes were much deeper.[58] In this sense, *Lemmon* was the culmination of a long and intense conflict over the place of slavery within the legal framework of the Union. The conflict was undoubtedly social and economic at its roots, but the arguments were often legal. And, as the law is both a molder of society and a product of it, these legal arguments were as important and real as the economic and social issues. The right to petition Congress about slavery, the right to discuss it openly, and the right to exclude it absolutely from any state were all cherished political ideals in the North. Similarly, the right of unmolested transit anywhere in the Union was a cherished right in the South. The issues at stake in *Lemmon* were very real and familiar to people on both sides of the Mason-Dixon line.

On another level, *Lemmon* was part of the larger social and political movements that ultimately led to the Republican party, the Civil

56. Ibid. 642.

57. Lincoln used this phrase in 1858, in his "House Divided Speech."

58. For another view, see Phillip S. Paludan, "The American Civil War Considered as a Crisis in Law and Order," 77 *American Historical Review* 1013–34 (Oct. 1972). Also, see Paludan, *Covenant with Death*, chaps. 1 and 2.

War, and Constitutional amendments ending slavery and making blacks full-fledged citizens. As a legal case, *Lemmon* was fought not between individual parties, but between the largest northern and the largest southern states.

Lemmon also served as a focal point for the threatening rhetoric of editors and politicians in both sections. As such it was the end result, in legal terms, of social and political pressures that had been building since *Somerset*. Between *Somerset* and *Lemmon* important social, moral, political, and economic ideas and forces changed and shaped the law—in the South as well as the North. At the same time, the law helped shape the development of these new ideas and the institutions that grew with them. The legal concepts of property and liberty were intrinsically tied to the emerging debate over slavery. Both as abstract values and as specific and immediate situations, these legal questions were present in the cases that culminated with *Lemmon* and *Mitchell* v. *Wells*. The right of the "eight colored Virginians" to a writ of habeas corpus that could secure their liberty and the right of the Lemmons to retain their most valuable possessions presented a very real dilemma. These competing claims brought the theoretical legal questions before the courts in the form of concrete problems demanding immediate and non-theoretical solutions. The law and the court systems thereby provided a forum where the issues of slavery and liberty could confront each other. As such, the law helped shape the arguments, tactics, and goals of those defending and attacking human bondage.

Cases like *Lemmon* and *Mitchell* v. *Wells* also contributed to the failure of federalism in the United States. Under the Constitution the Union could function and survive only if the states were willing to cooperate with each other. But, as the cases in this study show, federalism was impossible if some states held views that were morally and socially abhorrent to other states. The freeing of a slave by Ohio offended and threatened Mississippi; the owning of slaves and the interstate movement of them through free states offended and threatened the North. Acts of states in both sections led to mistrust and fear. Under such circumstances federalism and comity were impossible. Only a war, and a redefinition of the Constitution with three new amendments, could reestablish comity and federalism. This problem was defined in the antebellum courts, where the probable solutions were also discussed.

In the antebellum years the courts, at local, state, and national levels, became battlegrounds where the struggles over the issues of slavery and freedom could be fought. Ultimately, of course, the law proved inadequate to the task of solving the problem of slavery or of redefining federalism within the Union. But so did other institutions. No alternatives were left except the secession that Judge Handy suggested and the civil war that Justice Clerke predicted. Yet, even the war and the constitutional changes it brought about were framed in legal terms partially defined by the series of cases that began with *Somerset* and ended with *Lemmon*.

Chapter 10

The Implications of Comity and the Nationalization of Slavery

The State of Virginia threatened to appeal *Lemmon* to the United States Supreme Court, but that appeal was never initiated.[1] By the time the New York Court of Appeals decision was announced, in April 1860, the presidential campaign had preempted the political stage. Perhaps had Lincoln not been elected the case would have been pursued. It is always risky to predict a judicial decision, but given the record of the Taney court on slavery, it is not outrageous to think the decision would have been reversed and the right of slave transit in the North upheld.[2] This fear was certainly held by many northerners and was probably justified.

In 1854, in response to *Lemmon*, a New York State assemblyman proposed a bill to allow slave transit. The *New York Post* feared that "[g]angs of men and women, chained together may yet be seen, marching up or down Broadway or trembling on the Battery."[3] The debate over the Kansas-Nebraska Act heightened such fears. Abolitionists in Ohio saw both *Lemmon* and the Nebraska debates as "evidences of a resolve on the part of the slave power to extend its sway more entirely than ever before over the whole land," under the motto "*rule or union.*" Leading Free Soil politicians also feared that the new compromise "was part of a continuous movement of slaveholders to advance slavery over the entire North." Slavery, they predicted, would soon be forced on the free states.[4]

1. Eric Foner, *Free Soil, Free Labor, Free Men: The Ideology of the Republican Party before the Civil War* (New York: Oxford University Press, 1970) 98, indicates that the case was on appeal to the U.S. Supreme Court when the Civil War began. However, no record of such an appeal has been found during the course of this study.

2. A recent article by William M. Wiecek, "Slavery and Abolition before the United States Supreme Court, 1820–1860," 65 *Journal of American History* 34–59 (June 1978) argues forcefully that the Taney court was consistently proslavery.

3. Quoted in Richard H. Sewell, *Ballots for Freedom: Antislavery Politics in the United States, 1837–1860* (New York: Oxford University Press, 1976) 259.

4. Ibid. 258–59, Minutes of 12th annual meeting, Western Anti-Slavery Society, Minutebook, LC, 1854. For similar and earlier statements by politicians, see Salmon P. Chase to Dr. Norton S. Townshend, 2 May 1850, in Chase Papers, HSP; *New York Times*, 11 Sept. 1854, editorial entitled "A New Plot—Scheme for Nationalizing

As early as 1855 the ever-vigilant Charles Sumner tied recent events directly to *Lemmon.* He told a Republican convention in Boston that the "Slave Oligarchy . . . contemplates not merely the political subjugation of the National Government, but the actual introduction of Slavery into the Free States." He feared that "slaves will yet be counted in the shadow of the monument on Bunker Hill" and reported that "more than one step has been taken towards this effrontery." The first step in this conspiracy was the *Lemmon* case. Sumner told his audience that a "person of Virginia has asserted his right to hold slaves in New York on the way to Texas; and this claim is still pending before the highest tribunal of the land."[5]

Two years later the *Springfield Republican* glumly reported, "[T]he slaveholders are confident that the U.S. supreme court will give them this new accession to their growing power." Two months later the paper asked, "If slavery is a national institution, recognized, protected and carried into the territories, why does not the same authority recognize, protect and carry it into all the several states?" The paper predicted *Lemmon* would be to the free states what *Dred Scott* had been to the free territories:

> If a man can hold a slave one day in a free state, why not one month, why not one year? Why could not his "transit" be in-definitely lengthened, his "visit" a practical permanency? Who shall define the limits which the Union does claim for slavery? . . . It is the first step that costs, and having taken that, and overthrown the olden principle of the pure locality of slavery, all the rest follows after it, and slavery may exist by law, as well in Massachusetts as in Missouri, in Connecticut as in Kansas.[6]

Slavery"; and William Jay to S. P. Chase, 24 Mar. 1845, "There has been a favorite saying of ours that liberty must destroy slavery, or slavery will destroy liberty. If this be true according to present appearances, which is doomed to destruction? This is a momentous question & leads to *fearful & most painful conclusions*"; letter in Chase Papers, HSP.

5. George Frisbie Hoar, ed., 5 *Charles Sumner: His Complete Works* (20 vols. reprint of 1900 ed. New York: Negro Universities Press, 1969) 71. See also similar fears expressed before *Lemmon* became a major case, in Sumner's "Freedom National, Slavery Sectional" speech of 1852, in 3 ibid. 264–65.

6. *Springfield Republican*, 12 Oct. 1857 and 12 Dec. 1857. Even the conservative attorney George Templeton Strong feared the implications of *Lemmon.* In November 1860 he wrote in his diary: "If we accede to Southern exactions, we must re-open the slave trade with all its horrors, establish a Slave Code for the territories, and acquiesce in a decision of the United States Supreme Court in the Lemmon Case that will entitle every Southerner to bring his slaves into New York and Massachusetts and keep them there. We must confess that our federal government exists chiefly for the sake of Nigger owners. *I can't do* that. Rather let South Carolina and Georgia

In 1859 Salmon P. Chase expressed similar fears to an audience in Sandusky, Ohio. He claimed that if the Democrats won the presidency in 1860 *Lemmon* would "be decided in favor of the claim, just as after the election of Mr. Buchanan the Dred Scott case was decided in favor of the claim to carry slavery into the territories." He asked, "What will the decision be?"

> It will be just as they claim, that they can take their slaves into New York over the railroads of New Jersey, through Pennsylvania and through Ohio, Indiana, Illinois . . . to any state of the North, and that they can hold them there during all the time that it is convenient for them to be passing through. In other words it is a decision in favor, not of the African slave trade, but of the American slave trade, to be carried on in the free states.[7]

While the case was before the New York Court of Appeals, Horace Greeley's *New York Tribune* saw it as part of the "slaveocracy" conspiracy: "The slaveholders, it is perfectly well known, are aiming to reverse every legal decision hitherto made which prejudices their claims to make slavery universal. They are also aiming to shape the judgement of the Courts in this process, so as to shield them (the slaveholders) from all political action on the part of the people."[8]

Sumner, Chase, Greeley, and other Republicans all reflected the fears of their constituents and readers that the slaveocracy was about to take over the nation. As David Potter clearly demonstrated, the *Dred Scott* decision "made freedom local" and "it made slavery national, in the sense that slavery would be legal in any part of the United States where a state government had not abolished it."[9] For these and hundreds of other Republican leaders, it was only a short step to the nationalization of slavery by the Supreme Court.[10] For those who followed the *Lemmon* case, the danger seemed imminent. But even without mentioning *Lemmon*, many northerners saw omi-

secede. We will coerce and punish the traitorous seceders if we can; but if we can't, we are well rid of them"; entry of 2 Nov. 1860, Allan Nevins and Milton Halsey Thomas, eds., 3 *The Diary of George Templeton Strong* (4 vols. New York: Farrar, Straus, and Giroux, 1974) 57.

7. *New York Evening Post*, 31 Aug. 1859 carried the complete text of Chase's speech.

8. *New York Tribune*, 27 Jan. 1860.

9. David M. Potter, *The Impending Crisis, 1848–1861* (New York: Harper and Row, 1976) 293. Other Republicans, including the relatively conservative Simon Cameron and Lyman Trumbull, expressed similar fears. See Foner, *Free Soil, Free Labor, Free Men* 96–98.

10. Don E. Fehrenbacher, *The Dred Scott Case: Its Significance in American Law and Politics* (New York: Oxford University Press, 1978) 451.

nous threats to their free-state constitutions. An Indianapolis newspaper asked, "Can a Free State Constitution prevent slavery?" or, "can a slaveholder, defying our State Constitution, bring his slaves here in Indiana and hold them?"[11] The logic of *Dred Scott* was clear. If slaves were property, protected by the Constitution, then, in the words of Wisconsin's Senator James R. Doolittle, "no State Constitution or State law can abolish it, or prohibit its introduction." Doolittle feared that *Dred Scott* would carry "the law of slavery into every State of this Union."[12] A major exponent of this conspiracy theory would soon become the Republican party's leading politician and the nation's first Republican president. Thus, Abraham Lincoln's understanding of this problem must be examined at some length.

Even before the Supreme Court announced its decision in *Dred Scott*, Lincoln feared that it would lead to a nationalization of slavery in some form.[13] During his campaign for the Senate in 1858 Lincoln fully developed his theory of a conspiracy to force slavery on the North. He first outlined it in the "House Divided Speech," where he declared, "Either the *opponents* of slavery, will arrest the further spread of it, and place it where the public mind shall rest in the belief that it is in course of ultimate extinction; or its *advocates* will push it forward, till it shall become alike lawful in *all* the states, *old* as well as *new*—*North* as well as *South*." He added ominously, "Have we no *tendency* to the latter condition?"[14]

Lincoln detected this tendency in the Kansas-Nebraska Act, the *Dred Scott* decision, and the general trend of Supreme Court adjudications that might follow the *Dred Scott* case. Lincoln noted that in his concurring opinion in *Dred Scott*, Justice Nelson had declared that every state "had complete and absolute power over" slavery "except as restrained by the Federal Constitution." Similar language had been used in the Kansas-Nebraska Act, which declared that "the people of a *State* as well as a *Territory*, were to be left 'perfectly free'" to legislate on slavery "'subject only to the Constitution.'"

11. Ibid. 452.

12. *Congressional Globe*, 35th Cong., 1st sess., p. 665. See also speech of Senator James Harlan of Iowa in *Congressional Globe*, 35th Cong., 1st sess., pp. 384–85.

13. In October 1854, Lincoln spoke of a "covert *real* zeal for the spread of slavery"; Roy P. Basler, ed., 2 *The Collected Works of Abraham Lincoln* (9 vols. New Brunswick, N.J.: Rutgers University Press, 1953–55) 255. See also Basler, 2 *Works of Lincoln* 388, and Don E. Fehrenbacher, *Prelude to Greatness: Lincoln in the 1850s* (New York: McGraw Hill, 1964) 85–91. In a fragment of a speech that Basler dates as May 1858 but Fehrenbacher believes was written in December 1857, Lincoln claimed he expressed his "belief a year ago" that the nation would become all slave or all free; Basler, 2 *Works of Lincoln* 452.

14. Basler, 2 *Works of Lincoln* 461–62.

Lincoln asked his audience to examine the words of the act and of Justice Nelson: "Put *that* and *that* together, and we have another nice little niche, which we may ere long see filled with another Supreme Court decision, declaring that the Constitution of the United States does not permit a *state* to exclude slavery from its limits. . . . Such a decision," he warned, was "all that slavery now lacks of being alike lawful in all the states." Without a Republican victory in 1858 and 1860, Lincoln believed that "such a decision *is* probably coming, and will soon be upon us. . . . We shall *lie down* pleasantly dreaming that the people of *Missouri* are on the verge of making their state *free*; and we shall awake to the *reality*, instead, that the *Supreme* Court has made *Illinois* a *slave* state." Lincoln was convinced that the "logical conclusion" of *Dred Scott* was that what one "master might lawfully do with Dred Scott, in the free state of Illinois, every master might lawfully do with any other *one*, or one *thousand* slaves, in Illinois, or in any other free state."[15]

Throughout his debates with Douglas, Lincoln reiterated this theme and elaborated on the conspiracy. At Ottawa he asked, "Then what is necessary for the nationalization of slavery? It is simply the next Dred Scott decision. It is merely for the Supreme Court to decide that no *State* under the Constitution can exclude it, just as they have already decided that under the Constitution neither Congress nor the territorial legislature can do it." In this way, "slavery is to be made national."[16]

At Freeport Lincoln phrased the problem differently. He asked Douglas, "If the Supreme Court of the United States shall decide that States cannot exclude slavery from their limits, are you in favor of acquiescing in, adopting and following such a decision as a rule of political action?" This sober question was greeted by "loud applause" from the audience.[17]

At Galesburg he noted that the *Dred Scott* decision found the right to slave property "expressly affirmed in the Constitution." To this Lincoln added the Supremacy Clause of the Constitution and concluded three things. First, "[n]othing in the Constitution or laws of any State can destroy a right distinctly and expressly affirmed in the Constitution of the United States." Second, *"The right of property in a slave is distinctly and expressly affirmed in the Constitution!"* Thus, "nothing in the Constitution or laws of any State can destroy the right of property in a slave." Unless Republicans were elected, "a new Dred Scott decision, deciding against the right of the people of

15. *Dred Scott* v. *Sandford*, 19 Howard (U.S.) 393, 459 (1857); Basler, 2 *Works of Lincoln* 464–67.

16. Basler, 3 *Works of Lincoln* 27.

17. 3 ibid. 43.

the States to exclude slavery" would be made. He reiterated this point a week later in Quincy and reaffirmed the conspiracy "to make the institution of slavery national" in his last debate at Alton.[18]

Lincoln did not reject this theory after the election of 1858. In January 1859, for example, he wrote a correspondent that Douglas's policy "does inevitably lead to a nationalization of slavery." Five months later he wrote an Iowa attorney that "the o[b]ject of the Republican organization" was "*preventing the spread* and *national-ization* of Slavery."[19] What was once only Lincoln's theory had now become the "object" of his party.

And Lincoln did not limit this position to his private correspon-dence.[20] Between March 1859 and April 1860, Lincoln raised the specter of a "nationalization of slavery" in at least sixteen public speeches in nine northern states.[21] In 1859 he went into Ohio to campaign for Republican candidates. At Columbus Lincoln elabo-rated, broadened, and refined his theory. He told the audience, "[T]he Republican party, as I understand its principles and policy, believe that there is a great danger of the institution of slavery being spread and extended until it is made alike lawful in all the States of this Union."[22] The party, according to Lincoln, now not only accepted his "object" but also his fears.

Lincoln did not see this happening all at once. "The chief danger . . . is not just now the revival of the African slave trade, or the passage of a Congressional slave code, or the declaring of a second Dred Scott decision making slavery lawful in all the States." But he warned that a "new Dred Scott decision" would eventually "carry slavery into the free States" and "bring slavery up into the very heart of the North."[23]

While Lincoln was developing this "Nationalization of Slavery" theory, he emerged as a leading spokesman of his party. By 1860 he "had come to be regarded by a majority of Republican leaders as the candidate who best combined devotion to party principles with the ability to win."[24] In an age when audiences at political rallies and

18. 3 ibid. 230–32, 250–52, 299. For similar statements in debate at Jonesboro, 3 ibid. 116–17, 129–30; and in other campaign speeches, 3 ibid. 37–38, 78–79, 82–83, 86–90, 95–96, 329, 334.

19. 3 ibid. 349, 379.

20. For examples of private correspondence, see 3 ibid. 387–88, 390–91, 394–95, 519–20.

21. 3 ibid. 369–70, 463–64, 482, 484, 488–89, 493, 500, 503, 522, 548, 550–52; 4 ibid. 8, 13, 21, 28, 29, 42. Also, see major speech at Columbus, Ohio, 3 ibid. 404, 407–8, 420–21, 423–24.

22. 3 ibid. 404, 423.

23. 3 ibid. 404, 423, 421.

24. Fehrenbacher, *Prelude to Greatness* 2.

meetings "listened attentively to fine-spun technical arguments and lengthy rehashes of past utterances and events,"[25] Lincoln's constant reiteration of the prospect of a nationalization of slavery struck a responsive chord with both the party leadership and the rank and file. His audiences feared the "next Dred Scott decision" as much as he did.

While Lincoln was speaking and debating his way to national prominence, the "next Dred Scott case" was making its way through the New York courts. *Lemmon* was a nationally known case, which Lincoln would have heard of even in Illinois.[26] At least one New York politician predicted that *Lemmon* would provide "the material for agitation through the whole of the next Presidential campaign, from 1860 to 1864."[27]

In his Cooper Union address Lincoln predicted that the South would eventually demand the overthrow of the free-state constitutions, but had "not as yet" demanded it. However, in the printed version of the speech, Lincoln added a footnote containing the argument of Charles O'Conor before the New York Court of Appeals and concluded, "That demand has since been made." In the next paragraph of the speech Lincoln declared that if slavery was "right, we cannot justly object to its nationality." This statement too was footnoted with a reference to *Lemmon*.[28]

Less than two months after the Cooper Union speech, the New York Court of Appeals announced its five-to-three decision denying Lemmon the right to bring slaves into the state. Horace Greeley castigated the dissenting justices by asking, "[F]or how long a time and to what extent do the principles of justice and comity . . . operate?" He wondered if they would "demand us to tolerate on the part of the slaveholder the same power over his slave which he exercises at home?" While in New York could a master "commit rape on his female slave without any liability to be called to account for it?" And, if a slave gave birth in New York, would the child "be born slave or free born?" He thought it "pretty clear" that if there had been a majority of Democrats on the court "the right of every slave trader to parade his coffles of human merchandise through our streets, and call the roll of them either in Bunker Hill, Saratoga or any other battlefield of Liberty would have been established." Greeley, like Justice Clerke of New York and Justice Handy of Mis-

---

25. Ibid. 15.
26. Fehrenbacher, ibid. 93, suggested the case was *Ex parte Archy*, 9 Cal. 147 (1858). But it is unlikely Lincoln would have been disturbed by this obscure and distant case.
27. Eric Foner, *Free Soil, Free Labor, Free Men* 98.
28. Basler, 3 *Works of Lincoln* 548–49.

sissippi, sarcastically predicted where such decisions had to lead: "Only think of the 'gross violation of *justice* and comity' involved in our State law which declares every innocent man found on our soil and not a fugitive from some other State, the owner of himself! If we do not repent and repeal our law, may not Virginia be expected to make war on us?"[29] A year later Virginia would do just that.

The Republican Nightmare

It is easy to dismiss the fear of a nationalization of slavery as political rhetoric, as an "absurd bogey" designed to arouse northerners and gain votes.[30] Yet when a winning presidential candidate and hundreds of other successful politicians and editors place great emphasis on an idea or fear, it is incumbent upon the historian to consider their statements seriously. Indeed, had Lincoln's predictions been an "absurd bogey," it is doubtful that he would have won so many votes while making them. However absurd their fears of conspiracy may seem today, if some sense is to be made of the antebellum crisis, historians must try to understand the reasons for such a pervasive fear of a nationalization of slavery. Even if this fear were political rhetoric at its most cynical level, it does not explain the issue's attractiveness for northern voters and Republican politicians from all wings of the party.[31]

The benefit of over a century of hindsight confirms that no organized conspiracy to nationalize slavery operated at the time. It is less clear, however, that a decision of the Taney court would not give some protection to slavery in the free states. That this did not happen does not mean that it could not have happened. Indeed, the success of the Republican party in 1860 greatly diminished the chance that slavery would spread into the North. The outbreak of war eliminated that possibility. But the antebellum generation, which listened to arguments about the imminent nationalization of slavery and voted for a party committed to opposing this trend, had no way of knowing the outcome of the story. They could not know

29. *New York Tribune*, 25 & 26 Apr. 1860.

30. Allan Nevins, 1 *The Emergence of Lincoln* (2 vols. New York: Charles Scribner's Sons, 1950) 362.

31. Fehrenbacher, *Dred Scott Case* 486–88, argues that Lincoln used the conspiracy theory only when it became politically expedient to do so in his campaign against Douglas. This may or may not be true, but Lincoln did apparently believe in the threat of an ultimate nationalization of slavery. Douglas need not be seen as part of a conspiracy; in fact, the Republicans did not need even to envision a conspiracy to fear that slavery would be nationalized through actions by the Supreme Court, with the ultimate aid or tacit acquiescence of Congress and the president.

how weak the Democrats would be in 1860, that Lincoln would capture the White House, or that civil war would follow. The sequence of events they saw was far more disturbing: the Compromise of 1850, the Kansas-Nebraska Act, *Dred Scott*, the positive-good theory of slavery, and an aggressive slaveocracy or slave power conspiracy. The antebellum generation saw freedom on the defensive for the first time in American history. Until 1854 the North was satisfied that slavery was "in the course of ultimate extinction." But then came Kansas-Nebraska and *Dred Scott*.

Not only was freedom on the defensive, but for many it appeared that slavery was on the attack. In 1854 the proslavery ideologue George Fitzhugh asserted that "one set of Ideas will govern and control after awhile the civilized world. Slavery will everywhere be abolished, or everywhere be re-instituted."[32] Fitzhugh was only one of many southerners to extol the virtues of slavery and imply that it should be spread to the North. In the debate over the admission of Kansas to the Union, Senator James Henry Hammond of South Carolina argued for the superiority of slavery over free labor. He argued that the North would be better off with slavery, although he did not assert that the South was ready to force slavery on the North. But that was not long in coming. In November 1857, the *Washington Union*, the organ of the Buchanan administration, editorialized on the rights of slaveowners under the Constitution. First, the paper asserted that the purpose of government was the "protection of persons and their property." Thus the United States Constitution protected property in slaves. Under the Privileges and Immunities Clause, the paper argued, all citizens had the right to protection of *all* types of property, "any law of State to the contrary notwithstanding." This doctrine would of course protect slave property in transit through free states. So far the *Washington Union* had said nothing new. Such arguments had been made on behalf of slaveholders since the Founding. But, the *Union* followed the logic of this statement to a new, and for many northerners, ominous conclusion. The paper asserted: "[I]t follows that all State laws whether organic or otherwise, which prohibit a citizen of one State from settling in another and bringing his slave property with him, and most especially declaring it forfeited, are direct violations of the original intent of a Government which, as before stated, is the protection of person and property, and of the Constitution. . . ." Thus, "*the emancipation of the slaves*" in the North was "*a gross outrage on the rights of property* . . . an act of coercive legislation." Coming from the organ of President Buchanan and appearing as an "authoritative" state-

32. George Fitzhugh, *The Sociology of the South, or the Failure of Free Society* (Richmond, 1854) 94.

ment on administration policy, this article signaled a new attack on the laws of the free states.[33]

The political crisis that developed in 1860 further revealed a strengthening of slavery at the expense of freedom. Senator Robert Toombs of Georgia told his colleagues that the laws of nine northern states prohibiting slave transit were unconstitutional and should be nullified by federal legislation. After Lincoln's election Toombs suggested that the northern states be required to enforce slave codes when slaves were found in their jurisdiction, but that southern states would not have to respect the rights of northern free blacks. Comity, under Toombs's scheme, would be strictly a one-way affair. A similar demand was made by Senator Albert G. Brown of Mississippi, who thought slavery was legal *wherever* the American flag flew. Finally, in 1860 Senator John J. Crittenden of Kentucky proposed a constitutional amendment that would have invalidated all northern personal liberty laws, including, presumably, those freeing slaves in transit or attending sojourning masters.[34]

And coming behind this proslavery onslaught loomed *Lemmon* v. *The People*. Indeed, when the article in the *Washington Union* appeared, it led to a three-way debate on the floor of the Senate, which in part touched on *Lemmon*. Stephen A. Douglas attacked the article as an unwarranted attempt to subvert states' rights and northern liberties. Robert Toombs asserted that no slave-state representative had ever suggested forcing slavery on the North. Preston King of New York "was glad to hear" Toombs "disavow the doctrine" of the *Washington Union*. But King went on to say that the North did not fear legislative action. Rather, it was "through the judiciary that the doctrine is intended to be fostered on this Country." And if Toombs had not "heard of any pretension to that doctrine" of forcing slavery on the North, King could "inform him that the State of Virginia is now litigating in the courts the right of one of her citizens to hold slaves in the State of New York, the Lemmon case, well known throughout the country."[35]

By 1860 an appeal in *Lemmon* to the Taney court seemed imminent, and it took little imagination to predict how that court would decide the case. Even if the Taney court found only a limited right of

33. *Congressional Globe*, 35th Cong., 1st sess., p. 199, prints text of the *Washington Union* editorial attacking Senator Stephen A. Douglas (italics in *Congressional Globe*); Hammond speech at 68–71. Douglas attacked this editorial, at 199–200, and called it "authoritative" of the Buchanan administration.

34. *Congressional Globe*, 36th Cong., 2d sess., pp. 100–104, 112–14; also, Harold M. Hyman, *A More Perfect Union: The Impact of the Civil War and Reconstruction on the Constitution* (New York: A. A. Knopf, 1973) 23, 41, 43; Nevins, 1 *Emergence of Lincoln* 362; and Basler, 3 *Works of Lincoln* 24–26, 548n.

35. *Congressional Globe*, 35th Cong., 1st sess., p. 204.

slave transit, that would have provided the opening wedge Republicans feared. And, given the court's sweeping decision in *Dred Scott*, it is hard to deny that an appeal in *Lemmon* would not have led to some form of slavery in the North. As Fehrenbacher has argued, Lincoln's "warning that slavery might become lawful everywhere was . . . within its context, far from absurd."[36]

The context was really twofold. First was the stated presumption that the nationalization of slavery would happen only if the Republicans failed to win in 1860. This Lincoln constantly stressed, and of course this part of the issue was something the people of the North could control. Indeed, the whole purpose of Lincoln and other Republicans in stressing this issue was to have northerners control the problem by electing Republican leaders.

The second context was the Supreme Court. Here Lincoln and his party might not be able to effect a quick change. Indeed, as it turned out, without the Civil War it would have been impossible to achieve a radical change on the high bench until the late 1860s or 1870s.

The political scenario of the Republican nightmare is not difficult to imagine. In 1856 John C. Frémont failed to carry New Jersey, Pennsylvania, Indiana, Illinois, and California. In 1860 Lincoln would split New Jersey's electoral vote and carry the other four states, but win the election by a scant electoral majority of twenty-eight votes. Had Senator William H. Seward, the preconvention favorite, been nominated, he might easily have lost the election by failing to capture Pennsylvania, Indiana, and Illinois.[37] And, of course, even as late as 1860 there was no guarantee that Lincoln would face a splintered Democratic party, or that he could win no matter whom he faced. Until after the Democrats committed political suicide at their conventions in Charleston, Richmond, and Baltimore, the Republicans could not be sure they would win in 1860. Thus, it was not unreasonable for Lincoln and his party to be fearful of the next administration.[38]

The Supreme Court loomed as the real villain in this conspiracy. Even a Republican victory in 1860 would not immediately affect the court. Between 1860 and 1864 only three justices, Taney, McLean, and Daniel, died. Catron died in 1865 and Wayne in 1867. Thus not

36. Fehrenbacher, *Prelude to Greatness* 81.

37. Fehrenbacher, *Dred Scott Case*, 562–67.

38. When the Republican convention began, it appeared that Seward would win the nomination, and his reputation as a radical would have hurt his chances in the lower North. Of course, before 1860 there was no guarantee the Democrats would be unable to find a compromise candidate, as they had in 1852 and 1856. Lincoln's fears in 1858 and 1859 are thus based on the assumption the Republicans might not win the White House in 1860. See Potter, *The Impending Crisis* 426–30, and Fehrenbacher, *Prelude to Greatness* 143–61.

until 1865, and probably not until 1867, could an antislavery majority have been appointed to the court. Lincoln was able to accomplish this change by 1865 only because Justice John A. Campbell of Alabama, who lived until 1889, resigned when the Civil War began. If the geographic balance of the court were to be maintained in the 1860s, even accounting for the need to expand it to insure representation from the new western states, at least some of the new appointees would have been southerners. Of the five justices who died between 1860 and 1867, only McLean came from a free state. Thus, if *Lemmon* were to come before the Supreme Court before two successive Republican presidential victories chances were good that some type of slavery would have been forced on the North. In a major campaign speech on behalf of Lincoln in July 1860, Charles Sumner raised this ugly possibility before a New York audience:

> [A]n *Oligarchical Combination* of Slave-Masters . . . has entered into and possessed the National Government, like an Evil Spirit. This influence, which, wielding at will all the powers of the National Government, even those of the Judiciary, has become formidable to Freedom everywhere, clutching violently at the Territories, and menacing the Free States,—as witness the claim, still undecided in the court of the last resort, so audaciously presented by a citizen of Virginia, to hold slaves in New York on the way to Texas.[39]

A Counterfactual Approach to the 1860s

A thorough understanding of the fears of Republicans requires one only to hypothesize that secession did not take place in 1860–61 and that the Supreme Court was allowed to continue the kind of decision making that was begun with *Dred Scott*. And even if these fears turned out to be historically groundless, this examination may at least lead to an understanding of why so many people held them and how real or illusory the problems really were. In addition, such a hypothesis helps place the meaning of comity and slave transit in a larger perspective by showing the crucial importance of the question in the antebellum years and thus facilitates an understanding of the options and choices of judges, lawyers, and politicians during the period. Finally, such an analysis provides greater insight into events before and after the Civil War and some of the motivations for secession and the postwar amendments. As Harold Hyman noted, "One

39. Hoar, 6 *Charles Sumner* 325.

measure of the Civil War's impact is to gauge differences between what might have been, and what came to be."[40]

Some scholars may reject any counterfactual hypothesis as unhistorical. However, the technique offers the historian one more valuable tool for explaining the past. By showing what might have happened but did not, one obtains a better understanding of why events occurred as they did. As Oscar Handlin once pointed out, many "ingredients . . . determine the zigzags of history; and the historian can begin to understand its course only when he perceives that it is a line made up of a succession of points, with every point a turning point. . . . But at any given point there is no inevitability to the direction of the turning."[41] The following counterfactual study is presented as plausibly as possible. But historical plausibility is not its most vital aspect. While Lincoln's victory in 1860 may seem inevitable to the present generation of historians, it was by no means so to Lincoln's contemporaries. Thus the fears over *Dred Scott*, *Lemmon*, and the "slaveocracy" must be accepted as real and justifiable in the minds of those who entertained them. What follows is an attempt to see the possibilities as they appeared to those who lived with them and thus to understand better why men such as Lincoln, Chase, and Greeley spoke and acted as they did.

Precedents for the Nationalization of Slavery

In nationalizing slavery the Supreme Court could have relied on doctrine and dictum developed in *Groves* v. *Slaughter, Prigg* v. *Pennsylvania, Strader* v. *Graham*, and *Dred Scott*. The court might have begun where Justice Nelson left off in his concurring opinion in *Dred Scott*. Nelson asserted that "except as restrained by the Federal Constitution" every state had "complete and absolute power over the subject" of slavery. Lincoln, of course, noted in his "House Divided Speech" that "[i]n what *cases* the power of the *states* is so restrained by the U.S. Constitution, is left an *open* question . . . which we may, ere long, see filled with another Supreme Court decision, declaring that the Constitution of the United States does not permit a *state* to exclude slavery from its limits."[42]

Nelson ended his opinion with an even more foreboding statement: "A question has been alluded to, on the argument, namely:

40. Hyman, *A More Perfect Union* 47.

41. Oscar Handlin, *Chance or Destiny: Turning Points in American History* (Boston: Little, Brown and Company, 1955) 211–12.

42. Basler, 2 *Works of Lincoln* 466–67; *Dred Scott* v. *Sandford*, 19 Howard 393, 459 (1857).

the right of the master with his slave of transit into or through a free State, on business or commercial pursuits, or in the exercise of a Federal right, or the discharge of a Federal duty, being a citizen of the United States. . . ." This question was not before the court, but as if asking for a chance to answer it and in the process to respond to Lincoln's inquiry of "what *cases*," Nelson concluded his opinion: "This question . . . turns upon the rights and privileges secured to a common citizen of the republic under the Constitution of the United States. *When that question arises, we shall be prepared to decide it*" [emphasis added].[43]

The *Lemmon* case would have presented such a question to the court. In reversing the New York Court of Appeals decision, the court could have taken the first step toward nationalizing slavery. The court could have found for the Lemmons on two separate grounds: first, New York's statute was an unconstitutional interference with interstate commerce; second, the statute was also an abridgment of the comity guarantees of article IV.

With respect to the Commerce Clause issue three questions need to be answered: (1) is transit commerce? (2) in what areas of interstate commerce may the states legislate? and (3) while the Commerce Clause gives Congress paramount power, does it also give Congress exclusive power generally, and in this case in particular?

In *Gibbons* v. *Ogden* (1824)[44] Chief Justice Marshall said, "Commerce, undoubtedly is traffic, but it is something more; it is intercourse." Justice Baldwin elaborated on this point in his concurring opinion in *Groves* v. *Slaughter* (1841):[45] " '[C]ommerce among the states,' as defined by this Court, is 'trade,' 'traffic,' 'intercourse,' and dealing in articles of commerce between states, by its own citizens or others, and carried on in more than one state." In the broadest sense, interstate commerce would include the movement of citizens with their property from one state to another.[46]

In *Gibbons* Marshall also thought the Commerce Clause applied to "all external concerns of the nation and to those internal concerns which affect the states generally; but not those which are completely within a particular state, which do not affect other states." This opinion was modified slightly in *Cooley* v. *Board of Wardens of the Port of Philadelphia* (1851),[47] the last important commerce case decided before the Civil War. Here the court recognized essentially two

43. *Dred Scott* v. *Sandford* 468–69.
44. *Gibbons* v. *Ogden*, 9 Wheaton (U.S.) 1 (1824).
45. *Groves et al.* v. *Slaughter*, 15 Peters, (U.S.) 449 (1841).
46. Ibid. 511.
47. *Cooley* v. *Board of Wardens of the Port of Philadelphia*, 12 Howard (U.S.) 299 (1851).

types of commerce. One was purely local and required local regulation, while the other was national in scope and would "imperatively demand a single uniform rule." The interstate movement of slaves was an important national issue, and it would not have been unreasonable for the court to hold that it demanded a "single uniform rule." Indeed, the court could have argued that without such a rule the normal interstate movement of people and goods might break down.[48]

Justice Denio's opinion in the New York Court of Appeals acknowledged "that the transportation of slaves from one slaveholding State to another is an act of inter-state commerce, which may be legally protected and regulated by federal legislation." He felt, however, that until Congress acted the states were free to pass their own regulatory legislation. The Supreme Court could have held the opposite and perhaps quoted from the *Passenger Cases* (1849):[49] "[That] the [commerce] power is exclusive seems to be as fully established as any other power under the Constitution which had been controverted." As Justice McLean warned in *Groves*, "[I]f a commercial power may be exercised by a state because it has not been exercised by Congress, the same rule must apply to other powers expressly delegated to the federal government." Indeed, the *Cooley* decision reaffirmed that where commerce "imperatively demand a single uniform rule," congressional power was exclusive.[50] The court might have ended this discussion by resurrecting Justice Baldwin's discussion of the problem in *Groves*:

> If, however, the owner of slaves in Maryland, in transporting them to Kentucky, or Missouri, should pass through Pennsylvania, or Ohio, no law of either state could take away or affect his right of property nor if passing from one slave state to another, accident or distress should compel him to touch at any place within a state where slavery did not exist. Such transit of property, whether of slaves or bales of goods, is lawful commerce among the several states, which none can prohibit or regulate, which the constitution protects, and Congress may and ought to preserve from violation. Any reasoning or principle which would authorize any state to interfere with such transit of a slave, would equally apply to a bale of cotton, or

48. Ibid. 299; see also *City of New York* v. *Miln*, 11 Peters (U.S.) 102 (1837), and *Passenger Cases*, 7 Howard (U.S.) 283 (1849).

49. *Lemmon* v. *The People* 614; *Passenger Cases*, 7 Howard (U.S.) 238 (1851).

50. *Passenger Cases* 408; *Groves* v. *Slaughter* 504; *Cooley* v. *Board of Wardens of Port of Philadelphia* 299.

cotton goods; and thus leave the whole commercial intercourse between the state liable to interruption or extinction by state laws, or constitutions.[51]

This position was later supported by *Prigg* and *Dred Scott*, which held that slaves were property, protected by the Constitution.

The court could also rely on article IV to determine what privileges and immunities a traveling slaveowner brought with him to a free state and what "public Acts, Records, and judicial Proceedings" of the slave states had to be given "Full Faith and Credit" by the free states.

Five major objections to applying article IV to slavery had been raised by counsel or the bench in *Lemmon*.

First, one nation had no obligation to grant comity to citizens of another nation. It was done as a matter of convenience or reciprocity, not as a matter of settled law.

Second, "under the principles of the law of nations" comity does not "require the recognition and support of the relation of slaveowner and slave between strangers passing through" a state or nation.[52]

Third, it was a settled rule of law that a chattel adheres to the person of the owner (*lex domicilii*); thus, "the municipal law which makes men the subject of property is limited with its territorial jurisdiction." So, if the owner took his slave into a free state, the slave would become free because slave law cannot follow the chattel across state lines.[53]

Fourth, while a state might "voluntarily concede that the foreign law shall operate within her jurisdiction," there could "be no application of the principles of comity, when the State absolutely refuses to recognize or give effect to the foreign law" as "being inconsistent with her own laws, and contrary to her policy."[54]

Finally, there was the assumption that the "provision in relation

51. *Groves* v. *Slaughter* 516.

52. *Lemmon* v. *The People* 595, 597.

53. Ibid. 598. Some southerners completely rejected this view. Senator John M. Berrien of Georgia believed, "Slavery exists in the State where the owner dwells; it exists out of the State where the owner dwells. Once existing, it exists everywhere, until it comes within limits of a sovereignty which inhibits it"; quoted in Arthur Bestor, "State Sovereignty and Slavery—A Reinterpretation of Proslavery Constitutional Doctrine, 1846–1860," 54 *Journal of Illinois State Historical Society* 165 (1961). By Berrien's reasoning, if the court were to strike down state laws inhibiting slavery, it would in fact become national. The Georgia statute at issue in *In re George Kirk*, 1 Parker Cr. R. (N.Y.) 67 (1846), was an application of this theory, in that Georgia expected its slave code to have an extraterritorial effect in New York. See chap. 5 of this volume.

54. *Lemmon* v. *The People* 628–29.

to fugitives from service, is the only one in the Constitution that, by an intendment, supports the right of a slave owner in his own state, or in any other state. This, by its own terms, is limited to its special case, and necessarily excludes federal intervention in every other." Viewing the Fugitive Slave Clause in this manner was "not unreasonable, as the owner" could "voluntarily permit his slave to go within" a free state, "but he could not always prevent his slaves from escaping." The clause and the Constitution "went no further" because it "would naturally be supposed that if there were other cases in which the rights of slave owners ought to be protected in the States which should abolish slavery, they would be adjusted in connection with the provision looking specially to that case."[55]

The first two objections could be easily dismissed. By signing the Constitution, the states had agreed to grant comity to citizens of other states. "The framers," as one present-day expert has noted, felt that "the rules of private international law should not be left as among the states altogether on the basis of comity . . . but ought to be in some measure at least placed on the higher plane of constitutional obligation." The states could not use international law as a model, since they were not separate nations, but political units of the same nation. As Justice Clerke argued in his dissent in *Lemmon*, foreign nations might act as they pleased, granting or not granting comity and risk "a valid cause for resort to the only method by which nations can obtain redress after remonstrance or negotiation fails." But

> the relations of the different States of this Union towards each other are of a much closer and more positive nature than those between foreign nations. . . . They are one nation; war between them is legally impossible; and this comity, impliedly recognized by the law of nations, ripens, in the compact cementing these States into an express conventional obligation, which is not to be enforced by an appeal to arms but to be recognized and enforced by the judicial tribunals.[56]

Thus, the right of transit with constitutionally protected property—which included slaves—was a right protected, not by comity, but by the federal compact.

The third and fourth objections could be settled by an examination of the meaning of "Privileges and Immunities" and "Full Faith and Credit." This would begin, no doubt, with a restatement of Justice Bushrod Washington's enumeration of the privileges and

55. Ibid. 624, 606.
56. Ibid. 642. Edwin S. Corwin, ed., *The Constitution of the United States of America* (Washington, D.C.: Government Printing Office, 1964) 740.

immunities of citizenship as those "which are in their nature, fundamental . . . Protection by the Government; the enjoyment of life and liberty, with the right to acquire property of every kind, and to pursue and obtain happiness and safety. . . . The right of a citizen of one state, to pass through, or reside in any other state, for purposes of trade, agriculture, professional pursuits, or otherwise . . . to institute and maintain actions of any kind in the courts of the State; to take, hold and dispose of property, either real or personal."[57]

Under this interpretation it would seem that slave property, like any other property, could be brought in and out of states. Indeed, as Justice Clerke argued in his dissent, the New York decision could "only be maintained on the supposition that the compact which binds the States together does not recognize the right to the labor and service of slaves as property." Because by the "positive compact which regulates the dealings and intercourse" of the States, "things belonging to the citizens of any one State, recognized as property by that compact, are exempt, in their passage through the territory of any other State, from all interference and control of the latter." The majority in *Lemmon* was wrong, because slaves were "incontestably recognized as property in the Constitution of the United States."[58]

Here Justice Story's understanding of article IV could have been applied. He felt "it must have been" inserted "to 'form a more perfect union,' and to give each State a higher security and confidence in the other by attributing a superior sanctity and conclusiveness to the public acts and judicial proceedings of all." Thus, the "States were united in an indissoluble bond with each other. The commercial and other intercourse with each other would be constant and infinitely diversified." Or, as Charles O'Conor had told the New York Court of Appeals, the Privileges and Immunities Clause was designed "to exempt him [Lemmon] from State power, not subject him to it." The section existed "to secure to the citizen, when within a State in which he is not domiciled, the general privileges and immunities which, in the very nature of citizenship, as recognized and established by the Federal Constitution belonging to that *status* [as a "Citizen of the United States"]; so that by no partial and adverse legislation of a State into which he might go as a stranger or sojourner can he be deprived of them."[59]

Although no direct reference was made to the Full Faith and Credit provision of article IV in *Lemmon*, it could certainly have

57. *Corfield* v. *Coryell*, 6 F. Cas. 450, 456 (1823).

58. *Lemmon* v. *The People*, 637, 641, 643.

59. Ibid. 580–81; Thomas R. R. Cobb, *An Inquiry into the Law of Negro Slavery in the United States of America* (Philadelphia: T. & J. W. Johnson and Company, 1858; Savannah: W. Thorne Williams, 1858) 193–95.

been used by the Supreme Court. A contemporary southern legal expert, Thomas R. R. Cobb, claimed, "[T]hat the words 'public acts' refer to the laws of the several States, is admitted by all commentators upon this clause." Justice Washington, in *Green* v. *Sarmiento* (1810)[60] stated that the clause "was intended to give to the judgments of each State, within the other States, a more extensive force and effect than the rule of the law founded on mere comity." A free state, under this ruling, could not free a slave within its jurisdiction, but instead would be obligated to recognize and enforce those laws of other states that condemned men to bondage.[61]

The answer to the fifth objection was suggested by the objection itself. A provision was needed to secure fugitive slaves because there was some question as to their status. However, from the slaveowners' viewpoint no question arose about the status of slaves in the physical presence of a master, traveling in a free state. If they misbehaved or escaped, the master was there to punish or capture them. A special passage in the Constitution to allow slaveowners to bring their property with them while visiting the free states was not needed. This was taken for granted because it was common practice. The court could cite the early laws and decisions of Pennsylvania, Massachusetts, New York, New Jersey, Rhode Island, and Connecticut to show that in 1787 there was no need for a special clause protecting interstate transit with slaves because that right was freely given. Indeed, the court reviewing *Lemmon* could ask, if this were not the case in 1787 then why did the South agree to union in the first place? Indeed, why did any of the ten or eleven slave states agree to form a "more perfect union" if this right had not been secure?

With such reasoning, the Supreme Court could have reversed the decision in *Lemmon* and perhaps ordered New York to compensate the Lemmons for the loss of their slaves. The slaves themselves had been in Canada since shortly after they were freed by Judge Paine in 1852. In the future, slaveowners would have the right of transit,

---

60. *Green* v. *Sarmiento*, 10 F. Cas. 1117 (1810).

61. Ibid.; Cobb, *Inquiry* 189, 194; In the post–Civil War case of *Chicago & Alton Railroad* v. *Wiggins Ferry Co.*, 119 U.S. 615, 622 (1887), the U.S. Supreme Court came to just this conclusion. The court found that "[w]ithout doubt the constitutional requirement" of granting Full Faith and Credit implied "that the public acts of every State shall be given the same effect by the courts of another State that they have by law and usage at home." Although decided after the war, this decision was not based on any of the Civil War amendments and thus could have been reached by the Taney court. Had the court reached such a decision before the war, northern states would have been compelled to recognize the public acts of the South that created slavery. But under *Dred Scott*, southern states would not have been required to recognize the rights of free blacks.

with their human property, through any state in the Union. They could bring their slaves on business and pleasure trips, provided they remained in transit.

Successor Cases to *Lemmon*

It is possible to envision a long series of successor cases coming before the court. By suggesting one likely possibility and its outcome, the general trend of court decisions that Lincoln and others feared can be discerned.

Assume that a southern naval officer, assigned to the port of Boston, brought his slaves with him. Dred Scott's master was an Army officer, and other members of the military were often in such situations. At one time the Pennsylvania legislature was asked to consider amending the exemption from the six-months law that congressmen enjoyed to include other officers of the government, including, no doubt, military officers. It appears not to have been uncommon for military officers to bring slaves with them. Assume, further, that after a short time in Boston, the naval officer's slaves sued for their freedom and won. Assuming that the federal constitutional questions were properly raised by the naval officer, the case could be appealed directly from the Massachusetts Supreme Judicial Court to the Supreme Court of the United States.

The court could rely on its previous decisions in *Dred Scott, Lemmon,* and other cases to find for the naval officer. It would be possible to show that, as a military officer, the master was not a resident of Massachusetts and never intended to become one. Rather, he was only a temporary visitor and would remain so, even if he were stationed in Boston for twenty years. In this and *any other* residence case, temporal definitions of residence would be impossible. A United States citizen had the right to spend months, or even years, away from his home and still retain his home state citizenship. Indeed, the *Washington Union* had already argued that no matter how long a master stayed in a free state—even if he moved there to reside permanently—it would be unconstitutional for the free state to free his slaves.[62] If this reasoning—the "authoritative" reasoning of the Buchanan administration—were adopted by the court, then slaveholding, if not slavery itself, would be legal for anyone moving to a free state from a slave state.

In reaching such a decision, the Supreme Court would find Justice McLean's opinion in *Vaughn* v. *Williams* (1845) helpful.[63] In that

62. *Washington Union*, 17 Nov. 1857.
63. *Vaughn* v. *Williams*, 28 F. Cas. 1115 (1845).

case McLean affirmed "the principle that an owner of slaves who takes them into a non-slaveholding State, keeps them at labor for six months, announces his determination to become a resident of such state, and in pursuance thereof casts his vote at elections, thereby forfeits his right to them as slaves."[64] The declaration of "determination" combined with the act of voting caused the owner to lose his slaves. Thus, it could logically follow that if a slaveholder declared he had no intention of becoming a resident of a free state he could remain a sojourner and could retain his slaves.

After the "naval captain" case a master might go anywhere with his slaves and stay for an indefinite period of time. In order to be able to free slaves, a state would have to prove that the owner was actually a resident and was fraudulently trying to evade state law in order to keep his slaves.[65]

Another successor case could give masters even more rights. Imagine that several Virginians bought an iron foundry in Pennsylvania and used their slaves as workers. Every Christmas the foundry was closed for three weeks, and the slaves returned to Virginia.

Pennsylvania would claim that the slaves were residents of that state and should be freed. A proslavery Supreme Court might disagree, on the grounds that slaves were not legally persons and therefore could not be residents.[66] Only their owners might be residents, and they were clearly still residents and citizens of Virginia. Indeed, if the privileges and immunities of citizenship allowed "a citizen of one State" to travel in the other states and "to take, hold and dispose of property, either real or personal," then the Virginians would have had the right profitably to employ their slaves in Pennsylvania. What good, the court might ask, would article IV be if masters could take their slave property with them, but not make use of it? An industrial use of a slave was no different from a personal use, which had already been upheld in the "naval captain" case.

If the Privileges and Immunities Clause allowed the slaveowner to "take" and "hold" property, it also allowed him to "dispose of

64. Ibid. 1118.

65. *Arnold* v. *Marshal of the United States*, 1 F. Cas. 1181 (1828), held that a Rhode Island citizen could own a plantation in Georgia, spend his winters there, and still maintain his Rhode Island citizenship. Reversing these facts, it would be possible for a citizen of Georgia to spend most of his time in Rhode Island, or any other free state, and maintain his Georgia citizenship. This position would again be supported by the doctrine of *Vaughn* v. *Williams*.

66. For a contemporary Virginia decision supporting this position, see *Bailey & als.* v. *Poindexter's ex'or*, 12 Grat. (Va.) 132 (1858). There the Virginia Supreme Court held that slaves are "persons whose *status* or condition in legal definition and intendment exists in the denial to them of the attributes of any social or civil capacity whatever" (at 198).

property." Salmon P. Chase feared that a reversal in *Lemmon* would be "a decision in favor . . . of the American slave trade, to be carried on in the free states," while Horace Greeley predicted, "[W]e shall see men buying slaves for the New York market. There will be no legal power to prevent it."[67]

It is of course difficult for twentieth-century historians to view these fears as anything less than extreme paranoia. But in the 1850s practical and successful politicians believed them. Northerners could envision that the Taney court might rely on the Commerce Clause and the Privileges and Immunities Clause to uphold contracts for slaves sold in the free states. As a form of interstate trade, the court might declare that Congress had paramount and exclusive jurisdiction over the subject. Such a position would invalidate all state statutes prohibiting the trade, which would allow Congress to control or abolish the trade; until Congress acted, however, there could be no regulation whatsoever. Such an interpretation had been advanced by antislavery leaders who wished Congress to abolish the interstate slave trade. It could certainly be advanced by a proslavery court, which saw no chance that Congress would pass a restrictive law or that any president would sign it. And, in the 1850s such a decision appeared to have the support of the incumbent president, James Buchanan. His own organ, the *Washington Union*, had declared that all laws freeing slaves were "*a gross outrage on the rights of property.*"[68]

Thus, with the support of the White House, some northerners could even foresee the time when there would be both slaves and a slave trade in the free states. The buying and selling of slaves in the North of course would have been limited. Public opinion would have dictated that. Indeed, it is unlikely that anyone seriously thought a full-blown slave system could be forced on the North, or that it could be economically or culturally viable there. Few slaveowners would have risked their property by sending slaves to the North to be sold. But one or two might try it, just to assert their "rights." Indeed, if men were willing to die for the abstract right to bring slaves into Kansas, they might be equally willing to risk some of their property to protect their rights in the North. In the process New York might see the slave "market" that Horace Greeley feared.[69]

67. Speech by Chase in *New York Evening Post*, 31 Aug. 1859; Greeley, quoted in Foner, *Free Soil, Free Labor, Free Men* 98.

68. *Washington Union*, 17 Nov. 1857. Reprinted in *Congressional Globe*, 35th Cong., 1st sess., at 199. Emphasis in *Congressional Globe*.

69. For another view of this problem, involving the Migration and Importation Clause (Slave Trade Clause) of art. I, sec. 9, see Walter Berns, "The Constitution and the Migration of Slaves," 78 *Yale Law Journal* 198–228 (1968). Although Berns discusses an antislavery use of this clause to end the interstate slave trade, it could

The Supreme Court might have found it difficult to accept all the arguments postulated here. Members of the court, including Taney, might have been reluctant to push their proslavery ideologies and constitutional interpretations too far, for fear that it would lead to too severe a backlash in the North. Indeed, it may seem "incredible," as David Potter put it, "that nine sane justices could have contemplated" any decision nationalizing slavery. But, as Potter notes, before the *Dred Scott* decision "it might have seemed incredible that the Court could deny the power of Congress to regulate slavery in the territories. . . ." There was clearly no conspiracy to bring the hypothetical cases before the Supreme Court or to nationalize slavery. But precedent-setting cases, such as *Dred Scott* or *Lemmon* v. *The People*, are not always planned. They sometimes simply evolve out of the claims of individual litigants. Indeed, courts are often faced with decisions they would rather not make. Lord Mansfield, for example, suggested that the slave Somerset be liberated so the case would be mooted and not become a precedent.[70] Thus, even without a conspiracy of the "slaveocracy" and certainly without a conspiracy of Supreme Court justices, the possibility of nationalizing slavery through successive Supreme Court decisions might have existed. And whether that possibility actually existed or not, many northerners believed that it did.

Parts of this scenario, especially a successful appeal in *Lemmon*, could have been acted out if the Democrats had maintained power in the 1860s as they had done through most of the previous decade. At some point the logic of Stephen A. Douglas's "Freeport Doctrine" would have taken over, and slavery would have become untenable because of a lack of northern slave codes to support the institution. Slavery could not be maintained without popular and legal support, which did not generally exist in the North. And it would have been unrealistic to think that many slaveowners would have even wished

---

also have been used by a proslavery court. There would have been great difficulty in buying slaves in the North if free-state courts refused to enforce contracts for them. However, if such sales and contracts involved interstate commerce, they could be enforced in federal courts. For elaboration of this point, see Paul Finkelman, "The Nationalization of Slavery: A Counterfactual Approach to the 1860s," 14 *Louisiana Studies* [now *Southern Studies*] 235–37 (1975).

70. Potter, *The Impending Crisis* 351; William M. Wiecek, "*Somerset*: Lord Mansfield and the Legitimacy of Slavery in the Anglo-American World," 42 *University of Chicago Law Review* 102 (1974). See also Walter Ehrlich, *They Have No Rights: Dred Scott's Struggle for Freedom* (Westport, Conn.: Greenwood Press, 1979) 56, for a discussion of why *Dred Scott* was appealed to the Missouri Supreme Court. Ehrlich argues that as a "shrewd and prosperous businessman" John F. A. Sanford "was not going to lose property when he thought there was a good chance to retain it."

to force a complete slave system on the North.[71] But they would all want their constitutionally protected rights of transit and sojourn. For many northerners, however, enforcement of those rights would have been tantamount to making slavery "lawful in *all* the states." As long as a Democratic president could veto adverse legislation and appoint sympathetic justices, and as long as presidential vetoes would be sustained in the Senate, slavery could slowly spread to the North. Such were the fears of those who had lived through a recent past that included the Compromise of 1850, which nullified the habeas corpus rights of blacks in the North; the Kansas-Nebraska Act, which opened "free" territories to slavery; and *Dred Scott*, which denied blacks any rights under the Constitution and threatened freedom everywhere. Finally, the Supreme Court decision in *Ableman* v. *Booth and United States* v. *Booth* (1858)[72] showed that federal enforcement of the Fugitive Slave Law of 1850 could adversely affect whites as well as blacks.

States' Rights and Slavery

The decisions postulated here depart from the most basic tenet of the slaveocracy's ideology—states' rights. But decisions of the courts at the state and federal levels suggest that the states' rights doctrine, at least in the antebellum period, was often a two-edged sword, used by both proslavery and antislavery advocates. Indeed, states' rights was simply a philosophical screen to protect the South's real ideology—the maintenance of slavery. The issue was a convenient tool for rhetorical debates, easily discarded when no longer useful. Slavery, after all, and not states' rights, was "the cornerstone" of the Confederacy.

Thus, one has Justice Baldwin's strong federalist position in *Groves* v. *Slaughter*, Story's notion of a federally protected right of recaption of fugitive slaves in *Prigg*, and Taney's notion of "federal citizenship," which he denied to blacks in *Dred Scott*. Lastly, there is Taney's decision for a unanimous court in *Ableman* v. *Booth*. Here

71. Senator Robert Toombs made this argument in rebuttal to attacks on the *Washington Union* editorial; *Congressional Globe*, 35th Cong., 1st sess., app., at 203–4. Francis Lieber, a man who dearly loved the Union, nevertheless thought that encroachments by the South might eventually force the North to secede. This had of course been advocated by Garrisonian abolitionists for many years. That a unionist like Lieber would also consider it a realistic possibility indicates the depth of despair northerners felt after *Dred Scott*. For an analysis of Lieber's thinking, see Phillip S. Paludan, *A Covenant with Death: The Constitution, Law, and Equality in the Civil War Era* (Urbana: University of Illinois Press, 1975), especially 80–84.

72. *Ableman* v. *Booth and United States* v. *Booth*, 21 Howard 506 (1859).

Taney reprimanded a recalcitrant Wisconsin Supreme Court, which had released Booth, an abolitionist convicted of violating the Fugitive Slave Law. Taney's response to the states' rights position of the Wisconsin court was that such "propositions" were "new in the jurisprudence of the United States, as well as of the States." According to Taney, the founders felt the federal government "should be supreme, and strong enough to execute its laws by its own tribunals, without interruption from a State or from State authorities. . . . The language of the Constitution, by which power is granted, is too plain to admit of doubt or to need comment," for "the supremacy thus conferred on this Government could not peacefully be maintained, unless it was clothed with judicial power, equally paramount in authority to carry it into execution." Each state was pledged "*to support this Constitution.* And no power is more clearly conferred than the power of this court to decide ultimately and finally, all cases arising under such Constitution and laws."[73]

Such an emphatic defense of federal power was inconsistent with the states' rights philosophy of Taney's previous decisions. However, it was consistent with his previous defenses of slavery and with an interpretation of the Constitution as a slaveholder's document. Indeed, if the Constitution did support and protect slavery, as the court asserted, then forever after the South could logically support a strong federalist system. As long as the South could veto legislation and amendments that might threaten slavery, the South would want a strong central power, like the court, to protect and spread its institution. Powers held exclusively by Congress—for example, the regulation of the interstate movement of slaves—which could never be implemented against slavery, were well suited to the South's need.[74]

Starting in the 1830s the South found its "peculiar institution" under increasing attack from the North and the rest of the world. Outnumbered (although often neither outmaneuvered nor outvoted) in Congress, southerners looked to new sources for protection of slavery. In the federal courts they found a willing and creative ally in the person of Chief Justice Taney. By 1860, the Republican accusation that the Supreme Court was "the very citadel of American slavery" had much merit.[75]

73. Ibid. 541, 517, 525.

74. Arthur Bestor, "State Sovereignty and Slavery," argues (at 140–41) that Taney's opinion applied only to the supremacy of the federal judiciary. Taney was indeed strengthening the judiciary, but by implication he was giving the executive power to implement Supreme Court decrees. In taking more power for the judiciary, Taney was taking power away from the states. Thus, he was laying the groundwork for the decisions that could have led to a nationalization of slavery.

75. Potter, *The Impending Crisis* 294.

Taney saw slavery as a constitutionally sanctioned institution, which in some cases needed special protection not given to other forms of property. In *Dred Scott* he declared this protection to be the law of the land. In *Ableman* v. *Booth* he warned against state interference with those federal laws that protected slavery. The direction in which Taney was headed was clear.[76] *Lemmon* and the cases that might follow it threatened to push some form of slavery into the North. The fears of Lincoln and other Republicans on this issue were neither absurd nor unfounded. Rather, they reflected an analysis of the trend of events up to 1860. Republicans understood that comity and federalism would ultimately lead to a nation that was either all free or all slave. Ironically, it was the political success of that party in 1860 that makes Republican fears seem so unfounded. Fortunately, the election of Lincoln in 1860 averted the "tendency to the latter condition" that Lincoln and his party feared.

76. Unpublished (and often illegible) notes and drafts indicate that Taney may have already been preparing to write an opinion in *Lemmon* or a similar case, should one reach the court. Among other things, Taney wrote of an "obligation of all to respect the institution of slavery" and that the "free states of the union" had a "far greater" "obligation" to respect slavery than did European nations, who needed to respect it only out of comity. See "Oddments" file, Roger B. Taney Papers, (LC). See also Wiecek, *"Somerset"* 139. I am particularly grateful to Professor Wiecek for providing copies of the material he obtained from the Taney papers. A somewhat similar approach to this question has been taken by Harry Jaffa, *Crisis of the House Divided: An Interpretation of the Issues in the Lincoln-Douglas Debates* (Garden City, N.Y.: Doubleday and Company, 1959) 293.

Epilogue

From Comity to Civil War

At the time of the nation's Founding the new American states freely granted comity in cases involving sojourning slaves or those in transit. Some of the emerging free states, such as Pennsylvania and Connecticut, gave explicit statutory protection to slave property from other states. Those northern states not offering written guarantees nevertheless did not interfere with the master-slave relationship of visitors. In the South slaves were freed if they could establish a legitimate claim to the new status based on sojourn, residence, and sometimes even travel, in a free state.

The motivations for the slave-state policies were threefold. First, these motivations were supported by the common law of the nation as inherited from England. The implications of the *Somerset* decision—that a slave who touched free soil became free—were understood to be part of the common law of all the American states. Indeed, the arguments surrounding the Fugitive Slave Clause of the Constitution reveal an implicit acceptance of the *Somerset* rule that free states could free all slaves entering their domain, no matter how they arrived. Thus, in freeing slaves who had lived in or visited the North, southern courts were simply applying the law as they understood it. Second, they were supporting comity and interstate harmony. This in itself was an important reason for the early southern decisions. Finally, the willingness of southern courts to grant comity reflects an ambivalence toward slavery found in much of the South until at least the 1830s. In some southern courts this ambivalence lasted much longer, since the courts did not always reflect political and intellectual changes as quickly as the rest of the society.

The change in southern decision making is not difficult to understand. In the 1830s ambivalence over the morality or justice of slavery began to disappear. A notion that slavery was worthwhile—that it was a "positive good" for blacks as well as whites—replaced the libertarian ideology of an early generation of slaveholders. Acceptance of the "positive good" theory of slavery led to a rejection of the common law inheritance that placed such a high value on freedom and liberty for all men. Finally, comity with the free states began to lose some of its attractiveness as southerners saw their institutions attacked and vilified in the North. Gradually *Somerset* was exorcised from the legal heritage of most of the South. The South rejected its precedents that leaned toward freedom and at the same time moved more and more toward separation from the North. Southern decisions rejecting comity and cooperation helped pave the way to the dissolution of the Union in 1861.

From Comity to Freedom

For the North the process was similar to that in the South, but the motivations and results were in some ways reversed. In the beginning the North strove for comity, as did the South. But in the North this comity could be achieved only through the express rejection of *Somerset* and other common-law decisions favoring freedom. Comity and harmony within the Union were more important than the freedom of a few slaves or the adherence to basic principles found in common law and the free-state constitutions. A temporary suspension of the law of freedom in the North was a reasonable concession to make for the advantages of the Union. Underlying these concessions was a belief in the North that at some point the South would take steps to end slavery. The North looked forward to a time when the law of freedom could be reinstated without threatening the Union.

By the mid-1830s it was clear that slavery would not die out anytime soon. On the contrary, the new and aggressive proslavery ideology had replaced the more ambivalent southern position of the previous generation. At the same time, an aggressive antislavery movement began to pressure northern legislatures and courts to deny comity to the "peculiar institution." By 1860 these demands had succeeded in most of the North. Slaveholders found themselves unable to travel freely with their most precious possessions—their slaves. In these twenty-five years a minor revolution took place in northern jurisprudence. Comity, once freely granted, was now explicitly denied: transit with slaves was forbidden.

Two major factors led to this change. First, and most obvious, was the growth of the antislavery movement in the North. The revitalized antislavery movement of the 1830s brought cases before the bar and petitions to the legislatures to change the existing policies. In Massachusetts, for example, the precedent-setting *Aves* case was a direct result of abolitionist activism. In addition to the organized antislavery movement, strong sentiment grew against human bondage throughout the North. Even those who rejected extreme antislavery doctrine and were hostile to the abolitionist movement disliked the peculiar institution. Lawyers, judges, politicians, and citizens at large found slavery distasteful even if they were unwilling to oppose it actively. Later, in the mid-1840s and throughout the next decade, hostility to slavery merged with a general opposition to the South and the expansion of slavery into the new western territories. Republican politicians of the 1850s who were not abolitionists (indeed, few would so have classified themselves) feared that slavery would be pushed into the territories and then into the North itself: that a "slave power conspiracy" would lead to a "nationalization of slavery." Opposition to slave transit in the North was an important and critical way of preventing slavery's expansion. Whether one wanted to end slavery immediately (the abolitionist position) or simply halt its spread (the Republican position), the desirability of prohibiting all forms of slavery from the free states was clear. This led directly to the second factor in the movement away from comity in the North: the nature of the common law freedom in the North.

At the nation's Founding the *Somerset* decision was technically part of the common law of the former British colonies. In granting comity to visiting slaveholders the free states were explicitly rejecting (or at least suspending) their common law in favor of national harmony. In many cases the emerging free states were also rejecting—or suspending—parts of their constitutions and natural rights heritage. When the courts in the free states changed their decision making they were simply returning to the law as it had been—and as it theoretically should have remained—all along. When Chief Justice Shaw ruled in *Commonwealth* v. *Aves* that a slave voluntarily brought into Massachusetts was free, he was not creating new law; rather, he was returning the law of Massachusetts to its earlier philosophical position. Indeed, Shaw was surprised to discover that his decision was novel or precedent setting.

The jurisprudential change regarding slavery and comity in the North bears two interpretations. First, it may be viewed as a revolution in decision making, a dramatic reversal of precedent. This interpretation supports the notion of an effective antislavery movement converting judiciaries and legislatures to its views; or, if not converting these bodies, the antislavery movement at least put enough pressure on them to force a change in the law. From the radical perspective of the Garrisonian abolitionists the decision in *Aves* and its progeny was a great victory. The Garrisonians, after all, considered the Constitution to be a "covenant with death" and an "agreement in Hell." They argued for separation from the slave states—disunion—as the only morally correct method of resolving the contradiction created by their union under a Constitution that allowed slavery. The denial of comity could symbolize disunion and even spur it on. Not surprisingly, the Garrisonians were extremely active in pursuing transit cases. *Aves* was in court because of their activities.

A second way to interpret the change in northern decision making implies that the change was neither radical nor disunionist. Rather, it was a return to the law, the Constitution, and federalism as they were and should have remained. It was a partial acceptance of the antislavery constitutionalism of such men as Salmon P. Chase and William Jay. At the very least, this school of thought argued that the Constitution was neutral on the issue of slavery. More often, exponents of this position suggested that the Constitution was anti-slavery in spirit and could be applied that way in many cases, including those involving transit.

Both of these interpretations suggest a victory for antislavery activists in the northern denial of comity. Ultimately the more political abolitionists won the great victory. They, and their positions, were partially adopted by the Republican party. The denial of comity to slavery and the assertion of the law of freedom in the North became part of the larger movement to stop the spread of slavery. The political arguments generated by this movement helped elect Lincoln and that in turn led to secession, civil war, and emancipation.

The question of comity for slavery helped define the issues and problems that ultimately led to the Civil War. These issues also helped define the goals of the war and shaped its consequences. Much of the wording of the Fourteenth Amendment appears to be a direct response to the issues raised by the cases involving comity and interstate relations before the war. Perhaps the most important legacy of *Aves*, *Dred Scott*, *Lemmon*, and the other antebellum comity cases is this amendment. The men who witnessed these cases and others drafted an amendment that not only made freedmen citizens, but also demanded that their privileges and immunities be respected nationwide. In making the freedmen citizens of the nation, the amendment overruled *Dred Scott* and guaranteed the ex-slaves certain minimal federal rights. In making the freedmen citizens of the states in which they resided, the amendment accomplished two important goals. First, it required that the individual states recognize the rights of citizenship and therefore grant comity to blacks entering from other states. No longer could a southern state imprison a free black sailor from the North or, indeed, prohibit free blacks from entering their domain. Second, and perhaps even more important, the Fourteenth Amendment required that the states treat their black citizens as equals under the law, giving them due process and equal protection. Although it would take many years and a different generation of lawmakers and activists to enforce these regulations, the guarantees were written and waiting to be used. The lawmakers of the Civil War era knew that comity and harmony within the Union were possible only if there was equality.

Bibliography

The most important primary sources for this study were the reports of the state appellate courts. Most of these reports are available, state by state, in any good library. In addition, a number of other legal sources were used, including casebooks, treatises, and law journals. This material was supplemented with archival material whenever possible. The bibliography has been organized as appropriate for a book that is primarily a work in legal history. The first section contains important legal sources. It is followed by a list of pamphlets dealing with specific cases.

Legal Materials

American Jurist
American Law Journal
American Law Register
Catterall, Helen Tunnicliff. *Judicial Cases concerning American Slavery and the Negro*. 5 vols. Washington: Carnegie Institution, 1926–37.
Cobb, Thomas R. R. *An Inquiry into the Law of Negro Slavery in the United States of America*. Philadelphia: T. & J. W. Johnson and Company, 1858. Savannah: W. Thorne Williams, 1858.
Code Noir, ou Recueil d'Edits, Declarations et Arrets Concernant les Esclaves Négres de l'Amérique. Paris: Ches les Libraires Associez, 1743.
Huber, Ulric. *The Jurisprudence of My Time. (Heedensdaegse Rechts-geleertheyt.)* Translated by Percival Gane. 2 vols. Durban, South Africa: Buttersworth, 1939.
Hurd, John Codman. *The Law of Freedom and Bondage in the United States*. 2 vols. Boston: Little, Brown, 1862.
Kent, James. *Commentaries on American Law*. 4 vols. 5th ed. New York, 1844.
McBride, David N., and McBride, Jane N., eds. *Common Pleas Court Records of Highland County, Ohio (1805–1860)*. Ann Arbor: Edwards Letter Shop, 1959.
Monthly Law Reporter.
New York Legal Observer
Pennsylvania Law Journal
Pollack, Ervin H., ed. *Ohio Unreported Judicial Decisions Prior to 1823*. Indianapolis: Allen Smith Company, n.d.
Story, Joseph. *Commentaries on the Conflict of Laws*. 1st ed. Boston: Hilliard, Gray and Company, 1834.
Weekly Law Gazette
Western Law Journal

Western Legal Observer
Wheeler, Jacob. *A Practical Treatise on the Law of Slavery.* New York: Allan Pollock, Jr., 1837.

Reports of Cases

Benton, Thomas Hart. *Historical and Legal Examination of that part of the Decision of the Supreme Court of the United States in the Dred Scott Case, which declares the Unconstitutionality of the Missouri Compromise Act, and the Self-Extension of the Constitution to Territories, Carrying Slavery Along With It.* New York: D. Appleton and Company, 1857.

Birney, James G. *Examination of the Decision of the Supreme Court of the United States, in the Case of Strader, Gorman and Armstrong vs. Christopher Graham.* Cincinnati: Truman and Spofford, 1852.

Boston Female Anti-Slavery Society. *Right and Wrong in Boston #2: Annual Report of the Boston Female Anti-Slavery Society Being a Concise History of the Case of the Slave-Child Med.* Boston: Isaac Knapp, 1836.

Case of the Slave-Child Med: A Report of the Arguments of Counsel and of the Opinion of the Court in the Case of Commonwealth vs. Aves. Boston: Isaac Knapp, 1836.

Chase, Salmon Portland. *Reclamation of Fugitives from Service.* Cincinnati: R. P. Donogh and Company, 1847.

Chase, Salmon Portland. *Speech of Salmon Portland Chase in the Case of the Colored Woman Matilda.* Cincinnati: Pugh and Dodd, 1837.

Hildreth, Richard, ed. Lord John Campbell, *Lives of Atrocious Judges: Lives of Judges Infamous As Tools of Tyrants and Instruments of Oppression.* New York and Auburn: Miller, Orton, and Mulligan, 1856.

Holden Anti-Slavery Society. *Report of the Holden Slave Case.* Worcester: Colton and Howland, 1839.

Kane, John K. *Case of Passmore Williamson.* Philadelphia: Uriah Hunt and Son, 1856.

Narrative of the Facts in the Case of Passmore Williamson. Philadelphia: Pennsylvania Anti-Slavery Society, 1855.

New York Legal Observer. Report of the Case in the matter of George Kirk, A Fugitive Slave. New York: Legal Observer, 1847.

Report of the Lemmon Slave Case. New York: W. H. Tinson, 1860.

The State of Ohio vs. Forbes and Armitage, Arrested Upon the Requisition of the Government of Ohio on Charge of Kidnapping Jerry Phinney, and Tried before the Franklin Circuit Court of Kentucky, April 10, 1846. N.p., 1846.

Manuscript Sources

Attorney General's Papers, National Archives. Washington.
George Bryan Papers. Historical Society of Pennsylvania. Philadelphia.
John D. Caton Papers. Library of Congress. Washington.
Salmon P. Chase Papers. Historical Society of Pennsylvania. Philadelphia.
Salmon P. Chase Papers. Library of Congress. Washington.
Edwin Clarke Papers. New-York Historical Society. New York.
Edward Carey Gardiner Papers. Historical Society of Pennsylvania.
Philadelphia.
Jay Family Papers. Columbia University. New York.
Ellis Gray Loring Papers. Houghton Library, Harvard University.
Cambridge, Massachusetts.
Pennsylvania Abolition Society Papers, Microfilm ed. Historical Society of
Pennsylvania. Philadelphia.
Charles Sumner Papers. Houghton Library. Harvard University. Cam-
bridge, Massachusetts.
Roger B. Taney Papers. Library of Congress. Washington.
Western Anti-Slavery Society Minutebook. Library of Congress. Wash-
ington.

Other Contemporary Materials

*An Account of the Interviews Which Took Place . . . Between a Committee of
the Massachusetts Anti-Slavery Society and a Committee of the
Legislature.* Boston: Massachusetts Anti-Slavery Society, 1836.
Angle, Paul M., ed. *Created Equal? The Complete Lincoln-Douglas Debates
of 1858.* Chicago: University of Chicago Press, 1958.
Barnes, Gilbert Hobbs, and Dumond, Dwight L., eds. *Letters of Theodore
Dwight Weld, Angelina Grimké Weld, and Sarah Grimké, 1822–1844.* 2
vols. New York: Appleton-Crofts-Century, 1934.
Basler, Roy P., ed. *The Collected Works of Abraham Lincoln.* 9 vols. New
Brunswick, N.J.: Rutgers University Press, 1953–55.
Benton, Thomas Hart. *Thirty Years View.* 2 vols. New York: D. Appleton,
1857.
Chase, Salmon P., and Cleveland, Charles Dexter. *Anti-Slavery Addresses
of 1844 and 1845.* Philadelphia: J. A. Bancroft, 1867.
Coffin, Levi. *Reminiscences.* Cincinnati: Western Tract Society, 1876.
Curtis, Benjamin R., ed. *A Memoir of Benjamin Robbins Curtis.* 2 vols.
Boston: Little, Brown, 1879.
Dumond, Dwight L. *The Letters of James Gillespie Birney, 1831–1857.* 2
vols. New York: D. Appleton-Century, 1938.
Elliot, Jonathan, ed. *The Debates in the Several State Conventions on the
Adoption of the Federal Constitution as Recommended by the General
Convention at Philadelphia, in 1787.* 5 vols. Philadelphia: J. B.
Lippincott, 1896.

Farrand, Max, ed. *The Records of the Federal Convention of 1787.* 4 vols. New Haven: Yale University Press, 1937.

The First Annual Report of the New York Committee of Vigilance. New York: Piercy and Reed, 1837.

Fitzhugh, George. *The Sociology of the South, or the Failure of Free Society.* Richmond, 1854.

Fitzpatrick, J. C., ed. *The Writings of George Washington.* 39 vols. Washington: Government Printing Office, 1931–44.

Foner, Philip S., ed. *The Life and Writings of Frederick Douglass.* 4 vols. New York: International Publishers, 1950–55.

Hoar, George Frisbie, ed. *Charles Sumner: His Complete Works.* 20 vols. New York: Negro Universities Press, 1969.

Journal of the Congress of the Confederate States of America, 1861–1865. 7 vols. Washington: Government Printing Office, 1904–05.

Julian, George W. *Political Recollections, 1840 to 1872.* Chicago: Jansen, McClurg, 1884.

Lincoln, Charles Z., ed. *State of New York: Messages of the Governors.* 11 vols. Albany: J. P. Lyon Company, 1909.

Massachusetts Anti-Slavery Society. *Fifth Annual Report, 1837.* Boston: Isaac Knapp, 1837.

Needles, Edward. *An Historical Memoir of the Pennsylvania Society for Promoting the Abolition of Slavery.* Philadelphia: Merrihew and Thompson, 1848.

Nevins, Allan, and Thomas, Milton Halsey, eds. *The Diary of George Templeton Strong.* 4 vols. New York: Farrar, Straus, and Giroux, 1974.

Parrish, John. *Remarks on the Slavery of Black People.* Philadelphia: printed for the author, by Kimber, Conrad and Company, 1806.

Pennsylvania General Assembly. House of Representatives. Committee on the Judiciary. *Minority Report in Relation to the Rights of Transit of Slave Property Through This State.* [Philadelphia?], 1856.

Proceedings of the Anti-Slavery Convention of American Women Held in the City of New York, 1837. New York: William S. Dorr, 1837.

Report of the Committee on the Judiciary of the House of Representatives of Pennsylvania in Relation to the Rights of Transit of Slave Property Through This State. Harrisburg: N.p., 1856.

Rossiter, Clinton, ed. *The Federalist Papers.* New York: The New American Library, 1961.

Ruchames, Louis, and Merrill, Walter M., eds. *The Letters of William Lloyd Garrison.* 6 vols. Cambridge: Harvard University Press, 1971.

Schuckers, J. W. *The Life and Public Services of Salmon Portland Chase.* New York: D. Appleton and Company, 1884.

Seward, Frederick W. *William H. Seward: An Autobiography from 1801 to 1834 with a Memoir of His Life and Selections from His Letters, from 1831 to 1846.* New York: D. Appleton and Company, 1877.

Story, William W., ed. *Life and Letters of Joseph Story.* 2 vols. Boston: Little, Brown, 1851.

Warden, Robert B. *An Account of the Private Life and Public Services of Salmon Portland Chase.* Cincinnati: Wilstach, Baldwin, 1874.

Whittier, John G., ed. *Letters of Lydia Maria Child with a Biographical Introduction.* Boston: Houghton, Mifflin and Company, 1883.

Articles

"American Slavery and the Conflict of Laws." 71 *Columbia Law Review* 74–99 (Jan. 1971).
Arnold, Richard S. "The Power of State Courts to Enjoin Federal Officers." 73 *Yale Law Journal* 1385–1406 (1964).
Berns, Walter. "The Constitution and the Migration of Slaves." 78 *Yale Law Journal* 198–228 (Dec. 1968).
Bestor, Arthur. "The American Civil War as a Constitutional Crisis." 19 *American Historical Review* 325–52 (1964).
_____. "State Sovereignty and Slavery—A Reinterpretation of Proslavery Constitutional Doctrine, 1846–1860." 54 *Journal of Illinois State Historical Society* 117–80 (Summer 1961).
Bettle, Edward. "Notices of Negro Slavery as Connected with Pennsylvania." 1 *Memoirs of the Historical Society of Pennsylvania* 405–11 (1864).
Catterall, Helen Tunnicliff. "Some Antecedents of the Dred Scott Case." 30 *American Historical Review* 56–71 (1924).
Corwin, Edwin S. "The Dred Scott Decision in the Light of Contemporary Legal Doctrines." 17 *American Historical Review* 52–69 (1911).
Cushing, John D. "The Cushing Court and the Abolition of Slavery in Massachusetts: More Notes on the 'Quock Walker Case.'" 5 *American Journal of Legal History* 118–44 (Apr. 1961).
Eckert, Ralph Lowell. "The Ordeal of Passmore Williamson." 100 *Pennsylvania Magazine of History and Biography* 521–38 (Oct. 1976).
Ehrlich, Walter. "Was the Dred Scott Case Valid?" 55 *Journal of American History* 256–65 (1968).
Finkelman, Paul. "The Nationalization of Slavery: A Counterfactual Approach to the 1860s." 14 *Louisiana Studies* [now *Southern Studies*] 213–40 (Fall 1975).
_____. "Prigg v. *Pennsylvania* and Northern State Courts: Anti-Slavery Use of a Pro-Slavery Decision." 25 *Civil War History* 5–35 (March 1979).
_____. "The Treason Trial of Castner Hanway," in Michal R. Belknap, ed., *American Political Trials: The Role of Politicized Justice in United States History.* Westport, Conn.: Greenwood Press, forthcoming.
Flanigan, Daniel. "Criminal Procedure in Slave Trials in the Antebellum South." 40 *Journal of Southern History* 537–64 (1974).
Galbreath, C. B. "Anti-Slavery Movement in Columbiana County." 30 *Ohio Archaeological and Historical Quarterly* 355–95 (Jan. 1921).
Gerteis, Louis S. "Salmon P. Chase, Radicalism, and the Politics of Emancipation, 1861–1864." 60 *Journal of American History* 42–62 (June 1973).

Hammond, Isaac W. "Slavery in New Hampshire." 21 *Magazine of American History* 62–65 (1889).

Hindus, Michael. "Black Justice Under White Law: Criminal Prosecutions of Blacks in Antebellum South Carolina." 63 *Journal of American History* 575–99 (1976).

Horowitz, Harold W. "Choice-of-Law Decisions Involving Slavery: 'Interest Analysis' in the Early Nineteenth Century." 17 *UCLA Law Review* 587–601 (Feb. 1970).

Ketcham, Ralph L. "The Dictates of Conscience: Edward Coles and Slavery." 36 *Virginia Quarterly Review* 46–62. (Winter 1960).

Leslie, William R. "A Study in the Origins of Interstate Rendition: The Big Beaver Creek Murders." 57 *American Historical Review* 63–76 (Oct. 1951).

Nadelhaft, Jerome. "The Somersett Case and Slavery: Myth, Reality, and Repercussions." 51 *Journal of Negro History* 193–208 (July 1966).

Nash, A. E. Keir. "Fairness and Formalism in the Trials of Blacks in the State Supreme Courts of the Old South." 56 *Virginia Law Review* 64–100 (1970).

———. "A More Equitable Past? Southern Supreme Courts and the Protection of the Antebellum Negro." 48 *North Carolina Law Review* 197–242 (1970).

———. "Negro Rights, Unionism, and Greatness on the South Carolina Court of Appeals: The Extraordinary Chief Justice John Belton O'Neall." 21 *South Carolina Law Review* 141–90 (1969).

———. "Reason of Slavery: Understanding the Judicial Role in the Peculiar Institution." 78 *Vanderbilt Law Review* 7–218 (1979).

Northrup, A. Judd. "Slavery in New York." 4 *State Library Bulletin of History* 295–98 (May 1900).

Paludan, Phillip S. "The American Civil War Considered as a Crisis in Law and Order." 77 *American Historical Review* 1013–34 (Oct. 1972).

Philbrick, Francis S. "Law, Courts, and Litigation of Indiana Territory (1800–09)." 24 *Illinois Law Review* 1–19 (May 1929).

Riddell, William R. "*Le Code Noir.*" 10 *Journal of Negro History* 321–29 (July 1925).

Wiecek, William M. "Slavery and Abolition before the United States Supreme Court, 1820–1860." 65 *Journal of American History* 34–59 (June 1978).

———. "*Somerset*: Lord Mansfield and the Legitimacy of Slavery in the Anglo-American World." 42 *University of Chicago Law Review* 86–146 (Fall 1974).

Books

Barnes, Gilbert Hobbs. *The Anti-Slavery Impulse: 1830–1844.* New York: Appleton-Century, 1933.

Barrows, Chester L. *William M. Evarts: Lawyer, Diplomat, Statesman.* Chapel Hill: University of North Carolina Press, 1941.

Bartlett, Irving H. *From Slave to Citizen: The Story of the Negro in Rhode Island.* Providence: The Urban League of Greater Providence, 1954.

Berlin, Ira. *Slaves without Masters: The Free Negro in the Antebellum South.* New York: Pantheon Books, 1974.

Berwanger, Eugene H. *The Frontier against Slavery.* Urbana: University of Illinois Press, 1967.

Blassingame, John W. *Black New Orleans: 1860–1880.* Chicago: University of Chicago Press, 1973.

Brodie, Fawn M. *Thaddeus Stevens: Scourge of the South.* New York: W. W. Norton & Company, 1959.

Brown, William H. *An Historical Sketch of the Early Movement in Illinois for the Legalization of Slavery.* Chicago: Church, Goodman, and Donnelley, 1865.

Campbell, Stanley W. *The Slave Catchers: Enforcement of the Fugitive Slave Law, 1850–1860.* Chapel Hill: University of North Carolina Press, 1970.

Cardozo, Benjamin Nathan. *The Paradoxes of Legal Science.* New York: Columbia University Press, 1928.

Cavers, David F. *The Choice-of-Law Process.* Ann Arbor: The University of Michigan Press, 1965.

Chaddock, Robert E. *Ohio before 1850: A Study of the Early Influence of Pennsylvania and Southern Populations in Ohio.* New York: Columbia University Press, 1908.

Channing, Edward. *The Narragansett Planters.* Baltimore: Johns Hopkins University Press, 1886.

Child, Lydia Marie. *Isaac T. Hopper: A True Life.* 2d ed. New York: Dodd, Mead, and Company, 1881.

Cooley, Henry Schofield. *A Study of Slavery in New Jersey.* Baltimore: Johns Hopkins University Press, 1896.

Corwin, Edwin S., ed. *The Constitution of the United States of America.* Washington: Government Printing Office, 1964.

Cover, Robert M. *Justice Accused: Antislavery and the Judicial Process.* New Haven: Yale University Press, 1975.

Dargo, George. *Jefferson's Louisiana: Politics and the Clash of Legal Traditions.* Cambridge: Harvard University Press, 1975.

Davis, David Brion. *The Problem of Slavery in the Age of Revolution, 1770–1823.* Ithaca and London: Cornell University Press, 1975.

————. *The Slave Power Conspiracy and the Paranoid Style.* Baton Rouge: Louisiana State University Press, 1969.

Drake, Thomas E. *Quakers and Slavery in America.* New Haven: Yale University Press, 1950.

DuBois, W. E. B. *The Suppression of the African Slave-Trade to the United States of America, 1638–1870.* Cambridge: Harvard University Press, 1896.

Dumond, Dwight L. *Antislavery: The Crusade for Freedom in America.* Ann Arbor: University of Michigan Press, 1961.

Dunn, Jacob P. *Indiana: A Redemption from Slavery.* Boston and New York: Houghton Mifflin and Company, 1900.

Dyer, Brainerd. *The Public Career of William M. Evarts.* Berkeley: University of California Press, 1933.

Ehrlich, Walter. *They Have No Rights: Dred Scott's Struggle for Freedom.* Westport, Conn.: Greenwood Press, 1979.

Fairman, Charles. *Reconstruction and Reunion, 1864–1888, Part One.* New York: Macmillan Company, 1971.

Fehrenbacher, Don E. *The Dred Scott Case: Its Significance in American Law and Politics.* New York: Oxford University Press, 1978.

———. *Prelude to Greatness: Lincoln in the 1850s.* New York: McGraw Hill, 1964.

Fladeland, Betty. *James Gillespie Birney: Slaveholder to Abolitionist.* Ithaca: Cornell University Press, 1955.

Foner, Eric. *Free Soil, Free Labor, Free Men: The Ideology of the Republican Party before the Civil War.* New York: Oxford University Press, 1970.

Frankfurter, Felix, and Landis, James M. *The Business of the Supreme Court: A Study in the Federal Judicial System.* New York: Macmillan Company, 1927.

Franklin, John Hope. *The Militant South.* Cambridge: Harvard University Press, 1956.

———. *A Southern Odyssey: Travelers in the Antebellum North.* Baton Rouge: Louisiana State University Press, 1976.

Handlin, Oscar. *Chance or Destiny: Turning Points in American History.* Boston: Little, Brown, 1955.

Harris, N. Dwight. *The History of Negro Servitude in Illinois.* Chicago: A. C. McClure and Company, 1904.

Hart, Albert Bushnell. *Salmon P. Chase: The Political Abolitionist.* Boston and New York: Houghton Mifflin and Company, 1899.

Henderson, Dwight F. *Courts for a Nation.* Washington, D.C.: Public Affairs Press, 1971.

Higginbotham, A. Leon, Jr. *In the Matter of Color: Race and the American Legal Process, The Colonial Period.* New York: Oxford University Press, 1978.

Hilliard, Sam Bowes. *Hog Meat and Hoecake: Food Supply in the Old South, 1840–1860.* Carbondale: Southern Illinois University Press, 1972.

Hopkins, Vincent C. *Dred Scott's Case.* New York: Fordham University Press, 1951.

Hudson, Randall O., and Durham, James. *The New York Daily Tribune and Passmore Williamson's Case: A Study in the Use of Northern States' Rights.* Wichita, Kansas: Wichita State University, 1974.

Hyman, Harold M. *A More Perfect Union: The Impact of the Civil War and Reconstruction on the Constitution.* New York: A. A. Knopf, 1973.

Jaffa, Harry. *Crisis of the House Divided: An Interpretation of the Issues in the Lincoln-Douglas Debates.* Garden City: Doubleday and Company, 1959.

Jordan, Winthrop D. *White over Black.* Baltimore: Penguin Books, 1968.

Katz, Jonathan. *Resistance at Christiana: The Fugitive Slave Rebellion,*

Christiana, Pennsylvania: September 11, 1851. A Documentary Account.
New York: Thomas Y. Crowell, 1974.

Kenyon, Cecelia M., ed. *The Antifederalists.* Indianapolis: Bobbs-Merrill Company, 1966.

Kettner, James. *The Development of American Citizenship, 1608–1870.*
Chapel Hill: University of North Carolina Press, 1978.

Kiven, Arline Ruth. *Then Why the Negroes?* N.p.: Urban League of Rhode Island, 1973.

Krug, Mark. *Lyman Trumbull: Conservative Radical.* New York: A. S. Barnes, 1965.

Kutler, Stanley I., ed. *The Dred Scott Decision: Law or Politics?* Boston: Houghton Mifflin Company, 1967.

Lang, Meredith. *Defender of the Faith: The High Court of Mississippi, 1817–1875.* Jackson, Miss.: University Press of Mississippi, 1977.

Lee, Charles Robert, Jr. *The Confederate Constitutions.* Chapel Hill: University of North Carolina Press, 1963.

Levy, Leonard W. *The Law of the Commonwealth and Chief Justice Shaw.*
Cambridge: Harvard University Press, 1957.

Litwack, Leon F. *North of Slavery: The Negro in the Free States, 1790–1860.*
Chicago: University of Chicago Press, 1961.

Lynd, Staughton. *Class Conflict, Slavery, and the United States Constitution.*
Indianapolis: The Bobbs-Merrill Company, 1967.

MacNaul, Willard C. *The Jefferson-Lemen Compact: The Relation of Thomas Jefferson and James Lemen in the Exclusion of Slavery from Illinois and the Northwest Territory with Related Documents.* Chicago: University of Chicago Press, 1915.

McCloy, Shelby T. *The Negro in France.* Lexington: The University of Kentucky Press, 1961.

McColley, Robert. *Slavery and Jeffersonian Virginia.* Urbana: University of Illinois Press, 1964.

McManus, Edgar J. *Black Bondage in the North.* Syracuse: Syracuse University Press, 1973.

————. *A History of Negro Slavery in New York.* Syracuse: Syracuse University Press, 1966.

Morris, Thomas D. *Free Men All: The Personal Liberty Laws of the North, 1780–1861.* Baltimore: Johns Hopkins University Press, 1974.

Mullin, Gerald W. *Flight and Rebellion: Slave Resistance in Eighteenth-Century Virginia.* New York: Oxford University Press, 1972.

Nevins, Allan. *The Emergence of Lincoln.* 2 vols. New York: Charles Scribner's Sons, 1950.

Noonan, John T. *Persons and Masks of the Law.* New York: Farrar, Straus, and Giroux, 1976.

Nye, Russell B. *Fettered Freedom: Civil Liberties and the Slavery Controversy.* East Lansing: Michigan State University Press, 1949.

Oates, Stephen B. *With Malice toward None: The Life of Abraham Lincoln.*
New York: Harper and Row, 1977.

Paludan, Phillip S. *A Covenant with Death: The Constitution, Law, and*

Equality in the Civil War Era. Urbana: University of Illinois Press, 1975.

Phillips, Ulrich Bonnell. *American Negro Slavery.* New York: D. Appleton and Company, 1918.

Poole, William Frederick. *Anti-Slavery Opinions before the Year 1800.* Cincinnati: Robert Clarke and Company, 1873.

Potter, David M. *The Impending Crisis: 1848–1861.* New York: Harper and Row, 1976.

Quillin, Frank U. *The Color Line in Ohio: A History of Race Prejudice in a Typical Northern State.* Ann Arbor: George Wahr, 1913.

Richards, Leonard L. *"Gentlemen of Property and Standing": Anti-Abolitionist Mobs in Jacksonian America.* New York: Oxford University Press, 1970.

Robinson, Donald L. *Slavery in the Structure of American Politics, 1765–1820.* New York: Harcourt Brace Jovanovich, 1971.

Roseboom, Eugene H. *The Civil War Era: 1850–1873.* Columbus: Ohio State Archaelogical and Historical Society, 1944.

Sewell, Richard H. *Ballots for Freedom: Antislavery Politics in the United States, 1837–1860.* New York: Oxford University Press, 1976.

Spangler, Earl E. *The Negro in Minnesota.* Minneapolis: T. S. Denison and Company, 1961.

Swisher, Carl B. *History of the Supreme Court of the United States: The Taney Period, 1836–1864.* New York: Macmillan Company, 1974.

Taylor, Joe Gray. *Negro Slavery in Louisiana.* Baton Rouge: Louisiana Historical Association, 1963.

tenBroek, Jacobus. *The Constitution and the Right of Free Movement.* New York: National Travelers Aid Association, 1955.

Thornbrough, Emma Lou. *Indiana in the Civil War Era.* Indianapolis: Indiana Historical Society, 1965.

Trefousse, Hans L. *The Radical Republicans: Lincoln's Vanguard for Racial Justice.* New York: Alfred A. Knopf, 1969.

Trexler, Harrison A. *Slavery in Missouri, 1804–1865.* Baltimore: Johns Hopkins University Press, 1914.

Turner, Edward R. *The Negro in Pennsylvania: Slavery–Servitude–Freedom, 1639–1861.* Washington, D.C.: American Historical Association, 1911.

⸻. *Slavery in Pennsylvania.* Baltimore: Lord Baltimore Press, 1911.

Voegeli, V. Jacque. *Free But Not Equal: The Midwest and the Negro during the Civil War.* Chicago: University of Chicago Press, 1967.

Wade, Richard. *The Urban Frontier.* Cambridge: Harvard University Press, 1967.

Ward, W. E. F. *The Royal Navy and the Slavers: The Suppression of the Atlantic Slave Trade.* New York: Schocken Books, 1970.

Warren, Charles. *The Supreme Court in United States History.* 2 vols. Boston: Little, Brown and Company, 1922.

White, G. Edward. *The American Judicial Tradition: Profiles of Leading American Judges.* New York: Oxford University Press, 1976.

Wiecek, William M. *The Sources of Antislavery Constitutionalism in*

America, 1760–1848. Ithaca and London: Cornell University Press, 1977.

Wilson, Henry. *History of the Rise and Fall of the Slave Power in America.* 2 vols. Boston: James R. Osgood and Company, 1872.

Zilversmit, Arthur. *The First Emancipation: The Abolition of Slavery in the North.* Chicago: University of Chicago Press, 1967.

Unpublished Material

Finkelman, Paul. "A More Perfect Union? Slavery, Comity and Federalism, 1787–1861." Ph.D. dissertation, University of Chicago, 1976.

Index of Cases

Britain

United States

FEDERAL

UNITED STATES SUPREME COURT

Index